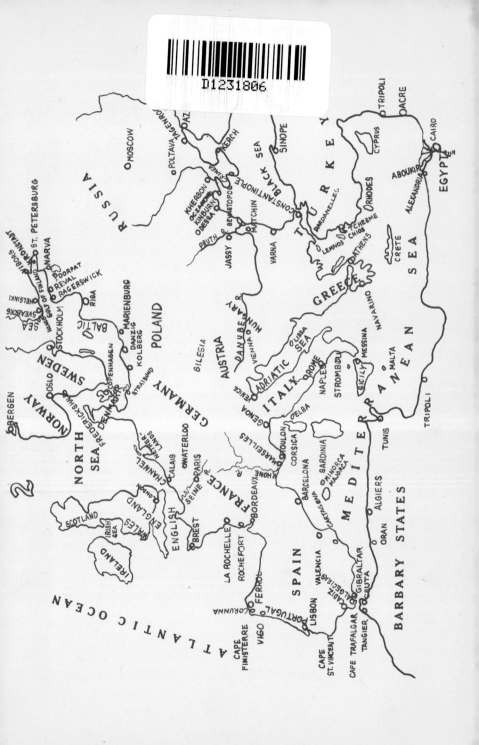

War at Sea
Book One, THE ANCIENT FLEETS
Book Two, THE AGE OF SAILS
Book Three, THE AGE OF STEAM

THE AGE OF

The story of naval warfare under sail

SAILS
1213 A. D.-1853 A. D.

JOHN VAN DUYN SOUTHWORTH

First President, Syracuse Council
Navy League of the United States
Associate Member of United States Naval Institute

AUTHOR OF
The Ancient Fleets
The Pirate from Rome
The Story of the World
Our Own United States
and others

TWAYNE PUBLISHERS
New York

Library of Congress Catalog Card Number: 68-17224

Manufactured in the United States of America

This three-book series, *War at Sea,*
is collectively dedicated to my earlier
"trilogy," a daughter and two sons.

⚓

Book Two, *The Age of Sails,* is
specifically dedicated to my elder son,
Edward Franklin Southworth, II

PREFACE

The Age of Sails is the second book of a trilogy dealing with naval warfare through the ages. The over-all title of the series is *War at Sea.*

In general, one can say that war upon the sea was first conducted under oars, then under sails, and finally under steam. Like most generalizations, this one is only partly true. There were long overlapping periods, especially between the first two of these catgories. The last important action between fleets of galleys did not occur until 383 years after the first important battle between fleets of sailing ships. During this period of nearly four centuries, both types of naval warfare were carried on in various parts of the world.

In the first book of this series, *The Ancient Fleets,* we gave consideration to all of the important naval actions fought under oars from the time of the first known Egyptian naval expedition, about 2600 B.C., to the repulse of the Japanese invasion fleet by the Korean and Chinese "turtle ships" in 1597 A.D. Actions fought principally under sails during this period were omitted, as belonging to a different developmental era.

In *The Age of Sails* we shall revert to the early thirteenth century, pick up these omitted sailing actions, then carry the story forward to the mid-nineteenth century, when steam power generally replaced the power of the wind. Actions involving engine-driven ships will, of course, be left for treatment in the third book of the series, *The Age of Steam.*

Basically, this series is a history of the world centered around the use and misuse of sea power. Every important naval battle ever fought is treated in one or another of the three volumes. Each is told in sufficient detail to bring out its drama, its tactics, and its significance. Land actions are mentioned only if they had a bearing upon the related naval activities; they are summarized as briefly as they can be without sacrificing needed continuity. Similarly, enough political history is included to make clear the causes and results of the naval actions included—just enough, and no more. The emphasis, throughout, is placed upon naval warfare.

Naturally, men as well as ships are included, since it is men who plan and fight. The ships are merely weapons. Most of the interest in any phase of history is human interest, supplied by the leaders, the heroes, the dupes, and the scapegoats. In this series, we come to meet and know a wide variety of human beings who have contributed, in one way or another, to the fascinating story of strife upon the waters of the world.

The author of this series hopes that the pleasure he has had in research and writing will be reflected in comparable pleasure on the part of the reader. It was fun to dig this material out and put it down. I hope it's fun to read it.

John Van Duyn Southworth

CONTENTS

List of Maps and Illustrations

1 A PERIOD OF TRANSITION

⚓

1.

Unlike other living organisms, the English navy had two fathers. The first was named Alfred; the second, John.

In the year 874 A.D., the Danes, or Vikings, had a firm foothold in England. In their long, seaworthy "dragon ships" they moved easily from one point of attack to another, utilizing mobility and surprise as effectively as force. England, at this time, was divided into many little kingdoms, each with its own minor king. Of all these rulers, only King Alfred the Great of Wessex was able to offer effective resistance to the invaders. Alfred organized a fleet—the first English navy—and used it to check the Danes upon the sea. It was effective, but when the Danish menace receded, the idea of a national navy was forgotten. More than three centuries were to pass before its revival.

As the thirteenth century began, King John sat upon the throne of England. His was an evil reputation, well and painstakingly earned. Before getting the crown, he had betrayed his father, King Henry II, and his brother, Richard I, and had had his nephew, Prince Arthur, put to death. Now, as king, he was running true to form by cheating his subjects, antagonizing his fellow monarchs, and scandalizing decent people everywhere. The climax was capped when he refused to accept Stephen Langton as Archbishop of Canterbury, though specifically instructed to do so by Pope Innocent III, head of the all-powerful Roman Catholic Church.

Innocent was perhaps the most vigorous man ever to occupy the papal chair. As "God's Vicar on Earth," he could not accept defiance from anyone, even a king. John was promptly excommunicated, and his country was placed under an interdict. To the superstitious people of the time, it appeared that the literal wrath of God was about to fall upon unhappy England.

The Pope did not depend upon God's wrath alone. As a doer of God's will, he selected King Philip Augustus of France, an old enemy of John's. Philip was promised divine help and absolution, plus whatever material spoils he could gain, if he would reduce the sinning monarch to subservience and bring him back into the family of God's obedient children.

It did not take King John long to conclude that this time he had gone too far. Across the Channel, Philip Augustus was busily gathering a great armament. Nearer at hand, the good English people were boldly raising their voices against an impious king so foolish as to defy the Lord's own anointed and thus deny his subjects those Church sacraments so necessary for the salvation of their souls. Unarmed and unadorned, the shaken king hastened into the presence of the Pope's legate, there to make complete and abject submission on all points. The legate, thoroughly delighted, went at once to France to call off the crusade for which Philip Augustus was so happily preparing.

Philip was anything but delighted at the news. Cried he, "I have already spent vast sums of money preparing this expedition, which I undertook at the Pope's definite orders, and for the remission of my sins." When the legate repeated that the expedition must not take place, the French king vowed that it would be done, whether the Pope liked it or not. The preparations continued.

2.

Though the withdrawal of the Pope's support did not give pause to Philip Augustus, it profoundly shocked one of his staunch allies, Count Ferdinand of Flanders. The loyalties of the feudal system clashed head-on with those of the Church. Philip Augustus might be Count Ferdinand's feudal lord, but the Pope was his spiritual lord, whose wishes must be obeyed. Without divine sanction, the armed forces of Flanders would not accompany those of France against the English.

Briefly, the idea of invading England was shelved until Flanders could be brought back into the fold. The great armament of France was turned northeastward, away from the Channel, against the little County of Flanders. In 1213, the French army laid siege to Ghent, while the fleet, which was to have carried the soldiers to England, sailed along the coast toward the river port of Damme, gateway to the more important city of Bruges.

King John, meanwhile, had not been idle. Now that he was once more on good terms with the Pope and with his own people, he bent his energies to preparing for the inevitable war with Philip. What better time could there be than the present, when Philip had his back turned and was preoccupied with the chastisement of Flanders? To strike at Philip, he had to have ships. He began at once to gather them.

Whatever else one may say about King John, one must admit that he was a first-rate organizer. His mind, though nasty, was orderly. His first step was to do away with the ancient and inefficient arrangement by which the so-called Cinque Ports of the counties of Kent and Sussex were permitted to profit from something closely resembling piracy in return for their services in resisting invasion from the sea. A true Royal Navy was needed in place of this hit-or-miss defense. Primitive dockyards were created at Portsmouth. Over the dockyards, the ships, and the personnel was erected a hierarchy of officials which was to develop, in time, into no less an organization than the British Admiralty. As the first top official of his navy, the king appointed William de Wrotham, Archbishop of Taunton, a thorough landlubber with a gift for organization.

The fleet which King John assembled consisted of some five hundred ships, the largest having a displacement of about eighty tons. All were round and tubby merchant ships, depending for their propulsion on a single square sail mounted on a mast set amidships. Except for a bit of caulking and the replacement of some doubtful boards or timbers, most remained unchanged, to serve as transports. A few of the larger ones were converted into warships. High walled platforms, or "castles," were built above the bows and sterns, and smaller "castles" were built around the masts, above the sails. From these points of vantage, men-at-arms could launch their arrows, darts, javelins, and rocks down upon the decks of any enemy vessels that might be encountered.

All of King John's ships—the converted and the unconverted—possessed one great advantage over the ships of earlier ages. From the sides of the sails, bowlines extended forward. These permitted the crews to adjust the angle of sail to wind and thus to perform the seemingly impossible task of tacking upwind.

3.

While the King and William de Wrotham remained at home, the new English fleet took to the sea under the command of Count William of Holland and of William Longsword, Earl of Salisbury. A course was set for the coast of Flanders.

The French fleet, meanwhile, had sailed up the river to the port of Damme, whose inhabitants gazed with fear at the formidable armament which had come against them. It was with distinct relief that the people of the town learned that the French proposed to leave them in peace in return for a modest ransom. The money was paid. The French pocketed it and then proceeded to loot Damme. That done, they fanned out farther into the countryside, to take anything worth taking from the subjects of the backsliding Count of Flanders.

Such was the state of affairs when King John's fleet approached the mouth of the River Rey on the last day of May, 1213. From a distance, it could be seen that the mouth of the river was choked with large ships and that others, finding no room in the river, were anchored off its mouth. Many of the smaller French vessels had been pulled up on the beach.

To gain further information, the English admirals sent some men close to the river mouth in small craft which could be mistaken for fishing boats. The scouts presently returned, bearing word that the French ships were undermanned, their crews being absent in search of loot.

Realizing that they were never likely to stumble on a better opportunity, the two Williams ordered an immediate attack. It was almost ridiculously easy. The undermanned ships were quickly taken, the skeleton crews being spared in recognition of their good sense in offering no resistance. Some of the smaller ships that had been beached were also refloated and captured, the remainder being stripped and burned.

Only up the river, in the harbor of Damme, was there any hard fighting. Here, returning French sailors manned whatever ships were still untaken and prepared to resist to the end. They were too few in number to succeed. English ships came swarming up the river, attacking the French vessels from all sides. Before nightfall, the victory was complete. King Philip's French fleet was no more.

A great tradition had been established. For the first time, English and French fleets had met in battle, and the English had won. So dismayed was Philip Augustus at the ineptness of his navy's leadership that he ordered the destruction of the rest of his fleet, personally applying the torch to some of his ships. "Alas, my Frenchmen know little of the ways of the sea!"

4.

For the English people, the naval victory over the French was the one bright spot in the sorry period of King John's misrule. The remainder of his reign was largely spent in controversy with his barons, who bitterly resented his illegal and highhanded methods of extortion. In 1215, at Runnymede, the king was forced to agree to the terms of the *Magna Carta,* in which he promised to give up certain of his unlawful powers. When it became evident that he had no intention of honoring the agreement, active civil war broke out between the monarch and the barons.

In their perplexity, the rebellious barons took the dangerous step of offering the English crown to Prince Louis of France, who was the husband of John's niece, Blanche of Castile. Louis, well pleased at the prospect, gathered a large army and a fleet of transports at Calais and set out across the Channel in May of 1216. Apparently, John's new fleet was caught napping, for the unguarded transports were not intercepted, though a few stragglers were picked up by the discredited privateers of the Cinque Ports. The greater part of Louis' army landed safely at Sandwich. Though King John was nearby with his army, he offered no opposition, merely retiring before the invaders. Seizing the initiative, Prince Louis promptly laid siege to Dover and Windsor castles.

It was not long before the English barons who had joined Prince Louis began to question the wisdom of their act. The French pretender treated them with disrespect, and soon he began to bestow titles and privileges upon his French followers, while granting his English associates nothing. Some of the barons quietly changed sides and moved into John's camp. No less important was a similar movement on the part of the citizens of some of the leading English seaports, who had formerly favored the invader. From several such ports, privateers set out to disrupt the French supply lines and bring Louis' loaded vessels into ports controlled by friends of King John.

The sudden death of King John, from a fever brought on by overindulgence in food and drink, completed the swing against Prince Louis. Almost to a man, the barons now threw their support to John's son, Henry III. Louis, however, was by no means ready to give up his claim to the crown. After suffering a defeat at Lincoln, he withdrew his forces into fortified London and sent word to his wife to rush him reinforcements and supplies as quickly as possible. On August 24, 1217, a fleet of eighty-one heavily laden French vessels set out from Calais, under the command of an old pirate named Eustace the Monk, who had once served King John but had betrayed his English master in order to serve the French.

One of the ablest of Henry's supporters was the king's Justiciar, Hubert de Burgh. To him, it seemed the essence of folly to wait until the French should land and unload their troops, equipment, and provisions. Might it not be better to meet them on the open waters of the Channel, where the heavily laden French vessels would be at a disadvantage? With characteristic energy, the Justiciar quickly gathered forty vessels, which he prepared for action by having strips of iron nailed across their bows—a process known as "bearding." This little fleet was manned by hastily gathered knights and bowmen, most of whom were reluctant to venture out on the unfamiliar open waters against such odds.

To the eyes of Eustace the Monk, all seemed to be going well. The day was clear and the Channel less choppy than usual. This was a fortunate thing, since his flagship was very heavily laden with men, supplies, and a huge and heavy *trebuchet,* for use in besieging castles. Not until the English coast was close at hand was there any sight of an English sail. Even when he saw the forty little ships issuing from Sandwich Harbor, he recognized no danger. These ships were holding a course parallel to his own, but in the opposite direction. Plainly, they were not going to attack him but were heading for Calais, to deliver a surprise attack in his absence. Let them go! The defenses of Calais would be more than adequate to drive them away.

For a time, the happy thoughts of Eustace the Monk seemed to be borne out. The English fleet held its course eastward, in apparent disregard of the French vessels wallowing past. Only when the last ships of the two fleets had passed and the entire English force lay upwind from the French, was there any change of course. Then, as one, the forty English vessels swung around, set their iron-reinforced bows toward the enemy, and drove in to the attack. The weather gauge more than made up for the difference in numbers. Running before the wind, the English were upon their opponents before the French could swing their overloaded vessels around to parry the attack. English arrows, sailing with the wind, plunged in among the Frenchmen long before French arrows could reach the English. Worst of all was the powdered lime, which drifted down in clouds before the attacking ships, blinding the Frenchmen and blistering their skins. Before the first boarder went over the rail, the French were more than half defeated.

Little effective resistance was possible. Blinded and demoralized, the Frenchmen fell easy prey to the boarders who came swarming onto their ships. The ordinary seamen were quickly killed; the knights and nobles were held for ransom. Eustace belonged to neither of these groups. As soon as he recognized the hopelessness of the situation, he dove through a hatchway and tried to bury himself in the cargo hold of his ship. He was found and dragged forth, pleading for his life and promising a rich reward for clemency. His words were not heeded, for there were too many black marks against his name. With little delay and no compunction, he was tied down to the rail of his own ship, and his head was severed from his body by the single slash of a sharp knife.

This English victory—variously known as the Battle of Dover, the Battle of Sandwich, and the Battle of South Foreland—contributed an important new idea to the English concept of defense. Hubert de Burgh had clearly proved his contention that the best place to meet a would-be invader of the island kingdom was on the sea, rather than on the beaches and the fields of England. From this time on, the stout wooden walls of England's ships were to assume increased importance as the nation's first line of resistance. Scarcely less important was the new tactical concept of gaining the weather gauge at the outset of a naval battle under sails.

What of Prince Louis, shut up in London and deprived of the reinforcements upon which he had counted? Correctly assessing the importance of his naval reverse, he quickly agreed to abandon his claims and his invasion and to return to France. The fighting ceased, leaving King Henry III free to consolidate his hold on the crown.

5.

For nearly ninety years, the waters of western Europe saw no further important naval activity. When at last another sea battle was fought, in 1304, it came as a result of a complicated quarrel involving

France, Flanders, and Holland. There is no need for us to investigate the causes. Suffice it to say that in 1304 much of Holland was overrun by Flemish troops and that a strong fleet commanded by Count Guy of Flanders lay off the Dutch seaport of Zierikzee, which was under siege.

In their distress, the Dutch appealed for help to King Philip IV of France, who quickly sent a fleet of twenty French sailing vessels and sixteen Genoese galleys, all under the command of Admiral Rinaldo di Grimaldi, of Genoa. These vessels rendezvoused with a swarm of small Dutch craft off the mouth of the River Maas, then proceeded toward Zierikzee, where the eighty large Flemish sailing ships lay at anchor.

Though the largest ships of the allied squadron were supplied by France, most of the fighting spirit was contributed by the patriotic Dutch, who felt that they were fighting for their homes and their freedom. As the fleets came together in the late afternoon of August 10, 1304, it was the Dutch who spearheaded the attack. As the range closed, Dutch arrows, then stones, assailed the Flemish sailors. Ships ground alongside, and the Dutch seamen swarmed over the rails wielding pikes, swords, and knives. The larger French and Genoese vessels played a comparatively minor part.

Night fell, but the battle went on by the uncertain light of the moon. It was not until after midnight that the outcome was clear. The Dutch, with their allies, were winning, and the Flemish fleet was doomed. The next day, a landing was made, and some five thousand of the besiegers of Zierikzee were rounded up among the sand dunes, where they had taken refuge.

The Dutch victory at Zierikzee led to peace between Flanders and Holland. The King of France, though, was not quite through with the war. He seized this opportunity to try to bring the Flemish people once more under his control. Surely, with their Count now in a cell in Paris, with their fleet taken, and with their army scattered, the low-landers would not presume to resist him. They did, though. A new Flemish army appeared, ready to resist to the utmost. "But it rains Flemings!" cried the astonished French king. Following the example of the Dutch, he made peace.

6.

We must now deal briefly with a feudal technicality which was to have most important results. In 1204, following his unsuccessful wars against Philip Augustus, King John had found it necessary to agree to a humiliating treaty by which he gave up most of the English lands on the continent and then received them back as fiefs, to be held under the overlordship of the King of France. Ever since that time the English kings had been, at least in theory, the vassals of their royal rivals across the Channel.

In 1327, vigorous Edward III came to the throne of England. He was by no means willing to acknowledge himself a vassal of the French king. On the contrary, he felt that he himself had a valid claim to the French throne, because his mother was the daughter of an earlier French king, Philip IV. Edward was outraged when his claims were disregarded and a new line of French kings took the throne of France after the Capet family petered out in 1328.

Instead of going to war at once, Edward III waited for a favorable opportunity. This occurred in 1337, when the French tried to disrupt the profitable wool trade between England and Flanders and the Flemish revolted against such arbitrary French control. King Philip VI of France promptly went to war with Flanders, and Edward went to war with Philip.

We need not concern ourselves with the military details of the very long war which followed. It is known as the Hundred Years' War, and the name expresses no exaggeration. With brief periods of truce, the war lasted for 116 years, from 1337 to 1453. Five kings of England, five kings of France, and at least three full generations of French and English citizens were to come and go without ever knowing the happiness of real peace. It will be sufficient for us to consider the rather limited naval affairs of this century-and-a-sixth of strife.

In addition to their armies, both Edward and Philip had large naval forces, which they were willing and anxious to use. The ships did not differ greatly from those which had fought off Sandwich and at Zierikzee. Each had a forecastle, an aftercastle, and a top castle, as before, from which could be discharged arrows, spears, rocks, powdered lye, and soap or lard to render the enemy's decks slippery. These structures, however, were of a more solid and permanent nature than those which the workmen of King John and Henry III had hastily added to commandeered merchant ships. An added feature was a bowsprit, extending forward on the starboard side of the stem timber. This was not used to support sails or rigging but, like the Roman *corvus,* served as a built-in boarding gangway. The rudders of these new ships were also set at the sterns instead of well aft on the starboard sides. As before, each ship had a single mast amidships to support a large square sail.

The real fighting of the Hundred Years' War opened on a naval note, after considerable pointless marching, countermarching, and jockeying on the land. In the spring of 1338, French squadrons raided the Thames estuary, Portsmouth, and the island of Guernsey, doing considerable damage. Edward struck back by a similar raid on the French seaport of Eu. Not long afterward, a small segment of the English fleet ran afoul of a larger French squadron off Walcheren Island and was defeated, with the loss of its two largest warships, the *Christopher* and the *Edouarda*. The captured ships made welcome additions to Philip's growing navy.

There was more desultory raiding in 1338 and 1339. The French burned Southampton. The English did the same to Le Tréport and Boulogne and also destroyed a few dozen ships in Boulogne Harbor, hanging all captured captains. In retaliation for this, a French fleet of galleys from Monaco then raided the English coast, capturing and mutilating a number of sailors and fishermen. The war, at this point, had become nasty but was still relatively pointless. The first significant blow was yet to be delivered.

7.

On June 22, 1340, King Edward set out for the Continent with almost his entire fleet. His intention was apparently to make a landing rather than to fight a naval engagement, for he took with him not only a large number of knights and foot soldiers but also many of the ladies of his court, who would hardly have been either safe or helpful in the event of a clash between fleets. A course was set for the mouth of the River Scheldt.

Unknown to the English, the French fleet had meantime been assembling at Sluys, a port at the mouth of the Scheldt estuary. Numerically, the French were much superior. In addition to their 140 large sailing vessels, they had a squadron of forty Genoese galleys and innumerable smaller craft. Their manpower totaled no less than 40,000. Their weakness lay in their command, for they had three admirals of equal authority. Two of these, Quiéret and Béhuchet, were political appointees who knew little of the sea. The third, Barbavara, was a Genoese pirate who knew what to do but was consistently outvoted, two to one.

As the English fleet approached the Estuary, King Edward noticed the great forest of masts, betokening a mighty fleet. He was informed that this was undoubtedly the French navy, which had caused him such trouble by the burning of his towns and the capture of his finest ships. At this, the king, disregarding the presence of the ladies and his earlier plan for an unopposed landing, resolved to have a go at Philip's sea power, in the hopes of eliminating it. Three daring English knights were sent ashore to reconnoiter. The report they brought back confirmed the identity of the ships, their numbers, and their formation.

The French, meanwhile, had become aware of the approach of Edward's fleet. Seeing the English ships sheer off and bear away, the two French admirals jumped to the conclusion that they were fleeing to avoid battle. Barbavara knew better, and his judgment was confirmed when he saw the enemy ships take a position which placed them both upwind and upsun from the French. Said he, "My Lords, the King of England and all his navy are coming upon us. I would advise you to steer for the open sea. If you stay here, while they have the sun, wind, and wave in their favor, they will hem you in so closely that you will be helpless and cannot maneuver."

To this good advice, the Frenchmen replied that their present position was ideal for defense. Béhuchet added, with some heat, "Let him who goes away be hanged! Here we will stay, and here we will take our chance!"

Barbavara shrugged. "I am sorry, my Lords, that you will not believe me. Personally, I do not propose to stay here and be destroyed. I am going to get myself and my ships out of this trap." So saying, he departed from the conference and had his oarsmen take their galleys out to sea while such a move was still possible.

The battle went precisely as Barbavara had predicted. In a misguided move to strengthen their defense, Quiéret and Béhuchet arranged their ships in four lines, each vessel being anchored and also being chained to those on either side. This, of course, made all maneuvering impossible. Heavy rocks were hoisted to the top castles, to serve as missiles, and bowmen were stationed on the forecastles and after castles.

The outcome of the fight was largely determined by morale. The English, being the attackers, had the greater "lift" on their side. This was further heightened by the recapture of the famous *Christopher* during the early minutes of the fighting. One by one, the ships of the first line were taken, after their crews had been thinned out by the accurate fire of bows and crossbows. At this point, unexpected reinforcements arrived as Lord Morley sailed into the battle with a squadron of English ships, which he had been quietly gathering in the seacoast towns of the northern counties. The attack on the second line was launched with real enthusiasm.

The morale of the French, already low, now received an added depressant. On the shore behind them appeared an army of Flemings, who had been attracted out of Bruges by the tidings of battle. Though these soldiers could take little active part in the capture of the French ships, their presence brought despair, for they effectively blocked all retreat inland. The battle became a slaughter, with no mercy granted. After nine hours of strife, the French fleet was in King Edward's hands and nearly 30,000 Frenchmen were dead. Quiéret tried to surrender but was cut down in cold blood. Béhuchet was hanged from the yardarm of his own ship. Only wise old Barbavara and his forty Genoese galleys managed to get away. All this was accomplished by the English with a loss of only two ships sunk and about 4,000 men killed.

Unlike King Edward, King Philip had not been present at the naval Battle of Sluys. For a while, no one dared tell him of the disaster which had befallen his fleet. At last, the dangerous and disagreeable task of breaking the news was forced upon the court fool. "Your Majesty," said the nimble-witted jester, "I must tell you that the English sailors are cowards. None of them had the courage to jump overboard as Your Majesty's French and Norman sailors did."

The naval victory of Sluys was followed by the unsuccessful siege of the French city of Tournay. Failing to take the town, Edward offered to settle the entire war by means of a personal combat with Philip. The offer was refused. A second offer was made, suggesting a battle between a picked group of one hundred English knights and a similar group of French knights. This, too, was refused. Thereupon, King Edward signed a two-year truce agreement with Philip and returned home to England.

8.

The war was technically renewed in 1342 and actively in 1344, when Edward reinvaded France. For a time, he kept his fleet with him, sailing along the coast while his army advanced against the seaport cities of La Hogue, Barfleur, Cherbourg, and Carentan. Everything and everyone of value taken by the army were put aboard ship for eventual transportation to England. When at last the army struck out inland, the fleet sailed home, laden with prisoners and loot.

The fleet was again used in 1347, during the siege of Calais. As the French garrison of the city began to suffer from starvation, King Philip made a strong effort to bring relief. A French fleet, attempting to bring supplies by sea, was intercepted by a larger English fleet under the Earl of Oxford and was captured intact. Attempts were then made by land. There were only two roads to Calais, one through the marshy land that backs up the city, the other along the shore. Edward erected strong towers along the former and stationed warships loaded with archers along the latter. Everyone who tried to pass by either way was sure to stop an arrow. No help reached Calais, which eventually surrendered.

9.

In 1348, the Spanish kingdom of Castile entered the war on the side of France. Soon armed Spanish vessels were intercepting English ships in the English Channel and the other "narrow seas" about the islands. King Edward was, of course, deeply concerned. When he heard news of a Spanish fleet at Sluys, under Don Carlos de la Cerda, he resolved to intercept the raiders as they began their voyage home. For this purpose he gathered a fleet of fifty ships, running perhaps 20 to 45 tons in burden, and carrying crews and fighting men totaling about 2,500 in number.

Froissart has given us a vivid picture of the expedition. The King, we are told, sat on the deck of his flagship, clad in a black velvet jacket and wearing a black beaver hat "which became him well." As the fleet sailed in search of the Spaniards, the King relaxed, enjoying to the full the songs chanted by his troubadour.

Late in the afternoon of August 29, 1350, the lookout in the top castle of the King's ship sighted a distant sail, then another, then a large number. It was the Spanish fleet, numbering some forty warships and transports. The King and his knights drank a toast to victory, then put on their helmets and prepared for battle. Seeing a large Spanish vessel bearing down upon his flagship, the *Thomas,* King Edward called out to his helmsman, "Set me against yonder Spaniard that is coming, for I wish to joust with him."

The King's instructions set the pattern for the battle—a ramming and boarding *melee* without plan or tactics. As King Edward's ship collided with its selected adversary, the Spaniard's bowsprit tore away the entire forecastle of the *Thomas* and caused some serious leaks through the gaps between sprung planks. Nor did the Spanish ship escape damage. Her mast toppled overboard, carrying with it the men in her fighting top. Attempts to grapple failed, and the vessels drifted apart and lost contact. Soon, however, the waterlogged *Thomas* found herself beside another Spanish vessel, to which her crew bound her fast. A boarding was effected, and the Spaniards were driven into the sea. Hastily, the King and his retinue transferred from their sinking flagship to this newly captured vessel, from which they continued the battle.

By a strange coincidence, the Prince of Wales had the duplicate of his father's experience. His ship, too, was badly damaged in a bow-on attempt at ramming. He, too, found it necessary to capture his antagonist, throw the crew overboard, and carry on the battle from her decks. In this endeavor, he was aided by the fact that another English ship, under the Earl of Lancaster, sent boarders into the Spanish vessel at the same time.

The crew of the English *Salle de Roi* found that they had a bear by the tail. In attempting to board a large Spanish vessel, they chained their ship firmly alongside but were unable to make a successful boarding in the face of Spanish resistance along the rails. To their chagrin, they found themselves being towed helplessly away as the larger Spanish vessel spread her sails. In the end, disaster was avoided by the captain's valet, who managed to make his way alone to the Spaniard's deck with a sharp knife in his hand. Once there, he quickly cut the halyards, thus letting the mainsail come crashing down. During the confusion which followed, the *Salle*'s crew made one more attempt at boarding. This time, they succeeded and captured their erstwhile captor.

The Battle of Winchelsea ended in an English victory. Fourteen of the enemy ships were captured, and the rest were put to flight. King Edward III emerged from the fray with the lyrical title, "King of the Seas."

10.

Philip VI of France died in 1350 and his successor, King John, in 1364. The new French king was Charles V. In England, Edward III held the throne until 1377, being succeeded by Richard II.

Early in the reign of Richard II, there was a brief renewal of naval activity. A French fleet raided the English coast, doing considerable damage. The English fleet, under the Earl of Buckingham, put to sea to intercept the raiders but missed them. John of Gaunt then succeeded to the command. His first endeavor was a raid that captured Cherbourg. This success was presently nullified. Off Cherbourg, he ran into a Spanish fleet, which defeated him and drove him home.

The defeat of the English squadron under John of Gaunt gave control of the "narrow seas" to the French and Spanish allies. They were quick to take advantage of it. A combined French and Spanish fleet visited the Firth of Forth, landing soldiers and also agents to stir up the Scots against their hereditary English enemies. The intrigue was successful. Presently a large squadron of Scottish, French, and Spanish vessels traveled south and raided Scarborough, taking away much booty and every English ship that lay in the harbor.

King Richard II and his admirals did nothing to counter the blow at Scarborough. This disgusted many Englishmen, including a public-spirited citizen of London named John Philpot. Philpot was a man of action. He started at once to raise money by private solicitation. With it, he scraped together a makeshift fleet of his own and sailed after the raiders. He found them, defeated them, and captured many of their vessels and their commander, a Scotsman named John Mercer.

John Philpot returned home in triumph, bringing with him all of the stolen ships from Scarborough and also fifteen captured Spanish warships. The English people hailed him as a hero, but the King's Council of Government took a different view. Philpot was haled before this body and was severely censured for his illegal actions. His offense, it seems, lay in not waiting for the issuance of an official permit!

11.

The cast of characters continued to change, while the war dragged on. Charles VI came to the throne of France. In England, Henry of Bolingbroke, Duke of Hereford, forced his royal cousin Richard to abdicate and took the throne as Henry IV. He was succeeded in 1413 by his son, Henry V.

The war had now been going on for seventy-six years, during which time there had been a rather profound change in the design of ships. Traders from northern Europe had observed in the Mediterranean a new and much more efficient type of vessel, known as the carrack. The carrack had a higher freeboard and was much more seaworthy than the earlier type of vessel it was beginning to replace. Its forecastle and aftercastle, though still raised platforms, were solidly walled and constructed and no longer had the tacked-on, crenelated look of the earlier fighting structures. There were three masts in place of one, the mainmast in the center carrying two sails and the mizzenmast, nearest the stern, carrying a triangular lateen rig. With some modifications, to make them better suited to rough northern weather, carracks were adopted by both the French and the English before the middle of the fourteenth century.

Although no one yet seemed to realize it, a turning point had been reached in naval design. The prototype of the "great ship" had been achieved—a vessel which could be armed with cannons and used for discharging broadside fire. Though cannons were added by the French as early as 1356, there were no artillery battles between fleets of carracks during the war. Blind to the opportunities, the seamen of both navies used their carracks as though they were galleys.

The English attack on Harfleur in 1415 is a case in point. To clear the way for his invasion of France, King Henry V sent his fleet of carracks, under the Earl of Huntingdon, to eliminate the French squadron in Harfleur Harbor. Apparently, the commanders of both fleets completely disregarded their artillery. The English, coming in fast before a favoring wind, headed directly for the French vessels in an old-fashioned ramming attack. The impact must have been terrific. We are told that some of the English carracks struck with such force that their own forecastles were ripped completely away, throwing the fighting men over the side into the water. Thereafter, the ships were quickly bound together by chains and cables, so that the crews could hack away at each other until one vessel or the other was captured.

The battle in the harbor lasted nearly an entire day before the French fleet was taken and the way opened for the capture of Harfleur by King Henry's army. The capture of Harfleur, in turn, cleared the way for the spectacular English victory over the French knights on the field at Agincourt.

12.

In our single-minded pursuit of the few naval actions of the Hundred Years' War, we have largely lost sight of the progress of the war as a whole. It can briefly be summarized. During the early years, the English won consistently. Their spirit and leadership were better, and they had developed a new style of fighting which it took the French an unbelievably long time to adopt. At Crécy in 1346, at Poitiers in 1356, and at Agincourt in 1415, English foot soldiers armed with deadly longbows slaughtered the heavily armored French knights, who charged in vain against their nimble and unarmored opponents. The third of these battles was fought sixty-nine years after the first. It took the French leaders all that time to realize that a longbow would drive an arrow through armor and that armored knights were out of date in war.

After the Battle of Agincourt, it appeared certain that England would win and that Henry V would make good his claim to the French throne. English armies now held the entire northern half of France. The French had experienced a long series of defeats, and their morale was extremely low. In 1420, King Charles VI of France officially admitted defeat by signing the humiliating Treaty of Troyes, appointing Henry V as his successor on the French throne. To strengthen his position still further, Henry took for his bride Charles's daughter, Princess Catherine of Valois. All that was necessary to bring France into the possession of the English kings was for thirty-three-year-old Henry V to outlive his fifty-two-year-old father-in-law. He failed to do so. Henry fell ill in 1422 and died a few weeks before Charles VI did—a fact which permitted Charles's son to declare the treaty void and to claim the throne of France for himself.

Unfortunately for France, the new ruler, Charles VII, was easygoing and incompetent. He showed little interest in defeating the English or even in being officially crowned King of France, since the English army was blocking the way to Rheims, where French kings were customarily crowned. Burgundy, an important French province, had broken away from France and had joined the English cause. There seemed to be no chance at all that France could win.

It was at this desperate time that a most remarkable and unexpected thing occurred. A French farm girl, known as Joan of Arc, became convinced that she heard the voices of saints and angels urging her to save France. At first, she was laughed at, but at last she won the confidence of Charles VII and was actually given permission to ride at the head of his armies and to help his commanders work for victory.

Joan of Arc brought about a wonderful change not only in the French army but also in the people of France. The soldiers became inspired and fought with new vigor, not for their feudal lords but for something new and glorious—for their country of France. For the first time, they began to experience strongly the feeling of nationalism, uniting men of the same country and the same language to drive from their soil these English-speaking foreigners. The same spirit spread to the common people of France, who had previously taken little interest in the war except as it affected them personally. Now they almost worshiped "the Maid," and they were willing to sacrifice much for her and for the cause of France. They, too, began to experience strong stirrings of nationalism.

When Joan first joined the army, one of the last French strongholds, the city of Orleans, was under siege by the English and was in imminent danger of being captured. Joan and her army fell upon the besieging English. After a long and desperate struggle, in which the Maid herself was wounded, they succeeded in breaking the siege. Other victories followed. Scarcely six months after Joan had assumed leadership, Charles VII was triumphantly crowned at Rheims. The tide of battle had definitely turned in favor of the French.

France and Charles VII had been saved, but the Maid herself was not so fortunate. Not long after the crowning of the king, Joan was captured by the Burgundians, who turned her over to the English. She was no ordinary prisoner of war, to be exchanged for other prisoners and restored to her army. This girl was dangerous! The English feared and hated her, for they realized that it was her inspiration that had aroused among the French the feeling of patriotic nationalism that had turned the tide of the war. The officials of the Church also disapproved of her. The girl had said that she received messages directly from saints and angels, without the help of the Church and the clergy. Such things could not be! Her enemies agreed among themselves that she must be destroyed. Charged with being a witch and a heretic, she was burned at the stake in the public square at Rouen. Lazy, ungrateful Charles VII made no effort to save the girl who had saved him, his throne, and his country.

After the death of Joan of Arc, everything went wrong for the English. The feeling of French nationalism that Joan had aroused did not die with her. The armies of France continued to fight an inspired war. Four years after the Maid's death, Burgundy made a separate peace with France. Eighteen years later, in 1453, King Henry VI of England also made peace. The English had lost all their possessions in France except the single seaport of Calais.

Yet the war did bring one benefit to England, for it stimulated English nationalism almost as much as it helped the nationalism of France. The armies that won so gloriously at Crécy, Poitiers, and Agincourt were made up, not of armored and mounted noblemen, as had been the case in earlier wars, but of unarmored bowmen, representative of the English commoners. This was especially true at Agincourt, where King Henry V led a "happy few" of his countrymen to a brilliant victory against tremendous odds. These ordinary foot soldiers had, for the first time, a share in the winning of victories for their king and country, and they shared with their commanders a feeling of patriotic elation. "Good old England" began to mean something to the common people.

The development of nationalism sounded the death knell of the feudal system and the other outworn institutions of the Middle Ages. The way was now clear for the emergence of true nations, with truly national armed forces for use on the land and on the sea.

13.

King Henry VIII, who mounted the throne of England in 1509, inherited a shadowy claim to the throne of France. When King Louis XII of France quarreled with Pope Julius II and sent a French army into Papal territory in 1511, Henry was one of several European kings who came to the assistance of the Church. Like most members of the Holy League, Henry had his own purposes in mind when he so nimbly volunteered to help with "the work of God." His heart was set on nothing less than the conquest of France.

During the first two years of the war, what little action took place between the English and the French was largely on the sea. English warships raided the French coasts, and French warships did the same to England. These were cannon-armed sailing vessels, carrying their heavy muzzle-loaders on their upper decks and mounted in their lofty forecastles and aftercastles, the same points of vantage from which the bowmen of earlier ages had launched their arrows. The disadvantage of a high center of gravity had not yet occurred to the ship designers of the day.

On August 12, 1512, an English squadron of fifty-one ships, under Sir Edward Howard, made a surprise raid on Brest. The twenty-one French warships in the port had so little warning of the impending action that some of them had to sail out to meet the enemy with their decks still crowded with men and women from the town who were being entertained aboard. These unhappy civilians experienced a most uncomfortable night as the ships rode at anchor in the choppy waters of the outer bay.

With the coming of dawn, the French admiral, Sieur de Clermont, decided that the odds were too great and ordered his fleet back into the inner harbor, leaving his largest ship, the *Cordelière,* to cover the retirement. Though hampered and distressed by the large number of panic-stricken civilians aboard his vessel, Captain Hervé de Portzno-guer maneuvered to keep his overcrowded warship between the retiring French and the oncoming English.

The *Cordelière's* gunners were well trained, and they used their sixteen big guns to good advantage. The first ship of the English line, the flagship *Mary Rose,* was driven ashore, shattered and sinking. Portznoguer had his eyes on the fourth ship in the English formation, the formidable *Regent.* Adroitly evading the second and third ships, he closed with this great opponent "like a dog seizing a rabbit." As the cannons roared, the ships were lashed together, blasting each other's hulls at point-blank range while the other English ships formed a circle and slammed cannon balls into their lone opponent. *Regent's* captain, Thomas Knyvet, died early in the struggle, his body severed by a cannon ball. Both ships burned furiously, and both blew up, in rapid succession, when the flames reached their powder magazines. It is recorded that as his ship exploded beneath him, Hervé de Portzno-guer leaped into the sea in full armor and was seen no more.

Cordelière had not gone down in vain. The English, shocked at the loss of their greatest ship, failed to follow up their advantage and retired from the action. The French squadron was saved.

For the remainder of the war, Brest was blockaded. The only naval action worthy of note was an attempt by Sir Edward Howard and a small group of followers to cut out six French galleys, seen lying at anchor in an exposed position in the outer bay. The attempt miscarried badly. As Howard and his men started to leap aboard an enemy vessel, their own ship drifted away, leaving the admiral and seventeen of his men trapped aboard the French galley. They were too few to withstand the counterattack of the French crew. All eighteen of the raiders were forced overboard and sank like iron stoves, being carried down by their armor.

The loss of the *Regent* was to have important effects, not only on the British Navy, but upon naval design and sea power in general. It would not do for the English public to learn that the greatest vessel in the fleet had been sunk in battle. For some time, King Henry VIII and his war minister, Cardinal Thomas Wolsey, kept the matter a close secret, not to be divulged until work on a replacement for the *Regent* was well under way.

The replacement was, indeed, an imposing vessel. Her displacement of 1,500 tons was half again that of the *Regent,* and she carried more than twice as many guns. Technically speaking, she was a "high-charged galleon," meaning that her forecastle and aftercastle towered up to dizzy heights at bow and stern. Her four lofty masts supported a cloud of sails. The name of this monster was *Henri Grâce à Dieu,* though she is more often known by her nickname, "the *Great Harry.*"

The *Great Harry* saw no action in the war, which came to an end in 1514 at about the time when the ship was launched. Six years later, in 1520, she was painted, gilded, and furbished up to serve as impressive transportation for her king and namesake when Henry VIII crossed the channel to meet King Francis I of France in the peaceful pageantry and negotiation of the so-called Field of the Cloth of Gold. Sped by her dozen sails of golden yellow, the great ship carried her king grandly across the Channel.

From King Henry's point of view, the voyage was anything but enjoyable. Overweighted by her lofty, gunbearing superstructure, *Henri Grâce à Dieu* gave frequent and unmistakable signs of capsizing. She never quite went over, but Henry was sufficiently shaken by the experience to return to England in another ship, less grand but far safer and more comfortable.

Despite her unseaworthiness, the great ship was too valuable to be discarded. King Henry's naval architects and carpenters worked on the problem and came up with a solution. Heavy guns were mounted on the lower decks, their muzzles protruding through closeable gunports in the ship's sides. This innovation both lowered the center of gravity and permitted an increase in the weight of artillery which could be carried. King Henry's precarious voyage to France had aided mightily in the development of sea power. The broadside-warship had made its appearance.

14.

Though "the Field of the Cloth of Gold" was a picturesque pageant, few real issues were settled there. Two years later, in 1522, war again broke out between Henry VIII of England and Francis I of France. In this struggle, Henry had a powerful ally in Emperor

Charles V of the Holy Roman Empire. Francis found himself so badly outclassed on the sea that he kept his fleet at home, confining himself mostly to land warfare in Italy, where he was defeated. The war came to an indecisive end in 1525, with beaten France losing little because the victors had taken to quarreling among themselves.

Henry VIII was not the sort of man who could long remain at peace with his neighbors. Between the years 1530 and 1532, he antagonized the Roman Catholic Church and, with it, most of Europe by forcing through an unsanctified divorce of his wife, Catharine of Aragon, and, when the Pope protested, by personally taking over control of the Church in England. Among those most offended was his old ally Charles V, who happened to be the nephew of the discarded wife. Tension mounted steadily, and in 1539 it appeared that Charles V and Francis I, urged on by Pope Paul III, might lead a great Catholic crusade against the royal English "backslider."

Faced by this danger, King Henry hastened to strengthen his defenses. Many new ships were built, including a new and more practical *"Great Harry"* of 1,000 tons and another comparable broadside warship, the *Mary Rose*. Among the smaller vessels built were a number of a type new to the English, galleasses, driven by sails and/or oars and mounting heavy guns in stout forecastles and aftercastles. The defenses of the principal harbors were strengthened by the building of strong stone towers and the emplacing of batteries of cannon. Though the invaders never appeared, the threat helped the king to prepare his country for an inevitable later war.

War broke out in earnest in 1544, following some growing hostilities in the previous year. On one side were Henry's England and Charles's Empire, opposing an informal alliance of France and Scotland.

Henry moved first. In May, 1544, an amphibious force commanded by Lord Lisle entered the Firth of Forth, debarked 12,000 troops against only token opposition, and quickly captured Leith and Edinburgh, except for the citadel. Simultaneously, an English cavalry detachment invaded Scotland from the south, and a second amphibious force crossed the channel to France and took Boulogne. The war seemed to be going extremely well for the English when suddenly word was received that Emperor Charles V had made a separate peace with the French and was pulling his forces out of the war.

Now the shoe was on the other foot. Francis I was no longer the underdog. His fleet was strong enough to carry on offensive operations in the Channel, and his army, equipped with an early form of musket in opposition to the English longbow, was more than able to hold its own. The English king and people found themselves faced with the specter of invasion. At about this time, an army of Scots increased the English feeling of insecurity by routing an English force at Ancrum Moor, very near the border between England and Scotland. It seemed prudent to prepare for a double invasion, and Henry VIII lost no time in doing so.

There could be little doubt where the French invasion would be attempted, for Portsmouth was the only well-equipped English naval base on the Channel. If it could be taken, or even bottled up securely, the English garrisons at Boulogne and Calais, on the French coast, could receive no supplies and reinforcements by sea and thus could quickly be starved out. The arrow must be aimed at Portsmouth.

It so happened that King Henry was having dinner aboard the *Great Harry* at Portsmouth on July 18, 1545, when the French invasion fleet was sighted. Being no sailor, he promptly went ashore to organize the land defenses, leaving the command of the ships in the able hands of John Dudley, Lord Lisle. As the English fleet was hurriedly readied for action, beacon fires flared on the hilltops, and the word traveled rapidly through the country that all men capable of bearing arms were urgently needed at the great naval base. So efficient was this pre-prepared warning system that men a hundred miles away were on the march within an hour of the first sighting of the French fleet.

The first French vessels sighted were four long, slender war galleys, the advance contingent of a squadron of twenty-five such ships which King Francis had brought up from the Mediterranean, under the command of Admiral Leone Strozzi of Rhodes. Following the galleys, at a distance, came three divisions of French sailing warships, 108 in all, the entire fleet being commanded by French Admiral Claude D'Annibault. The English fleet contained only 63 vessels, some of them very small in size.

The sighting of the four galleys led to a sortie by fourteen armed English sailing ships. Prudently, the galleys retired, attempting to draw the fourteen into the heart of the French fleet. When other sails were sighted, however, the fourteen little ships came about and returned to harbor.

July 19 dawned hot and windless—a perfect day for galley action and an impossible one for action by sailing ships. Strozzi, seizing his opportunity, took his twenty-five galleys boldly into Portsmouth Harbor and attacked the helpless sailing vessels as they lay at anchor. Avoiding the dangerous broadside batteries of the English ships, the galley commanders approached from bow or stern and used their own forward-firing guns with some effect. For the better part of an hour, no effective resistance was possible. The English crews merely endured the assault, answering back with the few light swivel guns that they could bring to bear.

The defenders on the shore, meanwhile, had not been idle. A number of light rowing barges were hastily equipped with single guns, firing over the bow, and were sent out to engage the galleys. Strozzi was quick to appreciate his danger. Though these improvised gunboats were tiny compared to his own great galleys, they were far more maneuverable. The long, slender galleys were hard to turn about, and their rams and their guns could be used only straight ahead. From astern or from the side, they were extremely vulnerable. Quickly, he ordered his galleys out of the harbor. As they retired, the English "rowing pieces," as they were called, followed and popped away with their light guns. At last, galled by this insolent attack, Admiral Strozzi took a chance and turned his own galley back toward the attackers. As the heavy guns roared out, the gunboats merely spun about and disappeared among the anchored English vessels. Strozzi continued his turn and followed his retreating galleys out to sea.

Now a sudden strong breeze swept the anchorage, and Admiral Lisle ordered his great ships to hoist sails and slip their moorings in order to pursue. As the fleet stirred into action, disaster struck. The gunports of the *Mary Rose* had been left open through someone's carelessness, and as the tremendous vessel heeled with the wind the starboard main battery was rolled down beneath the surface. King Henry shouted with dismay as he saw his second-largest vessel founder, taking down with her almost her entire crew. The pursuit of the French was called off.

The French, meanwhile, had landed a force of their dreaded musketeers at the eastern end of the Isle of Wight. In two days of desultory fighting, the English found that the longbow had lost none of its effectiveness as a weapon. Several arrows could be launched while a musketeer was reloading once, and a man struck by an arrow was just as dead as one struck by a bullet. The French invaders were driven out.

Admiral D'Annibault was not quite through. He took his fleet eastward and landed another force at Seaford, where they fared no better against the English bowmen than they had on the Isle of Wight. Admiral Lisle, noting that the French ships were anchored just west of a dangerous shoal known as The Owers, set forth with the first westerly wind that arose in the hope of driving the invaders' ships upon the rocks. The wind died, and the attack was abandoned. D'Annibault safely withdrew his fleet across the Channel. Lisle, having incurred royal displeasure for making an attempt without King Henry's specific approval, made no attempt to follow.

The French were back within a month. This time the fleets met, not in a harbor, but in mid-Channel. As before, the wind was too light to permit effective maneuvering by the sailing ships. Accordingly, Admiral D'Annibault sent his galleys ahead to attack the English. Admiral Lisle countered with a squadron of galleasses, under Captain William Tyrell. These oar-driven ships, though slower than the galleys, carried guns which could fire astern and abeam as well as straight ahead. Strozzi's French galleys were heavily battered and were kept away from Lisle's English sailing vessels. Both fleets anchored for the night, it being the general expectation that if the wind should arise during the night there would be a general engagement between the sailing fleets soon after daylight. The rising sun, though, revealed an empty sea where the French fleet had lain. D'Annibault had gone home.

Thanks to his foresight in building up an effective navy, King Henry VIII had won his war and had repelled the dangerous invasion attempt by the French. A treaty was signed in 1546. By its terms, King Francis had to pay King Henry a heavy indemnity.

With the war over, King Henry VIII did not allow his fleet to waste away. A permanent organization was set up to supervise the building, maintenance, and supply of ships. This was the genesis of the later Navy Board, so important in establishing England's long-time control of the seas. On the evidence of the recent hostilities, those in charge turned to "the great ship," with her sails and broadside cannon, rather than to the oared galleys, still so much in favor in the Mediterranean area to the south.

The pattern was set for English ascendancy, though one important factor could not yet be recognized. At about the same time when the new naval organization was holding its first meetings, the Drake farmhouse on the outskirts of Dartmoor was echoing to the squalls of a newborn baby boy whose proud parents had decided to name him Francis.

2

⚓

PORTUGUESE SEA POWER

1.

We must now go back in time and south in direction to pick up the story of Portugal's rise and eventual decline as a naval power. In its early stages, this development was strangely interlinked with that of England.

In the year 711 A.D., the people of the Iberian Peninsula began to suffer from the scourge of Mohammedanism, which had crept along the northern coast of Africa during most of the preceding century and then, like a forest fire crossing a creek, had vaulted across the narrow strait separating Africa from Europe. Tarik was the Moslem leader who established the first foothold in Europe. On a great rock on the northern shore of the strait he built a solid, square stone fortress, which still stands today. Gibral Tarik ("Tarik's rock") was the name he gave the great Nature-carved citadel which he had claimed. It is still called Gibraltar, having lost only the last two letters of its original name.

For nearly eight centuries, the people of the Iberian Peninsula were fated to fight the invaders in defense of their lands, their souls, and their very lives. To the true Spaniard or Portuguese, no more virtuous or praiseworthy act could be performed than to strike a blow at these menacing intruders of an alien faith.

In 1147, King Alfonso I of Portugal was besieging the great port of Lisbon, which had been taken by the Mohammedans. There seemed little prospect that the city could be taken. Indeed, the Portuguese forces were doing so badly that King Alfonso began to fear lest the defenders sally forth and take him and his army. At this point, a strange fleet came sailing up the Tagus River toward the city. The ships were definitely not Spanish or Portuguese. If they should prove to be Mohammedan, the whole cause would be lost. To the king's relief, they were English, carrying English, Flemish, and German knights to the Holy Land to take part in the Second Crusade. A sudden storm had turned them from their course, and they had entered the river in search of a safe anchorage.

King Alfonso did a magnificent job of salesmanship. "Why go so far to kill the infidels?" he asked. "We have plenty of them right here."

The crusaders debarked, joined the Portuguese, and helped them liberate the city. This was the beginning of a long and friendly relationship between the English and the Portuguese.

Forty-three years later, history repeated itself. Sancho I of Portugal, Alfonso's son, was engaged in desperate battle with the Mohammedans when another English fleet arrived in the nick of time and turned the tide in Sancho's favor. These Englishmen were also crusaders, members of the Third Crusade, on their way to the Holy Land. Small wonder the Portuguese and English became fast friends!

The close association became closer still when a Portuguese prince married an English princess. Prince John was the illegitimate son of King Pedro I. Though apparently excluded from the royal succession, he entered the picture when the crown seemed in danger of falling into Spanish hands. To keep Portugal free, he fought the Spaniards and defeated them, with some help from England. As a reward, he was elected king in 1385. His alliance with England was firmly bolstered by his marriage to Philippa, daughter of John of Gaunt of the royal English House of Lancaster.

King John I and Queen Philippa had many children, of whom five were sons—Duarte, Pedro, Henry, John, and Ferdinand. In one way or another, all were to make their mark in history. Growing into manhood, the five wished to win their spurs by taking the Mohammedan stronghold of Ceuta, across the Strait of Gibraltar. For a long time, King John opposed this ambitious undertaking, but at last he gave in and threw himself wholeheartedly into the preparations.

Although secrecy was necessary, word of the extensive military and naval buildup within Portugal eventually filtered across the borders and alarmed the European neighbors. Against whom would the blow be directed? King John would not say, lest the Moors be alerted, but he answered each foreign inquiry with the assurance that the inquiring nation was not the one which would be attacked. Of the likely targets, only Holland made no inquiry and hence received no assurance. This led to the widely believed rumor that the war was to be fought with Holland. Apparently, the Moors never considered the possibility that they were the designated recipients of all the attention.

2.

In the spring of 1415, when the fleet was almost ready to sail, a plague visited Portugal. Among the many thousands of victims was beloved Queen Philippa. As she lay dying, her thoughts were all of her husband and her sons and their great venture. A promise was extracted that her death would not be allowed to interfere. It did not. The fleet sailed in the summer. With the exception of the members of the royal family, no one knew the destination.

At dusk on August 19, 1415, the inhabitants of Ceuta were amazed and horrified to see a vast fleet of warships sail into their harbor. In a desperate but futile attempt to frighten the invaders, the Moorish governor, Salat ben Salat, ordered all citizens to place torches or candles in all windows and doors facing the harbor. In the gathering darkness, the lighted city looked tremendous. To counter this impression, King John ordered as many torches and lanterns as possible to be displayed on all of his ships. Together, the city and the fleet must have made a truly impressive sight.

At dawn, King John began a formal review of his fleet, in preparation for the general assault on the city. As a first order of business, he recommended to all that his third son, Prince Henry, should be given the honor of leading the first attack. That was all that Prince Henry and his older brother, Duarte, wanted to hear. Together, they slipped away, took a picked group of men, and set out for the beach while King John went on with the dull business of formal preparation. By the time he got around to issuing an order that under no conditions was the heir-apparent, Duarte, to go ashore, it was much too late.

The advanced landing party was met on the beach by a group of patriotic but somewhat discouraged young Mohammedans, among whom were two gigantic soldiers noted for their prowess. These two advanced ahead of their fellows, each swinging a heavy scimitar in unmistakable challenge. The challenge was accepted. Two experienced Portuguese soldiers drew their swords, stepped forward, and quickly cut down their selected opponents. The battle then became general when Prince Duarte led a charge which broke the Mohammedan lines. Prince Henry had favored waiting for the arrival of the main body, but he delayed no longer when he saw his brother's dangerous advance. Each led his men toward the city.

King John at last finished his review and sent his second son, Pedro, to tell Henry that he might now lead the attack. Imagine his surprise when word came back that both Henry and Duarte had gone ashore and had already succeeded in forcing their separate ways within the city. At once, the main Portuguese force swung into action, rushing to the assistance of the hard-pressed advance guard. It was just as well, for both brothers were having a hard time maintaining their positions. Prince Henry's situation was especially dangerous, for he and five of his knights found themselves backed into a *cul-de-sac,* fighting for their lives. The rumor spread that he was dead, but he was at last rescued, and the city was taken. Had the rumor been true, history since 1415 might have followed a very different course.

Thus Ceuta became a Portuguese stronghold on the northern shore of Africa. During the next three years, its governor, Prince Pedro, had to withstand almost daily counterattacks from the unhappy Moors. This he did successfully. During the fourth year, 1419, the Moors launched an all-out assault, aided by a Mohammedan fleet and army from Granada, in southern Spain. Fearing that this would be too formidable a force for the garrison to withstand, King John sent a strong fleet under Prince Henry and Prince John. The Portuguese relief expedition arrived without warning, while the Moors were busy attacking the city. The Mohammedan fleet in the harbor had been drained of its manpower and fell an easy victim to the princes and their cannon-armed carracks. When the Moorish fleet had been captured, the fighting men swarmed ashore and completely routed the attacking host. Ceuta was now secure.

3.

Although Prince Henry took part in the relief of Ceuta in 1419, his heart was no longer in such military expeditions. His burning enthusiasm was for exploration. Already, at the age of twenty-two, he had founded the seaport of Sagres near Cape St. Vincent, at the southwestern tip of his country. Already, he had begun his detailed study of maps, and his collection of mariners and geographers. Though he fought well at Ceuta, he could scarcely wait to get back to the stone tower at Sagres, which served him both as a home and as a studio-laboratory.

There were many motives, some visionary and some practical, that

led Prince Henry the Navigator to send out exploring expeditions—
the first two at his own expense, before his father's enthusiasm and
support were gained. The Portuguese currency had been debased to
the point of instability, and the treasury was desperately in need of
gold. It was believed that there were rich gold mines somewhere south
of the Sahara; indeed, legend spoke of a "river of gold" which
poured westward from the heart of Africa into the Atlantic. Discovery
of these gold fields would restore prosperity. There was also the need
for allies against the menace of Mohammedanism. Persistent rumors
spoke of a powerful Christian ruler, Prester John ("John, the
Priest"), who governed a rich land somewhere in Asia or Africa. If he
could be found and his favors gained, Christianity would be greatly
strengthened. Then there was the question of trade with the East,
whence came spices and other goods in great demand throughout Europe. Venice and Genoa controlled the only known routes to the East,
partly by sea and partly by land from the eastern Mediterranean.
Might not an all-sea route be found which would eliminate transship-
ment and give Portugal a monopoly? In later years, this last motiva-
tion received increased importance, as the Ottoman Turks tightened
their grip on the eastern Mediterranean and began to monopolize the
Asiatic trade for themselves.

At the time when Prince Henry began to send out his explorers,
little was known about the greater part of the African continent.
There was no first-hand knowledge of the lands or seas south of Cape
Nun, on the coast of what is now Morocco. Since progress toward the
Torrid Zone brought higher temperatures, it was widely believed that
the seas south of Cape Nun consisted of boiling water, which no mariner could cross. Long forgotten was the expedition which King Necho
II of Egypt had dispatched under Phoenician command more than
two thousand years before—an expedition which had completely cir-
cumnavigated Africa from the Strait of Suez, south through the Red
Sea and the Indian Ocean, around the cape, north through the Atlantic Ocean, through the Strait of Gibraltar, thence east through the
Mediterranean to Egypt. Herodotus, in writing of this epic three-year
voyage, records as the one doubtful item the very fact which proves it
true in light of modern astronomical knowledge: ". . . They related
(which I myself do not believe, though perhaps some others may)
that as they rounded Africa they beheld the sun on their right hand."

All this had long been forgotten, washed out along with other cultural and scientific achievements by the eroding effects of ignorance and superstitious preoccupation with religion during the darker parts of the Middle Ages. Now it all had to be discovered over again, and Prince Henry was there, ready to play a leading part in its rediscovery.

At first, Prince Henry's sailors, venturing timidly south along the rugged African coast, accomplished little. Not far south of Cape Nun was dreaded Cape Bojador, whose sheer rock cliffs rose from a seething mass of foam-covered reefs. Those who came within sight of this abode of death turned back in terror. Farther west, though, there were some results. Madeira was discovered and settled in 1418, and in 1432 the Azores were discovered and claimed—actually *re*discovered, since Phoenician ships had regularly visited them as early as seventeen centuries before. Visits were also made to the Canaries, but these islands could not be claimed for Portugal because it soon developed that a Spanish expedition had gotten there earlier, in 1402.

The death of King John I in 1433, and the accession of Prince Duarte to the throne, brought no interruption in Prince Henry's expeditions. Duarte proved to be as liberal a patron as his father had been. In 1434, a daring captain named Gil Eanes rounded terrible Cape Bojador and discovered, to his amazement, that he and his men were still alive. His ships had not foundered on the reefs, nor had he encountered tremendous monsters or boiling seas. The way was open for further exploration to the south. Soon thereafter, another captain, venturing still farther south beyond the Cape Bojador, found what he believed to be the mouth of the famous "river of gold." Actually, it was not a river but a mere opening in the line of reefs, and it yielded no gold at all. Its name, however, still appears upon the maps of Africa as Rio de Oro.

4.

In 1437, there was a tragic interruption. Prince Ferdinand, the youngest of the five brothers, had been too young to take part in the attack on Ceuta. Thirsting for glory, he strongly urged King Duarte to let him lead an attack on Tangier, another important African stronghold of the Mohammedans. Prince Henry strongly supported the demand, which was opposed by Prince Pedro. Duarte, uncertain of the rights of the matter, appealed to the Pope, who could see no justification, since the Moslems had been making no attacks on Christians or their possessions. Nevertheless, a decision was reached in favor of the war, on the grounds that all Christian monarchs were under oath to do everything possible "for the greater glory of God."

The Cortes and the people of Portugal were decidedly lukewarm on the question of the attack on Tangier. As a result, few men and few ships were provided. This made no difference to Prince Henry and Prince Ferdinand. Was not one Portuguese more than equal to two, or three, or even four Mohammedans? Short-handed and underequipped as it was, the expedition set sail on August 22, 1437.

Arriving at Ceuta, the brothers divided their forces, Prince Henry leading a group by land and Prince Ferdinand commanding the fleet. Both forces reached Tangier without incident and reunited to begin the siege. From the very beginning, everything went wrong. The members of the first wave of Portuguese to reach the walls found that their scaling ladders were too short to reach any openings into which they could be hooked. There was nothing to do but fall back. Now they were attacked by increasing numbers of angry Moors who had come swarming from the many Mohammedan strongholds located nearby. The pressure and the odds became too great. Prince Henry issued orders to resist strongly until dark, then to fall back to the shore and take refuge on the ships. This plan might have succeeded but for the treachery of Prince Henry's own chaplain, the priest Martin Vieyra, who stole away and informed the Mohammedan leaders. As a result, the Portuguese force was quickly cut off from the sea.

Soon, lack of food and water brought terrible suffering to the entrapped invaders. To save the lives of his men, young Prince Ferdinand offered himself as a hostage. The offer was accepted, but even after the prince had delivered himself to the enemy the Mohammedans launched further attacks, making it necessary for the Portuguese survivors to fight their way back to the beach and to the safety of their ships.

It soon became evident that the Mohammedans intended to make the greatest possible use of their royal hostage. With scorn and insults, they rejected the idea of exchanging him for any prisoner or combination of prisoners in Portuguese hands. Only the captured stronghold of Ceuta would be considered as a fair exchange. The news prostrated Prince Henry, who was at Ceuta preparing to return to Lisbon. Prince John hastened to his side, and together they agreed that, much as they loved their brother, they could not recommend the surrender of the great African base. King Duarte was even more seriously affected by the worry and sorrow of the situation. Unwilling to make so grave a decision himself, he called a meeting of the Cortes (parliament) and turned the question over to the members. After spirited debate, a majority voted to retain Ceuta, but to use every effort to ransom Prince Ferdinand with money. The decision carried double death. King Duarte, overcome with worry and remorse, sickened and died in 1438. Five years later, the insults, injuries, and deprivations experienced by Ferdinand at the hands of his Mohammedan captors brought welcome death to the miserable royal hostage.

5.

The death of King Duarte bestowed the throne on his six-year-old son, Alfonso V. Since the new king was much too young to rule, Prince Pedro was made regent. He did a good and conscientious job, but enemies in the court undermined his reputation and laid the ground work for his eventual overthrow when Alfonso should reach his fourteenth year and become, by Portuguese law, a grown man, ready to rule in his own right.

In 1441, Prince Henry was able to renew his expeditions, which had been interrupted by the tragedy at Tangier and by his brother's death. Prince Pedro, as regent, gave him all possible assistance, including a complete monopoly of all claims and profits made south of Cape Bojador.

One voyage after another was made, each going farther than the last. South of Rio de Oro, a Moorish settlement was reached, and trade in sealskins and seal oil was instituted. A little farther south, contact was made with Negro tribes possessing gold. Here was a double source of revenue—the gold and the Negroes themselves! The infamous African slave trade began with this voyage in 1441. On subsequent voyages, Cape Blanco, the Senegal and Gambia rivers, and Cape Verde were reached.

Prince Henry found it necessary to discontinue his explorations in 1446, in order to play a pacifying role in the now-bitter quarrel between his brother Pedro and his nephew, King Alfonso. The attempt failed. After three years of growing friction, a small battle was fought, and Pedro was killed. Young Alfonso and his dubious counselors were left in power.

Dismayed and disheartened, Prince Henry returned to his lonely tower at Sagres, where he received more unhappy news. The gist of the reports that trickled in was that numerous illegal Portuguese expeditions had been violating his West African monopoly, sowing distrust among the natives, and making an even more odious traffic out of his small-scale slave trade.

Resuming his life where it had been interrupted, the Prince sent out a number of additional expeditions. Attempts were made to sail up the Senegal and Gambia rivers to the land of Prester John. Rapids in the rivers defeated both attempts. A few more probings were made along Africa's westernmost shoulder before advancing age, diminishing finances, and a renewal of the Portuguese campaign in North Africa forced this great pioneer explorer to bring an end to his significant hobby.

6.

The victory, it seems, does not always go to the strong. Alfonso V was one of the weakest of Portuguese kings, yet he succeeded where many of his stronger predecessors had failed.

Alfonso had long dreamed, as had many Portuguese, of a campaign to avenge the martyred Prince Ferdinand. This dream might well have come to nothing had not an additional stimulus been received. In 1453, the Ottoman Turks captured Constantinople, brought the Eastern Roman Empire to an end, and completed the blocking of the trade routes to the East. At once, a belated wave of fervor swept western Europe. A league was formed for the express purpose of driving the heathen Turks back into central Asia, where they could no longer trouble Christians. Portugal was a member of the league. It occurred to Alfonso that the capture of the Mohammedan bases in North Africa would constitute an important contribution to Christendom, to the league, and—last but by no means least—to Portugal.

Alfonso wanted to attack powerful Tangier, but his advisers knew better. They convinced him that it would be far wiser to capture a small base than to fail in an attempt against a large one. Consequently, the target was shifted to the little city of Alcacer-Seguier, and plans were rushed for the creation of an overwhelming force.

In September, 1457, 200 vessels—mostly carracks and caravels—set sail, carrying some 20,000 picked Portuguese soldiers. This was more than three times the force which had been sent twenty years before against the much stronger city of Tangier. Taken along, somewhat against his will, was poor old Prince Henry, who would far rather have been spending his time and energy preparing further voyages of exploration.

The Moors were taken entirely by surprise. No fleet appeared to bar the progress of the Portuguese transports, nor was there any effective resistance on the beaches. Scarcely had the formal siege of Alcacer-Seguier begun than the city surrendered. It was a worthwhile victory, but it yielded little honor and no glory. All in all, the quick surrender smacked strongly of anticlimax.

Prince Henry's day was done. He died in 1460 without having the opportunity to outfit any more expeditions. He had sent out, in all, more than fifty explorations and had materially increased man's knowledge of the world.

7.

The resources of Portugal were now poured freely into preparations for an attack on Tangier. The easy success at Alcacer-Seguier had made an equally easy conquest of its greater neighbor seem almost certain.

The attack was launched in 1464. Again, no Mohammedan fleet appeared, and the landing was made with little difficulty. Here all resemblance to the Alcacer-Seguier campaign ceased. Determined attacks upon the strong and lofty walls of Tangier were driven back with frightful losses. The flower of the Portuguese army beat itself to pieces against the city. Then came the inevitable circling movement, and once more a Portuguese expeditionary force found itself trapped before Tangier. Far from avenging Prince Ferdinand, Alfonso found himself in grave danger of emulating him.

In desperation, the entrapped Portuguese made an all-out attempt to cut their way through to freedom. Thousands died, but the king and a group of his followers managed to fight their way through the Moorish lines and reach the sea, where Portuguese warships joined in the fight and aided the escape. Had not the fleet cooperated well, there would have been few if any survivors.

It took nearly seven years for King Alfonso to overcome the terror occasioned by his narrow escape. Probably he would never again have made an attempt upon the Moslems had not his son, Prince John, begun to dream of glory and to urge his royal father to erase the stain on his and his country's name. Eventually, the needling had its effect.

In 1471, a tremendous expedition of more than 30,000 soldiers in

308 carracks and caravels set sail from the harbors of Portugal for North Africa. The target this time was Arsilla, a small city on the Atlantic coast. Small cities, it seemed, were easier to take than large ones, and a victory—any victory—was badly needed.

The people of Arsilla did their best to resist, but the odds were too great. The Portuguese swarmed in, bent on erasing memories of Tangier. King Alfonso and Prince John assumed the lead in the erasing process, which consisted of a complete, cold-blooded massacre. In this most un-Christian orgy of blood-letting, nobody was spared, regardless of age, sex, or willingness to surrender.

It would seem that the king and the prince deserved nothing good from this slaughter of the innocents. Desserts are not always just; sometimes they are most surprising. Word of the slaughter reached Tangier and caused a general panic. The strong city, which had twice repulsed the best of Portuguese effort, now became a victim of its own fears. The people hastily gathered what they could of their possessions and went away, leaving Tangier open to bloodless conquest. Surprised but happy, Alfonso and John occupied the city. It was subsequently peopled by imported Christians. As a result of his unexpectedly and undeservedly successful campaign, Alfonso was honored by the title Africanus, which must have sounded, at times, a bit sarcastic, even to him.

8.

Alfonso V died of the plague in 1481. He was followed on the throne by his son, John II—commonly known as "John the Perfect" —under whom Portuguese explorers obtained their greatest successes and the country reached the height of its power.

King John was a man of direct and vigorous action. Typical of his methods was the handling of a case of piracy. A Portuguese vessel was taken on the high seas by a French pirate. Although the identity of the buccaneer was known, the French government for some reason declined to take any action. At once, King John ordered the seizure of all French ships in Portuguese waters. When the French protested, they were told that the ships and their crews would be held until the Portuguese vessel, together with its crew, passengers, and cargo, should be returned to its owners. At once, the dilatory French stirred themselves, and it was not long before the ship returned to its home port. The French vessels were not released. When representatives of the French king protested, they were told that a parrot which had been aboard the Portuguese ship was still missing. Not a French vessel would be permitted to sail until that parrot should be returned. Once more, the high French officials bestirred themselves. The parrot was found and delivered to its owner, and an important international incident came to an end. Like Alexander the Great before him and Theodore Roosevelt after him, King John II of Portugal knew how to cut through red tape and opposition and get things done.

9.

Early in his reign, King John came to appreciate the value to Portugal of the discoveries which had been made as a result of Prince Henry's earlier impetus. What if some other nations should send ships to take advantage of Portugal's explorations? Many steps were quickly taken to protect the monopoly. A strong fort was erected at Mina on the Guinea coast to discourage all foreign visitors. Carefully exaggerated accounts of the dangers and terrors of African voyages were widely circulated, to lessen the zeal of unwanted navigators. Three experienced Portuguese pilots who deserted the king's service and fled to Castile were pursued in the best cloak-and-dagger tradition; two were murdered, and the third was spirited back across the border and quartered, to the horror of all others who contemplated such defections. Finally, an expedition which was being prepared in England was halted through the method of a direct appeal from King John II of Portugal to King Edward IV of England. Wherever possible, in short, rival expeditions were nipped in the bud.

While competitors were being discouraged, Portuguese explorers were receiving every encouragement. Year by year, it was becoming more evident that a new route must be found if Portugal and its royal house were to grow wealthy from Europe's growing taste for spices and other Eastern luxuries. King John and his advisers were convinced that India could be reached by passing around the southern tip of Africa. The fact that the coastline slanted eastward just south of Cape Verde was regarded as a sign that the continent did not extend much farther to the south. It was hoped, in fact, that the Portuguese fort which had been constructed at Mina was at or near the southernmost point. Great was the disappointment, then, when later explorers reported that the coast again turned southward beyond Mina.

Still, the king did not give up. In 1482, he sent Diego Cao to go as far south as possible, planting marble crosses as he went to establish Portuguese claims to any new shores discovered. On this first voyage, Cao discovered the mouth of the Congo and passed beyond it. On a second voyage, two years later, he went still farther, reaching Cape Cross and establishing one of his markers there.

King John was now sure that it would not be long before one of his explorers would pass around the Cape and definitely establish the direct ocean route to the East. What would happen then? To pave the way, he sent two of his most trusted emissaries eastward through the Mediterranean, across Suez, and down the Red Sea. Both were well versed in Mohammedan ways and spoke the Arabic tongue fluently. One man, Pero de Covilha, was then to go on to India by the known Mohammedan trade route; the other, Alfonso de Paiva, was to become familiar with the eastern coast of Africa, then strike inland to Ethiopia, whose inhabitants were said to be Coptic Christians. Might not *this* be the origin of the legend of Prester John?

Covilha had the greater success. He reached India, learned what he could, then returned to Cairo, exploring the East African coast as he went. Here he learned that Paiva was dead. Soon he was found by two Jewish travelers, bearing a letter for him from King John. The king, it seemed, wanted him to go at once to Ethiopia and establish friendly relations. Not wishing to risk the loss of the valuable information he had gained in India, he wrote a long and detailed letter to the king, entrusting it to one of the Jewish travelers. Then he set off into the heart of Africa and disappeared. His letter eventually reached the king and proved most valuable in the formulation of his plans.

10.

King John, meanwhile, was continuing to send his explorers southward. In the summer of 1487, Bartholomew Diaz set sail from Lisbon. South, then east, then south again he went, past Mina, past the Congo, past Cape Cross. More than three hundred miles beyond the farthest point previously reached, he came upon a broad bay, now known as Luderitz Bay. Farther than this, he dared not go. As he was turning homeward, a sudden storm swept down from the north. There was no possibility of bucking it. The only safety lay in reducing sail and running before the monstrous waves. For thirteen tumultuous days, the little vessel fled southward before the storm. When at last the wind died down, Diaz swung his ship to the eastward to reach the

African coast. Days passed, and there was no land ahead. The coast had disappeared! Was it possible that the southern tip of Africa had been passed? The course was changed again, this time to due north. At last, land appeared ahead. An anchorage was found at Mossel Bay. A short voyage to the east definitely established the fact that the coastline steadily curved northeastward, toward India.

As soon as possible, Diaz set sail for home, rounding the Cape in a roaring storm that came close to reducing this expedition, like so many others, to the status of an unsolved mystery of the sea.

Back in Lisbon, the explorer lost no time in reporting to his king. Because of the stormy conditions under which he had seen Africa's southern tip, he spoke of his landfall there as "the Cape of Storms." King John gently chided him. Said he, "Let us rather call it the Cape of Good Hope, for there is now good hope that we have at last found our route to India."

11.

One would have thought that King John would immediately fit out a new expedition and send it out under Diaz, to complete the voyage to India and open up the much-desired new trade route. King John did not do so. Instead, he set Diaz to work developing a more seaworthy type of vessel than the frail carracks and caravels in which the early explorers had made their journeys. The need for such a vessel had been noted in the report which Diaz had rendered to the king. The result, after some years of experimentation, was a strong and seaworthy craft known as a *nau*. In appearance, a *nau* somewhat resembled a large carrack, but had even more rounded lines and far greater height. Above the bow platform, which had now become the overhanging head, towered a solid forecastle. The aftercastle was also increased in height by one full deck. These improvements, besides adding seaworthiness, also provided the opportunity for mounting more broadside guns. The *nau* was a far better warship than her earlier relatives.

While Diaz was still puttering around with his shipbuilding experiments, distressing news reached the court of Portugal. According to the reports, received in 1492, Spain had beaten the Portuguese in making the first all-water voyage to the Far East. A Genoese navigator named Christopher Columbus had been the one to do it. King John remembered him well. Back in 1484, Columbus had appeared at the Portuguese court with a visionary plan for reaching the countries of the East by sailing west, around the world. The king had listened to his story but had declined to back him, feeling that his own plans for sailing around Africa were far more practical than this fantastic thought of going around a world which might or might not prove to be round. Columbus had then gone to Spain, where King Ferdinand and Queen Isabella had given him ships, men, and money. Now he was back—without spices or rich oriental goods, to be sure—claiming to have reached the islands of the Indies by sailing a mere 3,000 miles westward across the Atlantic. If his story proved true, Spain had a far shorter water route to the East than Portugal could hope to find around Africa!

Nevertheless, King John did not give up hope. Preparations continued to be made for an expedition of four ships, three of them being of the newly developed *nau* design. The king chose Estevao da Gama to command the little fleet. In bypassing Diaz, he was following a rather pointless pattern which had been developed as early as the times of Prince Henry the Navigator—that of not permitting the same commander to head two consecutive voyages. Whatever such a plan might gain in eagerness to outdo a predecessor would be more than offset, it would seem, by the sacrifice of hard-gained experience.

Death dealt a double blow to the plans. First, King John died. Though still a young man of only forty, he had been sadly stricken by the accidental death of his only legitimate son. Shortly afterward, Estevao da Gama also died. It began to look as though the long series of Portuguese explorations might come to nothing.

12.

The new king, Manuel I, was the brother of Queen Leonor of Portugal. Fortunately, he, too, had an interest in finding the long-sought trade route. One of his first acts was to appoint, as new commander, Vasco da Gama, the son of the deceased admiral. Bartholomew Diaz, though again passed over for the command, was engaged to accompany Da Gama on the voyage. In July, 1497, the ships set out on the first leg of their voyage, to the Cape Verde Islands.

Leaving the islands on August 3, Da Gama and Diaz combined their talents to perform a daring and, for that day, an almost miraculous feat of navigation. Instead of hugging the coast, as all previous explorers had done, they set out for the Cape on a great semicircular course designed to avoid the hampering northward currents along the shores of Africa and to take advantage of the southern belt of prevailing westerlies. Without any device for determining longitude, and with only the crude astrolabe to indicate approximate latitude, this was an almost foolhardy thing to attempt. For 97 days, the little ships plowed along through unknown seas. When at last they sighted land, it was at St. Helena Bay, less than one hundred miles north of the Cape for which they had been aiming. To this day, experienced navigators marvel at this tremendous feat of dead reckoning.

Arrival at the Cape showed the wisdom of preparing the new and stronger type of ship. So vicious a storm arose that for three full days the ships were all but overwhelmed by the mountainous seas that poured across their decks. The upperworks were badly battered and the holds half flooded. It became necessary to jettison a good deal of the cargo just to stay afloat. But stay afloat they did, and at the end of the third day the storm lifted.

When once around Africa's southern shore and headed north, Vasco da Gama began to make good use of the old letter which Covilha had sent to the king, telling of his discoveries in India and Africa. It was extremely useful, though it could not inform him of all the dangers and problems he would face.

The first sound of cannon fire to echo across the waters of the Indian Ocean was heard early in 1498 when some natives who had seemed friendly suddenly launched an attack on a Portuguese landing party. They were quickly and bloodlessly dispersed by a few cannon balls fired over their heads. More dangerous were the Mohammedan merchants who were encountered a little farther north along the coast, in Mozambique and elsewhere. These men, who openly welcomed Da Gama through his Arab interpreter, soon recognized him as a deadly competitor for the rich Eastern trade. On several occasions, they planned native attacks, which were frustrated only by a combination of luck and vigilance. In this first casual contact lay the seeds of a most bitter rivalry.

At Melinde, which he reached in March, 1498, Da Gama had the rare good fortune to meet an experienced Arab pilot named Ahmed-bem-Madjid. Guided by this man, he struck out boldly across the Indian Ocean and was able to steer a direct course for Calicut, India, which he reached on May 20. The local ruler, Samoudri-Rajah, received him cordially but became cool when he learned that the explorer had not come laden with suitable gifts. The Mohammedan merchants, of whom there were many, hastened to exploit the coolness and to intensify it. As a result, Da Gama was unable to establish good trade relations and had to leave India on a note of frustration. He eventually reached home about September 1, 1499, having been gone a little more than two years. The way was now open for the development of sea-borne trade between Portugal and the East and for the outbreak of a merciless naval war on the waters of the Indian Ocean.

13.

In the meantime, an extraordinary international development had taken place. Portugal had discovered lands and trade routes to the south and to the east. Spain, in the person of Christopher Columbus, had discovered lands and routes to the west. Sooner or later, it seemed certain that the two nations would clash over some mutually claimed territory. Pope Alexander VI was deeply worried over this probability. In 1493, the Pope issued a bull arbitrarily stating that Portugal should have any new lands discovered east of an imaginary demarcation line extending north and south from pole to pole 300 miles west of the Cape Verde Islands. Spain was to have any new lands discovered west of the line. A year later, in 1494, the Spanish and Portuguese governments signed a treaty incorporating the Pope's provision but moving the demarcation line 810 miles farther west.

Although Portugal and Spain were the only two European nations that had yet shown an interest in exploration, the Pope's bull and the treaty which followed it were received with something less than enthusiasm by the rulers of the other nations of Europe. Most indignant of all was King Francis I of France, who sarcastically demanded to be shown Father Adam's will dividing the world between Spain and Portugal.

14.

The return of Da Gama brought joy to King Manuel. Now, at long last, the hoped-for route to India had been found. At once, he made plans for sending out a great expedition of thirteen ships, headed by Alvarez Cabral. The fleet set sail in March, 1500. In attempting to duplicate Da Gama's feat of navigation, Cabral encountered strong winds from the east, which carried him far west of his intended course. When land was at last sighted, it turned out to be the easternmost tip of South America. Cabral landed and claimed the land for Portugal, giving it the name Brazil because of the many brazilwood trees which he saw growing there. By a strange coincidence, this eastward-jutting landfall was the only part of either American continent which lay on the Portuguese side of the famous demarcation line.

Cabral reached Calicut on September 13, 1500. An audience was arranged, and the Portuguese went, dressed in their best outfits, to overawe the natives. Instead, it was the Portuguese who were overawed by the jewels and wealth and sumptuousness of the Rajah's court. Though neither group trusted the other, the Rajah finally assented to the idea of a Portuguese trading post in Calicut. It was duly established. When the fleet had sailed, however, the ever-present Mohammedan traders stirred up the natives, who burned the trading post and killed the fifty Portuguese who had been left to man it.

Somehow, word of the massacre reached Cabral, who had not yet left the shores of India on his return voyage. Back he came, with blood in his eye. On the way, he encountered a fleet of ten Mohammedan galleys. It was not a fair test of galley against sailing ship, for the Mohammedans were utterly unprepared for the broadsides which were poured into their ships at close range. It seems probable that these particular Mohammedans knew nothing of the cause of the admiral's fury. Overwhelmed, they quickly surrendered. They might better have continued to fight. Cabral cold-bloodedly slaughtered every man on every ship. Then on he went to Calicut, bombarded the city, and burned it.

In January, 1501, Alvarez Cabral set sail for Portugal, his ships bulging with cargoes of pepper and cinnamon. Behind him he left a sullen but fearful India, whose people were beginning to understand the true nature of the smiling Christian traders who came from across the sea.

15.

Neither the Hindus nor the Mohammedan traders were given an opportunity to forget the Portuguese and their methods. Early in 1502, a fleet of twenty armed trading ships set out from Lisbon, bent upon making clear to all that Portugal owned both the lands and the seas of the East. It was now Vasco da Gama's turn to command again. With him, in subordinate command, he took his nephew, the young and energetic Vincente Sodre.

Even before India was sighted Da Gama had an opportunity to place the imprint of his personality upon the voyage. In the Arabian Sea he encountered a Mohammedan merchant vessel carrying more than two hundred traders, with their wives and children. The ship was attacked without provocation and taken without difficulty. After stripping the ship, passengers, and crew of everything worth taking, Da Gama herded the unfortunate Mohammedans into the bow, set the ship on fire, and abandoned them to perish by burning or drowning, as each preferred. If the commander's purpose in this early example of *spurlos versenkt* was to eliminate witnesses and evidence, he failed miserably. Though no Mohammedans survived, many of his own crew recorded in their private journals both the event and the feelings of horror which it aroused.

Arriving at Calicut, Da Gama soon determined that Samoudri-Rajah was in no mood to welcome him. The scars left by the bombardment and fire of the previous year were still much in evidence. So were the Mohammedan traders, who had not failed to point out to the ruler the many advantages of their own, more gentle method of dealing. The coolness of the reception did not daunt the Portuguese commander. At once, he sent word ashore that Samoudri-Rajah must at once expel all Mohammedans, together with their families. Having a shrewd idea of the answer he would receive, Da Gama at the same time sent groups of soldiers in small boats to round up all local merchants they could find. These unhappy people were brought back to the Portuguese fleet and held as hostages.

As anticipated, Samoudri-Rajah flatly refused to expel the Mohammedans. Very well! He could be made to regret it! At once, the inoffensive hostages were brought to the deck of the flagship. In turn, each had his hands chopped off and his ears sliced from his head. The mutilated men were then dumped into a small boat and permitted to drift ashore as a bloody commentary upon their ruler's lack of cooperation.

To Da Gama's mind, the maiming of a few hostages was by no means an adequate answer to Samoudri-Rajah's "insolence." The more substantial part of the Portuguese answer quickly followed. The twenty ships, anchored in a long line off the city, ran out their guns and began a systematic bombardment of defenseless Calicut. Resistance was hopeless. The native soldiers had only spears and arrows with which to oppose the cannon balls which came thundering in from the ships. There was nothing for them to do but huddle in whatever shelter they could find while their city was hammered to pieces about them.

Calicut was now obviously no fit place to serve as Portuguese head-quarters in India. Not far down the coast was the rival city of Cochin. Thence Da Gama sailed when he was through with Calicut, and there he left part of his fleet under Vincente Sodre when he, himself, returned to Portugal with a fine sense of Christian duty done.

During his uncle's absence, young Sodre divided his time between the practice of selective piracy and a campaign to bring about open war between his hosts at Cochin and his old enemies at Calicut. Both activities were successful. On the sea, his vessels succeeded in intercepting and robbing large numbers of Mohammedan vessels and in killing their crews. At the same time, the Rajah of Cochin lent an attentive ear, and the war with Calicut broke out actively. These events were duly reported by a ship dispatched to Lisbon.

16.

In April, 1503, another large fleet set sail from Portugal under the command of Alfonso de Albuquerque. Arriving at Cochin, Albuquerque had his men set to work at once building a strong stone fort with which to nail down Portuguese control. When the fort had been finished, the admiral returned to Portugal, leaving his soldiers and most of his ships under the command of a veteran soldier named Duarte Pacheco. We should note this man well, for he was one of the few admirable characters connected in any way with Portugal's conquest of the East.

Pacheco's ships gave him command of the sea, but this was a minor advantage in dealing with Samoudri-Rajah, who preferred to fight on land and avoided the coast. As a result, Pacheco was forced to bring his big guns ashore and use them as field artillery. It was well for him that he did, for he soon discovered that his allies from Cochin were very much afraid of their enemies from Calicut and needed little excuse to launch an enthusiastic retreat. With only seventy men of his own, and with fainthearted allies, he found himself facing a huge army which he estimated at 50,000 men. Turning to his brother officers, he wryly commented, "Gentlemen, all now lies with the artillery."

All did lie with the artillery. When the big guns cut loose at the tightly packed lines of the enemy, the slaughter was tremendous.

Pacheco won a smashing victory, and control of India belonged to Portugal.

One would think that the king and the people of Portugal would have been profoundly grateful to this simple, hard-fighting soldier who had done so much. Instead, he received the same ungrateful treatment that Clive of India was to receive two and a half centuries later at the hands of Britain, and for even less cause. Pacheco's offense was his honesty and simplicity. He refused to accept graft, and he disdained pomp and luxury. The contrast with his associates was too marked; it made them look bad. Enmities were quickly aroused, charges were trumped up, and poor bewildered Duarte Pacheco was carried back to Portugal in chains to die in poverty and undeserved disgrace.

17.

The evident wealth of India soon caused the Portuguese king to designate the country a viceroyalty. For his first viceroy, King Manuel selected Dom Francisco de Almeida, an intelligent administrator and a resourceful leader in war. His main problem, as he saw it, was the elimination of the "new races," by which he meant the Arabs, Turks, and others who had slid in ahead of Portugal by the Red Sea route and had established prosperous commerce with the natives of India. Said he, "Let us establish our strength at sea, rather than occupying the land. With lands so distant, it is not desirable for us to attempt the old-fashioned type of conquest. Let us eliminate these new races and restore the authority of the original inhabitants of the coast. Let us use our navy to secure control of the sea and so protect the natives, through whom we may, in effect, rule India. It will do no harm for us to build a few forts along the coast, but these must be maintained solely to protect our trading posts from attack. Our chief safety will lie in the friendship of the native rulers, whom we shall place upon their thrones and support and protect by our navy. We must undo the anarchy, death, piracy, and disorder which have marked our procedure in the past."

Almeida soon had an opportunity to put his naval policy into operation. At the head of the Red Sea appeared a formidable fleet, which had been assembled by two unlikely allies—the Mohammedan ruler of Egypt and the Christian Doge of Venice. Though dissimilar in all other ways, these two men had one common characteristic, an intense desire to eliminate the newly arrived Portuguese from the Eastern trade that had long been so profitable to their own governments. In their fleet were cannon-armed Venetian galleys, Egyptian *feluccas,* and a vast assembly of minor vessels of slight draft and small tonnage. Southward through the Red Sea they swarmed, intent upon taking the Portuguese Viceroy and his forces by surprise. A double blow was to be struck, for the little fleet of Calicut was to launch an attack upon the Portuguese at the same time.

Fortunately for Dom Francisco de Almeida, a dark-skinned, turban-wearing stranger sought him out at Cochin and told him of the impending attack. Though apparently a Moslem, this man was actually a Christian, from Bologna, Italy. His disguise had enabled him to observe the preparations at first hand and to slip on ahead and give the warning.

At once, the Viceroy swung into action. A squadron of his cannon-armed *naus* was sent to Calicut, under his son Lourenco. Without preface or warning, these ships sailed into Calicut Harbor and used their guns to blast the fleet of Calicut into uselessness. On sailed Lourenco, north along the coast, scouting for signs of the enemy. No ships being sighted, the young man took his squadron into the harbor of Chaul and there dropped anchor.

The Egyptian-Venetian fleet was not so far away as Dom Lourenco imagined. Already, Diu had been occupied, and the enemy ships were even then on their way to Chaul, where he lay. They caught him with his anchors down, his guns in, and his crews away from battle stations. Though the Portuguese sailors fought hard, their ships were taken. Young Lourenco Almeida fell dead while directing the defense of his flagship.

18.

The news of the defeat at Chaul roused the viceroy to a fury. His beloved son was dead! A Portuguese squadron had been taken! His country's prestige had been damaged in the eyes of these Indian rajahs, who must at all costs be impressed with Portuguese invincibility! The enemy must be struck hard, at once. In frantic haste, he readied his fleet for sea.

The allies, now back at Diu, heard that he was coming and prepared to receive him. They crowded the shores with armed men and stationed a fringe of their smaller craft in the shallow inshore waters. Their main vessels were temptingly anchored in the harbor, to invite boarding. As soon as a Portuguese ship should come alongside one of their vessels and grapple, the anchor ropes were to be cut so that both vessels would drift onto the beach, where the waiting light-draft vessels and the soldiers could subdue the Portuguese warship.

As he entered the harbor, experienced old Almeida quickly perceived the possibilities. Somehow, he got word to his captains to be ready to drop their stern anchors before grappling. His plan worked to perfection. When the time came to board, the Portuguese on each ship dropped their stern anchors just as the enemy was cutting cables. As a result, it was only the allied ships that drifted into the shallows and grounded. Almeida then swung his ships about and delivered repeated broadsides into the confused mass of enemy ships. It was a complete and overwhelming victory. Portuguese prestige was restored beyond the most optimistic of expectations.

But Lourenco was dead! This personal tragedy was allowed to upset both the personality and the wise plans of the viceroy. He was now an embittered man, bent on revenge. The prisoners taken at Diu were bound across the mouths of his cannons, and the waterfront was splattered with the fragments of their bodies. There followed a reign of terror all up and down the northwestern coast of India, marked by sudden attacks upon native cities thought to be unfriendly to the Portuguese. There was now no mercy in the heart of Dom Francisco de Almeida, and little balance in his brain.

Inevitably, reports of the viceroy's activities filtered back to Portugal and brought dismay to the court. Alfonso de Albuquerque was appointed in place of Almeida and was sent eastward with all haste. Though his credentials were all in order, Albuquerque was clapped into a cell and held prisoner while the former viceroy proceeded with his bloodletting. At last, yielding to fate, Almeida gave up and set sail for home, knowing in his heart that imprisonment or death awaited him in Lisbon. Perhaps it was this consideration that caused him to conduct a final raid as his ship neared the southern tip of Africa. Advancing too boldly against the natives, he was transfixed by a spear and instantly killed. It was the kindest thing that could have happened to him.

19 .

During Almeida's term as viceroy, it had become increasingly evident that the spices and other rich oriental goods did not come from India at all but from some place much farther to the east. India was merely a way station for the shipment of such goods to Europe. Before being deposed in 1509, Almeida had sent an expedition eastward under Diogo Lopes de Sequeira to seek the origin of the spices. Sequeira reached the Strait of Malacca and went ashore to establish a Portuguese claim. The natives proved to be unfriendly. They ambushed the Portuguese, who suffered many casualties and were lucky to get away at all. Returning to India, the leader found that Almeida was dead and that Albuquerque was the new viceroy.

To Alfonso de Albuquerque goes the major credit for building up the Portuguese Empire in the Far East. He went about it systematically. Surveying the various cities of India, he selected Goa as the best to serve as his capital. Goa was defended vigorously by the native inhabitants, who were driven out after much hard fighting. Back they came, and retook their city. Not daunted, Albuquerque once more attacked Goa, and once more took it. This time, it remained in his hands, to serve as a capital and base of operations.

It was Albuquerque's intention to gain complete control of the Indian Ocean, thus inhibiting all foreign trade competition. By carefully studying the map, he determined that this could be accomplished by gaining possession of three key seaports. Aden would give him control of access from the Red Sea. Ormuz would control access from the Persian Gulf. Malacca would furnish the key to the eastern approaches. With these three serving as bases for Portuguese sea power, there could be no competing trade in the rich spice lands.

In 1511, the viceroy sent a fleet eastward to take Malacca. The excuse, if one were needed, was the part allegedly played by the Malaccans in the resistance to Sequeira's landing two years earlier. The Portuguese warships met strong resistance and failed in their first attack. Knowing that these persistent Europeans would return, the Sultan of Malacca appealed for help to Wu Tsung, the Emperor of China. Wu Tsung, in turn, passed the buck to King Phra Borom Raxa of Siam, requesting that Siamese forces drive away the Portuguese. This the King of Siam was by no means willing to do. He had recently been quarreling with the Sultan of Malacca and was in no mood to pull his late enemy's chestnuts from the fire. Instead, he made overtures to the Portuguese which led to the signing of a trade treaty. Deprived of aid, Malacca soon passed into Portuguese hands.

Strategically located Malacca proved to be an ideal base of operations. From it, Portuguese ships fanned out through the East Indies, to the Moluccas, to China, and to Japan. Trading posts were established in all these lands, and rare and desirable products began to flood back from them to Malacca, thence to Goa and to Lisbon. Not only was the spice trade now a Portuguese monopoly; the "Spice Is-lands" themselves were becoming known as the Portuguese East Indies!

In connection with the acquisition of the Moluccas, we should note the name of Antonio de Abreu. Albuquerque sent this resourceful captain eastward from Malacca in 1511. En route to the Moluccas, he took his ships through the waters of the western Pacific. Though the history books give Vasco Nunez de Balboa of Spain the sole credit for discovering the Pacific Ocean, there can be no question that this neg-lected Portuguese navigator actually had his ships on Pacific waters a full two years before Balboa looked down from a mountain top in Panama and claimed "the great South Sea" for Spain.

Aden was to be the next point of conquest. Albuquerque hoped to surprise the city, but the Mohammedan inhabitants were ready for him. The big guns on his ships were answered by equally big guns in the stone forts of the city. After much furious cannonading, the Portu-guese withdrew in order to avoid further damage to their fleet. Instead of returning at once to Goa, they sailed northward up the Red Sea, where they found nothing worthy of their attention. Frustrated for the first and only time in his career, Albuquerque cast about wildly for some method of striking at his enemies. He even considered briefly an inland excursion to the headwaters of the Nile, for the purpose of diverting the river to a new course and thus destroying Mohammedan Egypt through lack of water. Fortunately, he reconsidered.

The conquest of Ormuz proved to be easy. On a previous voyage, some years before, Albuquerque had made an armed landing at this key Persian base and had forced the ruler to acknowledge Portuguese supremacy. As a result, the people of Ormuz regarded themselves as having special and friendly ties with the Portuguese. It so happened that Albuquerque's fleet arrived off the city during a dispute over local leadership. Far from resisting, the city fathers invited Albuquerque to serve as arbitrator in settling the dispute. He came ashore, surrounded by armed men, quickly surveyed the situation, had his men kill one of the disputants and dispossess the other, and took formal possession of the city in the name of the Portuguese king. A little later, when the ruler of Persia sent to Ormuz for his accustomed tribute, Albuquerque sent him a bundle of bullets and swords, accompanied by a message: "This is the coin in which Portugal pays her tribute."

While Alfonso de Albuquerque was building up Portugal's rich empire in the East, his enemies were undermining his reputation in the court at Lisbon. Unhappily, King Manuel believed the lies that were told. Without warning, the viceroy learned in 1515 that he was being displaced by a personal enemy, Dom Lopo Soares. The shock completely unnerved him. He sailed at once from Ormuz to Goa, brooding on the injustice and misfortune of the situation. As his ship entered the harbor of Goa, he died.

20.

The sixty-five years following the death of Albuquerque were years of decline and decay for the Portuguese Empire. In 1515, Portugal was the leading colonial nation of the world, with rich possessions in Asia, Africa, South America, and island groups in the Atlantic, Pacific, and Indian oceans. By 1580, she had lost not only her great colonial empire but even her own national sovereignty.

In large measure, the Portuguese themselves were to blame. Their troubles stemmed directly from their own incompetence, arrogance, and greed. Cruelty to the natives destroyed confidence, bred resentment, and weakened the Portuguese hold upon the colonies. Greed led to the building of ever larger ships to carry greater cargoes—ships so huge as to be completely unseaworthy. Records indicate that of every six Portuguese ships that set out on a voyage to or from the Indies, one never reached port. The Portuguese anthology, *Historia Tragico-Maritima,* is full of harrowing accounts of the danger, privation, and death of crews and passengers who embarked on Indies-bound Portuguese merchant vessels. The inevitable result was a steady weakening of the bonds holding the colonial possessions to the Mother Country.

Worse things were happening at home. A succession of weak kings and regents, ruling for their own pleasure and gain, steadily loosened the grip by which the Portuguese government held its land and its people. In 1580, as a result of a carefully managed series of intrigues, King Philip II of Spain managed to make himself the King of Portugal, as well. Soon thereafter, the energetic Dutch began to take away, one by one, the distant possessions of which Portugal had been so proud.

After sixty years of "Babylonian captivity," under Spanish control, the Portuguese managed to regain their independence. By that time, most of their empire had passed out of their hands for good. Portugal had become a second-class nation.

3

⚓

SPAIN'S DAY OF GLORY

1.

As in the case of Portugal, Spain began her period of naval and colonial supremacy with a royal marriage. Before it took place, there was, in fact, no Spain as such—merely a collection of little Spanish kingdoms and a powerful though decaying Moorish area. When Isabella of Castile married Ferdinand of Aragon, in 1469, the foundation was laid for a strong and united Spain.

One of the chief problems facing the royal pair was the Mohammedan occupation of a large part of the Iberian Peninsula. As devout members of the Church, it was the plain duty of Ferdinand and Isabella to drive out the infidels. As rulers of the now-united kingdoms of Aragon and Castile, they could see the desirability of uniting the entire peninsula under their control.

The Moors themselves precipitated the war in 1481 by surprising the Spanish town of Zahara and enslaving the entire Christian population. Reprisal followed quickly, when a Spanish force assaulted Alhama, captured the citadel, and slaughtered the garrison. The decisive struggle had begun.

During the eleven years which followed, there was much fighting on the land and none upon the sea. The Moorish zeal for conquest had burned low, and their armed strength had been sapped by a dynastic quarrel within their ruling house. In 1492, the Moorish stronghold of Granada fell before the armies of Ferdinand and Isabella. The Moorish state in Spain was doomed.

It so happened that the happy outcome of the Moorish war was achieved just at the time when Christopher Columbus was seeking aid in the Spanish court. No doubt the expansive feeling which accompanied the tidings of victory had much to do with the Queen's willingness to back the visionary explorer. The outfitting of a small expedition was slight in cost compared to the steady, heavy drain on the now-terminated war. Columbus received his ships and men.

It has been said of Christopher Columbus: "Before he set sail, he did not know where he was going; when he arrived, he did not know where he was; when he returned, he did not know where he had been." In the most literal of senses, this was true. Though he made three subsequent voyages, the explorer insisted to his dying day that he had reached "the Indies"—by which he meant the Portuguese spice islands. It was, he thought, just bad luck that he had found none of the wealthy cities which he had sought.

2.

Other Spanish explorers, following Columbus, came to realize that he had discovered a vast and largely uncivilized New World, which lay athwart the desired route to the Indies. Settlements were made in the islands lying south and southeast of the mainland—the islands which in time came to be known as the *West* Indies. From these settlements, explorers set out westward. In 1513, Ponce de Leon discovered and claimed the peninsula of Florida, which he took to be a large island. In the same year, Vasco Balboa crossed the narrow Isthmus of Panama and beheld the vast "South Sea," which he claimed, with all the lands it touched, for Spain. Neither the claim—the largest ever made by man—nor the name stuck; today, we call this body of water the Pacific Ocean.

In 1519, Hernando Cortez led a Spanish expedition from Cuba, landed on the eastern coast of Mexico, and after frightful dangers and much hard fighting conquered the empire of the civilized Aztec Indians. Here, for the first time, the Spaniards found what they were looking for—gold and jewels in enormous quantities. A few years later, Francisco Pizarro sailed from the Isthmus of Panama, landed on the Pacific coast of South America, and succeeded in conquering the empire of the Inca Indians of Peru, who were even richer than the Aztecs.

Perhaps the greatest of all explorers was Ferdinand Magellan, a Portuguese nobleman who sailed in the service of Spain. The Spaniards were extremely anxious to find a water route through the barrier of the American continents, through which ships could sail to the wealthy East. In 1519, Magellan set out in search in the desired passage. Under his command were five stout ships, much like the *nau* type which the Portuguese had devised.

Without much difficulty, Magellan reached the coast of South America. He sailed southward, examining every bay, inlet, and river in the hope that it might prove to be the passage which he sought. His first winter was spent in a sheltered bay on the Atlantic coast of what is now Argentina. Here, he found it necessary to put to death the leader of a dangerous mutiny, who wanted to turn the expedition back to Spain.

Near the southern end of the continent, Magellan at last found the passage of which explorers had long been dreaming. It was narrow and dangerous and much farther south than he would have liked, but it did provide a navigable waterway. In attempting the passage of this "Strait of Magellan," one of the explorer's ships was wrecked and another was forced to turn back. The other three sailed on and at last reached the waters of a great ocean to the west.

There are few stormier places in the world than the stretch of ocean at the western end of the Strait of Magellan. It was a strange quirk of chance that led Magellan's ships, after five weeks of exhausting and dangerous battling, to sail out onto a body of water so calm and un-ruffled that he gave it the name Pacific Ocean. It would be hard to think of a less fitting title!

Not even dreaming of the vast size of the Pacific, Magellan struck out boldly across it, in spite of a shortage of food and drinking water. It was nearly a fatal mistake. The food gave out, and what little water was left became a greenish, jelly-like mass, swarming with maggots. In their desperation, the members of the crew were forced to eat their belts and the leather fittings from the rigging in order to fill their stomachs and relieve the agonizing pangs of hunger. Some were dead and the rest in desperate shape when a group of islands was reached. While the famished Spaniards ate and drank, the island natives came aboard and stole almost everything that could be taken. It was this which caused Magellan to name the islands the Ladrones ("the robbers") when he claimed them in the name of Spain.

Sailing on, Magellan and his men reached and claimed a much larger island group, which later became known as the Philippines, after King Philip II of Spain. Here, the leader made the mistake of joining in a native war, with the result that he and many of his men were killed. The survivors took the best of the remaining ships, sailed to the Portuguese East Indies, and took aboard a load of spices.

In 1522, eighteen half-starved men—all that were left of the 270 who had set out so boldly three years before—arrived in a Spanish port, having completed the first voyage ever made around the world. Of the five vessels that had started, only one had returned with a cargo, yet so valuable were the tropical products this ship brought back that the men who had financed the expedition made a tremendous profit. This gives us some indication of the margin of profit yielded by the rich products of the East.

Was Magellan the first man to sail around the world? It is often said that he could not have been, since he died before the voyage was completed. This view overlooks the fact that on an earlier voyage, under the flag of Portugal, Magellan had sailed farther east than the point at which he died on his westward voyage. Thus, as parts of two different voyages, Magellan did actually pass around the world, and was the first man to do so.

Much of what is now the southern part of the United States became known to the world because of the explorations of two bold Spaniards, Hernando de Soto and Francisco de Coronado.

De Soto and a group of followers landed in Florida in 1539 and made their way northward and westward, searching for wealthy cities to conquer. No cities were found, but in 1541 De Soto and his men reached the mighty Mississippi, which had never before been seen by any white man. Crossing the river on crude rafts, the Spaniards pushed on farther westward, still seeking vainly for cities to conquer. Whenever Indians were encountered, the Spaniards seized them as slaves. This, naturally, aroused opposition and led to reprisals. At last, weariness and the almost constant attacks by hostile Indians halted the party and turned it back toward the river. De Soto died on the banks of the Mississippi. His companions quietly buried him in the waters of the great river he had discovered. They then released their surviving captives and their horses and traveled southward along the river, at last reaching a Spanish settlement in what is now Mexico.

Tradition has it that the vast herds of wild horses which later inhabited the western plains were the descendants of the mares and stallions turned loose on the De Soto expedition. Apparently, the plains Indians quickly discovered for themselves the tremendous and varied usefulness of the horse. When white men again penetrated the region in later years, they found themselves opposed by fast-moving bodies of horsemen instead of the plodding and comparatively helpless walking Indians whom De Soto had encountered.

While De Soto was probing inland from Florida, Coronado and his men were pushing northward from Mexico, searching for seven mythical cities of enormous wealth. They found no such cities, but they did explore endless miles of the southwestern plains, from what is now Arizona to what is now Kansas. Two side expeditions, sent out by Coronado's main party, added further valuable discoveries. One, under Melchior Diaz, struck westward to the mouth of the Colorado River and found a message left by another Spanish expedition under Alarcon, who had sailed northward through the Gulf of California and had discovered that Lower California is not an island, as had been assumed, but is a peninsula. The second side expedition, under Cardenas and Tovar, traveled northwestward and came upon the awe-inspiring Grand Canyon of the Colorado River.

3.

As a result of her explorations, Spain laid claim to vast lands in the New World. Included in this rich new empire were most of the West Indies Islands; all of South America except Brazil; Central America; Mexico; and the entire southern part of what is now the United States, from Florida on the east to California on the west. From these new lands a golden harvest could be reaped. Holding the wealth would be quite another problem, for the dearth of Spanish products caused an unfavorable balance of trade which drained the treasure out across the borders almost as fast as it came in and caused a growing boom among Spain's neighbors. Still, as long as she had her empire, Spain could look forward to a flood of gold, and her empire would be safe as long as she could control the sea.

The period of Spain's overseas empire coincided with the development of a new type of sailing ship—the galleon. Despite the popular conception, the galleon was not introduced by the Spaniards. In fact, Spain was one of the last major powers to adopt it. The first galleons were built in Italy. Both France and England had squadrons of galleons before Spain possessed a single one. But the ship was so well adapted to Spain's needs in this period of overseas expansion that large numbers of them were built almost as soon as the virtues of the first one came to be appreciated. The galleon became so integral a part of Spanish sea power that today few people think of the noun "galleon" without adding the adjective "Spanish."

Specifically, the galleon was a large sailing ship with a high forecastle and a towering enclosed poop structure at the stern, sometimes three or four decks high. There was at least one gun deck, pierced with gun ports and armed with heavy broadside cannons. Normally, there were three masts, two bearing square sails and the third a triangular lateen rig. Though awkward and unwieldy, the galleons were the largest and most seaworthy ships that had yet appeared. Properly handled, they were formidable as fighting craft.

As the coffers of the Aztecs and the Incas began to yield their golden harvests, it became customary for fleets of galleons to gather at the Isthmus of Panama and in the harbors of eastern Mexico to receive their cargoes of gold, silver, and jewels. These "plate-fleets," as they were called, presented a tremendous temptation to pirates, including some very special pirates who represented joint-stock companies in England and elsewhere. One such company had among its seagoing employees such characters as Francis Drake and John Hawkins. Among its stockholders was no less a personage than Queen Elizabeth I of England!

4.

King Philip II, who came to the Spanish throne in 1556, had many reasons for disliking England. He had been married to the English queen, Mary Tudor, and had planned with that ardent Catholic ruler to undo her father's work and make England once more a Catholic country. Prospects had seemed bright while the lady lived, but in 1558 she had died and had been succeeded by her strong-minded and archly Protestant half-sister, Elizabeth. Now England was swinging strongly away from Catholicism, to the unutterable horror both of Philip and of his spiritual mentor, Pope Sixtus V. There was also the vexing question of England's "piracy" against the Spanish plate fleets. Not the least of the sources if indignation was the aid and comfort which England was furnishing to the heretic rebels in the Netherlands.

Philip had inherited the Netherlands, as well as Spain, from his father, Emperor Charles V. With his northern lands he had also inherited a thorny religious problem. The teachings of the Protestant reformers had taken firm root in the fertile Dutch soil. Philip's answer was savage persecution of all "heretics"—by which term he meant any who differed in even the slightest degree from the teachings of the Roman Catholic Church. The dreaded Inquisition was called upon to root out heresy and to compel complete compliance.

The Netherlanders first tried to gain relief by reason. A group of leaders representing the leading Dutch families appeared before Philip's regent and submitted a moderate request that their grievances be considered. They were contemptuously dismissed as "a band of beggars." The term was cheerfully taken up by Count Brederode, one of the Dutch leaders. A beggar's wallet became the symbol of resistance. Those who now took up arms against the Spaniards gloried in the twin terms, "Beggars of the Land" and "Beggars of the Sea."

We need not dwell upon the growing violence which characterized, on both sides, the outbreak of armed conflict between the Spaniards and their resentful Dutch subjects. Our interest must be confined, in the main, to happenings upon the sea—to the campaigns of the vigorous Dutch "Sea Beggars."

Long familiarity with the sea had made the Dutch a nation of sailors. It was natural, then, that as bitterness turned to violence, many of them should take to the sea in order to strike at their oppressors. William of Orange, the leader of the Dutch rebels, issued letters of marque to give his seamen the legal status of privateers, but the Spaniards insisted upon regarding and treating the "Sea Beggars" as common pirates.

In 1568, the quarrel which had long been brewing between Queen Elizabeth of England and King Philip of Spain was intensified when the queen seized a Spanish vessel in Plymouth Harbor and confiscated its treasure of coin, intended to pay the Spanish soldiers in the Netherlands. Philip struck back by seizing all English property and ships in the Netherlands. This, in turn, led Elizabeth to open her ports to the Dutch privateers, who thus enjoyed, for the first time, safe harbors into which they could retire.

For nearly four years, the Dutch "Sea Beggars" used the harbors of England as bases from which to strike the Spaniards. It was a bloody period. The Dutch admiral, William de la Marck, bore a personal grudge against all things Spanish and all things Catholic. On the many occasions when he captured Spanish vessels, no mercy was shown. More attention was paid to the wholesale cutting of throats than to his secondary objective, the taking of supplies and treasure. Spanish cruelty was repaid in kind.

In 1572, the "Sea Beggars" lost their snug haven. Thanks to one of the characteristic quirks of international diplomacy, England and Spain resumed friendly negotiations. As a result, Admiral de la Marck and his squadron of twenty-four Dutch privateers found themselves ejected from the once-friendly harbors of England. To make matters worse, they were not permitted to purchase supplies before they sailed, so they made their departure with hollow stomachs and empty holds.

Where could they go? The ports of their own country were in Spanish hands. England was now forbidden territory. Certainly, no other country would dare the wrath of mighty Spain by offering such "pirates" sanctuary. Lacking an objective or a plan, they sailed toward the Netherlands, taking two Spanish merchantmen on the way. Still without a plan, they entered the estuary of the river Maas.

On an island near the river's mouth stood the fortified town of Brill, with stout stone walls and a broad harbor. It so happened that the commander of one of De la Marck's ships was William of Blois, who knew the town well, since his father had once been governor of the island. After much earnest argument, this young man at last persuaded his admiral to try a daring plan—no less than an assault upon the defenses of Brill. Concealing their small numbers, the rebels first delivered a bold demand that the town be surrendered to them, then quickly followed with a two-pronged attack upon the two main gates. With the aid of fire and of improvised battering rams made from the old masts of ships, both groups succeeded in gaining entrance. They met in the midst of the town, a mere 250 men who had succeeded in capturing an important stronghold.

The Spaniards struck back at once. No sooner had the news of the capture of Brill been received when a Spanish fleet set out to retake the town. The defenders were few in number, but they were determined to hold tightly to this first little foothold of free Dutch soil. As the Spanish forces disembarked and deployed toward the gates, a brave Dutch carpenter snatched up his ax, plunged into the water, and swam to one of the main sluices in the dike that kept the sea waters away from the walls of Brill. At the same time, William of Blois and a friend named Robol led a little flotilla of rowboats against the anchored Spanish fleet. The startled Spaniards on the island simultaneously became aware of a torrent of sea water pouring through the shattered sluice and of columns of flames rising from several of the anchored ships. Other vessels, their anchor ropes cut, were seen to be drifting onto the shallow bars near the island. In the sudden panic, the Spaniards turned and ran toward their surviving ships. Many were drowned, but most escaped, leaving Brill to serve as a nucleus for the new free Dutch Republic.

The taking of Brill led to successful revolts on the part of other Dutch towns and cities. Flushing, Walcheren, Enkhuisen, and many other communities drove out their Spanish garrisons and joined the cause of William of Orange and Dutch freedom. Though there was little bloodshed in these revolts, there was much whenever the Spaniards retook a defected town. At Mechlin, for example, the town was given up to butchery, execution, rape, and looting, climaxed by the mass drowning of five hundred townsmen. The same thing happened at Naarden. The result was steadily rising Dutch anger and a resolve to fight to the very end.

5.

Soon after the slaughter at Naarden, a unique naval battle was fought near Amsterdam. Caught in a sudden cold snap, a small fleet of Dutch warships became trapped in the ice, immobile and apparently helpless. The news was conveyed to Don Frederick, son of the oppressive Duke of Alva. Here was an opportunity not to be missed! A picked force of Spanish arquebusiers was hastily assembled and dispatched over the ice toward the imprisoned vessels. The Dutch crews, meanwhile, set frantically to work chopping ice so as to make a moat surrounding their fleet. In only a few places were bridges of solid ice left, sufficiently firm to support the weight of bodies of men.

As the Spaniards approached the moat and began to deploy around the fleet, they were amazed to see groups of Dutch sailors leave the ships and move with incredible speed across the ice bridges which had been left. These men were not running, but were gliding on skates, an old Dutch custom with which the Spaniards had had no previous experience. Like mounted Indians around a wagon train, they swiftly circled the amazed Spaniards, dashing in from time to time to discharge a volley then darting away again as the helpless Spaniards attempted to wheel about on the slippery footing and bring their heavy weapons to bear. Leaving several hundred of their men dead upon the ice, Don Frederick's arquebusiers retreated in panic. Next day, a warm wind melted the ice, permitting the Dutch ships to escape to Enkhuisen.

The Duke of Alva, though much distressed, was tremendously intrigued by the possibilities of war on skates. As he wrote his king, " 'Twas a thing never heard of before today, to see a body of arquebusiers thus skirmishing upon a frozen sea." At once, he ordered 7,000 pairs of skates for his own soldiers and immediately instituted skating lessons. Though the Spanish soldiers eventually learned to skim about upon the ice, the Dutch never gave them a chance to employ their new-found skills in warfare.

The war continued. Haarlem was besieged by the Spaniards and desperately defended by the Dutch, who introduced the novel weapon of flaming hoops dropped around the necks of soldiers climbing up the walls. After seven months of siege, and the death of 12,000 of his men, Don Frederick took the city and put to death 2,300 of its surviving inhabitants. The Dutch merely became angrier and more determined.

Among the important incidents in the siege of Haarlem was a naval engagement fought in the lake which lay beside the city. Control of the lake would give the Spaniards a stranglehold on all communication lines between Haarlem and the outside world and would lead to the eventual starving out of the garrison. Accordingly, Spanish Admiral Bossu built a fleet of 100 small but powerful ships in nearby Amsterdam and introduced them into the lake by breaching a dike. The Dutch, under Martin Brand, managed to gather about 150 small vessels. The fight was long and fierce, being characterized by boarding and much hand-to-hand action. At last, after the loss of more than 2,000 of his men and the capture of twenty-two of his boats, Brand was driven from the lake and the city was doomed.

The Dutch did not forget Admiral Bossu and his part in the sufferings of Haarlem. Doggedly, they set to work to build a fleet which could meet his on even terms, or better. Their chance came on October 11, 1573, when Bossu took thirty of his largest vessels out into the open waters of the Zuider Zee. Out after him went twenty-five vessels commanded by Dutch Admiral Dirkzoon. The Spaniards had better cannon, which at first they used successfully in battering the Dutch ships at long range. Dirkzoon kept boring in, taking his punishment and striving for a chance to board. At last, a shift in the wind gave him the opportunity he sought. With the wind blowing from directly astern, down he came upon the Spanish fleet, which tried in vain to avoid close contact.

Seeing the enemy so close upon them, the Spaniards gave way to panic. Five of their ships were quickly taken, and twenty-four bore away in flight. Only the flagship, the huge and heavily armed *Inquisition,* remained to oppose the four small Dutch vessels which had not gone off in pursuit of the fugitives. A broadside from the *Inquisition*'s heavy guns shattered one of these small assailants, but the other three ranged alongside and were soon firmly fastened to the Spanish flagship.

An epic battle followed, a battle which lasted without interruption from three in the afternoon until eleven the next morning. During all this time, navigation and tactics were completely impossible. The one great vessel and the three smaller ones drifted aimlessly, while bloody hand-to-hand fighting raged on the *Inquisition*'s decks. Time after time the Dutch came aboard, attacking with burning hoops, boiling oil, molten lead, and the more usual arquebus and sword. Time after time, they were repulsed with heavy losses by the armor-protected Spaniards. The grounding of the four vessels on a shoal brought no interruption. At daybreak, a daring Hollander, John Haring, forced his way to the *Inquisition*'s flag halyards and hauled down the Spanish flag. His heroism went for naught; he was shot through the body, and the battle went on. It was not until eleven o'clock that Admiral Bossu and his 300 surviving crew members, exhausted by their efforts in a hopeless cause, gave up. The prisoners were taken into captivity unharmed—a remarkable fact in view of the bloody nature of the war and the hatred in which this Dutch-born admiral of Spain was held by his countrymen.

The success of the Sea Beggars proved so damaging to the reputation of the Duke of Alva that he presently resigned his regency and returned to Spain. He was replaced by Don Luis de Requesens.

6.

One of the most pressing problems facing Requesens was the relief of Middleburg, which was being held by a Spanish force under Mondragon. A Dutch fleet under Admiral Boisot was maintaining such a tight blockade on the city that its surrender must come soon unless the blockade could be broken. To effect this, Requesens gathered a fleet of seventy-five large ships, which he entrusted to the command of Julian Romero, despite that young man's protests that he was a soldier and not a sailor. This large Spanish fleet was to join with another group of thirty vessels under Sancho d'Avila and advance against the Dutch.

Requesens himself took a position on a dike, whence he could watch the inevitable victory of his ships. As they passed by him, each of Romero's ships fired a salute in his honor. When this formality was over, there were only seventy-four Spanish ships, one having set off an explosion of its magazines while in the act of honoring the regent.

It so happened that Captain Schot, of the Dutch flagship, lay dying of fever, "so weak that he could scarcely blow a feather from his mouth." As the Spaniards approached, he somehow staggered aboard his ship and reclaimed the command from Captain Klaafzoon, who had been appointed as his substitute. Klaafzoon's order that the men should remain below decks until after the first Spanish volley was angrily countermanded by Schot, who stationed his men on the decks, ready for instant boarding. As a result, the first and only Spanish broadside resulted in heavy casualties among the Dutch sailors. Both Schot and Klaafzoon were killed, and Admiral Boisot lost an eye. Thereafter, the battle was a hand-to-hand conflict with pistol, dagger, pike, and battle-ax. There was no quarter. Those who tried to surrender were instantly killed and tossed overboard. When the Spanish losses reached fifteen ships and 1,200 men, the battle became a rout.

Admiral Romero himself had a difficult time. His flagship, fleeing with the rest, ran aground and was boarded by a swarm of Sea Beggars. As the vengeful Dutch broke in his cabin door, the Spanish admiral squeezed out through a porthole and dropped into the water. Apparently, he was a strong swimmer, for he managed to reach the dike upon which Don Luis de Requesens still stood, disconsolately surveying the rout of his fleet. With the water dripping from his face and clothes, Romero bowed to the Regent. "I told your excellency," he said, "that I was a land fighter and not a sailor. If you were to give me command of a hundred fleets, I believe that none of them would fare better than this one has."

Romero's defeat sealed the fate of Middleburg. Within a few weeks, the stronghold capitulated.

7.

Leyden, meanwhile, had been placed under siege by the Spaniards. In many respects, its situation was much like that of Middleburg. There was, however, one important difference, for it was fifteen miles from the sea. It seemed the height of folly for Admiral Boisot to attempt its relief by means of his fleet.

Leyden could not be brought to the sea, but it was barely possible that the sea could be brought to Leyden. Dikes were breached, and sea water flowed through the gaps, flooding the fields beyond. "Better a drowned land than a lost land!"

As the waters rose inch by inch over the flooded lowlands, Boisot and his men assembled a strange war fleet, more than two hundred vessels strong. Most were flat-bottomed barges, armed with cannons and propelled by oars. The flagship, especially designed and hastily built for the occasion, was a masterpiece of ingenuity. The *Arke van Delft,* as she was named, was an armored barge driven by hand-cranked paddle wheels. In this strange craft, Admiral Boisot led his men in their forlorn attempt to relieve Leyden.

Progress was discouragingly slow. Each row of dikes involved a new landing operation, much hard fighting, and extensive work with pick and shovel. When the wind was from the east, the waters would recede and leave the ships stranded, sometimes for days. On such occasions, the starving people of Leyden would gaze forlornly at their weather vanes and tighten their belts, while the confident Spanish besiegers would taunt those on the walls with the chant: "As well can the Prince of Orange pluck the stars from the sky as bring the ocean to the walls of Leyden."

October 1, 1574, found Boisot's fleet stranded, still many miles from the city. Three weeks of inching inland had apparently accomplished nothing except the entrapment of the ships in soggy meadows. Then came the change—a violent storm from the west. The ocean rolled in through the shattered dikes, and the ships at last floated free. Oars were plied, the paddle wheels of the flagship turned, and the squadron went on toward Leyden.

At Zoeterwoude, which was reached after dark, armed Spanish picket boats were encountered. Boisot's Zeeland sailors brought their cannons into play, the flashes of the explosions clearly revealing the tree branches and the farmhouse roofs and chimneys which extended upward through the flood waters. The Spaniards were routed, not only those in the picket boats, but also those manning the formidable Zouterwoude forts. The garrisons, panic-stricken at seeing their last routes to safety disappearing beneath the rising flood, abandoned their guns and rushed along the slippery dikes toward firmer ground. Few of them made it; most of the fugitives were brought down by the harpoons of the wild Zeeland sailors.

The next day, with Leyden actually in sight, a final obstacle was encountered. This was the dike at Lammen, surmounted by strong forts and guarded by well-armed Spanish forces. Admiral Boisot had too few men to risk a direct assault. As night was falling, he withdrew his ships from the neighborhood of the dike to consider possible moves.

During the night, fate took a hand. The flood waters, seeping through the dikes, reached the base of the Leyden city wall. Suddenly, during the small, dark hours, a section of the wall collapsed with a thunderous roar. At first, no one knew the cause of the uproar, and everyone suspected the worst. The citizens of Leyden awoke to the startled conviction that the Spaniards were upon them and that all was lost. The Spaniards outside the walls were equally frightened, thinking that the roaring crash portended a desperate sally from the city. The rising waters about their ankles added to their panic, and they fled. Likewise, the Spanish garrison at Lammen, hearing the distant rumble, assumed that they were about to be cut off. With all haste, they quitted their positions and sought safety.

With the first light of day, Admiral Boisot found his problem solved. Lammen was deserted, its dike undefended. The Spaniards were gone from before the walls of Leyden. There remained only the slight task of breaching the last dike and sailing with arms and food supplies through the rising waters to the city walls.

The Prince of Orange had not plucked the stars from the sky, but his fleet had brought the ocean to the walls of Leyden.

8.

During most of his regency, Don Luis Requesens had suffered from inadequate naval forces, which considerably limited his activities in this low-lying and easily flooded land. He had continuously besought King Philip II for additional ships and seamen, but he had received few. Despairing of achieving naval superiority, he now cast about for ways of subduing the Dutch revolt by other means.

The result was an exploit compounded of equal measures of daring and deceit. Zeeland, though the source of many of the most fanatical of Dutch freedom-fighters, was not without its traitors. Somehow, Requesens' agents reached some of these and from them learned of a mud bar extending from the mainland to the important island of Schouwen, upon which was located the patriot stronghold of Zierik-zee. Under normal conditions, the water upon this bar was shallow enough to permit the passage of men who did not mind wading up to their necks in water. The nearby shoals would prevent the approach of the large ships of the Dutch blockading squadron.

The passage was made on the night of September 27, 1575. Through the shallow water, slipping and sliding on the treacherous footing of the bar, went three thousand picked Spanish and Walloon infantrymen. A violent thunderstorm lighted their way fitfully and also revealed them to their enemies. For each individual soldier, the passage must have been a frightful experience. Many a man slipped from the narrow pathway and drowned as his companions inched forward, almost within arms' reach. Cannon balls from the Dutch men-of-war ripped holes in the slender formation. Along the edges of the bar ranged small Dutch boats, bearing Zeeland defenders armed with pikes and harpoons. Spaniards were transfixed, or were wounded and forced off the narrow footing. Nevertheless, the march continued, and a considerable portion of the men essaying the crossing at last arrived on the firm ground of Schouwen Island.

Once on the islands, the Spaniards laid violent siege to Brouwershaven, Bommende, and Zierikzee. The first two quickly fell and suffered the massacre of their populations and garrisons. Zierikzee, however, was defended strongly through the autumn, the winter, and the following spring, despite the growing privation within the walls. Spanish success in this campaign was greatly aided by the traitorous activities of certain Zeelanders, who not only actively opposed the efforts of the defenders but also effectively paralyzed the high command by assassinating General Charles van Boisot, who was in charge of the military establishment on Schouwen.

As the siege lines tightened around Zierikzee, the importance of saving the city became increasingly evident to the Dutch. The Spanish land forces were too strong; relief, therefore, must come from the sea. The command was entrusted to Admiral Boisot, who had so successfully engineered the relief of Leyden.

General Mondragon, in charge of the Spanish besieging forces, had anticipated the possibility of naval attack. To prevent it, he had clogged the harbor with sunken hulks, with pilings, and with strongly anchored chains. Boisot's flagship, the *Red Lion,* smashed boldly into this impediment. It did not give way. Instead, the *Red Lion* became hopelessly entangled. Seeing this, the crews of the Spanish vessels in the harbor made a sudden attack upon the smaller vessels surrounding the stricken flagship. The supporting Dutch vessels were driven off, and the *Red Lion* was left to its fate. The combination of a falling tide and increasing Spanish attacks made the end inevitable. As his ship heeled over, Boisot and three hundred of his surviving seamen went over the side, entrusting themselves to the sea rather than to Spanish mercy. Most of them, including the admiral, were drowned. With them died the last hope of saving Zierikzee.

While the siege of Zierikzee was still going on, Requesens died suddenly of a fever. This made it necessary to select a new Spanish regent for the Netherlands. The man chosen was Don John of Austria, illegitimate half-brother of King Philip II, born of a strange affair between Emperor Charles V and a sweet-voiced, sour-tempered washerwoman of Ratisbon. Don John was Spain's greatest naval hero, having commanded the allied fleet of Spain, Venice, and the Vatican in the defeat of the mighty Mohammedan navy at Lepanto in 1571.

Under Don John, there was a brief period of peace while attempts were made to find some common ground that would satisfy both the Spanish king and his Dutch subjects. Things had gone much too far. Fighting was resumed early in 1578—mainly land fighting, with little naval action. The young regent's armies did well, but he himself did not. In October, 1578, he died of a fever at the age of thirty-three. He was succeeded by his nephew, the Duke of Parma.

9.

In 1580, King Philip II of Spain committed a thundering error. The ruler of the small neighboring country of Portugal died without issue, leaving a contest for his throne. Philip was able to conjure up a claim of his own; it became decisive when backed by the full military and naval might of his country. Portugal fell into the hands of Philip, who thus became, at one and the same time, King Philip II of Spain and King Philip I of Portugal.

Spain's relations with Portugal and with the Netherlands were more closely linked than at first appeared. Dutch merchants had long been carrying on a profitable trade in spices and other exotic goods from the Portuguese East Indies, buying these goods in Lisbon and selling them at a large profit throughout northern Europe. One of Philip's first acts as sovereign of Portugal was to cut off this trade by forbidding Dutch ships to enter Portuguese harbors. The result was that the stubborn Dutch went directly to the source of supplies. The Dutch conquest of the East Indies, which followed as a direct concomitant of

Philip's seizure of Portugal, will be considered in detail in the next chapter.

10.

Meanwhile, the war in the Netherlands dragged along without either the Dutch or the Spaniards being able to gain a decided advantage. The assassination of William the Silent, Prince of Orange, was a serious blow to the Dutch cause, though his son Maurice and others carried on the struggle as best they could. Most of the fighting was on the land.

We should, however, note one campaign in which naval activities played a role. Many of the most important cities of the Netherlands lay like a string of beads along the great river Scheldt. It occurred to the Duke of Parma that if he could gain control of the river he could cut off these cities from outside assistance and could take them, one by one. The campaign was launched, and soon Dendermonde, Ghent, Brussels, and Mechlin were in Spanish hands. Antwerp was the chief target which remained. Parma wasted no time in placing it under siege.

Antwerp was not easy to take, for Dutch ships regularly sailed up the Scheldt, bringing food and munitions to the city. Cannon fire from the banks was ineffective against these vessels, and the Spaniards had insufficient naval power to form a blockade. To isolate the city, Parma determined to construct a "bridge of boats" across the river below Antwerp.

It should not have been difficult for the Dutch fleet to prevent the building of the bridge. Repeated orders were sent to Admiral Treslong to take his warships up the Scheldt and destroy the incomplete structure and the two forts which were being built at its ends. Always, the orders were answered by protests, alleging that Treslong's fleet was not strong enough for such a venture. By the time Treslong's secret and treasonable cooperation with the Spaniards was revealed to the Dutch authorities, the bridge and the forts were finished and the problem had become materially harder to solve.

Treslong's place was taken by Justin of Nassau, the illegitimate son of William of Orange. Together with the Count of Hohenlohe and some of the defenders of Antwerp, he formed a scheme that appeared to offer much promise. Fireships and explosive-laden barges were to be sent down the current from the city against the bridge. When word was received by Justin and Hohenlohe that the bridge had been breached, the fleet was to come up the river, complete the work of destruction, and reopen the way to Antwerp.

The people of Antwerp did their part remarkably well. In the city, there lived an Italian mechanic named Gianibelli, to whom the details were entrusted. The city fathers furnished thirty-two scows and two small ships, the *Fortune* and the *Hope*. The scows were converted into ordinary fireships, for use against the long raft which the Spaniards had constructed along the upstream side of the bridge of boats in order to discourage assaults. The *Fortune* and the *Hope* became "Hell-burners." In the hold of each, a stone chamber was prepared, filled with 7,000 pounds of gunpowder. Around and over the magazine fragments of heavy material were distributed. The explosive in the *Fortune* was to be activated by a long, slow fuse; that in the *Hope* by a clockwork device.

On the night of April 5, 1585, the destructive flotilla was started on its way, the fireships first, followed by the two "Hell-burners." Seeing the danger to their bridge, the Spaniards hastened to fend off the fire-ships and to battle the flames which poured from them. In this, they were extremely successful—far too successful for their own good. The fireships were discovered not to be dangerous, and the "Hell-burners," when they arrived, were regarded as just two more fireships.

The *Fortune* lodged against the outer edge of the raft and was promptly boarded by Spanish soldiers anxious to put out her fire. The *Hope* fared better, passing through a break in the raft and lodging against one of the bridge supports. Both blew up in quick succession. The explosion of the *Fortune* killed only the small group of men who had climbed aboard, but that of the *Hope* was catastrophic. A tremendous gap was blown in the bridge, and no fewer than 800 Spanish soldiers were torn to pieces. The Duke of Parma narrowly escaped sharing the fate of his men; he had left the bridge mere seconds before the "Hell-burner" went off. Even so, he was injured when thrown down by the force of the explosion.

All was now up to the fleet. The roar and glare of the explosions were clearly evident from the Dutch position downstream. At once, a boat was dispatched to determine whether the bridge had been breached or whether the explosions had been premature. Unfortunately, the commander of the scout boat lacked audacity. Not daring to approach the bridge, he took a hasty and distant look and returned with the erroneous news that the plot had failed and the bridge was undamaged. The Dutch warships therefore made no advance, and the opportunity was lost. By the time the true facts were known, Parma's men had repaired the damage.

Within a few weeks, Gianibelli tried again, this time with heavily weighted flatboats that acquired so much momentum from the current that they burst through raft and bridge alike. This time, the fleet, though alerted and willing, was unable to work upstream against a contrary wind. "The Archimedes of Antwerp," as Gianibelli was coming to be called, was playing in very bad luck.

When Parma rebuilt his bridge a second time, he provided a defense against current-borne vessels. This was a gate which could be swung back to permit such destructive objects to sail harmlessly through. Spurred on by this, Gianibelli and his assistants devised what was probably the only vessel in history to be equipped with underwater sails. Beneath a weighted raft was affixed an inverted mast with yards and a large square sail, to be pushed by the rushing river current rather than the wind. It worked to perfection. Borne by the full force of the current, the raft held to the middle of the river and traveled so swiftly that the Spaniards were unable to open their water gate. The raft smashed right on through. Poor teamwork again defeated the effort. The fleet did not put in an appearance. Once more, the bridge was rebuilt.

Gianibelli was hard at work on a new "Hell-burner" when the plans were changed and all attempts against the bridge as such abandoned. A new thought had occurred to the Dutch high command.

The new plan was actually a revival of the strategy that had brought relief to Leyden. The Cowenstein dike was to be breached and the countryside flooded, thus permitting the fleet to bypass the bridge and reach Antwerp across formerly dry land. Unfortunately for the Dutch, Parma had long anticipated the move and had both fortified and garrisoned the dike. The fleet and the forces from Antwerp moved in coordination. There was much hard fighting, involving everything from naval bombardment and the use of fireships to hand-to-hand conflict on the dike. For a time, the issue hung uncertain, and then the attackers were driven off. The dike remained untaken, and Antwerp was doomed. The city was surrendered to the Spaniards in August, 1585.

11.

Antwerp had fallen, but the Netherlands as a whole remained unsubdued. There now began to arrive in the low countries an increasing body of English soldiery, under the general command of the Earl of Leicester. The fact that these men came with the permission and blessing of Queen Elizabeth leads us to turn once more to a consideration of the delicate relations between Spain and England—between that most Catholic of all monarchs, Philip II, and his capricious Protestant sister-in-law, Elizabeth I.

There were many reasons for the growing hostility between Spain and England, some chronic, some acute. Among the former were the religious antipathy between Catholic Spain and Protestant England and the long-building rivalry between the two countries for trade and maritime supremacy. Among the latter were the damaging raids being made on Spanish commerce by Sir Francis Drake and the discovery of the Babington conspiracy to assassinate Queen Elizabeth and replace her on the English throne with her Catholic cousin, Mary, Queen of Scots. The conspiracy itself angered Elizabeth, and the subsequent beheading of Queen Mary infuriated her well-wisher, King Philip. Before the end of 1585, Philip had decided on war with England. Only the timing and the details remained to be arranged.

It must be understood that legally Sir Francis Drake was not a pirate, despite his taking ways and his warlike acts against a supposedly friendly nation. Like many shipmasters of his time, he went forth under the protection of Letters of Reprisal, issued by his Queen. In theory, at least, such letters were issued to shipmen who had lost valuable ships and cargoes through illegal seizure by a foreign power. A Letter of Reprisal gave such a seaman the right to prey upon the shipping of the offending power until his own losses had been redeemed. Drake and his kinsman, John Hawkins, had suffered such losses when a fleet of slaving ships under their command had been taken by the Spaniards in 1567 in the Spanish colonial harbor of San Juan de Ulua. Their Letters of Reprisal were, therefore, perfectly legal by the laws and usages of that day, even though the interrupted slave-selling expedition had not been.

It was King Philip's intention to invade England during the summer of 1587. The full energies of his kingdom were marshaled to this end. By the early spring months, the Spanish harbors had begun to fill with warships, while the waterfronts bulged with munitions and equipment. In charge of all this preparation was the man who was to command the invasion itself—the Marquis of Santa Cruz, who had brilliantly distinguished himself at Lepanto.

12.

To Francis Drake it was abundantly clear that the best place to stop an invasion is in its home base and that the best time to stop it is before it has been launched. He and his supporters used every argument at their command to gain permission for a raid on the Spanish coast. For some time, they were unsuccessful. Queen Elizabeth and many of her advisers continued to hope for "a prosperous peace." Others who offered opposition did so in the fear that Catholic France might launch an invasion across the channel in revenge for the execution of Mary, Queen of Scots. Discouraging weeks and months went by, while King Philip's preparations neared completion.

Suddenly, for reasons never made completely clear, Queen Elizabeth changed her mind. Drake was given a fleet of twenty-three stout ships and a commission "to impeach the joining together of the King of Spain's fleets out of their several ports . . . and particularly to distress the ships within the havens themselves." Overjoyed, he began at once to equip his vessels and to lay his plans in detail.

The mercurial Queen did not hold long to her resolve. Promises from Spain and timid advice from her courtiers led her to water down the commission. New orders were drawn, including the discouraging directive: "You shall forbear to enter forcibly into any of the said King's ports or havens; or to offer any violence to any of his towns or shipping within harbouring; or to do any act of hostility upon the land." All that these orders left for Drake to do was to cruise the seas, looking for Spanish ships far from port.

Impelled by advanced information or a shrewd hunch, Drake put to sea with his preparations still incomplete before the Queen's courier reached his base at Plymouth. Officially, he was still under his original orders. A fast ship was sent after him, commanded by the illegitimate son of his friend and kinsman, John Hawkins. Adroitly, the young man managed not to find the departing squadron and returned home, confessing failure but convoying a rich Spanish prize to soften the Queen's anger.

Two weeks after sailing, Drake encountered a fleet of Flemish merchant ships, not far from Lisbon. From the captains of these friendly vessels, he learned that the harbor of Cadiz was crowded with ships being readied for the invasion of England. Most of them were nearly ready to sail to their rendezvous port of Lisbon. For Cadiz, then, he set his course.

The Cadiz anchorage consisted of a harbor beyond a harbor, the two being separated by a narrow spit of land pierced by a channel a mere half mile in width. An old castle and two batteries of heavy guns guarded the outer harbor. Of more immediate concern to the attackers was the presence of twelve large galleys, fully manned by experienced crews.

Before the time of Drake's raid on Cadiz, there had been little opportunity to compare the fighting merits of the galley and the "great ship." There had been that brush off the Isle of Wight in 1545 between English sailing ships and a squadron of French galleys, but it had been indecisive. Off Prevesa, in 1540, the great *Galleon of Venice* had used her guns effectively to smash back repeated attacks by Turkish galleys. At Lepanto, in 1571, it had been the galleys of Christendom which had destroyed the oar-propelled sea power of the Mohammedans. Don John's few large sailing ships had been held back by adverse winds, but even if they had been present he would probably not have used them, for he was known to feel that against galleys a sailing ship was more of a liability than an asset. In general, the naval men of the sixteenth century felt that the galley was the more effective fighting ship, especially in protected waters and in times of calm, when the oared ship could readily move about and employ its ram and its heavy bow guns while the sailing vessel lay immobile. Small wonder, then, that many of Drake's crewmen, including Vice-Admiral Borough, shrank from the perils of entering a harbor protected by such highly regarded fighting craft.

There was nothing timid about Sir Frances Drake. Galleys or no galleys, he was going into Cadiz. At four o'clock on the afternoon of October 19, 1587, his flagship *Elizabeth Bonaventure* led the line of English ships in past the outer breakwater.

It must be remembered that England and Spain were not then at war, despite King Philip's obvious intentions. This squadron, so boldly sailing in, *might* be on a peaceful mission. Two Spanish galleys came rowing out to learn the facts. They quickly succeeded. Smashing broadsides from the leading English ships sent the galleys limping back, badly damaged and laden with dead and wounded Spaniards. The visit was obviously not a friendly one.

The sound of cannonading threw the harbor of Cadiz into confusion. All ships in the outer harbor which could do so got under way at once, cutting their anchor cables in order to flee to the presumed safety of the inner harbor. At the same time, the remaining ten galleys came out and rowed at full speed toward the line of English ships. The next few minutes settled once and for all the question of superiority between galley and "great ship." Taking four of his best ships, Drake sailed across the front of the advancing line of galleys, delivering smashing broadsides. Shattered and shaken, the Spanish vessels fled into the shallows, leaving the shipping in the outer harbor at Drake's mercy. Only the ineffective batteries on the shore could now oppose him.

Before darkness halted his operations, Drake had taken care of all ships that had not been able to escape to the inner harbor. Serviceable ships equipped with sails were added to his fleet. The others were set afire and cut loose, to drift upon the shore and burn. To the Admiral's intense regret one of the largest of the Spanish ships, a forty-gun galleon, had to be subdued by cannon fire and sank before it could be captured.

Timid Vice-Admiral Borough was horrified to learn that Drake had no thought of putting out to sea and escaping while he could. The English ships and the vessels they had taken anchored just out of reach of the Spanish batteries and spent the night in the outer harbor. Early in the morning, the bold leader was once more in action, personally leading a raid by boats and small ships across the bar into the inner harbor. A great galleon belonging to the Marquis of Santa Cruz himself was one of the vessels burned. Before withdrawing in the late morning, Drake had spread through the inner harbor destruction comparable to that wrought in the outer harbor the evening before.

At noon, as the English force was at last preparing to leave the harbor, the wind died out completely. Taking heart, the Spaniards made a last attempt to destroy the raiders. Fire ships were sent drifting down the ebbing tide toward the stationary English vessels, and the damaged galleys were sent out once more under conditions made to order for their operation. The attempts were fruitless. The fire ships were fended off, and the galleys were further blasted by gunners who took full advantage of the calm to place their shots precisely where they wished. For fourteen hours, the Spaniards did their best, but it was not good enough. At two the next morning, a wind sprang up, and Drake led his squadron out of Cadiz Harbor. With him he took six well-loaded ships which he had captured. Behind him in Cadiz, thirty-one large ships and uncounted smaller ones lay on the harbor's bottom or smoldered on the shore. "I have singed the beard of the King of Spain," said Francis Drake, with satisfaction.

13.

The raid on Cadiz, though the most spectacular, was not the only blow struck by Drake against King Philip's preparations. He even went so far as to capture Sagres Castle, near the tip of Cape St. Vincent, and he made it into an English stronghold within the Spanish borders. Though he could not take strongly defended Lisbon, he anchored off the harbor mouth, capturing all ships which tried to enter the harbor and openly daring the Spanish galley fleet to come out against him. The lessons of Cadiz had been well learned. Not a galley ventured out.

The net result of Drake's operations was a delay of a year in the timetable of Spanish invasion. Instead of 1587, 1588 must now be the year of decision. Instead of vulnerable galleys, galleons and caravels must bear the brunt of the sea fighting. A part of the lesson had been learned, but not all of it. The Spanish ships on which preparations were now rushed were armed with broadside guns, but most of these were of the short-barreled, short-range variety instead of the longer-range, harder-hitting "long guns" favored by Drake and the English. Spain was proud of her foot soldiers, reputed to be the best in the world. She could not conceive of a long-range naval battle, in which boarding tactics would not play the major role.

Overworked and bullied by his king, the Marquis de Santa Cruz died early in 1588. Casting about for a successor, Philip II at last selected the young Duke of Medina-Sidonia, noted for his vast fortune, his unwavering piety, and his complete ignorance of all things maritime. The horrified nobleman protested in vain. He had been chosen by his sovereign, and nothing which he could say would alter Philip's decision.

14.

On May 30, 1588,[1] King Philip's fleet—the "Invincible Armada" —set sail from Lisbon and began the laborious voyage northward along the Portuguese coast. Bad food and seeping sea water troubled the expedition from the start. After two weeks of bucking strong headwinds, the ships had still progressed no further than Corunna. At this point, a sudden storm scattered the fleet. Many of the ships put into Corunna Harbor. Others sought shelter at other points along the northern Iberian coast. A few continued onward toward the point of rendezvous near the Scilly Islands. It took more than a month to round up the stragglers and to put the Armada once more in condition to sail against England.

When it once more set out to sea, on July 23, the Armada was one of the largest and most impressive fleets ever to sail the seas. It included 137 great vessels, mostly galleons, though there were also some caravels, galleys, and galleasses. About half of this total were warships, the rest being transports, supply vessels, and miscellaneous auxiliaries. The total number of guns was 2,431. The Armada was manned by some 8,050 seamen and upwards of 2,000 galley slaves, laboring at the oars. It carried about 19,000 soldiers, plus 1,400 priests, volunteers, and other supernumeraries.

Awaiting the Armada at Dunkirk was an army of 17,000 veteran Spanish troops, under the Duke of Parma, reputed to be the leading soldier of Europe. This was the force which was to be ferried across the Narrow Seas and was then to accomplish the conquest of England for Philip, for Spain, and for the Roman Catholic Church.

The plan which had been handed ready-made to Medina-Sidonia by his king was the essence of simplicity. The Armada was to sail eastward through the English Channel and the Straits of Dover to Calais. The Duke of Parma, meanwhile, was to load his troops upon the barges he had collected at Dunkirk and ferry them along the coast to Calais, where he would succeed Medina-Sidonia as commander in chief of the expedition. As far as possible, naval action was to be avoided until the forces had been joined. After the juncture, it would

[1] This date and the others which follow in the account of the Armada are those of the modern, or Gregorian, calendar, which had been adopted in Spain in 1582 but was not recognized in England until 1752. Since the two calendars were ten days apart in 1588, the Spanish dates, here given, are ten days later than those given in the contemporary English reports.

be a simple matter for the powerful Armada to sweep away any British or Dutch ships which tried to oppose a crossing to the coast of England.

To Philip's way of thinking, the deed was as good as done when the plan had once been formulated. The reward of a million scudi, which Pope Sixtus V had promised him as soon as a single English seaport should be in Spanish hands, was as good as in his pocket. His own claim to the English throne, which the best Spanish lawyers had been carefully reviewing and bolstering, awaited only the extinction of the English House of Tudor. Last, but by no means least, heretic England was about to be restored to the arms of Mother Church, to the great benefit of the eternal soul of Philip of Hapsburg.

In England, meanwhile, there was much confusion. Word of the death of Santa Cruz and of the scattering of the Spanish fleet by the storm off Corunna had led to rumors that the proposed invasion had been postponed for at least a year and perhaps forever. Disarmingly friendly communications from the Spanish and French courts seemed to add substance to the rumors. Queen Elizabeth, for one, was completely deceived by this "peace offensive." Always eager to cut down expenses, she quickly sent word to her Lord High Admiral, Charles Howard, to decommission four of the largest of her warships and send them to the dockyard for extensive overhauling.

Fortunately for England, Admiral Howard was not as easily deceived as his sovereign. Though he himself was an ardent Catholic, he had no wish to see his native land, Protestant though it was, overcome by a foreign Catholic ruler. At the risk of his head, he wrote to the queen's secretary, Sir Francis Walsingham, "It is to me a strange treaty of peace, but the end is like unto the beginning. For the love of God, let the narrow seas be well strengthened, and the ships victualed for some good time."

The next day, Howard wrote directly to the queen: "For the love of Jesus Christ, Madam, awake thoroughly, and see the villainous treasons round about you, against your Majesty and your realm, and draw your forces round about you, like a mighty prince to defend you."

On the same day, he wrote again to Walsingham: "Let Her Majesty trust no more to Judas' kisses; for let her assure herself there is no trust to French King nor Duke of Parma. Let her defend herself like a noble and mighty prince, and trust to her sword and not to their word, and then she need not fear, for her good God will defend her. Good

Mr. Secretary, let the narrow seas be well strengthened. What charge is ill spent now for surety?"

These letters, which still exist in the Naval Archives of Great Britain, reach across the intervening centuries with an urgent message for us who live today.

Receiving no reaction whatever from his daring communications, Admiral Howard took it unto himself to sustain and provision the ships in question from his own resources. He also summoned to Plymouth, for consultation and discussion, some of the leading seamen of England, including Sir Francis Drake, Sir John Hawkins, and Sir Martin Frobisher—men who knew the Spaniards well.

On July 29, 1588, as Drake, Hawkins, and Frobisher were enjoying a game of bowls on the green at Plymouth, a small Scottish privateer raced into Plymouth harbor, with all sails set. Her captain bore exciting news. Not only had the Armada sailed, but it was even now off the English coast. He himself had seen the vast fleet of Spanish ships sailing eastward along the coast of Cornwall. The enemy was at hand!

Tradition has it that, as panic spread, Drake's icy attitude restored confidence. He insisted that the bowling match be finished. "There's time for that," he said, "and to beat the Spaniards after."

The end of the bowling game was followed by hours of intense activity. As soon as darkness fell, a long-prepared beacon fire was lighted at Plymouth. Its glare was seen by watchers farther east along the coast, who in turn lighted a beacon of their own. Thus the word spread quickly, beacon by beacon, so that by morning most of England knew that the dreaded Spaniards had at last arrived.

In the meantime, Howard, Drake, and the other English master seamen had been warping their ships out of Plymouth Harbor and making for a point of rendezvous in the shelter of a nearby headland. There they lay, sixty-seven in number, throughout the night and the long next morning, their officers and lookouts straining for a sight of Spanish sails on the western horizon.

15.

So much has been written about the vast Armada and the tiny English fleet which was gathered to resist it that, in the interest of fairness, one should look the facts squarely in the face. The ships of the Armada were 137 in number, nearly half of which were merely armed transports and supply ships. Queen Elizabeth's navy, at this time, consisted of thirty-four warships. The country's peril, however, had brought many privately owned ships temporarily into service, eventually swelling the number to 197. Thus, in total numbers, the English had the advantage. The greater part of these English ships were small, some being mere fishing boats, totally unfitted for action and never brought close to the Armada. If we count only fully qualified warships of 300 tons or more, the Spaniards had 62, averaging 727 tons each, against 23 English vessels, averaging 552 tons. The English ships, on the other hand, were faster and more maneuverable, and a higher percentage of their cannons were "long guns," suitable for long-range action. In total manpower afloat, the Spaniards outnumbered the English nearly two to one. Thus, there were advantages on both sides, making it difficult to strike a balance. The evaluation must depend upon the results.

Lord High Admiral Charles Howard, though himself an experienced seaman, had the rare good sense to defer to the superior judgment of his Vice-Admiral, Sir Francis Drake. Drake, for his part, was not above courting the opinions of Hawkins, Frobisher, and others of the group. Thus the little English fleet of 67 vessels which first engaged the Spaniards had the advantage of perhaps the greatest collection of fighting sea lore ever to guide an embattled squadron. In the long run, such lore counted for far more than mere manpower or weight of broadside.

As the Spanish fleet hove into sight, there were those among the English defenders who favored an all-out attack upon the invaders. The great galleons should be boarded and the Dons driven into the sea! Such a course would have played directly into the hands of the Spaniards, with their deckloads of trained soldiers and their heavy, short-range artillery. Howard, Drake, and the others in command had the intelligence to employ to the utmost their own advantages and avoid at all costs those of the Spaniards.

16.

The Armada passed Plymouth as a great, slow-moving crescent[1] of mighty ships. From tip to tip, the tightly packed formation measured a full seven miles. The English seamen let it pass, then fell in behind it

[1] In all probability, this widely described "crescent" formation was actually the famous "flying eagle" formation which had won at Lepanto.

with their 67 vessels. By this move, Drake and his companions gained
the weather gauge on their opponents.

The first real action began about nine in the morning of July 31.
Using their upwind position, the English ships opened a long-range
cannonading of the Spanish fleet, which was unable to reply effectively. As the action continued, a few of Philip's floating palaces began to show signs of damage. Still, little was accomplished until an
accident of navigation separated a group of Spanish ships in the rear
division farther than usual from the main body. At once, the English
ships closed, sailing in line ahead, and poured a heavy fire on the
unfortunate group of Spaniards. With great difficulty, some ships from
the main Spanish body beat upwind to the rescue of their compatriots,
who were escorted in badly damaged condition toward the now-
ragged formation.

At this point, Admiral Howard signaled a breakoff of activity. The
Spaniards were now safely past Plymouth, which was no longer in
danger of invasion. The English fleet was too short of men, ships, and
ammunition to risk too close or too prolonged an engagement. As
Howard later wrote, "We durst not adventure to put in among them,
their fleet being so strong."

The Spaniards, meanwhile, were having their troubles. Aboard the
great galleon *San Salvador,* a Flemish gunner was undergoing punishment for wasting ammunition during the day's action. Resentful,
bruised in body and spirit, he crept away and planned a frightful revenge. Within the ship's magazine, he lighted a slow fuse. Then he
leaped overboard and disappeared. Minutes later, the *San Salvador*
blew up with a thunderous roar. Within the shattered and burning
wreck were the treasure chests from which the Armada's entire complement was to be paid.

An attempt was made to save the ruined treasure ship. Within the
main body of the fleet, certain galleons swung their bows about in an
attempt to beat back upwind to their wounded sister vessel. The attempt resulted in collision. A galleon commanded by Don Pedro de
Valdez crashed against another ship, sustaining grievous injuries. The
foremast was weakened and sagged against the mainmast, entangling
most of the rigging in a useless cat's cradle of snarled lines. In panic,
the other Spaniards struggled free, abandoning the crippled galleon to
her fate. Later, in reporting the matter to his king, Don Pedro wrote
bitterly: "He [the Duke of Medina-Sidonia] left me comfortless in

sight of the whole fleet. Greater inhumanity and thanklessness was never, I think, heard of among men."

Seeing the glare of the burning *San Salvador*, Admiral Howard changed his plans and ordered a night pursuit of the Spaniards. A lantern was hung on the stern of Drake's flagship, the *Revenge*, to serve as a guide beacon for the English ships. On they sailed, following the light. Suddenly, there was only darkness. The lamp was gone. Blindly, during the rest of the night, the English vessels groped eastward in the Armada's wake. It was sheer good fortune that none of them blundered to destruction among the great Spanish ships.

With the coming of daylight, Drake's disappearance was explained. He had come upon Don Pedro's crippled galleon and had closed to capture it. For the time being, the pirate in Drake's soul had overcome the admiral. Here was rich loot, not to be shared with any other captain. The lantern was quickly doused so that the work of capture and acquisition could go on unobserved. Sir Francis Drake has never entirely lost the stain upon his name caused by this episode in which he so callously jeopardized the safety of England for his own gain.

17.

Now that Plymouth had been passed by the Armada, the next likely point of attack was the Isle of Wight, some 120 miles farther to the east. About half way between lay Portland, a little seaport on the shore of a long peninsula, or "bill."

On August 1, the day after the battle off Plymouth, there was no important fighting between the fleets. The Armada continued to sail slowly eastward, dogged by the prowling English squadron, which continually grew in size as small ships from the various English ports put out with volunteer crews to help repel the invaders. Miraculously, the shattered treasure ship *San Salvador* was still afloat and was still with the Armada, its fires extinguished and its many leaks kept somewhat under control by continuous pumping.

Both fleets were beginning to run short of ammunition. The Spaniards hoped to replenish their supply when they should complete their juncture with Parma at Calais. The English should have found the supply problem simpler, but they did not. On the last day of July, Howard had sent a frantic appeal to Walsingham: "Sir, for the love of God and our country let us have with some speed some great shot sent us of our bigness; for this service will continue long; and some powder with it." As a result of this and other appeals, a wagon train was organized and sent to the Tower of London, where the Queen had large stores of munitions. Here the twin serpents of red tape and stupid bureaucracy raised their ugly heads to unprecedented heights. The great enemy Armada was at hand. Invasion appeared imminent. The English fleet was fighting for the nation's life. The Admiral's request for needed munitions was refused because the requisition was not in proper form!

The one important activity of August 1 was the cutting out of the damaged treasure ship. During the day, it became evident that the sea was gaining on the pumps. Evidently, the *San Salvador* was going to sink. An attempt was made to salvage useful goods, but the treasure chests were deep in the flooded hold and could not be reached. Some *feluccas*—small, lateen-rigged sailing ships—were detailed to sink her to prevent her capture by the English. As the *feluccas* lingered behind to complete their assignment, they were pounced upon and driven off by a little group of English warships, Howard and Hawkins both being present in person. The *San Salvador* was boarded and taken in tow. Thanks to the prodigious efforts of the prize crew, she was at last brought safely into Weymouth Harbor, where her treasure of 100,000 ducats was extracted.

To the Spanish captains, August 1 must have seemed a day of ill omen. The snatching of the treasure was bad, but worse from the captains' point of view was the assigning of a hangman to each ship of the Armada. These grim crewmen all had the same order from the Duke of Medina-Sidonia: "Hang any captain whose ship deserts its assigned place in the formation."

18.

Tuesday, August 2, was a day of frantic though disorganized activity. It began long before sunup as the two fleets lay becalmed. Noting that a group of English ships had become separated from the others, the Spanish admiral ordered Don Hugo de Moncada, commander of his galleasses, to make an attack under oars. It so happened that Don Hugo had previously made a request to be permitted to attack, and had been rebuffed. Now he would not cooperate. His ships got under way but bypassed their intended prey and accomplished nothing.

With daylight came a wind from the northeast. This deprived the galleasses of their stationary target but, at the same time, gave the weather gauge for the first time to the Spaniards. Seeing an opportunity to close with his elusive adversaries, Medina-Sidonia changed course and bore down upon the English ships off Portland Bill.

In trying to regain the weather gauge, Admiral Howard came very near to becoming entrapped. Leading a small group of ships, his flagship, the *Ark Royal,* tried to slip past the landward edge of the Spanish formation. At once, Medina-Sidonia moved to head him off, forcing Howard to come about and head seaward. There was little room for maneuver. With his eight strongest ships in line ahead, Howard passed across the bows of the nearest Spanish vessels, which were coming at him in line abreast, effectively masking each other's fire. As Howard delivered a terrific, short-range raking fire at his pursuers, the weaker ships of his squadron, shielded by the English battle line, made good their escape.

Meanwhile, Frobisher in the *Triumph,* leading five other vessels, had gotten himself into just as tight a trap, between the Spaniards and the shore. Led by four galleasses, a large body of Spanish ships bore down upon them. To all concerned, Frobisher seemed doomed. His men prepared to sell their lives as dearly as possible.

Now occurred Sir Francis Drake's opportunity to regain the favor he had lost. Aided by a lucky switch of the wind, he led a group of fifty ships to the seaward wing of the Spanish formation and attacked vigorously. The startled Spaniards found themselves attacked from behind while fickle Nature was depriving them of the weather gauge. At the same time, Howard, having fought free of his own predicament, led six of his largest ships to the rescue of Frobisher, who was still battling gallantly against the four great galleasses.

In the confusion of battle, the *San Marcos,* flagship of the Duke of Medina-Sidonia, became separated from the group of galleons with which it had been operating. As the great galleon bore down upon Frobisher's squadron to reinforce the four galleasses, it had the misfortune to encounter Howard's line of warships, also hurrying to take part in the same fray. As they passed, each of Howard's ships treated the *San Marcos* to a devastating broadside. Not long afterward, another string of English ships, headed by Drake's *Revenge,* happened upon the damaged flagship. Once more, the Duke's galleon received a frightful mauling. The wonder is that the ship stayed afloat at all. In the end, however, she succeeded in rejoining the main body of the Armada.

After twelve hours of furious cannonading, in which many ships were damaged but few were sunk, both admirals were glad to break off hostilities. Ammunition was very low in both fleets, and the men were exhausted. Both sides claimed a victory.

The addition of volunteers had now swelled the English fleet to more than 100 ships. The confusion of the battle had shown organizational weakness. The next day a meeting was held aboard the *Ark Royal* to bring order out of chaos. The fleet was divided into four squadrons, of approximately equal size. Each contained a nucleus of the queen's warships and a supporting group of volunteered vessels. Howard, Drake, Hawkins, and Frobisher took command of the four groups, each of which was to operate as a unit. All four units followed the Armada eastward, continually feinting as though to attack but veering off, because of the shortage of powder and shot. The only cannonading occurred early in the morning, when one large Spanish ship was badly damaged but could not be taken.

Toward the end of the day, a little badly needed ammunition was ferried out to the English fleet—only about enough for one sharp engagement. The parsimonious queen was evidently fighting her war for survival on the installment plan!

19.

The dawn of Thursday, August 4, found the two fleets drifting in a dead calm off the Isle of Wight. The Duke of Medina-Sidonia knew this as the most vulnerable spot on England's southern coast—an easily taken spot where he could land and maintain himself until receiving definite word that the Duke of Parma was ready and waiting for him at Calais. This dreaded possibility was not lost upon Howard and his English associates.

The first activity occurred when Sir John Hawkins detected two Spanish galleons, the *San Luis* and the *Santa Anna,* drifting at some distance from each other and from the other ships of the Armada. At once, he ordered several of his vessels to be towed by their small boats toward the vulnerable Spaniards. At this, three galleasses and a Levantine galley came rowing out to oppose Hawkins. This led Howard to order the *Ark Royal* and the *Golden Lion* to be towed into the fray. In the fight that followed, the galleasses succeeded in rescuing the two isolated galleons, though all three galleasses were badly damaged.

The cannonading attracted the *San Marcos* and other galleons from the main body of the Armada. It also attracted Frobisher's flagship *Triumph,* which succeeded in getting itself isolated in the midst of the enemy with no wind for its sails and with an unshipped rudder. The Spaniards made a strong attempt to board but were frustrated when Frobisher ordered out eleven longboats to tow his ship away, while daring workmen scrambled down his vessel's stern to work on the rudder. Providentially, a wind sprang up, and the *Triumph* escaped.

The Armada had, meanwhile, been edging in toward its immediate objective, the Isle of Wight. While Howard and Frobisher were engaged with the Spanish rear guard, Hawkins took advantage of the southerly wind to slip away and join Drake to seaward of the main Spanish body. To reach the Isle of Wight, the Spaniards had to pass between the two English squadrons and a dangerous reef, the Owers, toward which the wind was now blowing ever more strongly from the southwest. At just the proper moment, the English ships attacked the *San Mateo,* the Spanish galleon which stood farthest out to sea. As the *San Mateo* was driven into the Spanish fleet, crowding developed, and there was a growing danger that the inner fringes of the Armada would be forced upon the reef. To avert this threatening disaster, Medina-Sidonia swung his flagship to the eastward, out to sea. The other vessels followed his lead. The reef was safely passed, but so was the opportunity to make the planned landing on the Isle of Wight.

Writing to his queen that night, Lord High Admiral Charles Howard reported with satisfaction: "Their force is wonderful, great and strong; and yet we pluck their feathers, by little and little."

20.

Worried and frustrated, the Duke of Medina-Sidonia guided his great, ungainly fleet on eastward. No longer was it possible to seize the Isle of Wight and wait there for news of Parma. There was nothing to do now but cross the Channel to Calais, hoping that the Duke and his reinforcements were waiting there.

Late the next afternoon, Calais was in sight. Anxious eyes scanned the shore, but there was no sign of Parma, his barges, or his men. Into the open and unprotected roadstead sailed the Armada. Anchors plunged into the water, and the great fleet came to rest.

Where *was* Parma? We now know that he was at Dunkirk helplessly tied down by a blockading squadron of Dutch ships, supplemented by an English squadron under Lord Henry Seymour. Gladly would he have gone to Calais to meet Medina-Sidonia, but he could not. He was completely devoid of naval protection, and, as he subsequently pointed out, his fleet of barges could easily have been rounded up and destroyed by any four ships of the blockading squadron.

Aboard the English fleet, at anchor just out of cannon range to seaward of the Armada, a meeting was being held to determine the best way to dislodge the Spanish vessels from their anchorage before Parma should devise some way of fighting his way overland to effect a junction. To Sir William Winter, captain of the *Vanguard,* is credited the suggestion: "Considering their hugeness, 'twill not be possible to remove them but by a device." The "device" he then suggested was the use of fireships.

Under cover of darkness, eight old merchant ships, contributed by the various leaders from their squadrons, were smeared with pitch, loaded with combustibles, and towed to a point off the harbor mouth from which both wind and tide bore directly toward the Spanish fleet. Each was set afire and was sent on its way toward the mass of Spanish shipping. Aboard each fireship was a single intrepid steersman, who was to guide the ship as long as he dared, then escape over the stern into a small boat, which was being towed along.

Aboard the Spanish vessels, the appearance of the flaming fireships produced a panic all out of proportion to the actual danger. Many of the Spaniards had been present when the "hell-burners" from Antwerp had exploded against the bridge on the Scheldt River. The dreadful memory of death and destruction was still fresh in their minds. Gianibelli was known to have escaped to England. Doubtless he was with the English fleet. Cries of "The Antwerp hell-burners!" rang out. There was no time to haul up anchor to avoid the disaster. Axes were wielded, and the great galleons and galleasses were cut free from their ground tackle. There was confusion and jamming. Glancing collisions were common. One galleon ran solidly aground. As each Spanish crew fought to avoid the danger, open water appeared through which the fireships sailed harmlessly to the shore.

Harmlessly? Though no Spanish ship, save the grounded galleon, had met disaster, yet all were in bad shape, free of their anchors and with no choice but to beat out to sea away from the lee shore. In darkness and disorder, the Armada put to sea.

21.

Morning found the Spanish ships widely scattered, with no semblance of formation. Driven by the southwest wind, they had drifted eastward along the shore, their crews striving only to keep them from grounding. The greater part of them lay off the little port of Gravelines, midway between Calais and Dunkirk. Should they succeed in reorganizing, there was grave danger that they might yet effect a junction with Parma by putting in at the latter port.

The English commanders had no intention of letting the Spaniards reform their squadrons. All six divisions—Seymour's and Winter's groups having joined the other four—swept eastward in pursuit. Once more, as off the Isle of Wight, the Spanish ships seemed to be in grave danger of being forced upon a rugged lee shore. Only by standing straight off the coast and toward the advancing English were they able to avoid the threatened disaster, but at the cost of heavy hammering by the English guns. As usual, it fell to Medina-Sidonia and his much-battered flagship *San Marcos* to set the course and receive the worst of the punishment.

This time it was Lord High Admiral Howard himself who deserted his post on the right wing and so weakened the English attack. The largest of the Spanish galleasses, a rich, rare prize, was detected limping along the shore line, trying to escape. Disdaining the over-all strategy in order to pluck another feather, Howard led his ships out of formation and took the prize. Had he not done so, it is possible that the Spanish Armada might then and there have been destroyed.

As it was, the Spanish ships, still striving for some sort of formation, were harried and chivvied along the coast, past Dunkirk and out into the misty reaches of the North Sea. The disconsolate Duke of Parma, standing on the waterfront, saw the fleet that was to have guarded his way to England receding farther and farther to the north until it was lost to sight.

Had the Spaniards but known it, the English pursuers were now completely harmless. The last supplies of powder and shot were gone. There was nothing to prevent the Armada from retracing its course to Dunkirk, to Calais, or back through the Channel to England or to Spain. Nothing, that is, but ignorance of the true situation. The English were still there, still following doggedly, still apparently ready to deal out more of the punishment with which they had been so liberal for the past week and more. For three days, the Spaniards fled northward, and for three days the English followed menacingly, forcing the would-be invaders farther and farther from the ports of England.

When at last the half-starved English turned homeward, Medina-Sidonia was at a loss. He dared not try to return through the Channel. For a while, he considered wintering on the coast of Denmark or Norway, to resume the invasion attempt in the spring. The thought of the unprotected Spanish coasts, at the mercy of Drake and his raiders, forced the abandonment of the plan. In desperation, he decided to return home by passing north of Scotland, around the British Isles into the Atlantic.

In the treacherous seas off Scotland and Ireland, Nature took a hand. Tremendous storms battered what was left of the Armada. Ships that might have ridden out the storms at anchor were swept upon the shore, their officers bitterly regretting the loss of their anchors in Calais Harbor. Scores of ships were wrecked, and thousands of men were drowned. Survivors who managed to fight their way through the surf to the Scottish or Irish coasts found little help. Most had their throats cut; the few who lived were turned over to the English as prisoners. Of the 137 great ships that had so proudly sailed from the ports of Spain, only fifty managed to return. Of the 30,450 men who had set forth, only about 10,000 lived to see their homes again. It was one of the great naval disasters of all time.

We must say for Philip II that he was magnanimous in his defeat and disappointment. He might have held the unfortunate Duke of Medina-Sidonia completely responsible. Instead, he laid the blame chiefly upon the storms, saying, "After all, one cannot fight against God himself." He also saved a bit of the blame for the English, whose long-range cannon work appeared to him to be mere cowardly trickery. Why could they not have gone down bravely to a close-range defeat before the pikes of the Spanish boarders, as the Turks had done at Lepanto?

What of the cost to the English? Drake concludes his famous written account with the words: "With all their great and terrible ostentation, they did not in all their sailing round about England so much as sink or take one ship, barque, pinnace, or cock-boat of ours, or even burn so much as one sheep-cote on this land."

22.

The defeat of the Armada dealt the death blow to Spanish naval power. It took a few years, however, for death to claim its victim. After the heavy blows of the joust in the Channel, the misericord had to be applied a few times before the twitching stopped.

In 1589, Drake commanded an expedition against Spain and Portugal which was successful in its naval aspects but proved costly and disappointing when land fighting was undertaken. Corunna was taken and sacked, several warships and merchant vessels being captured. A land attack upon Lisbon failed, as did an attempt to stir up the Portuguese in revolution against Spanish control.

In August of 1591 occurred a sea fight which has never been matched for gallant disregard of odds. A squadron of six English warships, under Admiral Howard, lay off the island of Flores, in the Azores, taking on water and supplies. On the horizon appeared a fleet of fifty-three Spanish ships, fifteen being large warships. The odds were too great. In haste, Admiral Howard ordered his squadron to sea and set a course to avoid the Spaniards.

Five of the English ships escaped. The sixth—Drake's old flagship *Revenge,* commanded by Sir Richard Grenville—did not. Ninety of her crew of 190 were sick ashore, and Grenville took the time to bring these men aboard to save them from the usual Spanish "mercy" extended to heretics. The Spanish fleet was now close at hand. Instead of trying to flee along the coast, Grenville sailed boldly toward his enemies, in an evident attempt to fight his way through their fleet and out to sea.

The attempt failed. As the little *Revenge* tried to pass through a gap in the Spanish formation, the great galleon *San Philip* loomed up to windward, completely cutting off the wind from the English sails. Slowed so that she "could neither make way nor feele her helm," the *Revenge* prepared to sell her life dearly. As enemy ships gathered about her, she discharged a broadside of "crosse bar shot" into the *San Philip*'s towering sides.

The action started shortly before three in the afternoon—one lone English ship in the midst of fifty-three enemy, all armed, fifteen being larger warships than herself—one hundred able-bodied Englishmen against ten thousand Spaniards. Eight hours later, the battle still went on, the *Revenge* hurling her shot into the solid wall of surrounding vessels and receiving frightful punishment in return. Before midnight, Grenville lay dying of two wounds, but he had had the satisfaction of seeing two of his largest assailants go down from the blows he had delivered, of seeing numerous Spanish boarding attacks beaten back with heavy loss.

With the coming of daylight, the little *Revenge* still floated defiantly in the midst of her enemies, now one fewer from the sinking of a third galleon in the night. Her cannon were silent, for the powder was gone. Too few men were left alive to repel the next attempt at boarding. The end was in sight.

With almost the last strength in his body, Grenville called upon his master gunner to "split the ship and sink her." Hastening to do as he was commanded, the loyal gunner was seized by others of the crew, who wished to live to fight another day. So the *Revenge* was taken, and the few of her crew who remained alive were made prisoners. The Spanish admiral, overcome with admiration, had the dying Grenville removed from "this marvelous unsavory ship, filled with blood and bodies of dead and wounded men, like a slaughter house."

In the end, the *Revenge* amply justified her name. About two weeks after Sir Richard Grenville's burial at sea, a hurricane of tremendous force struck the Spanish fleet, now grown to some 140 vessels by the addition of a convoy from the Indies. The *Revenge* went down, with her prize crew and her fifty English prisoners. So did nearly one hundred of the Spanish ships, including all fifty of the battered vessels which had exchanged shots with the *Revenge* during the fifteen hours of her death struggle. Like Samson, she had brought down a host of her enemies in the moment of her own destruction.

Probably no ship in history ever dealt so great a blow to the prestige and confidence of an enemy nation.

23.

In that same year of 1591, there was another sea fight which proved destructive of Spanish morale. Near Gibraltar, the English ship *Centurion,* convoying a group of small merchant vessels, was attacked by six Spanish galleys. As Captain Robert Bradshaw of the *Centurion* prepared for battle, all but one of his convoy sought safety in flight. The tiny *Dolphin* alone remained with her protector.

Together, the *Centurion* and the *Dolphin* received the attack. Five of the galleys concentrated on the warship while the sixth assailed the little merchantman. Though the *Dolphin*'s crew resisted bravely, they had neither the manpower nor the armament to match a galley. At last, facing capture, her captain blew up his ship, destroying it and all on board.

The *Centurion* had a crew of only forty-eight, yet she fought the Spanish galleys to a standstill. When the Spanish powder gave out after six hours, the little English ship was still resisting. As a final gesture of frustration, each of the Spanish galleys rowed by their defiant enemy, pelting the *Centurion*'s surviving crewmen with hammers and with chains taken from the galley slaves. Then they went away, leaving the battered little warship alone, free to limp on home to England.

24.

History repeated itself in 1596, when word reached England that King Philip II was preparing another great Armada to succeed where the first had failed. A fleet of seventeen English and twenty Dutch warships, accompanied by numerous supply vessels, set out for the Spanish coast. Lord High Admiral Charles Howard was in command, with the Earl of Essex and Sir Walter Raleigh serving under him. Once more, Cadiz was assailed and taken. This time, though, the rich prize of shipping in the harbor did not fall into English hands. The local commander—none other than the ill-fated Duke of Medina-Sidonia—regretfully put the torch to the shipping in both the inner and outer harbors when the success of the English attack seemed assured. In the fire which followed, Spain lost thirteen great warships besides innumerable merchant vessels and vast stores of supplies. The king's beard had been singed again!

Philip of Spain died in 1598. In the first thirty-two years of his reign, he had seen his nation become the strongest in the world, holding the world's greatest empire and drawing from it a golden harvest. Spanish galleons sailed everywhere. Sea power was the key. In the final ten years of his life, he had seen Spanish sea power smashed at the hands of two nations whose people were far more at home on the deep than Spaniards could ever be.

Spain's day of glory was over. It was left for the English and the Dutch to determine which nation should next be Queen of the Seas.

4 THE RISE
OF DUTCH NAVAL POWER

1.

The people of the Netherlands had a natural affinity for the sea. Much of their low-lying country had actually been a part of the North Sea bottom, and had had to be painfully conquered by means of dikes, polders, windmills, and pumps. The herring, which formed an important part of the Dutch diet, had to be taken from the stormy waters of the fishing banks by the sturdy Dutch fishermen. The prosperity of the little country depended upon trade, and trade depended upon sailors and fleets of merchant ships. The sea was, at one and the same time, the great enemy and the great ally of the Dutch.

Before 1580, Dutch merchant shipping existed on only a very modest scale. The Portuguese were the great traders. It was they who had found the route to the Indies and had taken for their own the fabulously wealthy Spice Islands, south and southeast of Asia. Portuguese vessels brought the pepper and other spices to Lisbon, where they were offered for sale to all buyers. Dutch merchants bought the goods in Lisbon, transported them to northern Europe, and resold them at a markup sufficient to guarantee a modest profit. At this point, the Dutch were playing jackal to the Portuguese lion.

Meanwhile, as we have seen, the Portuguese were having troubles of their own. Almost everyone, from king to merchant, seemed to be trying to follow the motto of one Portuguese Viceroy of India: "Send pepper to Lisbon, then lie down and sleep." The empire was rapidly disintegrating, and the home government was weakening to the point where it would soon pass, almost by default, into the hands of King Philip II of Spain.

Philip's seizure of Portugal in 1580 came at the time when he was bending every effort to suppress a revolt in the Netherlands. By way of striking a blow at his disobedient Dutch subjects, he promptly closed the port of Lisbon to all Dutch vessels. This blow to the Netherlands' economy was to have surprising and important results.

The resourceful Dutch had no intention of being deprived of their profitable trade in spices. If they could no longer get their cargoes in Lisbon, it seemed self-evident that they must go directly to the original source—to the Spice Islands themselves. Portugal, having been absorbed by Spain, was no longer in a position to defend her long-guarded monopoly. As for Spain herself, she was already doing the Dutch all the harm she could. Here was a chance to strike back at her. In increasing numbers, Dutch ships set out for the Far East to take on forbidden cargoes.

The death of Philip II in 1598 did nothing to reduce the friction between the Spaniards and the Dutch. If anything, the new king, Philip III, was more repressive than his father. One of his first acts was to seize all Dutch ships in Spanish-controlled harbors and imprison their crews. Though some of the unfortunate sailors were later released, others were tortured, and some were chained to the rowing benches of Spanish galleys. Not long afterward, King Philip issued an edict forbidding the inhabitants of all Spanish lands to trade with the Dutch. If the rebels would not yield to force, they might give in when faced by starvation and the strangulation of their trade.

The Dutch accepted the challenge. Though it strained the resources of the little country to the utmost, they assembled a fleet of seventy-three warships and sent it out under the command of Peter van der Does. His instructions were flexible. In general, they provided for doing as much harm as possible to Spain and as much good as possible for the Dutch cause.

The first point of contact was at the port of Corunna. A Spanish fleet lay in the harbor, protected by heavy artillery in the forts. The Dutch could not go in, and the Spaniards would not come out. After some maneuvering and deploying, Admiral van der Does decided that nothing constructive could be done at Corunna. He then sailed to the Canary Islands, made two landings, and acquired a modest amount of loot.

Striking south from the Canaries, Van der Does sailed along the northern coast of the Gulf of Guinea, coming at last to the island of Saint Thomas, a Portuguese colony. The island was taken without resistance, but scarcely had the looting begun when a tropical fever struck down hundreds of the Dutch invaders. Admiral van der Does was among those who died. He was buried on the island, his grave being protected from desecration by a vast mound of masonry, consisting of the ruins of an entire town which the Dutch destroyed for this sole purpose.

Sorrowfully, then, the Dutch sailed homeward, losing another thousand men to fever during the voyage. The results achieved by the great fleet had fallen far short of expectations. Nevertheless, an important step had been taken. The seafaring Dutch had started the systematic dismemberment of the Portuguese Empire.

2.

During the next few years, there was much hard fighting on the land between the Dutch and the Spaniards, but little on the sea. The most important event of this period was the death of Queen Elizabeth I of England, in 1603. She had been a somewhat uncomfortable and unpredictable friend of the Dutch, but a friend, nevertheless. Her successor, King James I—son of the ill-fated Mary, Queen of Scots—was not a friend at all.

The enmity of King James for the Dutch stemmed from the fact that he had just made peace with Spain. By way of demonstrating his sincerity, he went out of his way to antagonize his late allies in the Netherlands. Spanish ships and even the vessels of illegal pirate groups operating out of Dunkirk and other Channel ports were permitted to seek sanctuary in English harbors when pursued by Dutch warships. The Dutch, on the other hand, were not permitted to visit English harbors under any conditions.

The situation came to a head in 1605, when a Dutch fleet under Admiral Hautain encountered a larger Spanish fleet of warships and transports off the English port of Dover. Many of the Spanish vessels were quickly taken; the rest fled toward the sanctuary of the "neutral" harbor. Unfortunately, the Dutch had endured too much at the hands of Spaniards to be much inclined to show mercy. The captured Spaniards were bound back to back, in pairs, and were thrown into the sea. This was not a sudden inspiration on the part of the Dutch. It was an established policy of their government, adopted for use against the Channel pirates and the Spanish invaders of the Netherlands. Dutch sailors and naval officers were under firm instructions to apply *voet-spoelen* (literally, "feet washing") to all captured pirates and Spanish soldiers on transports. Often they did it reluctantly. In the end, the custom was discontinued as a result of a strike among Dutch sailors, who refused to go to sea until the orders enforcing *voetspoelen* were rescinded.

On this day, however, *voetspoelen* was applied with a vim which shocked the crews of English ships which had come out from Dover to witness the battle. Though most of the Spaniards were drowned, some were fished from the water and borne to safety by the compassionate English.

The fleeing Spanish ships which had escaped from the battle were meanwhile making all possible speed for Dover, closely pursued by that part of the Dutch fleet which had not paused to take and drown prisoners. As the Spaniards neared sanctuary, the great guns of the Dover forts boomed forth, hurling their cannon balls at the pursuing Dutch. Direct hits were scored, more than one hundred Dutch sailors being killed in this unexpected attack by English gunners. The incident drove a wedge between the formerly friendly countries of England and the Dutch Republic, creating a split which was to grow steadily wider during the next half century and more.

In the meantime, the Dutch were extending their activities into a rich and distant area. As early as 1597, a Dutch merchant named Cornelis de Houtman had taken a trading ship to the East Indies, despite the vigilance of Spaniards and Portuguese, and had returned with a rich cargo of spices. This had led other Dutch merchants to send out fleets of vessels especially designed "to outrun the Spanish and outcarry the English." In 1602, this prosperous but disorganized trade was brought together under a single administrative authority by the creation of the Dutch East India Company, with its headquarters in Amsterdam.

3.

For the first few years, the activities of the Dutch East India Company were furtive and strictly illegal. The riches of the Spice Islands were generally regarded as being the rightful possession of the Portuguese traders and their Spanish overlords. Spanish authority was carefully circumvented and avoided, rather than challenged. The Dutch were looked upon as poachers.

In 1605, the great change began. To stop the illicit trade in the Far East, King Philip III sent out a powerful fleet, under Admiral Hurtado. The eight galleons and thirty-two galleys which Hurtado took to the coast of India should have been strong enough to suppress anything that the Dutch had in those waters. The Dutch, however, had had their fill of running away. When a fleet of only five Dutch vessels, under Wolfert Hermandzoon, came upon the Spanish squadron off the Malabar coast, he attacked instead of retiring. The boldness of the Dutch in defying odds of eight to one completely unnerved the Spaniards, whose morale had been sinking ever lower since the defeat of the Armada. Two Spanish vessels were taken and the others driven away in unceremonious flight. The astounded Hermandzoon found himself master of all he surveyed.

Now that the Spaniards had been brushed aside, Admiral Hermandzoon sailed on boldly to the East Indies. Landing on the Banda Islands, noted for their rich spices, he made a treaty with the local ruler, guaranteeing to protect the natives against the Spaniards and the Portuguese in exchange for a monopoly of the Banda spice trade. It was this agreement which formed the basis of the later Dutch claim to the entire East Indies area.

In October, 1606, there occurred a battle very reminiscent of the last fight of the *Revenge*. A Dutch fleet of thirteen ships, under Admiral Hautain, was cruising off Cape St. Vincent, in the hope of intercepting the Spanish plate fleet from the New World. The sight of many sails on the western horizon sent the Dutch vessels hurrying in that direction. Closer inspection showed that it was not the plate fleet but a squadron of Spanish warships, including eighteen galleons, eight galleys, and a number of smaller vessels. The odds looked unattractive, even after a rising sea forced the galleys to leave the Spanish formation and make for the shelter of the shore. The Spanish fleet was coming from directly upwind, with everything in its favor. Valuing discretion above valor on this day, Admiral Hautain ordered his ships to scatter and escape.

All got away except the ship commanded by Vice-Admiral Klaazoon, who apparently chose to sail directly toward the Spaniards rather than flee. There was a brief exchange of cannon fire at close range before Klaazoon's mainmast went by the board. Now he could not escape. Nothing was left but to fight to the death. For two days and two nights the crippled Dutch ship exchanged fire with her eighteen powerful adversaries. To all demands for surrender, all promises of quarter, the Dutch Vice-Admiral turned a deaf ear. At last, with only sixty men left alive and the ship sinking, he called his survivors together and announced his decision to die rather than give up. All offered agreement. After a moment of kneeling in prayer on the blood-soaked decks, Klaazoon hurled a torch into the magazine. The ship blew up. Only two living survivors were fished from the water by the awe-struck Spaniards, who heard the story of the Vice-Admiral's last minutes, then heard themselves roundly cursed before the two seamen died of their frightful burns.

4.

Early in 1607, the Dutch won a brilliant victory, then passed up a golden opportunity. Admiral Jacob Heemskerk, in command of a fleet of twenty-six small Dutch warships, went cruising off the Spanish and Portuguese coasts in search of treasure fleets. He found none, but he did hear tidings of a strong Spanish naval squadron at anchor in the harbor of Gibraltar. Twenty-one Spanish ships were there, including ten enormous galleons. Though numbers favored the Dutch, tonnage, weight of broadside, manpower, and location favored the Spaniards. To sail into Gibraltar Harbor against those odds appeared to be the height of folly.

Don Juan Alvarez d'Avila, the Spanish admiral, certainly thought so. When he saw the little ships entering the harbor mouth, he was overcome with amazement at the daring of a Dutch commander who would sail so close to a fleet so greatly superior. To those about him, he observed that his flagship alone was more than a match for all those little Dutch cockleshells.

As the Dutch advanced, some of D'Avila's confidence left him. Why, that leading Dutch ship seemed to be headed straight for his own *St. Augustine!* Hastily, he ordered the anchor cables cut, so that the flagship could slip deeper into the Spanish formation and thus avoid the first contact with those foolhardy sailors from the north. The flowing tide carried the *St. Augustine* in among the other Spanish vessels, but Heemskerk's *Aeolus* followed her right in.

As the ships neared, the *St. Augustine* fired a broadside at her smaller adversary. The *Aeolus* held her fire until her bowsprit touched the Spanish ship, then fired her bow chasers and loosed a volley of musketry. As the firing became general, a cannon ball carried away one of Admiral Heemskerk's legs. He had time for only a few orders and instructions before his life drained away. By that time, D'Avila also lay dead.

As the battle spread throughout the harbor, the Dutch strategy became evident. Two Dutch ships would attack each of the Spanish galleons, one from either side, first cannonading at close range, then boarding. Spanish ships not yet engaged were completely ignored in the single-mindedness of this assault. Their turn would come quickly enough.

The captain of one of the Dutch ships had taken with him his ten-year-old son, to serve as cabin boy. As the battle waxed hot, the boy followed his father's instructions and remained in the comparative safety of the cabin, listening with anxious ears to the roar of cannon and the shattering of planks and timbers. At last, able to stand his confinement no more, he rushed out on the deck just in time to see his father fall dead upon the deck. The Spanish galleon with which his father's ship had been engaged was drifting away, but it is said that the Dutch crew, inspired by the boy's grief and rage, increased their efforts and took the Spanish vessel.

We should note this boy well. His name was Marten Harpertzoon Tromp. We shall meet him again.

All over the harbor, the Dutch were gaining the upper hand. As the battle became a rout, the victorious Dutchmen were driven almost to madness by three bits of information which passed from ship to ship. Their beloved Admiral Heemskerk and Vice-Admiral Alteras both lay dead. An attempt had been made to massacre the Dutch prisoners lying chained in the holds of the Spanish ships, to prevent their rescue by their countrymen. Finally, papers had been found, signed by King Philip III, ordering death by torture for all captured heretics. Such cruelty must be met by cruelty! Small ships were sent to skirt the shores, to prevent the landing of fleeing Spanish crews. Even drowning Spaniards in the harbor were sought out and harpooned by the vengeful Dutch.

By sunset, it was all over. The badly damaged *St. Augustine* was in Dutch hands. The other twenty Spanish warships had been sunk, burned, or blown up. Thousands of Spaniards were dead. All night, the victorious Dutch fleet lay in Gibraltar Harbor. By the glare of the burning ships, the populace of the doomed fortress city could be seen fleeing inland, taking with them such possessions as could hastily be snatched up.

Morning brought a revulsion of feeling to the Dutch, who were completely spent and satiated from their bloodletting of the day before. With uncomprehending eyes, they saw helpless before them one of the great strategic fortresses of the world, theirs for the taking. Had Heemskerk or Alteras lived, doubtless the possibilities would have been exploited—the seizure of Gibraltar and the launching of a land expedition to take Cadiz from behind. All this was lost upon the victors, who wanted only to go home. Cutting the damaged *St. Augustine* free to drift upon the shore, they sailed away, leaving the amazed Spaniards still in possession of their fortress on the strait.

5 .

Though the Dutch failed to pick up the jewel of Gibraltar when they found it lying at their feet, there were few other treasures that they missed. All through the wealthy East, Dutch expeditions were busily prying loose the fingers of the Portuguese and making treaties and trade arrangements with the local rulers. In India, on Ceylon, along the Malay Peninsula, and throughout the East Indies, outposts of the Dutch East India Company appeared—centers of trade and of imperial expansion. Besides the trading posts, there were way stations, to serve as an aid and protection to navigation. Perhaps the most important of these was the settlement at Table Bay, on the Cape of Good Hope, founded in 1652.

The Dutch looked westward, too. Navigators such as Henry Hudson, Cornelis Mey, and Adrian Block skirted the eastern coast of North America, claiming bays and rivers beside which would soon appear such Dutch settlements as Fort Orange (now Albany, N.Y.), New Amsterdam (New York City), and Bergen (Jersey City, N.J.). A strong but unsuccessful effort was made to wrest Brazil from its Portuguese proprietors; though this failed, other Dutch settlements took root along the Caribbean coast of South America—Surinam (Dutch Guiana) and Curacao. To administer these promising western possessions, the Dutch West India Company was created in 1621, as a commercial rival to the prosperous Dutch East India Company.

In 1639, Spain made a last, desperate effort to bring the Netherlands back under Spanish control. A Spanish fleet of sixty-seven warships—the greatest naval concentration since the Armada—set out for Dunkirk to join forces with those old enemies of the Dutch, the Channel pirates. The Spanish ships were not only numerous, but large. The great *Mater Theresa,* the largest warship the world had ever seen, displaced 2,400 tons and carried seventy guns and a crew of 1,200. The fleet as a whole mounted 2,000 guns and carried

24,000 men. In the opinion of King Philip III, this new Spanish Armada could not fail.

The little boy who had wept and had shaken his fist at the Spaniards in 1607 was now a man of forty-two—Vice-Admiral Marten Harpertzoon Tromp of the Netherlands navy. As the Spaniards approached the Channel, they were sighted by his little squadron of thirteen ships. The odds being too great, he shadowed the enemy until he was joined by other squadrons under Witte De With and Adrian Banckers. Now he had thirty-one ships with which to oppose the enemy's sixty-seven. A conference was held aboard Tromp's ship. Were the odds too great for all-out battle? "Not at all!" thundered De With. "There is room at the bottom of the sea for all those Spanish ships, and the sooner we start sending them there, the better!" The other two agreed.

Admiral Oquendo of Spain was used to orthodox naval tactics, but they were of little use in fighting the Dutch. During the remaining daylight hours, when an attack might have come, he watched the enemy carefully, but nothing happened. When the sun went down, he should have been safe until morning, but he was not. By the light of a full moon, the Dutch launched a midnight attack. Heavy cannonading damaged the Spanish ships and threw the crews into demoralizing confusion.

Dawn found the Spanish fleet in full retreat toward the English coast. It was Oquendo's hope that he could reach Dover, where he would be protected by the big guns of the English forts. He fell short of his goal. Harried and chivvied by the Dutch, his great warships finally took refuge behind a long bar known as Goodwin Sands, within English territorial waters. Not wishing to attack so close to a neutral shore, Tromp divided his ships into two squadrons, one at either end of the bar, and clamped a tight blockade on Admiral Oquendo's Armada.

News of the blockade brought numerous small Dutch ships hurrying across the Channel, swelling Admiral Tromp's fleet to 110 vessels. The news also brought an English fleet under Admiral Pennington, whose orders were to prevent any breach of English neutrality. Pennington served as an intermediary. Through him, Tromp issued a challenge to Oquendo to meet in formal battle in the open sea. Oquendo replied that he was too short of powder for such an engagement. Tromp offered to let Oquendo have half of the Dutch squadron's powder supplies. Oquendo thanked him, but added that several of the Spanish ships needed new masts. Tromp offered to supply them. As the incredible negotiations continued, it became clear to everyone that Admiral Oquendo was actually afraid to bring his great ships out to do battle with the Dutch.

The Spaniards, however, could not remain behind Goodwin Sands forever. Admiral Tromp and the Dutch might respect English neutrality, but the next big storm would be unlikely to do so. The open roadstead at Goodwin Sands would become a death trap. On October 20, the Spanish fleet tried to run the blockade and reach Dunkirk.

The so-called Battle of the Downs, which followed, delivered the *coup de grâce* to Spain's life as a major power. Spanish seamanship and Spanish gunnery proved to be no match for those of the Dutch. Admiral Oquendo was helpless before the deft maneuvers of Admiral Tromp. It was a running fight, with the Spaniards doing all of the running. One after another, the huge Spanish vessels were cut out of the fleet, hammered into helplessness, and either sunk or boarded. Of the sixty-seven vessels which left the haven of Goodwin Sands, only eighteen managed to get safely to Dunkirk. Most of these were badly damaged ships, with decimated crews.

The defeat of this second Armada was followed by general collapse. The very next year, Portugal managed to regain her independence. A dying grip was held for a few years on the Netherlands, but by the Treaty of Munster, in 1648, the independence of the Dutch was formally acknowledged. They had been independent in all but name for fully half a century.

6.

What of English sea power, during these years while Spain was declining and the Netherlands were rising to maritime supremacy?

It lay neglected. Under Howard and Drake, Queen Elizabeth's Tudor Navy had wrested the control of the seas from Spain. With the Queen's death, all was permitted to fall into decay. King James I hastened to make peace with the erstwhile enemy, Spain. By the terms of his hastily drafted treaty, the licensing of English privateers was specifically prohibited. At the same time, the tiny Royal Navy, which should have formed the nucleus of England's sea power, lay at its piers without repair or upkeep. "The wise fool of England," as the scholarly James was called in derision, could not see the value of naval supremacy to a sea-girt country.

While James argued about religion, antagonized the Scots, and urged his scholars on in the translation of his own edition of the Bible, the defenses of the country were neglected. English merchant shipping died on the vine. Piracy flourished. The Dutch and the French did what they pleased on the high seas. The sea might which James had inherited steadily dwindled.

Though King Charles I was not quite so blind as his father, he made the error of trying to support both the fleet and the royal purse by illegal taxation, unsanctioned by Parliament. This threw the navy directly into politics, where no armed service belongs. When a prominent Englishman named John Hampden refused to pay the king's "ship money," he was sent to prison without a trial and thus became a martyr for the Parliamentary cause. While the quarrel between the king and Parliament grew in intensity, the fleet languished. It was not until King Charles had been overthrown and put to death by the Parliamentary forces under Oliver Cromwell that there was an opportunity to do something about control of the sea. This was in 1649. By this time, the Dutch commercial empire had been well established.

The English looked askance at the thrifty Dutch, who had risen so fast and grown so rich on the world's trade. As Sir William Temple, an English ambassador to Holland, expressed it: "Never any country traded so much and consumed so little. They buy infinitely, but 'tis to sell again. They are the great masters of Indian spices and Persian silks, but wear plain woollen and feed upon their own fish and roots. They sell the finest of their own cloth to France and buy coarse out of England for their own wear. They send abroad the best of their own butter and buy the cheapest out of Ireland for their own use. They furnish infinite luxury which they never practice, and traffic in pleasure which they never taste. Their common riches lie in every man's spending less than he has coming in."

There is admiration in Sir William Temple's words, but there is far more of fear and envy. The Dutch were doing what England felt herself destined to do.

In a very real sense, the fleet which King Charles I had built with the illegally extracted "ship money" was England's first truly national navy. Earlier fleets had been built around small numbers of "King's ships" or "Queen's ships," supplemented by others contributed by seacoast communities and by private individuals. Charles' greed in taxing inland areas as well as those along the coast had led for the first time to national support of English sea power. It was ironic that the king's little national navy did not stand by him but sided with his Parliamentary foes, maintaining an efficient blockade which kept him from receiving aid from France and other mainland countries.

7.

Following the defeat and execution of King Charles, his nephew, Prince Rupert, seized a part of the English navy and put to sea, in defiance of Cromwell and the victorious Parliamentary forces. This semipiratical endeavor, strongly reminiscent of the activities of Sextus Pompey in Roman times, faced the English government with a serious problem. In Ireland, in Barbados, in Virginia, and elsewhere there was much royalist sentiment which might be crystallized against the Commonwealth should Prince Rupert gain control of the sea. As rapidly as possible, Cromwell mobilized what was left to him of the navy, placing it in the charge of three converted soldiers, whom he designated "Generals of the Sea."

Robert Blake, one of the three, proved to be a remarkable choice. For ten years before the war, he had been a quiet instructor of Greek at Oxford University, with no other aspiration than that of a full professorship. During the struggle between king and Parliament, he had served as a colonel of militia in Cromwell's New Model Army. When he was appointed to his naval command, he was fifty years old and had never set foot on a ship. Yet this unlikely man was destined, in the remaining eight years of his life, to establish himself as one of England's greatest naval heroes.

During the organization of Cromwell's fleet, Prince Rupert had been enjoying a field day, seizing English commerce in the Channel. At the appearance of the fleet under Blake, Deane, and Popham, he fled, taking refuge in the harbor of Kinsale, Ireland, where royalist feeling was strong. Balked by heavy batteries on the shore, the pursuing fleet performed the double duty of blockading Kinsale and guarding the transports carrying English troops to Ireland, where they waged a successful land campaign marked by many unnecessary cruelties for which the Irish have never forgiven Oliver Cromwell.

The approach of Cromwell's land forces to Kinsale forced Prince Rupert to make a break for it. Suddenly emerging in the midst of a storm, he burst through the blockading squadron and escaped, with the loss of three of his ships.

Unable to shake off the dogged pursuit of his enemies, Prince Rupert put in at Lisbon, Portugal. Soon Blake appeared with eighteen men-of-war, demanding the right to sail into the harbor and destroy "the pirate." The Portuguese king refused permission. When Blake tried to force his way in, Portuguese batteries opened fire and drove him back out. He was not, however, to be balked so easily. A large Portuguese convoy approaching Lisbon was attacked by the English warships, and seven merchant ships were taken as prizes. Alarmed at this, the King of Portugal changed his mind and ordered Prince Rupert's fleet to depart.

Once more, Prince Rupert succeeded in running the blockade, but it did him little good. A sudden storm caught his ships off the southern coast of Spain and dashed most of them upon the shore. His largest vessel was wrecked soon afterward in the Azores. Westward he sailed to the West Indies, where he maintained himself for awhile by piracy. The endeavor had now sunk to insignificance. Seeing no future in the course of action he had undertaken, Prince Rupert gave up and sailed to France, where he sold his two remaining vessels to the French government.

8.

In the meantime, the once-cordial relations between England and the Netherlands had deteriorated. William II, hereditary *stadtholder* of the Dutch government, had taken as his wife Princess Mary, the daughter of the late King Charles I of England. William was naturally opposed to those who had beheaded his father-in-law and who were forcibly keeping from the throne Prince Charles, William's brother-in-law. The sudden death of William II by smallpox in 1650 did nothing to improve the situation. His embittered wife was left to hold the country for his posthumous son, William, who was born soon afterward.

There were other sources of irritation, even more important than the feelings of the Dutch ruling family. Chief among these was the growing commercial rivalry between England and the Netherlands. This was intensified in 1651, when Parliament passed the Navigation Act, forbidding the importation into England or any of her colonies of any goods brought by ships which were not English. Though aimed directly at Dutch commerce, this act also had a pleasingly adverse effect upon the trade of France and Spain. At about the same time, notices were issued that all vessels encountering English warships in the Channel were to dip their colors in salute and that all Dutch fishing vessels in English waters were to turn over to the English one-tenth of all herring caught.

In considering these highhanded decrees issued by the Lord-Protector of the Commonwealth, we should keep in mind that Oliver Cromwell was seeking neither peace nor justice. His eyes were on English commercial supremacy by whatever means. Another contributing factor was a deep and burning resentment felt throughout England over an event which had occurred some twenty-eight years before. This was the massacre in 1623 at Amboina of a group of employees of the British East India Company by a private army sent by the Dutch East India Company. Since this was company rather than government business, neither James I nor Parliament had taken any official action. The more realistic English people, however, had never ceased to resent this unavenged massacre of their fellow countrymen by the Dutch.

Probably we shall never know who was responsible for the actual outbreak of hostilities between the English and the Dutch. The official reports are so contradictory that it is evident that somebody lied. It is known that about the middle of May, 1652, Dutch Admiral Marten Tromp led out forty-two small Dutch warships in order to escort an expected fleet of Dutch merchant vessels through the privateer-infested Channel. The contact was made without incident, but on the way home the Dutch encountered a fleet of fifteen large English warships under Blake. Thus far, the accounts agree.

According to Tromp's report, he was preparing to dip his flag in the required salute when the English flagship fired three successive solid shots into his vessel. After the third shot had ripped through his planking, Tromp protested by firing a high shot which cut a hole through Blake's flag. The English replied with a full broadside, and the fight was on.

Blake, on the other hand, asserts that he fired three warning shots across Tromp's bow. The first two were completely ignored, and the third was answered by a Dutch broadside. One can take one's choice of accounts. In either event, a fierce general battle promptly developed. As the noise of the cannonading reached the shore, eight additional English vessels put out from the Downs to join the embattled fifteen.

Darkness put an end to the fighting after four hours of furious battle. One Dutch ship had gone down, and another had been captured. The English had lost no vessels. They had not, on the other hand, succeeded in taking the rich convoy, which was shepherded safely into port by Tromp's surviving ships.

The First Anglo-Dutch War had begun.

9.

Wishing to harass his enemy at as little cost as possible, Blake now led his warships out against the Dutch herring fleet. This was, of course, no battle. Most of the herring ships were captured and their much-needed catches seized.

The hardship of a herring shortage brought the Dutch people face to face with imminent war—a war for which they were poorly prepared. No nation had better seamen than the Dutch, but the English had far better ships. Dutch vessels had to be small and of shallow draft in order to sail over the many mud bars and through the narrow river and harbor entrances of the Netherlands. England's ships were large, seaworthy, and powerfully armed—ideal fighting craft for a nation of rising blue-water sailors. An even more important disadvantage of the Dutch was their vulnerable position on the mainland. Their country was ringed by enemies, real and potential. Much of the Dutch energy and wealth had to be devoted to maintaining border forts and an army of 57,000 men on the frontiers. England was troubled by no such considerations.

The Dutch government, unimpressed by the odds, promptly declared war and sent out Admiral Tromp with seventy warships "to sweep the English from the sea." Tromp's luck was bad. He had just located an English squadron under Sir George Ayscue, and had managed to maneuver himself into a favorable windward position, when the wind fell to a dead calm, leaving both fleets immobile. When once more the wind sprang up, it blew from the opposite direction, and Ayscue managed to escape.

Onward went Tromp, still looking for English vessels to attack and destroy. Somewhere to the north, he knew, was the squadron with which Blake had attacked the herring fleet. This time it was a storm instead of a calm which upset his plans. Strong winds and giant waves scattered the little Dutch vessels, forcing the admiral to return home with a dispersed and badly damaged fleet. The complete lack of accomplishment so disappointed the members of the States-General that

Tromp was relieved of his command, which was bestowed on Admiral Michael Adrianzoon de Ruyter, whom Mahan describes as the foremost naval officer of that age.

The new Dutch admiral soon had a chance to show what he could do. With thirty-eight small warships, he set sail for the Channel to guard an incoming group of Dutch merchant ships. Off Plymouth, he encountered Admiral Ayscue with an English fleet of approximately the same numbers but, as usual, of somewhat larger size. Ayscue's plan of action was sound, but something went wrong with his system of communications. His flagship burst through the center of the Dutch line, thus dividing his enemies. To his consternation, however, he soon discovered that only nine of his ships had followed him through the gap, the remainder of the fleet having sheered off and run completely out of the battle area. Faced with heavy punishment and possible capture, Ayscue hoisted retirement signals and succeeded in fighting his way clear of the action and in leading his now-outnumbered squadron into Plymouth Harbor. De Ruyter tried to follow him in, but the wind shifted to the north and prevented him from doing so. Thereupon, the Dutch admiral gathered his forces and his convoy and went on home, lucky to be victorious.

The battle off Plymouth cost both commanders their jobs. Ayscue was removed from command and retired on a pension, not for inefficiency but for suspected royalist leanings. De Ruyter, though he continued active, was placed under the higher command of Admiral Cornelis de Witt.

10.

On September 28, English Admiral Blake saw a large fleet of Dutch warships approaching the mouth of the Thames. Wind and water presented some knotty problems; in order to maintain the weather gauge, Blake had to station some of his deep-hulled ships dangerously near a shoal known as the Kentish Knock. He took the chance, dividing his ships on the two sides of the navigable channel so that the Dutch would have to pass between the English groups and receive fire from both sides at once.

As feared, Blake's flagship and two other vessels of his squadron were grounded for a time, but they continued in action and at the same time served as markers to guide the other English ships away from the shoal waters. De Witt's smaller vessels were roughly handled, but the Dutch continued to battle stubbornly until darkness put an end to the fighting. Dawn found the Dutch fleet in full retreat. Blake pursued the enemy across the Channel and into Dutch waters, finally abandoning the chase near the island of Goeree, where shoal waters offered sanctuary to the shallower-draft Dutch vessels.

The victory off the Kentish Knock apparently made the English overconfident. The Dutch appeared to be beaten. Cold weather was coming on, when all naval action customarily ceased. These considerations led the English powers-that-be to divide the fleet into twenty small squadrons, some to be detached for convoy duty in distant and warmer areas, some to be consigned to dockyards for overhaul and refitting. Blake was left with only forty-five ships, manned and fit for duty.

Admiral Tromp had now been restored to command of the Dutch navy. Seasons and customs meant little to him. If the English chose to dismantle their fleet, so much the better! On November 30, the Dutch admiral sailed with seventy-three warships and a few armed auxiliaries to convoy three hundred merchant vessels through the Channel. Though his primary objective was to see the merchant ships safely through the dangerous passage, he was by no means adverse to the idea of meeting the English fleet.

Admiral Blake was on the horns of a dilemma. If he brought his fleet out to fight, he faced almost certain defeat because of the disparity in numbers. If he remained safe in port, he not only let the Dutch convoy pass through England's narrow seas with impunity but also opened up the English shores to Dutch raiding parties. He chose to fight, but in waters of his own selection—deep waters, where the larger English ships would be at their best. Accordingly, he left port and sailed southwestward through the Channel, with Tromp's fleet in full pursuit.

The chase continued for the balance of the day, without near enough contact to bring about fighting. The wind steadily increased in strength, becoming so strong by sundown that both fleets anchored to ride out the growing storm. All night, both Blake and Tromp battled the gods of the weather and disregarded each other. By mid-morning, the storm abated somewhat, and the chase was renewed. At three in the afternoon, off Dungeness Head, Admiral Blake found the situation he desired and turned to fight. The water was deep, and he had the weather gauge.

As the battle opened, Tromp's flagship, the *Brederode,* and Blake's *Triumph* passed on opposite courses, exchanging broadsides. Tromp swung his ship toward the English line, passing astern of the *Triumph* but colliding with the *Garland* and locking fast to her. As the two ships battled at close range, the English *Bonaventure* attacked the *Brederode* from the other side and grappled. The battle might well have opened with the capture of the Dutch admiral and his flagship had not Vice-Admiral Evertsen seen the danger and brought his ship alongside the *Bonaventure*. The four ships, closely locked together, fought a fierce, hand-to-hand battle within a battle, which ended with the Dutch capturing both English vessels.

The *Triumph,* meanwhile, found herself surrounded by a horde of enemies. At one time, she was exchanging broadsides with no fewer than twenty Dutch men-of-war. Three times the *Triumph* was boarded by Dutch sailors, and three times her desperate crew drove them out again. In the end, she was saved from capture or destruction by the timely help of the *Victory,* the *Vanguard,* and the *Sapphire.*

Admiral Blake had fought a gallant fight against odds that had proved too great. Painfully wounded, and seeing nothing ahead but destruction, he hoisted signals of retirement and managed to disengage what was left of his fleet. Three of his ships had been sunk, one burned, and two captured. The Dutch had lost no vessels, though one was suffering from a stubborn fire which would, during the night, reach her magazines and blow her up.

It was unquestionably a victory for the Dutch, who were left, at year's end, in complete command of the Channel. On the day following the battle, Tromp's fleet managed to intercept and take a fourteen-gun English warship, returning from an overseas voyage. The Dutch convoy was speeded safely on its way. Tromp then added insult to injury by sending parties of Dutch sailors ashore to rustle English cattle and forage for supplies and by sailing along the English coast, displaying a broom at his masthead as a symbol of having swept the seas clean of his enemies. This is said to be the origin of a famous naval tradition.

Admiral Blake, despondent over his defeat, wrote out and submitted his resignation. It is to the credit of the English Council of State and the leaders of Parliament that it was not accepted. With uncharacteristic honesty, the politicians shouldered the blame for the unprepared condition of the English fleet and commended Blake for doing the best possible job with what he had on hand.

As the year 1652 came to an end, the little country of the Netherlands had gained for herself the mastery of the seas.

11.

As winter clamped down, both England and the Netherlands were faced with the problem of preparing for the struggle ahead. England did it better. Blake's fleet was greatly strengthened, and some able under-officers were assigned to him. At the same time, suspected royalists were weeded out of the service. The Dutch States-General, meanwhile, passed a resolution providing for 150 new warships. Nothing came of it, chiefly for financial reasons. All that was actually accomplished was the patching and repair of ships already in being.

One of the great disadvantages under which the Dutch labored was the necessity of offering battle, ready or not, whenever a large Dutch convoy approached the Channel from either direction. To keep the country alive, Dutch commerce had to keep flowing past the enemy's shores. Little English trade, on the other hand, passed close to the Netherlands.

Late in February, 1653, Tromp's fleet made contact with an inbound Dutch convoy of about 200 ships off Land's End, the southwestern tip of England. To intercept this rich prize, Blake divided his English fleet of some 80 ships into six divisions, which he spaced across the Channel near Portland. He personally commanded the two squadrons of the "red group"; Admiral William Penn[1] commanded the two "blue" squadrons; and Admiral George Monk (also spelled Monck) commanded the single "white" squadron, farthest to the southeast. This division of forces, while excellent for patrolling, was not the best formation for fighting a battle.

Tromp, groping eastward in a fog, stumbled upon Blake's red division. A commander more prudent than Blake might have sheered off and postponed action until he could gather his scattered forces. Such a course apparently never crossed the English admiral's mind. He bored right in, discharging a broadside at Tromp's flagship. This was answered by three broadsides, as Tromp's crew, reloading rapidly and sailing nimbly, made a complete loop around Blake's *Triumph*. At the first impact, Blake's red division was split into two groups and thrown into genuine peril.

Admiral Blake was saved by the superior training and indoctrination of his officers. Without hesitation, Rear Admiral Lawson led the separated segment of the red division into contact with Vice-Admiral Penn's blue division, which he joined. Together, Penn and Lawson

---

[1] Father of the Quaker William Penn who founded Pennsylvania.

performed a circling maneuver which brought them from the south squarely through the heart of the Dutch fleet and against Tromp's starboard flank. Now it was Tromp who found his squadron split in two, and who was hard pressed to prevent disaster. Only by performing the difficult maneuver of a simultaneous tack was he able to extricate his division from its precarious situation.

In the meantime, De Ruyter, in charge of the port Dutch column, found himself heavily engaged with the ships which had followed Blake into the heart of the action. Though his flagship was only a small vessel of twenty-eight guns, he did not hesitate to attack and board the English ship *Prosperity,* of fifty-four. What is more, he captured her, after being once repulsed in a boarding attempt. All at once, from an unexpected direction, De Ruyter found himself assailed by the ships which Penn and Lawson had brought circling around from the south. To avoid being overwhelmed, he had to abandon the crippled *Prosperity* and fight his way clear.

Far off to the southeast, Monk, in charge of the English white division, heard the cannonading and set his course toward the battle. On the way, he encountered a column of Dutch ships, led by Jan Evertsen. For two hours, a separate battle was fought, at the end of which Monk succeeded in fighting his way past Evertsen and joining the main struggle.

As Monk's ships arrived from the southeast, darkness forced a break in hostilities. Each side had had two warships sunk and many damaged. Among the worst damaged of the Dutch vessels was the flagship of Vice-Admiral De Ruyter.

During the hours of darkness, the Dutch worked hard to bring order out of confusion. They succeeded. The first light of dawn revealed the Dutch merchant fleet sailing in a dense, close-order formation with the warships following them in a crescent, interposed between the English and the convoy.

The action during this second day of the "Three-Day Battle of Portland" was largely indecisive. As the fleets moved slowly past the Isle of Wight, the English contented themselves with long-range cannonading, aimed high in order to bring down masts and rigging and force individual ships to lag behind. Whatever advantage there was lay with the English, for the powder supplies of a number of the Dutch ships began to run low. On a few of the ships, the ammunition was completely gone before darkness again brought an end to the fighting.

The final day was one of desperation. Admiral Tromp was all too well aware of the growing helplessness of his fleet, as his powder supplies dwindled. Blake, on the other hand, could see that the great Dutch convoy was drawing slowly but steadily nearer to the shallow waters off the Flanders coast, where his ships of deeper draft could not follow. Like a boxer who sees the final round coming to an end before he can score a knockout, Blake tried, on this third day, every maneuver at his command. He himself led his red division on a circling course, trying to pull ahead of the Dutch formation and block them off from safety. This was foiled by Tromp's skill in countermaneuvering. At the same time, Vice-Admiral Penn led a strike directly at the middle of the protective crescent. After much hard fighting, some of his ships broke through and found themselves in the midst of the convoy, like wolves in a flock of sheep. Much damage was done before Tromp managed to drive the raiders out again in a spirited action which saw much heavy close-range cannonading between the flagships of Tromp and Penn.

Late in the day, the exhausted English drew off to regroup. Then back they came, in a final try for the knockout. As Tromp reported in his account of the battle: "Blake, having gathered all his forces, came on as though he would attack us once again. Seeing this, I reefed my sails to let him know that I was ready to recommence the fight with him. After the vanguards of the two fleets had charged one another for some time, the English sheered off to seaward, and Blake, being out of cannon shot, came at us no more."

It had been an expensive battle for both sides. The Dutch had lost fifty merchant ships and twelve men-of-war, sunk or captured, in comparison to the English loss of six warships. In casualties, the figures ran the other way. The Dutch had had six hundred men killed, the English two thousand. In addition, large numbers were wounded on both sides, including Admiral Blake and Vice-Admiral Deane of the English fleet.

12.

The wounding of Admiral Blake led directly to an important development in English sea power. As he lay on his bed, recuperating from his wound, he had plenty of time to think about the battle and to assess the reasons why he and his fellow admirals had been unable to take the entire Dutch convoy. If only there could be a set of rules, based on experience, to cover all contingencies! The result was a handbook of naval lore, entitled *Fighting Instructions*. From the date of its issuance, in March, 1653, it was to serve, with many subsequent modifications, as the Bible of the English naval officer, bolstering the weak and uncertain but at the same time shackling the initiative of the daring and imaginative. Henceforth, it would be a bold officer indeed who would venture to fight his battles otherwise than "by the book."

Three months after the issuance of *Fighting Instructions* came the first chance to apply the new rules to warfare. Tromp's fleet, this time not impeded by a convoy, appeared off Dover and bombarded the English forts. Since Blake had not yet returned to duty, Vice-Admiral Monk and Vice-Admiral Deane led out a fleet of about one hundred English ships to hunt down the raiding squadron, which was about equal in numbers. The two fleets came together off the mouth of the Thames, near a shoal known as the Gabbard. The Dutch were sailing in three parallel divisions, a time-honored formation which was supposed to give maximum protection against boarding. The English, thanks to Blake's thoughtfulness, were far more concerned with maximum firepower and with protection against raking fire from bow or stern. Accordingly, they came into action in fleet line ahead, all ships following Monk's flagship in a single unbroken line.

Since Tromp's ships were smaller than the English and much inferior in firepower, the Dutch admiral tried to fight a retiring action, while slanting away from the enemy downwind. At the same time, he kept a sharp eye peeled for any circumstance which would permit him to throw his entire force against a portion of the enemy's line. A sudden shift of the wind appeared to give him the advantage he sought. Now in possession of the weather gauge, he turned and closed rapidly with the English van, cannonading as he came on. It was during this phase of the action that Vice-Admiral Richard Deane was killed, leaving the entire English command on the shoulders of George Monk.

Nature had played a cruel trick upon the Dutch. As rapidly as it had shifted, the wind shifted again, this time favoring the English. To his dismay, Tromp saw the entire English line bearing down upon his fleet, while from the mouth of the Thames was issuing an additional squadron of eighteen English warships, with the foremost vessel bearing the flag of Admiral Blake. The stricken admiral had risen from his bed at the sound of cannonading and had put to sea to take part in the battle.

To make matters worse for Tromp, he himself was heavily engaged at the time of the shift of fortune. An attempt by his crew to board the ship of Vice-Admiral Penn had failed, and his men were now desperately trying to repel English boarders, which swarmed upon his deck. Feeling that all was lost, the Dutch admiral dashed below, seized a torch, and hurled it into the powder magazine. There was a terrific explosion. The decks of the flagship were hurled violently upward, bringing death to boarders and crewmen alike. In the midst of the holocaust, Admiral Tromp himself miraculously survived, with only minor burns!

The battle was an English victory, for Tromp lost twenty-five warships and 1500 men before the remnant of his fleet found safety in the Flemish shallows. The Dutch, discouraged, sued for peace. Cromwell, overplaying his hand, laid down terms so severe that they could not be accepted. An actual surrender of Dutch independence would have been involved. The war went on.

13.

Although the Netherlands government was near the end of its resources, every energy was devoted to refitting the fleet for another major effort. While the English navy under Monk maintained a tight blockade of the Dutch coast, ninety-five warships were readied at Flushing and thirty at Amsterdam. To prevent the junction of these two fleets, Monk kept a heavy concentration of ships near the island of Texel, at the mouth of the Zuider Zee.

On July 30, Tromp led his ninety-five ships out of Flushing and sailed for Texel, where he was presently sighted by Monk. As the English took off in full cry, Tromp skilfully retired, drawing the blockaders far enough from Texel to enable the smaller Dutch fleet, under De Witt, to escape out to sea, where it was able to join forces with Tromp the next day.

In the Battle of Scheveningen, which followed, each fleet had approximately 125 ships. Both fleets employed the fleet line ahead, Tromp having observed the advantages of this formation as employed by the enemy at the Battle of the Gabbard. Both fleets, therefore, sailed in parallel courses, tacking almost in unison, and cannonading each other heavily. So near were the lines that not only cannons but also muskets were employed in the general firing—a fact which cost the life of Admiral Tromp, who fell dying with a musket ball near his heart. For reasons of morale, his flag was kept flying from the masthead of his flagship.

Hour after hour, the two fleets blasted away at each other, meanwhile sailing a zig-zag course of some forty miles along the coast. Damage was heavy on both sides. Early in the afternoon, the Dutch powder supply began to give out, and soon thereafter the wind shifted so as to give the English line the weather gauge. At this, certain of the Dutch captains showed a tendency to escape downwind toward the shallows. Admiral De Witt tried hard to arrest this movement, even going to the extreme of firing on Dutch ships which broke formation. It was no use. The tide of battle had turned, and the Dutch had to retire.

Again, it had been an expensive victory for the English. They had lost eight ships sunk and 1,100 men killed or wounded. The Dutch had lost ten ships and about 1,800 men. The English fleet had suffered such damage that the blockade could not be maintained, but the Dutch were too badly hurt to take much advantage of it. Once more, the Dutch sued for peace. This time, Cromwell modified his demands, leaving the Dutch their independence and their territory. On this basis, the Treaty of Westminster was signed, April 5, 1654.

But Admiral Tromp was dead! "By his death," said one of his associates, "the Dutch fleet became as a body without a soul."

The First Anglo-Dutch War marked a turning point in naval affairs. For the first time, great fleets had worked together as units to carry out the over-all plans of such master strategists as Blake and Tromp. Order had been substituted for the chaos of the earlier piecemeal actions. For the first time, the science of naval warfare had been reduced to simple, comprehensive rules of action, through the issuance of Blake's *Fighting Instructions*. For the first time, definite lines of battle had appeared, working as units to secure the greatest amount of usable firepower. From this point on, we hear a new term applied to those vessels large enough, strong enough, and powerfully enough armed to deserve a place in the battle line. They are "ships-of-the-line," "line-of-battle ships," or simply "battleships."

The war also marked the high-water mark of Dutch naval power. Technically, at least, the Netherlands were not an independent nation until the signing of the Treaty of Munster, in 1648. Only four years later, after the victory off Dungeness Head, the little country had become the leading naval power of the world. By the very nature of things, it had to be a brief period of domination. By war's end, in 1654, the balance had already begun to shift.

5 "TO BEAT THE DUTCH"

⚓

1.

Neither the English nor the Dutch were to enjoy a long period of peace following the signing of the Treaty of Westminster in 1654. Even during the brief interval between their wars with one another, there were other enemies to be fought.

England was the first to find herself engaged in further armed conflict. Cromwell—never a peaceful man—had acquired a long list of real or fancied wrongs to be avenged. The question was not whether to have war or peace, but rather with whom to have the first reckoning.

In October, 1655, Admiral Blake (now largely recovered from his wounds) was sent to the Mediterranean in charge of a squadron of thirty ships. His first port of call was Leghorn, in northwestern Italy. Five years earlier, Prince Rupert had put in at Leghorn and had sold three captured English merchant ships to representatives of the Duke of Tuscany and of Pope Innocent X. Damages, said Admiral Blake coldly, were now due in the amount of 60,000 pounds. The Tuscan and Papal representatives looked at the rows of frowning cannons on Blake's thirty warships and promptly paid.

While England had been engaged in her struggle with the Netherlands, the Barbary Pirates of North Africa had seized the opportunity to capture a number of English ships and imprison their crews. A settlement of this question was the next item on Blake's agenda. Accordingly, he sailed directly from Leghorn to Algiers, where the local Dey received him peacefully enough but gave him little satisfaction.

Leaving the negotiations at Algiers incomplete, Blake sailed to Tunis. Here he found what he wanted—open and insolent defiance. The Dey of Tunis withdrew his ships into the strongly fortified harbor of Porto Farina and sent word to the English admiral that if he wished to talk about settlement of his claim he must first silence the great batteries in Goletta and Porto Farina castles. In apparent discouragement, Blake weighed anchor and sailed away, leaving the Dey smug, happy, and overconfident.

Blake's withdrawal had been for the double purpose of achieving surprise and awaiting favorable conditions. On April 4, 1656, he suddenly reappeared and launched a furious bombardment of the two great castles which guarded the narrow harbor mouth. The wind was blowing strongly inshore, so the smoke of the bombardment completely blinded the city's defenders. Having battered the forts into helplessness, he availed himself of this same onshore wind and sailed boldly and swiftly into the harbor. The nine Tunisian warships were quickly boarded and burned. When Blake's ships, largely undamaged and with only small losses in manpower, sailed out once more, "impregnable" Porto Farina had become a bee without a stinger.

Word of Admiral Blake's exploit rapidly traveled throughout the Mediterranean area. The Deys of Algiers, Tunis, and Tripoli tumbled over themselves in their eagerness to release English prisoners, pay damages, and give guarantees of future immunity. To echo the words of Sir Geoffrey Callender, "Blake's cruise did so much for English prestige in the Mediterranean that he deserves to be regarded as the creator of British influence within the Straits."

2.

Oliver Cromwell, meanwhile, had been trying to make up his mind whether to pick a quarrel with France or with Spain. He selected Spain. A peremptory demand was sent to the Spanish court that England should be permitted to share in the profits of trade with the Spanish colonies. To nobody's surprise, the demand was refused. Said Cromwell, piously, "Providence seems to lead us to an attack on the West Indies."

Guided by Providence, or by a sure instinct for profitable trade, Cromwell promptly dispatched a fleet of thirty-eight ships under Admiral Penn and an army of 6,000 men under General Robert Venables to Spain's West Indies islands. It was anything but a brilliant expedition. Penn and Venables quarreled bitterly over priority of command and failed to cooperate whenever possible. Typical was the attack on Santo Domingo, where Penn landed Venables' army and then refused to support it by fire from his ships' guns. The result was near disaster, with the invaders being driven out and nearly captured by the Spaniards. The only real accomplishment of the entire expedition was the capture of Jamaica, in the face of very weak opposition.

So disgusted was Cromwell with the performance of Penn and Venables that, upon their return, he had them both confined in the Tower of London. He did not hesitate, however, to keep possession of Jamaica, which has been a prized English possession ever since.

3.

Though by no means a well man, Admiral Blake was given no opportunity to rest and recuperate when he returned to England. Almost at once, Cromwell sent him out again, this time to blockade the Spanish harbor of Cadiz. He did his usual superlative job. Without the advantage of copper sheathing for his ships and without a nearby naval base into which to retire, he nevertheless kept Spain's great seaport closed for six consecutive months during the fall and winter of 1656–57. Besides the negative value to England of keeping the enemy's port inactive, a fine positive value materialized. Part of the Spanish plate fleet, loaded with silver ingots from the New World, blundered into Blake's blockade and was captured. The ingots, shipped to London, did much to defray the costs of the war.

In April, 1657, word reached Admiral Blake of a rich Spanish treasure fleet en route to Spain from Mexico by way of the Canary Islands. Promptly, he set sail for the Canaries, hoping to arrive before the Spanish ships and head them off. He arrived too late. The ships were already in the harbor of Santa Cruz, on Teneriffe Island. They appeared to be completely safe, for Santa Cruz Harbor had a narrow, treacherous entrance protected by strong forts on either side. On the far shore of the harbor were other batteries, placed to command the entire water surface. There were few more strongly defended harbors in the world.

Before launching his attack, Admiral Blake studied the defenses long and carefully through his telescope. He noted that the castles beside the entrance stood on lofty bluffs and that several of the ships within the harbor had been moored where they masked the fire of the batteries on the shore. Having weighed these facts, he waited for a favoring wind and a flowing tide and made for the entrance.

As usual, careful planning paid off. The smoke of Blake's cannons drifted down upon the defenders and blinded them. Arriving at the entrance, he led his column of ships as near as possible to the right-hand shore, meanwhile continuing to shell the castle opposite. As he had hoped, the gunners in the nearest castle could not depress their guns enough to get at his ships. He went through almost unscathed and at once attacked the Spanish galleons, taking or destroying them all and gaining much of the treasure. So well timed was the endeavor that he finished his work of destruction and looting just as the tide began to ebb. As a result, his ships were able to drift safely out of the harbor in spite of the inshore wind. He had lost no ships and had suffered casualties of only 50 killed and 120 wounded.

Back on station off Cadiz, Admiral Blake at last received the welcome word that he was to go home on leave. He did not quite make it. As his flagship entered Plymouth Sound, he died. Oliver Cromwell recognized his services by burying him in Westminster Abbey, where only England's greatest lie.

4.

The Netherlands, too, got themselves embroiled in a war between their struggles with the English. This came under the head of "Unfinished Business."

Back in the 1630's, while the Thirty Years' War was still going on, neutral Denmark had assumed the duty of policing the important straits which passed beside her shores. To do this required the building of a navy. This, in turn, took money, which the Danes raised by placing high tariffs on all goods passing through the straits between the Baltic and North Seas. Among the countries whose trade was most hurt by these tariffs were Sweden and the Netherlands. Sweden also had a grudge against King Christian IV of Denmark, whose work in promoting an end to the Thirty Years' War had, it was felt, robbed Sweden of much benefit from her participation. Thanks to Denmark, Sweden's hero-king, Gustavus-Adolphus, had died in vain! Queen Christina's famous minister, Oxenstierna, planned revenge.

Thus it happened that in 1644 Denmark was attacked by a Swedish army and by a combined Dutch and Swedish fleet. In this emergency, King Christian, though nearing seventy years of age, took personal command of his fleet of thirty Danish warships and went out to meet the forty-six vessels of the invading squadron. The Battle of Kolberg, which followed, was an epic struggle. King Christian was wounded early, losing an eye and several teeth and being badly lacerated by flying splinters. Nevertheless, he maintained his position, covered with blood and supported by his sword, until at last darkness forced an end to the fighting and the enemy retired, badly battered.

Unfortunately, King Christian's heroism availed his country little in the end. Denmark now had only seventeen ships left in usable condition, whereas the enemy had reserves upon which to draw. Not long afterward, a fleet of sixty-four Dutch and Swedish ships caught Denmark's seventeen and annihilated them, after a bitter fight. Denmark was beaten, and had to surrender some land to her enemies and to exempt both Sweden and the Netherlands from the tariffs.

All this had happened in the years before the First Anglo-Dutch War. Now the situation had changed. Sweden was Mistress of the Baltic and was making plans to seize the Danish straits for her own advantage. It now behooved the Dutch to support their late enemy against their late ally.

The Dutch forces were almost too late in bringing aid to the Danes. Already, the Swedes had seized the powerful fortresses of Kronborg and Elsenborg, commanding the straits, and had taken the island of Funen by advancing across the ice. Funen had been gained despite unique defensive measures by the Danes, who had bowled down large numbers of Swedish soldiers by means of cannon balls fired flat across the ice. With these three strongholds in Swedish possession, the task of the Dutch would be that much harder. Even worse, the Danish capital of Copenhagen was presently placed under siege.

Shaken by the suddenness and violence of the Swedish attack, King Frederick III of Denmark considered surrender. His courage was restored by the words of the Dutch representative in the Danish court, who remarked that "the oaken keys of the sound lie in the docks of Amsterdam." Thus reassured of Dutch naval support, the king continued his resistance.

On October 29, 1658, a squadron of thirty-five Dutch ships entered the Sound, which is the easternmost channel lying between Denmark and Sweden. In command was Admiral Jacob van Wassenaer, Lord of Obdam, an old man suffering from gout but imbued with that bulldog tenacity which made the Dutch such formidable opponents. Under him served Vice-Admiral Witte de With, in command of the leading division of ships, and Vice-Admiral Pieter Florizoon, in command of the rear division. Waiting for them in the Sound was a Swedish fleet which outnumbered and outgunned the Dutch at a ratio of nearly three to two. It was under Swedish Admiral Karl Gustaf Wrangel, whose flag flew from the *Victoria.*

Witte de With opened the battle. In the *Brederode,* he led the advance against the Swedes, entirely disregarding the heavy fire from forts on both sides of the channel. Straight for the *Victoria* he sailed, more than willing to match his 59 guns against the heavier and more numerous guns of his great adversary. For a time, the two ships exchanged broadsides; then Obdam arrived in the *Eendracht,* and the smaller *Brederode* left the two flagships to fight it out while she took on opponents more nearly her own size. There were two of these, the *Drake* and the *Leopard. Leopard* was driven off, burning and sinking, but soon thereafter *Brederode* ran aground. The *Drake* and the *Wismar* took positions off the helpless warship's bow and stern and raked her with broadsides. *Drake* presently withdrew from this unequal contest, going to the assistance of the hard-pressed *Victoria,* but *Wismar* continued for a full two hours, receiving in return only an occasional shot from *Brederode's* chasers. When at last the Swedes boarded, they found that most of the Dutch crew were casualties. Witte de With, though mortally wounded, tried to use his sword against the attackers. Subdued and taken aboard the *Wismar,* he mourned the capture of his famous ship. When informed that the *Brederode* had gone down with the flag of the Netherlands still flying, he smiled and died.

The battle, meanwhile, had degenerated into a desperate *melee,* without plan or organization. Admiral Florizoon's *Joshua* attacked the Swedish *Cesar* but was beaten off with the admiral and many of his crewmen dead. *Victoria* and *Eendracht,* the flagships of the two top admirals, slugged it out until Swedish Admiral Wrangel was forced to take his shattered vessel into Helsingor Harbor to keep her from sinking. There was no respite for Obdam. Presently the *Eendracht* found herself battling four Swedish ships. She took heavy punishment until three Dutch ships came to her assistance, driving off two of the attacking vessels and capturing two, one of which quickly sank.

Five hours after the opening shots had been fired, the wind freshened, and the rising waves threatened many of the damaged ships. Obdam somehow managed to extricate his squadron and to reach the harbor of Copenhagen. Because of this Dutch retirement, the Swedes claimed the victory, but they had little justification. Obdam had succeeded in breaking the siege of the Danish capital and had captured or destroyed five of Wrangel's first-line warships while losing only one himself. The Swedish army on Funen was cut off and was subsequently forced to surrender. All in all, it must be regarded as a Dutch victory, though it was gained at a heavy cost in manpower. Hundreds of seamen had been lost on both sides. In addition, Dutch Vice-Admirals Witte de With and Pieter Florizoon had been killed, and ailing old Admiral Obdam was so used up that he should never have served again.

A year later, Admiral Michael de Ruyter followed up Obdam's victory, leading another Dutch fleet into the Sound, bringing added reinforcements to Copenhagen, and ending for all time Sweden's attempts to close the Baltic straits to outside trade.

5.

Oliver Cromwell died in 1658 in the midst of a terrific thunderstorm, stirred up, said his enemies, by the Devil as he came to London to reclaim his own. With him ended a period of strong leadership and of harsh, uncompromising Puritan morality. The Lord Protector's son, Richard, who followed him in office, was too human and too lenient to maintain his father's iron grasp. In the face of growing pressure from all sides, Richard soon resigned. The mantle of power fell upon the shoulders of that steadfast "General of the Sea," George Monk.

Had George Monk so desired, he could have taken over as dictator of England. He had no such desire. As soon as possible, he scheduled a free election of Parliament—the first in twenty years. Many of the successful candidates were young men who had known little of life in England except during the drab period of the Protectorate. They wanted a change, a swing back to the pleasures of the "good old days" of the kings. The pleasures, it seems, were remembered better than the crimes, the corruption, and the injustice.

By a large majority, the members of the new Parliament voted to restore the monarchy. In 1660, Prince Charles, son of the executed monarch, returned from his exile on the Continent and took his place on the throne as King Charles II of England. One of his first acts was to bestow on deserving George Monk the title of Duke of Albemarle.

Though no more honest than his father, King Charles II was far more intelligent. He also had a good sense of humor, which helped him to realize his ambition "to keep my head on my shoulders and my seat on the throne."

One of the important new figures in the direction of the English navy was the king's younger brother James, Duke of York. Though stubborn and unimaginative, the Duke was far from unintelligent in naval affairs. One of his early activities was the revising and strengthening of Blake's *Fighting Instructions,* to take advantage of the experience gained in the recent wars.

The issuing of the revised *Fighting Instructions* brought into the open a quarrel which had long been simmering beneath the surface of the English admiralty. All of the leaders were in agreement that a fleet should go into action "in line ahead," with all ships sailing in a single column for greatest broadside firepower and greatest protection against raking tactics. The dispute arose over what was best to do when action had once been joined. The Formal School, headed by the Duke of York and Admiral Penn, maintained that the fleet line ahead should be held throughout the entire engagement, to enable the admiral to retain control over the movements of all ships and, in case of defeat, to extricate a maximum number of his vessels with the least confusion. The *Melee* School, headed by the newly appointed Duke of Albermarle and by Prince Rupert (now back in favor, thanks to the Restoration), maintained that when action had been joined, the ships should separate, with each ship or small division being on its own to do the greatest possible damage to the enemy.

The argument thus begun was to have a strong influence on naval planning, not only in the seventeenth century but also in the eighteenth, nineteenth, and twentieth centuries!

6.

England's victory in the first Anglo-Dutch War had done little to lessen the rivalry between the two nations. The Dutch navy had again been built up to formidable proportions, under Admiral De Ruyter. The Dutch colonial empire was continuing to expand. Most important of all, the Dutch merchant fleet was making greater and greater inroads upon England's commercial prosperity. King Charles II resolved to use his navy to change all this.

James, the Duke of York, had even more reason than his brother to regret the activities of the Dutch. As head of a commercial company dealing in gold and slaves, he resented bitterly the competition offered in these same lines by the Dutch East India Company. Accordingly, he sent out a company-owned war fleet under Sir Robert Holmes to tip the scales in England's favor. Holmes quickly captured the Dutch trading posts at Cape Corse and Cape Verde, on the west coast of Africa.

King Charles now performed an act of generosity almost unmatched in history. To his brother James he presented a complete colony, including a number of large and prosperous towns. The only trouble was that the colony did not belong to him, but to the Netherlands. England had almost no real claim at all to this valuable territory, which she coveted because it lay between her New England and her southern colonies in North America. The understanding between the brothers was that James could have New Netherland if he could get it.

In May, 1664, the inhabitants of the town of New Amsterdam, at the southern tip of Manhattan Island, were amazed to see a fleet of four English warships sail into the harbor. The gun ports were opened, and the guns were run out in evident preparation for a bombardment. Sir Richard Nicholas, in command of the English squadron, sent ashore a message demanding immediate surrender of the colony.

Peter Stuyvesant, the Dutch Governor of New Netherland, ordered his handful of soldiers to man the guns of the fort and to resist to the end. His people did not back him up. They could see that the odds against them were very great, and they were also more than a little weary of Stuyvesant's heavy-handed paternal rule. The Governor could not hold the colony alone. Though his rage and his language were spectacular, he was forced to surrender New Netherland to the English, who soon divided it into three colonies which they named New York, New Jersey, and Delaware.

When word of the English seizures reached the Netherlands, a message was dispatched to Admiral De Ruyter to take his fleet and remedy the situation. It so happened that De Ruyter and English Admiral Lawson were in joint command of a combined Dutch and English fleet patrolling the Mediterranean to suppress piracy. It was necessary for De Ruyter to collect his ships quietly and slip away without letting his fellow admiral know what was afoot. He succeeded in this, but Lawson accurately surmised the Dutch intentions and sent a message of warning to London.

Admiral De Ruyter's cruise was successful, as far as it went. Without difficulty he retook the trading posts on the African coast. He then sailed westward across the Atlantic, apparently with the thought of retaking New Netherland. Reaching the West Indies, he found English merchant shipping so heavy that he stayed there, capturing twenty well-filled ships. New Netherland remained under English control.

The Duke of York, meanwhile, was taking full advantage of the strained state of affairs. His warships patrolled the Channel, quickly taking no fewer than 130 Dutch merchantmen. It became evident that a formal declaration of war could not be long delayed.

7.

In March, 1665, King Charles II formally declared war against the Netherlands, thus belatedly giving an aura of lawfulness to his brother's earlier acts.

In April, an English fleet of ninety-eight warships sailed for the Dutch coast, under the personal command of the Duke of York. Neither the Dutch fleet nor many Dutch merchantmen were in evidence. After about a month of fruitless sailing and blockading, the English fleet returned home.

The Dutch, meanwhile, were frantically preparing for a war which they did not want. Since Admiral De Ruyter was still away with his section of the fleet, the command was bestowed on ailing old Admiral Obdam, who was given definite instructions to sail for England and engage the enemy. Late in May, he set out with 103 warships. A few days later (June 3, 1665) he encountered the English fleet off Lowestoft.

Extensive preliminary maneuvering gave the English the weather gauge. Down they came upon the Dutch, sailing in line abreast. When within range of the Dutch fleet, the ships tacked in unison to form a line ahead, following the Duke's flagship *Royal Charles*. The two fleets were therefore sailing parallel courses, in accordance with the dictates of the Formalist School. The Dutch, apparently, had other theories. Before the cannonading could commence, their line, which had drawn slightly ahead, reversed course, all ships following Obdam's flagship *Eendracht* in a U-turn. As a result, the two lines passed each other quickly, in opposite directions, with consequent lessening of the effectiveness of the cannon fire.

To counter the Dutch maneuver, the individual English ships, on order, came about and reversed both their direction of sailing and the head and tail of their line. The Dutch then repeated their original maneuver, so that the lines once more passed one another, cannonading furiously. Little damage was done to either fleet during these first two brushes.

Once more the two fleets came about, each in its own manner. This time there was a difference. The captains of a number of ships in the midst of the Dutch line flinched from the hail of shot and bore away to leeward, opening a gap in the line. Seeing his opportunity, the Earl of Sandwich broke formation and led a column of English ships through the heart of the Dutch fleet. The formal battle became a desperate *melee,* with little plan or unity.

The Dutch got all the worst of it. Early in the action, Lieutenant-Admiral Egbert Cortenaer received a mortal wound. The captain of his flagship, panic-stricken, fled eastward, with the admiral's flag still flying. He was followed out of the battle by a dozen Dutch warships, whose captains did not know that the admiral was dead and thought that they were following him in a battle maneuver.

Seeing his fleet disintegrating about him, Admiral Obdam made a desperate effort to snatch victory from defeat by taking or destroying the enemy's flagship. At his orders, the *Eendracht* made directly for the *Royal Charles.* As the ships came together, the Duke of York had the narrowest of escapes from death. A single chain shot killed three noblemen standing beside him, showering him with their blood and wounding him with a flying sliver of skull. Calmly, he held his position, directing the repulse of three efforts by the Dutch to board and take his ship. As the flagships drifted apart, he ordered his gunners to fire successively, at point-blank range, into the *Eendracht's* hull. There was a sudden column of flame, and the *Eendracht* was gone, with Admiral Obdam and all but five members of her crew.

More trouble was in store. A sudden attack by English fireships caused great destruction. One of these craft, encountering four Dutch ships with their rigging entangled, burned all four. Four others were singly destroyed by individual fireships. It appeared that the entire Dutch fleet was on the verge of annihilation.

In the moment of disaster, two able Dutch seamen acted quickly to save what was left of their fleet. Lieutenant-Admiral Jan Evertsen managed to extricate some forty ships from the battle and to lead them to safety in the estuary of the Maas River. At about the same time, Vice-Admiral Cornelis Tromp, son of the revered hero, was gathering and extricating an equal number of ships, which found sanctuary in the lee of Texel Island.

It had been a serious defeat for the Dutch, who had lost eighteen ships and some 7,000 men, in comparison to the English losses of one ship and 600 men. By a strange coincidence, each fleet lost four admirals killed—a high number unmatched in any other battle.

Feeling that his brother's elaborate opening maneuvers had accomplished only a delay and a lessening of the victory, King Charles II removed the Duke of York from command of the fleet, replacing him with the Duke of Albemarle (Admiral Monk) and Prince Rupert, both of whom favored the formless *melee* as the best type of sea fight.

The Dutch admiralty, not content with mere demotion, brought charges against those captains who had shown cowardice in action. Four were executed. Others were dismissed from the service "with dishonor."

8.

The only other action of 1665 was a peculiar and most irregular incident involving a conspiracy between the Earl of Sandwich and the government of Denmark, which at that time controlled Norway. Word got out that a large group of richly laden Dutch merchant ships were lying at anchor in the harbor of the neutral Norwegian Port of Bergen. The Earl of Sandwich took his British squadron there by way of Copenhagen, stopping to propose to the Danish court a division of the spoils if the Danish authorities at Bergen would cooperate in the contemplated raid. Cupidity prevailed, and the agreement was made.

Rumors of the plot quickly reached Bergen, but official orders did not. In the absence of orders to the contrary, the Governor of Bergen —who seems to have been an honest and conscientious man—decided to do his duty as he saw it. When the Earl of Sandwich reached the Norwegian port and sailed boldly in, his ships were fired on by the big guns of the fort and were forced to beat a hasty retreat. Subsequently, Dutch Admiral De Witt appeared with a powerful squadron to convoy the merchantmen home. Only the occurrence of a sudden storm, which scattered the convoy, made it possible for the Earl to make any captures at all. He was much disappointed in the small value of his ill-gotten gains, and his disappointment gave way to dismay when he was censured for his irregularities and was removed from command.

Bad as conditions always were in the fleet, the English sailors of 1665 were the luckiest citizens of England. The "Black Death"—actually, bubonic plague—was sweeping the country, killing such numbers of people that many of the dying had to lie unattended and many of the dead unburied. In London alone, more than 100,000 died within six months. The plague failed to reach the fleet, which prudently avoided the centers of population. Otherwise, the war might well have ended in a Dutch victory in 1665.

9.

France, now actively guided by the young and impetuous Louis XIV, entered the war in 1666 as an ally of the Netherlands. Rumor had it that a French fleet of thirty-six warships was lurking in the vicinity of the Isle of Wight. To counter this menace, Prince Rupert took twenty ships and set out to look for the Frenchmen, leaving the Duke of Albemarle with only fifty-four. As usual, division of forces in the face of the enemy proved to be a serious mistake. The French squadron was actually in its home port of Brest, but De Ruyter was coming with about one hundred Dutch ships with the dual purpose of destroying the English fleet and of making a landing on the coast of England.

Fog briefly postponed the battle, causing the Dutch to anchor somewhere off the Downs without having established contact. Though De Ruyter did not know it, Albemarle's fleet was also at anchor, not far to the west. Thus the two hostile fleets lay in close proximity during the night of June 10, 1666.

By morning the fog was gone, and the two anchored fleets were found to be within sight of one another. Albemarle moved first. In spite of the numerical odds against him, he weighed anchor quickly, hoping to take advantage of the weather gauge to strike and defeat the Dutch van under Cornelis Tromp before the rest of the Dutch fleet could form and beat upwind to the rescue. The Dutch, seeing their danger, got under way quickly, some of the captains slipping or cutting their anchor cables in their haste. Not being able to form upwind in the face of the enemy, they sailed rapidly downwind ahead of the English toward the coast of France. As they went, they formed a battle line, led by what had been their rear squadron and with Tromp's original van squadron in the rear.

Shortly after noon, the first thirty-five ships of Albemarle's fleet drew up within cannon range of Tromp's division and opened fire. A running fight developed, during which the Dutch discovered an unexpected advantage in not having the weather gauge. In the rising wind, the ships of both battle lines heeled sharply. As a result, the English dared not open their lower gun ports on the side toward the enemy and were thus unable to use some of their biggest guns. The Dutch, having no such disadvantage, were able to do considerable damage during this stage of the battle and to sink one English ship of fifty guns.

The arrival of both fleets at the shoal waters off the Flanders coast caused a change of pattern. The deep-draft English ships had to sheer away to avoid grounding, while the shallower Dutch vessels continued on unpursued and were able, for the first time, to regroup their squadrons effectively. This done, they came out again and attacked with vigor. In the *melee* that followed, three English ships, including Vice-Admiral Berkeley's flagship *Swiftsure,* were separated from their fleet, surrounded, and taken. As the boarders swarmed aboard his ship, Admiral Berkeley himself led the defense until mortally wounded by a musket ball in the throat.

Another English officer who fought as gallantly as Berkeley, and with more success, was Rear Admiral John Harman. When his flagship, the *Henry,* was grappled by a fireship, the admiral's lieutenant, Thomas Lemming, leaped aboard the flaming menace and managed to cast it loose and escape back to his own vessel. Another fireship set the *Henry* ablaze, causing a panic, but Admiral Harman drew his sword and forced the crew to fight the fire, which was eventually brought under control. A spar, falling from a burning mast, broke the admiral's leg, but he supported himself on his sword and maintained command. Coolly, he directed his gunners as they sank a third fireship. Came then the flagship of old Vice-Admiral Cornelis Evertsen, demanding the surrender of the stricken *Henry.* Harman refused— "No! No! It has not yet come to that!"—and fired a broadside that killed Evertsen and damaged his ship. In the end, indomitable John Harman managed to take his crippled flagship safely back to England.

On the second day of the battle, a dead calm prevented action until about noon, when a moderate wind sprang up. This was a day of formal naval activity, with the fleets passing one another on opposite tacks and exchanging broadsides. The effectiveness of the Dutch was considerably lessened by a difference of opinion between Admiral De Ruyter and Vice-Admiral Cornelis Tromp, who felt that he should have been placed in command. Feeling that the Dutch battle line was poorly constituted, with some ships masking the fire of others, Tromp, on his own initiative, took his van ships through the English van to attack the enemy from the other side. This resulted, for a time, in a strange, three-sided engagement between Albemarle's English battle line and two independently operating Dutch lines, one to windward and one to leeward. Taking advantage of this situation, Albemarle succeeded in isolating five of Tromp's ships and was rapidly hammering them into submission when De Ruyter, leading the main body of the Dutch fleet, broke through the English line and came to the rescue of his uncooperative subordinate. Six English ships were sunk and one burned during this reversal of fortune.

The third day was one of retreat for the English, who formed their fleet into a long line abreast and headed for home, with the Dutch pursuing and nibbling at the flanks. The chief incident was the grounding of the ninety-gun *Prince Royal,* flagship of Vice-Admiral Sir George Ayscue, on the Galloper Shoal. Rather than break his defense formation and bring on another *melee,* Albemarle sailed on and left Ayscue to his inevitable fate. After a brief resistance, the abandoned Vice-Admiral was forced to surrender when menaced by a ring of enemy warships, including two Dutch fireships.

As he neared the mouth of the Thames, Albemarle was joined by Prince Rupert's squadron, returning from its fruitless patrol to the southwest. This brought the total of English ships to sixty. The Dutch, having sent home many of their disabled vessels, now had seventy-eight.

In the morning, the reinforced English fleet came out, attacking upwind in the face of a stiff southwesterly breeze. After much furious fighting, Albemarle succeeded in performing the difficult task of cutting upwind through the enemy battle line. It availed him little, for the Dutch were sailing in two parallel columns, between which the English ships were trapped. The remainder of the engagement consisted of Albemarle's attempts to undo what he had done and fight his way clear. After heavy losses, he succeeded in doing so. At this, in the face of rising winds and seas, the Dutch withdrew and sailed for home.

In his *Influence of Sea Power upon History,* Mahan speaks of the Four Days' Battle as "the most remarkable, in some of its aspects, that has ever been fought upon the ocean." Certainly, for length and for close, continuous, heavy action it has seldom been equaled. The losses were heavy, especially for the English, who had seventeen ships burned or sunk and six captured by the enemy. Their loss in man-power was 9,000, of which about two-thirds were killed and one-third captured. The Dutch lost seven vessels and about 2,000 men. The Dutch had won a resounding victory over the English fleet, but they had not succeeded in making their landing on the English coast.

10.

The Dutch leaders did not give up the idea of invading England. Indeed, the idea took firmer root after the Four Days' Battle, thanks to a growing conviction that the English people were dissatisfied with their government and needed only an excuse to overthrow it. Preparations were rushed for an invading force that would provide the excuse.

Late in July, Admiral De Ruyter sailed with eighty-eight warships, bearing troops as well as fighting crews. The plan was to sail up the Thames to the vicinity of London before making a landing. This, however, proved to be impractical. A large English fleet, which had been hastily refitted after the late defeat, occupied the river mouth. Along the shore were numerous fireships, ready to be ignited and sent forth against the invaders. Worst of all, the English had removed the channel buoys, and the Dutch had no pilots sufficiently familiar with the local waters to guide a fleet safely in past the numerous shoals. De Ruyter had to content himself with prowling along the shore, hoping that an English fleet would come out and fight.

On July 22 he got his wish. A fleet of about eighty English ships under the Duke of Albemarle came out and engaged the Dutch in the vicinity of a large shoal known as the Gunfleet. After some elaborate sparring and maneuvering, the two fleets settled down on an easterly course, each in line ahead, with the Dutch line to windward. So they continued, cannonading briskly, until suddenly Cornelis Tromp swung his ship to starboard and led the rear of the Dutch line through the English line, separating the English rear division, under Sir Jeremy Smith, from the rest of the English force. The two rear divisions bore off to the south, fighting their own private battle and leaving the remainder of the two fleets to get along as best they could. Both battles raged indecisively until stopped by darkness.

During the night, confusion developed within the Dutch fleet. Dawn found Admiral De Ruyter, with only seven ships, surrounded by twenty-two of the enemy. All seemed lost. The cannonading was terrific, once being marked by the firing of simultaneous broadsides from seven enemy vessels into the Dutch flagship. De Ruyter, however, re-tained his composure, fought shrewdly, and in the end managed to break through the ring of his enemies and retreat with the greater part of his fleet toward the sheltering shallows of the Dutch coast. At about the same time, Cornelis Tromp, out of sight to the south, was doing the same thing.

The English fleet pursued the Dutch across the Channel and estab-lished a blockade of the Dutch coast. It had been a distinct victory for the Duke of Albemarle. The Dutch had lost twenty ships and had had 7,000 men killed or wounded, the English but a single ship and a few hundred men. Among the Dutch casualties was Vice-Admiral Jan Evertsen, whose father, son, and four brothers had already died in the war. A casualty of another sort was Cornelis Tromp, who was dis-missed from the service for failure to cooperate with his commanding officer.

11.

The victory won at the Gunfleet did the English far more harm than it did the beaten Dutch. Charles II regarded the naval war as good as won. Already he had reduced the size of the army in order to save money, always in scarce supply with the spendthrift king. Now it was the turn of the navy. At the king's insistence, many of the best English warships were decommissioned and their crews dispersed. The function of the English navy was reduced from one of fleet action and control of the seas to one of convoying and commerce raiding.

On June 7, 1667, the folly of the new policy became evident to all. Admiral De Ruyter appeared at the mouth of the Thames with eighty-one warships. While the greater part of the fleet blockaded the river mouth and took and looted the naval base at Sheerness, a squadron of twenty-two ships under Lieutenant-Admiral William Joseph van Ghent sailed up the river toward the anchorage where most of the remaining warships of the English navy lay at anchor.

Apparently, Admiral Van Ghent was not the most enterprising of leaders, for he soon found himself checked by shore batteries and by a chain across the river, held up and guarded by a row of hulks. For four days, he hesitated before this barrier, accomplishing nothing. At last De Ruyter, weary of the delay, came up the river and quickly solved the problem. Well-directed fireships set the hulks ablaze and let the chain drop to the river bottom. The Dutch warships poured through the gap and quickly captured a fifty-gun English warship stationed not far beyond. Regarding this captured ship as expendable, the Admiral sent her in to blast the shore batteries at close range. They were quickly put out of action.

The wolves were in the sheepfold, and the slaughter was terrific. The startled citizens of London heard steady cannon fire and saw the eastern sky alight with the flames of burning ships. Many fled from the city, fearing that the Dutch might attack even great London itself. In the end, De Ruyter withdrew, taking with him enormous quantities of stores and two captured English warships, the flagship *Royal Charles* and the *Unity*. Behind him he left the smoldering wrecks of countless English ships and a populace that had been deeply shocked and frightened.

How did the playboy king react to this damaging raid on his navy, to this daring incursion to the very edge of his capital city, to this capture of the great flagship on which he had made his triumphant return from exile? In his famous diary, Samuel Pepys, an official in the naval office, records: "The night the Dutch burned our ships, the King did sup with my Lady Castlemayne, at the Duchess of Monmouth's, and they were all mad in hunting a poor moth."

12.

In July, 1667, the second Anglo-Dutch War suddenly seemed to lose much of its importance. On the Continent, King Louis XIV of France was flexing his muscles and was showing unmistakable signs of preparing for a war of conquest. In the face of this new menace, the trade differences between the English and the Dutch suddenly seemed insignificant.

The result was the signing of the Peace of Breda. Theoretically, the negotiations were between England, on the one hand, and the Netherlands, France, and Denmark, on the other. Actually, King Louis XIV of France freely used his influence and his persuasive tongue to gain as many advantages as possible for England—a potential ally or neutral—and as few as possible for the Netherlands, a prospective victim. As a result, the English Navigation Acts were only slightly revised, to permit Dutch ships to carry to England European exports brought from the interior of the Continent down the Rhine. Territorially, the Dutch signed away much and received little. England retained New Netherland in exchange for some territory of little value adjoining the

Dutch settlements in Guiana (Surinam). France received back Acadia, which had been taken by the English, but surrendered to England a few islands in the West Indies.

England had not won a clear-cut victory over the Netherlands. Every resource had had to be strained and every bit of determination and energy expended to fight the Dutch on even terms and thus to gain a position from which a favorable peace could be extracted with King Louis' strong outside help. Though not defeated on the sea, the Netherlanders had lost the battle of the conference table. The Netherlands' brief period as a leading naval power was at an end.

Among the English gains from these wars was a most expressive phrase, added to the English language. Colloquially speaking, an effort carried on to the utmost of one's ability is an effort made "to beat the Dutch."

6 THE GLORIOUS DREAM OF LOUIS XIV

⚓

1.

We have already caught some glimpses of Louis XIV, the glittering French monarch who came to the throne in 1643, at the age of five. Now we must make his closer acquaintance.

For the first eighteen years of his reign, Louis was content to let his great minister, Cardinal Mazarin, govern for him. This period ended abruptly in 1661, when Mazarin died. King Louis took over. From that day until his death forty-nine years later, every important decision made by the French government was his. Whether or not he actually said, "L'Etat, c'est moi," his every act clearly showed that he believed that he was, in fact, the French government. Believing firmly in "the Divine Right of Kings," Louis was sure that he had been put in charge of France personally and directly by God. It followed that any questioning of his words, acts, or decisions was out-and-out heresy.

The two great aims of Louis' life were the supremacy of France and of the Roman Catholic Church. Most of the things he did were aimed at achieving one or both of these objectives.

Though France was predominantly a Catholic country, it did contain a rather large number of Huguenots, or French Protestants. An earlier king, Henry IV, had issued the Edict of Nantes in 1598, guaranteeing to these people the right to worship as they wished. Since then, they had lived quiet, useful lives, and France had been undisturbed by religious conflict. Such tolerance seemed sinful to King Louis. In 1685, he suddenly revoked the Edict of Nantes, thus subjecting the Huguenots to further persecution and driving large numbers of them from the country.

Louis also dreamed of expanding his borders as far as possible, in order to make France the strongest nation in Europe and the center of a world-wide empire. This would, of course, involve wars of conquest, which would provide an opportunity for the winning of much glory. France had a great army, a strong navy, and some very able military and naval leaders. Let the wars begin!

Louis' first war—the so-called War of Devolution (1667–68)—was fought against Spain for possession of the Spanish Netherlands. It was entirely a land war and was not particularly successful. The French armies conquered some of the fringes of the Netherlands and overran the border territory of Franche Comté, but that was all. It was not the Spaniards who halted the conquest, but the growing alarm in Europe. The menace of Louis' conquering armies had led England and the Netherlands to sign the Peace of Breda. Now the two recent enemies hastened to join with Sweden in a triple alliance against the new would-be conqueror. Hastily, Louis brought the War of Devolution to an end before it could turn into a general European conflict.

2 .

Before he could continue his conquests, Louis felt it necessary to disassemble the triple alliance. This proved to be easier than expected. Some heavy bribes in the right quarters led the Swedish government to change its mind and to withdraw. His purpose was to isolate the Netherlands, the next target of conquest. England, therefore, must also be won away from the alliance.

King Louis XIV played very skilfully upon the weaknesses and needs of King Charles II. Charles needed money. Louis had plenty. Charles had a secret hankering to be a Catholic. Louis was in a splendid position to serve as an intermediary with the Church. The result of all this temptation was the Secret Treaty of Dover, signed in 1670. By its terms, Charles promised to become a Catholic, secretly at once, openly when he dared, and to work to convert his country to Catholicism. He also promised to abandon his Dutch allies and to help Louis in the proposed French conquest of the Netherlands. In return, Louis promised Charles a yearly pension large enough to make it unnecessary for him to go to Parliament for funds.

The royal plotters laid their plans most carefully, in order to keep the people of the Netherlands from knowing of the fate in store for them. England was to strike the first blow by seizing a rich Dutch convoy from Smyrna, as it tried to pass through the Channel. The English and French fleets would then combine and would descend upon the Dutch coast while the French army was making a lightning land invasion from the south. March, 1672, was the time selected.

As so often happens, the plans did not work out exactly as laid. The Dutch, not without reason, had begun to suspect treachery. As a result, the Smyrna merchant flotilla entered the Channel with an escort of seven Dutch warships. At the approach of the raiding squadron under Sir Robert Holmes, the Dutch opened fire and managed to stave off the English forces. The convoy escaped intact. The opening move had been badly bungled. The English had been detected in an act of piracy—and unsuccessful piracy, at that!

3.

Now that the mask was off, England and France made haste to declare war on the Dutch. Reasons were given, but nobody took them very seriously. It was recognized by all as a clear case of naked aggression.

Faced with annihilation, the Dutch moved swiftly. Admiral De Ruyter led out the Netherlands navy of 91 vessels, in the hope of defeating the English before they could be joined by the French. He was not in time. When well at sea, he found the allied fleet, 101 vessels strong—68 English under the Duke of York and 33 French under Vice-Admiral Jean d'Estrees. In the face of these more numerous and larger units, the Dutch admiral fell back to the shallow waters off his own coast, where they dared not follow. Having thus driven the Dutch from the sea, as they supposed, the allies then sailed to the east coast of England and anchored at Southwold Bay, or Solebay, in apparent security.

Admiral De Ruyter had staged a magnificent feint. No sooner had the allied fleet quit his shores than he had emerged and followed them. The watchers on the cliffs had scarcely had time to shout their warnings when the Dutch fleet came pouring into Southwold Bay in two columns, borne on by an easterly wind which gave them the weather gauge and trapped the allies against a dangerous lee shore. In frantic haste, the allied captains slipped their anchor cables and tried to claw out from the shore. Following the lead of the Duke of York's flagship, the *Prince,* the English ships straggled into a ragged line and moved north, on a starboard tack. D'Estrees and the French, meanwhile, moved south on a port tack.

Having thus separated his enemies at the very outset, De Ruyter sent one division of his ships, under Vice-Admiral Adrian Bankert, to keep the French occupied while he and Lieutenant-Admiral William van Ghent went after the English.

Bankert had little difficulty with the French, who were happy to settle for a relatively harmless long-range artillery duel against the greatly outnumbered Dutch division opposing them. The purpose of this southern segment of the battle was thus easily achieved; the French were kept from coming to the assistance of the English.

The fighting in the northern part of the bay was very different. In spite of the presence of the formalist Duke of York, the battle quickly degenerated into a *melee*. The Duke himself, in the thick of the action, found it necessary to transfer his flag from the disabled *Prince* to the *St. Michael* and, later, to the *London*. The *Royal James,* flagship of the Earl of Sandwich, became heavily engaged with the flagship of Admiral Van Ghent and with three Dutch fireships. At the end of two hours, Van Ghent was dead and two of the fireships had been fended off and had burned out harmlessly. The Earl was not to escape. The third fireship crashed into the *Royal James* and stuck fast, spreading flames throughout the flagship. The Earl tried to transfer to another ship, but his small boat was swamped and he was drowned.

A shift of the wind in favor of the allies caused Admiral De Ruyter to withdraw from the scene of action. He had lost three ships, the English one, and the French two—these having gone down during D'Estree's one half-hearted attempt to break through Bankert's line. The losses of men were heavy on both sides. Though the statistics seem even, the over-all advantage rested with the Dutch. They had so damaged the allied fleet that its contemplated moves against the Netherlands had to be postponed by more than a month. Besides gaining time, De Ruyter, retiring from the battle, seized the opportunity to escort a large fleet of Dutch merchantmen safely past the dangerous shores of England and home. Nobody came out of Solebay to challenge him.

One more item about this battle deserves our notice. On several of the English ships were units of specially trained foot soldiers, members of "The Duke of York and Albemarle's Maritime Regiment of Foot." They proved effective in action. In the Duke's report of the battle, to his royal brother, appears this sentence: "Those Marines, of whom I soe oft have wrote to you, behaved themselves stoutly." This is the first known use of the term "Marines" to describe the soldiers of the sea.

4.

In the meantime, the French invasion of the Netherlands had gotten off to a good start. Huge French armies, nominally led by King Louis XIV but actually directed by the great Generals Condè and Turenne, swarmed across the borders and drove back the Dutch. Many forts were taken, and the quick subjugation of the little country began to look certain.

The confusion and panic of the emergency led to the overthrow of the Dutch government. Since the death of the *Stadtholder,* Prince William II of Orange, in 1650, the government had been administered by Jan De Witt, the head of the republican faction of the States-General. Fearing the creation of a monarchy, the De Witts—Jan and his brother Cornelis—had engineered the passing of the Exclusion Bill, aimed at keeping the late *Stadtholder*'s son William from holding the same title. Though the law had been popular when passed, there was now a growing sentiment in favor of young Prince William. Unfounded charges were made against the De Witts, who were presently arrested, then literally torn apart by a mob which stormed their prison. Prince William, who had nothing to do with this crime, suddenly found his country's future resting in his hands. With the repeal of the Exclusion Act, he became Prince William III, with the title of *Stadtholder.*

Under their new leader, the Dutch revived and stiffened their defenses. Sluices in the dikes were opened, and the sea became the ally of the people in checking the invaders. The glittering armies of Louis XIV slid to a soggy halt.

Propaganda was tried. French and English representatives tried to impress upon Prince William the desirability of surrendering, to avoid seeing the ruin of his country. "There is one means," he replied, "which will save me from the sight of my country's ruin. I will die in the last ditch."

5.

In the realm of naval affairs, Admiral De Ruyter was playing a very cagey game. The combined English and French fleets skirted the Dutch coast, trying to tempt him out for a decisive battle. Knowing that the safety of his country depended upon the maintenance of his fleet-in-being, he refused the offer but sailed the shallows to interpose his force between the enemy and the land. This blocked aggression from the sea as effectively as the open dikes were blocking it by land, for the English and French admirals knew the dangers of contending at the same time with the treacherous shoal waters of the Netherlands coast and with the small but aggressive Dutch navy.

In the end, the English and French lost patience and decided to try a sea-borne invasion without first eliminating the defenders. De Ruyter was ready to oppose them to the end, but it proved to be unnecessary. A combination of adverse winds and tides kept the invasion force away and at last forced it to turn back. This was widely regarded as a sign that Providence had shown its favor to the Dutch cause. Wishing to be on the right side, Spain, the Holy Roman Emperor, and the Elector of Brandenburg began to contribute to the defense of the Netherlands. Louis XIV, tired of a static campaign without glory and of the discomfort of wet feet, withdrew his armies and returned to the more beguiling pleasures of his palace at Versailles.

The war went on upon the sea. Early in 1673, the Dutch made an attempt to trap the English in their lair by sinking stone-laden hulks in the channels at the mouth of the Thames. Had this succeeded, the next step would have been an all-out attack on the French, in order to destroy their fleet before the English could come to their assistance. It did not succeed. Though a Dutch squadron entered the Thames estuary, an English squadron under Prince Rupert met it and drove it out again, leaving the channels still unblocked.

In June, Prince Rupert and French Admiral D'Estrees made another attempt to invade the Netherlands from the sea. Together, the allies had 91 fighting ships, as opposed to the current Dutch fleet of 64. It was felt that if De Ruyter could be tempted out to fight he could easily be defeated. Six thousand English troops were waiting at Yarmouth to embark and invade as soon as word of victory was received. The only real fear was that the Dutch admiral would not come out from his sheltered inland seas.

The allies found the Dutch fleet at anchor off Schoenveldt, in the estuary of the Scheldt River. In order to dangle an irresistible bait, the Prince sent into the estuary a squadron of thirty-five of his smaller warships. The bait was taken with alacrity—so rapidly, in fact, that the venturesome thirty-five were barely able to get back out to sea ahead of their pursuers. As Prince Rupert and Admiral D'Estrees strove frantically to organize for this lightning-like attack, the squadron of thirty-five came back in full flight and completely upset what little order had been achieved. Worse, from the allies' point of view, was the fact that the retreating squadron completely masked all fire at the pursuing Dutch until the two fleets were almost in contact.

In the *melee* which followed, the smaller Dutch fleet gave a good account of itself. Only Cornelis Tromp somewhat spoiled the picture by getting cut off from the other Dutch divisions and having to be rescued by a desperate sortie by Admiral De Ruyter. In the end, the Dutch retired into their safe anchorage. Neither fleet had had any ships captured, though the French had two of theirs sunk and the Dutch one. The loss of life had been heavy on both sides. The allied invasion was called off for the time being.

A week later, taking advantage of an offshore wind, the Dutch came out again. The allies saw them coming and hastened to get under way, some having to cut their anchor cables to do so. Hoping to tempt their enemies far from shelter, the English and French set their course northwestward, in line ahead. Not until 5 P.M. did the Dutch catch up. A running fight then followed, raging indecisively for about five hours. By this time, the fleets were far from the Dutch coast and well on their way to England. Fearing a trap, Admiral De Ruyter broke off action and turned about to go home. He had lost no ships but had sustained considerable damage and some casualties. The allies, battered even worse, held their northwesterly course for another two hours, then swung around and, at a safe distance, made a brief gesture of pursuing the Dutch. This done, they reversed course again and went to their home ports for refitting, repairs, and supplies.

In mid-August, the combined English-French fleet came back with the triple purpose of intercepting and capturing a richly laden Dutch convoy from the East Indies, of landing troops on the Netherlands coast, and, if possible, of drawing out and destroying that pestiferous Dutch fleet. Prince Rupert and Admiral D'Estrees missed the merchant ships, which managed to reach port in safety, but off the island of Texel they did find the Dutch fleet under Admiral De Ruyter. The allied fleet outnumbered the Dutch eighty-eight ships-of-the-line to sixty, each battle line being accompanied by the usual auxiliaries, frigates, and fireships.

Admiral D'Estrees' column of thirty French ships was leading the allied line, with Prince Rupert in command of the center division and

Vice-Admiral Sir Edward Spragge in command of the rear. Counting on D'Estrees' reluctance to fight any harder than he had to, De Ruyter ordered Vice-Admiral Bankert, with only twelve ships, to take care of the allied van. Bankert succeeded brilliantly, breaking through the French line, edging the French ships away from the action, then returning to the conflict while the French, having had enough, withdrew.

In the meantime, the rear segments of the two fleets had gone away to enjoy a private battle by themselves. Cornelis Tromp and Vice-Admiral Spragge, the rival commanders, were alike in their love of combat, their dislike of regimentation, and their utter detestation of each other. Another factor was the promise Spragge had made to King Charles to defeat Tromp and bring him to England, dead or alive. For some hours, these rival gamecocks fought without any marked advantage for either. Both of their flagships were disabled early in the fray, causing each leader to transfer to a second ship. The turning point came when Spragge attempted to transfer himself and his flag yet again. He was halfway between the *St. George* and the *Royal Charles* when a cannon ball demolished his small open boat. After Spragge's death, Tromp gained the upper hand.

The center sections of the two fleets were also fiercely engaged. Here, too, there was at first no advantage, De Ruyter and Prince Rupert finding, each in the other, a worthy opponent. Then Bankert came back, having removed the French, and Prince Rupert found the going very hot. Seeing that Spragge's rear division was having trouble in the distance, he shifted his course to join forces with it. At this, De Ruyter broke off action and led his fleet into the shelter of the Zuyder Zee.

At first glance, the clash off Texel looks like a drawn battle. No ship of either fleet had been sunk, though many in each fleet had been so badly shattered as to be useless for further action. Loss of life, heavy on both sides, had been heavier for the allies, whose ships had been crowded with soldiers intended for the invasion. Though it was the Dutch who withdrew, the victory was theirs. The blockade was broken, and the idea of a sea-borne invasion of the Netherlands was given up. What is more, the demonstration of Dutch naval prowess brought new allies—Spain, Lorraine, and the Holy Roman Empire—openly into the war on the side of the Netherlands.

What can we say of Admiral Michael de Ruyter that can top the tribute made by his enemies? The official historian of the Royal Navy said it best: "Never, perhaps, did a commander of inferior forces handle them with greater tactical ability, or more skilfully create for himself a temporary local superiority."

Protests by the English people and growing friction with his French allies at last forced King Charles II to drop out of King Louis' war with the Dutch. The Treaty of Westminster, signed in February, 1674, gave England far more than she had won by force of arms. The Dutch paid a heavy indemnity, agreed to salute the English flag in the Narrow Seas, and assented to the terms of England's Navigation Acts. They also restored to English control the North American colony of New Netherland, which Lieutenant Admiral Cornelis ("Devil") Evertsen had retaken from the English in 1673. The English, for their part, gave up only the island of Tobago, off the northern coast of South America, which they had recently captured from the Dutch.

Once more, the Netherlands had won a war and lost a peace.

6.

Though the Netherlands had made peace with England, the war with France went on. Louis XIV still held to his dream of adding the little low countries to his domains.

The removal of England as an enemy proved disastrous to Dutch sea power. The performance of the French navy in the war had been so bad that the Dutch felt no sense of challenge from that direction. Their navy was permitted to deteriorate, full concentration being placed on the defense of the land frontiers.

Early in the spring of 1676, Prince William, in his capacity of *Stadtholder,* ordered Admiral de Ruyter to take the fleet into the Mediterranean, to help the Spanish allies suppress a revolt in their colony of Sicily and, at the same time, to keep the French from taking the island. In vain, the admiral protested that he had only eighteen ships fit for service. When he appealed to the States-General, he was told that he must be growing timid in his old age. Regretfully, foreseeing disaster, he put to sea.

On January 7, 1676, off the island of Stromboli, De Ruyter encountered the French fleet—twenty ships-of-the-line and six fireships to oppose his eighteen Dutch and one Spanish ships, four fireships, and a squadron of Spanish galleys. Feeling that conditions would never be better, and having the weather gauge, the intrepid Dutchman bore in to the attack. He was unsuccessful, for French Admiral Abraham Duquesne gave way before him and kept the range open. Night fell, and nothing had been resolved.

During the night, the wind changed in direction and rose in intensity, forcing the unseaworthy Spanish galleys to run for shelter in the lee of an island. Now the odds favored the French, and Duquesne attacked, sending his battle line in at a slant against the Dutch line. It was a poor way to attack, for the French ships came into action one at a time as the lines converged, and they suffered heavily from the concentrated fire of the well-ordered Dutch battle line. One French ship was sunk, and many were badly damaged. French casualties were heavy, too, Admiral Duquesne being among the wounded. Though the victory was not clear-cut for either side, the more numerous and heavier French ships had been so roughly handled that they were unable to interfere with the orderly Dutch retirement to Palermo. With the action over, the Spanish galleys reappeared and proved their value by towing to port some of the more badly damaged Dutch vessels. All arrived safely except the *Essen,* which sank during the night.

De Ruyter's time of service had run out. He was supposed to return home, but at the last moment he received word from Prince William that he was to stay six months longer, cooperating more closely with the Spaniards. Spain needed him—a fact which he used to secure the release of a group of "heretic" Lutheran pastors whom the Spaniards had condemned to brief life-sentences swinging the oars of galleys. The Spaniards added ten ships to his battle line, but there was a string attached. With them came Admiral Don Francisco Pereira, who was to exercise command over the combined fleet.

Admiral De Ruyter and his Spanish allies sailed against the French in mid-April. Knowing that the Spaniards had little stomach for close, hard sea warfare, he had suggested that the Spanish vessels be spaced throughout the Dutch battle line. Don Francisco overruled him. De Ruyter's own division would be the van, followed by the Spanish division, with Vice-Admiral Jan de Haen's Dutch squadron in the rear. It proved to be the worst possible arrangement.

The French, too, had received reinforcements, bringing their total strength up to thirty-three ships-of-the-line and seven fireships. Nevertheless, De Ruyter led his squadron boldly in against them, hoping against hope that the Spaniards would follow his lead. They did not. Instead, the Spanish squadron held back, and by so doing they also kept the rear division out of action. The heavy early fighting fell upon

De Ruyter, with odds of more than three to one against him. Early in the battle, he was struck by a cannon ball which broke his right leg in two places, carried away most of his left foot, and hurled him across his quarterdeck and down to the deck below, with severe injuries to his head. Concealing his wounds as best he could, he continued to give orders and even dispatched a boat to the Spanish flagship with a note begging Don Francisco to play a more active part in the fight. Don Francisco did. So, as a result, did De Haen. After some hours of cannonading, it was the French who drew away, their fleet so badly battered that it would be out of action for months. Admiral de Haen pursued them briefly, then rejoined the main body of the fleet, which was retiring toward Palermo.

Admiral De Ruyter was alive when the action was broken off, and he was able to send a full report of the battle to his prince. A week later, he had joined Marten Tromp in death. The two greatest leaders were gone. This was a double blow from which Dutch sea power could not recover.

Without De Ruyter's guidance and inspiration, the Dutch-Spanish Mediterranean squadron deteriorated. Later in the year, a French squadron caught it off guard and at anchor in Palermo Harbor and destroyed most of it.

The war went on for another two years without any notable activity on the sea. On land, the French were successful in nibbling away at the fringes of the Netherlands, threatening to engorge the country in a series of little bites. It was a wearisome campaign for both sides, particularly for the Dutch.

The eventual peace came in a peculiar way. Princess Mary, eldest daughter of the Duke of York, and niece of King Charles II, was an eligible spinster and a significant pawn on the chessboard of international relations. Prince William of the Netherlands expressed interest in the lady and was invited to England, where he found, to his delight, that she was personally attractive to him. After some fevered negotiation, the marriage was arranged.

Now that his late enemy was a member of the family, King Charles II made every effort to serve as an intermediary and end the war. He was successful. By the Treaty of Nijmegen (August, 1678), Louis gave up his conquests on the borders of the Netherlands, and peace was restored.

Events in England now strongly affected affairs in the Netherlands.

When King Charles II died in 1685, he was succeeded by his brother James, the erstwhile Duke of York. Though James II was an avowed Catholic, his two daughters were not, so there seemed no danger of a new Catholic succession in Protestant England. All this changed when James married a French princess and had a son, who was baptized into the Catholic Church. Might this not presage another strong Catholic regime, like that of "Bloody Mary" Tudor, in which Protestantism would be suppressed? Something must be done at once!

To his surprise, William, Prince of Orange, received a letter from a group of prominent Englishmen inviting him and his wife to become the rulers of England. They graciously accepted. Though King James tried to keep them out of the country, he was unable to do so, as most of his people and a large part of his army declared themselves in favor of the new rulers from the Netherlands. James fled to France, and Parliament declared that the throne was vacant because King James II had "withdrawn himself out of the kingdom." Queen Mary II and her husband, William III, became the new royal family, to rule jointly.

William and Mary were now the rulers of two countries, England and the Netherlands. In many ways, the two countries worked as partners. One of England's assignments was to retain control of the seas. There seemed to be little point in reviving the Dutch navy.

7.

While England and the Netherlands had been engaged in their life-and-death struggle for naval supremacy, the prize had imperceptibly slipped from the grasp of both. In France, Jean Baptiste Colbert, Chief Minister of Louis XIV, had been quietly at work building up a magnificent French fleet. In 1678, when the Treaty of Nijmegen brought an uneasy peace to Europe, the French navy was greater in numbers of ships, in weight of broadside, and in manpower than the English and Dutch fleets combined. On paper, at least, France had become the leading naval power of the world.

Since the middle of the seventeenth century, steady evolution had been taking place in the design of warships. Gone, now, were the towering galleons, the galleys, and the galleasses. The gilt, the gingerbread, and the decorated sails had largely been sacrificed in the interest of practicality. Through a series of intermediate types, there now appeared the basic classes of warships which would dominate naval architecture for the next century and three-quarters.

The mainstay of every important fleet was the ship-of-the-line. She was tall, broad, and solid, with thick, strong wooden sides. Through her rows of gun ports peered as many and as large guns as could be crowded into her hull. She was a slow sailer, except in the briskest of winds, but this was comparatively unimportant, because she was seldom called upon to pursue another ship, and she almost never had to flee. Her function was to sail in stately procession with other ships-of-the-line, dealing out a devastating volume of cannon fire with which to overwhelm and destroy the units of another line of battleships. Nothing except another ship-of-the-line could hope to stand up to her successfully in ship-to-ship combat.

In 1652, when the first Anglo-Dutch War began, the greatest ships-of-the-line were two-deckers, mounting approximately sixty guns. Five years later, in 1657, the first three-decker was built. In the years which followed, these multilevel ships appeared in greater numbers and in greater size. Though a fourth gun deck was seldom added, for reasons of stability, the number of guns tended to increase until ships with 90 or even 110 guns or more were not unusual.

Ships-of-the-line which grew old and infirm were sometimes scrapped, sometimes rebuilt into approximately their original condition, and sometimes cut down, or razed. This latter practice gave rise to a new class of ship, the *razee,* or cut-down ship-of-the-line. Usually, a *razee* had two decks in place of three and mounted correspondingly fewer guns. She retained, however, her solid side walls, and she was somewhat more manageable than a full three-decker.

Next to the ships-of-the-line and *razees* in size and power were the frigates. These were flush-decked vessels with only a single gun deck, bearing from 24 to 50 heavy guns. Faster than ships-of-the-line, under ordinary conditions, the frigates served as cruisers, ranging far and wide, scouting, picketing, raiding commerce, and attacking other frigates as well as lesser types of warships.

Below the frigates came the smaller and less powerful types—brigs, sloops, schooners, ketches, snows, and other minor vessels, each with its own uses, virtues, and limitations. All carried guns, but in these lesser types they were apt to be few and small.

Since some warships were considerably more powerful than others of the same general type, it became important to provide more exact designations, so that, for example, a 60- or 74-gun ship-of-the-line would not find itself opposed in battle formation by a 90- or 110-

gunner. Accordingly, the British admiralty divided its warships into six ratings, the first-rate ships being those with the most guns and the sixth-raters those with the least. Only vessels of the first three ratings were entitled to a place in the formal line of battle and to the name of "ship." Even the powerful and useful frigates did not merit these two distinctions. As the system was set up, a first-rate ship was one of 90 guns or more; second-rate, 80; third-rate, 50; fourth-rate, 38; fifth-rate, 18; and sixth-rate, 6. Though minor adjustments were made from time to time, these categories did not change very much.

The seventeenth century was now in its closing years. France, with her great navy, seemed to be the unquestioned Queen of the Seas. Looking across the oceans, Louis XIV began to dream of colonial greatness—of an expanding French empire, secured and defended by his magnificent ships-of-war. Who, after all, could check him on the sea?

8.

The expulsion of James II from the English throne made it certain that peace in Europe could not last very long. Louis XIV, an ardent Catholic, was shocked and dismayed at the spectacle of a Catholic king being dethroned in favor of a Protestant successor. Though he made no attempt to prevent the crossing of William and Mary from the Netherlands to England, he eagerly welcomed the exiled James to his court and spent long hours plotting with him for the restoration of the House of Stuart to the English throne. Inevitably, Colbert's splendid French fleet must play a leading part in any such attempt.

Ireland, being close to England and to France, seemed the logical point of attack. As a Catholic country, it was strongly in sympathy with James and hostile to his Protestant successors. A French fleet carried James to Kinsale, Ireland, in March of 1689.

James must have been greatly encouraged by his reception in Ireland. Scarcely had he left ship when he was joined by very considerable forces under the Duke of Tyrconnel, who had been busy for many weeks weeding all Protestants out of the army and out of various government positions. This work was almost done. Fearing for their lives, the Protestants of Ireland had taken refuge in the two weakly fortified towns of Londonderry and Enniskillen. With the taking of these places, Ireland would be solidly Catholic and practically unanimous in favor of James and his cause.

James and Tyrconnel confidently led their army northward to take Londonderry. They had not counted on the resolution of desperate men. The 7,000 defenders would neither surrender nor give an inch, in spite of odds of more than two to one against them. When attacked, they killed nearly 9,000 of the attackers at a cost of 3,000 of their own lives. Badly disconcerted, James and Tyrconnel drew back their forces and began a formal siege, counting on starvation and shortage of ammunition as their strong allies.

Meanwhile, at Enniskillen, much the same thing was taking place. Attacked by superior numbers, the defenders resisted bitterly and forced the attackers to institute a siege. Against all probability, neither place had yielded to assault.

King William's navy had thus far done nothing to prevent the invasion of Ireland or to relieve the beleaguered Irish Protestants. Now, belatedly, a squadron of nineteen third-rate ships-of-the-line was sent out under Admiral Arthur Herbert to intercept and, if possible, to destroy the French squadron which had brought James to Kinsale. Since the French squadron had already returned to Brest, there was little for Herbert to do but cruise around. He was still doing this when the French returned, bringing supplies for James's army.

When sighted, the French ships were just entering Bantry Bay, near Ireland's southwestern tip. Though outnumbered in ships-of-the-line twenty-four to nineteen and in frigates five to none, Herbert boldly led his fleet into Bantry Bay to do battle with the French, who had everything in their favor, including the direction of the wind.

As soon as he saw the English ships entering the bay, the French admiral, the Marquis de Château-Renault, formed his ships into line and sailed boldly downwind toward Herbert's squadron, which was having difficulty holding its formation while tacking upwind. There followed six and a half hours of cannonading, chiefly remarkable for the fact that no ships were sunk in either fleet, though many were badly damaged. At five in the afternoon, having suffered casualties double those of the French, Herbert led his ships out to sea with the thought of regrouping and coming back if the wind should change. The wind did not oblige. With darkness falling, the English admiral then took his fleet back to Portsmouth.

Word reached King William that the morale of the English sailors was low as a result of the poor showing of their fleet at Bantry Bay. With all speed, he traveled to Portsmouth, where he dined with Admiral Herbert and his officers and spoke highly of their "accomplishment." Before leaving, he knighted two of the English captains and distributed ten shillings to each of the sailors. Not long afterward, Admiral Herbert was made the Earl of Torrington. Whether deserved or not, the rewards had the desired effect. In the minds of the English people, the dismal battle of Bantry Bay was magically transformed into a victory!

Late in July, 1689, the English fleet—its morale now strengthened —again went into action. A squadron under Sir George Rooke sailed up Lough Foyle toward Londonderry until checked by a well-defended log boom across the river. Under heavy fire, the ships dropped back to the river mouth and lay at anchor for weeks, while the inhabitants of Londonderry despaired. Wrote one, in his diary, "Next Wednesday is our last, if relief does not arrive before it."

Relief did arrive, on the very next day. Two supply ships and the frigate *Dartmouth* came up the river, engaged in a bloody duel with the batteries at the ends of the boom, and forced their way through to hard-pressed Londonderry. Three days later, the besiegers gave up after 105 days of constant pressure and withdrew their forces, not only from Londonderry but also from Enniskillen.

In June, 1690, King William at last led his army to Ireland, to suppress the revolt that had been going on there for more than a year. At his appproach, James and his Irish allies fell back to a strong position on the bank of the River Boyne, near Drogheda.

King William, never one to shrink from personal danger, was guilty of a foolhardy act which almost cost him his life. Reconnoitering with a small group of companions, he rode into an ambush. A concealed cannon was discharged at him at point-blank range. The ball struck the king in the right shoulder, ripping away cloth and flesh and hurling him to the ground. Despite his painful wound, he quickly leaped to his feet, remounted his horse, and fled. Bullets filled the air around him, but he managed to escape.

The next day, against the advice of his doctors, King William led his troops into battle. Grasping his sword in his left hand and guiding his horse with his half-crippled right, he led the charge against the enemy position. James fled from the field and from Ireland, once more taking refuge in the court of France.

Before the end of July, 1690, the French-backed Irish revolt against King William and Queen Mary was over.

9.

While King William and his father-in-law were contending in Ireland for the English throne, important affairs were taking place in other areas.

The Battle of Bantry Bay had been fought by two nations which were, technically at least, at peace. Obviously, under the conditions, the peace could not last long. The battle itself, the open encouragement given by King Louis XIV to former King James, and the presence of French troops among the Irish forces supporting the pretender all served to nudge England and France toward a state of open war. The war was formally declared on May 7, 1689, about a week after the affair at Bantry Bay.

In declaring war, England was entering more than a mere struggle with France. For some time, Louis XIV had been at war with the Holy Roman Empire, Bavaria, Saxony, the Palatinate, Sweden, and Spain—a group of nations which had banded together and had formed a defensive alliance, the League of Augsburg, to check French aggression. Now King William was adding his own two nations, England and the Netherlands, to the ring of enemies surrounding mighty France. In Europe, this struggle was known as the War of the League of Augsburg. In the English colonies in America, to which it eventually spread, it was simply called King William's War.

10.

When King William departed for Ireland, leaving the conduct of his government in the hands of Queen Mary, King Louis XIV thought he saw his chance to bring about an invasion of England. Word was sent to the commander of the French squadron at Toulon to take his ships to Brest and join the larger squadron there under the Count de Tourville. Thus reinforced, Tourville would then set about to clear the Channel of English sea power.

The English, meanwhile, were doing much of Tourville's work for him. Their fleet was being divided and sent away in various directions. A squadron under Sir Cloudesley Shovell had already gone to Ireland with King William. Another squadron, under Rear Admiral Edward Russell, was now detached for the purpose of escorting Queen Maria Anna of Spain to meet her husband, King Charles II, to whom she had just been married by proxy. When this errand should be completed, Russell was instructed to sail on to Toulon and blockade the French squadron stationed there. The departure of these two squadrons left the Earl of Torrington (the former Admiral Herbert) with only fifty-seven warships, including twenty-two Dutch vessels under Lieutenant-Admiral Cornelis ("Devil") Evertsen. It was hardly an adequate fleet with which to control the Channel and repel a threatened invasion.

From the very first, Queen Maria Anna proved to be a difficult passenger. As a spoiled Austrian princess, she was accustomed to having her own way. Having heard of the physical ugliness, the imbecility, and the lasciviousness of her new husband, she was in no hurry to meet him in person. Consequently, she made Admiral Russell's life miserable with not-to-be-ignored royal demands to take this detour and that. Adverse weather further complicated the problem. By the time the fleet had reached Spain, had deposited its capricious passenger, and had hastened on to Toulon, the French squadron had long since departed and was well on its way to Brest.

While the English had been dividing their naval forces, the French had succeeded in consolidating theirs.

11.

On June 13, 1690, the Count de Tourville sailed from Brest with seventy-two large men-of-war—the most powerful French fleet that had ever put to sea. After nine days of reconnoitering, he anchored his ships in a bay near the southwestern tip of the Isle of Wight. It so happened that Torrington's English fleet was anchored in another bay near the eastern end of the island. During the night of the 22nd, neither commander knew of the near presence of the other.

With the dawn came word to each commander that the enemy was near at hand. Torrington called a conference of his officers, English and Dutch. Together, they decided that they were not strong enough to risk a decisive battle. Timorous as this decision sounds, it was backed by good reasoning. Should the smaller English-Dutch fleet engage and meet disaster, the way was wide open for a French invasion of the British Isles. As long as there was an English fleet-in-being, able to fight even against odds, King Louis would be in no position to launch a sea-borne invasion, which might be intercepted and annihilated.

With these thoughts in mind, the Earl of Torrington put to sea and sailed slowly eastward along England's southern coast. The French followed, looking for a favorable chance to engage in battle.

Word reached Queen Mary in London concerning the conduct of her fleet. Her husband was away in Ireland, fighting valiantly for their throne. Here was her chance to strike a blow. Knowing nothing about strategy and little about the sea, she at once dispatched a peremptory message to Admiral Torrington to stop his retreat and to fight the French. He had no recourse but to obey.

On the morning of June 30, the English fleet turned upon its ene-mies, some ten or twelve miles south of the promontory known as Beachy Head. With the wind in his favor and a sound plan in mind, the Earl of Torrington bore down upon Tourville's long line of French ships. The English admiral had strengthened his rear division at the expense of the center. What he planned was to hold his van—the twenty-two Dutch ships under Evertsen—and his weakened center away from the French line while sending his strengthened rear divi-sion in to crush the rear of the French formation. Under the circum-stances, such a maneuver presented the least risk and the greatest chance of victory.

As so often happens, things did not work out precisely as planned. Torrington was about to swing his central section to starboard, away from the French, when he saw a wide gap open in the French line. His first impulse was to lead his ships through the gap, thus severing the French formation. The orders had been given and the swing toward the gap had begun when he thought better of it, decided to retain his original battle plan, and bore away to cannonade at long range.

For some reason never made clear, Evertsen, in the English-Dutch van, swung his twenty-two ships to port and engaged the French at close range. Perhaps he had misunderstood the original plan because of the difference in languages or had been misled by Torrington's im-petuous swing to port instead of starboard. More likely, this youngest of the fighting Evertsen dynasty simply preferred to fight the kind of close-up, slam-bang action to which he had long been accustomed. Whatever the reason, his ships took a frightful mauling, not only from the strong French van but also from some ships of the French center which hastened forward, little impeded by Torrington's long-range fire. Disaster threatened when the leading ships of the French van drew ahead of Evertsen's formation and doubled around it. It seemed certain that the Dutch squadron would be surrounded and annihi-lated. Then, all at once, the wind died out completely.

As the sudden calm froze the ships into immobility, the Earl of Torrington hoisted the signals that saved his fleet. Leaving their sails aloft to flap in the dying breeze, all of the English and Dutch ships dropped their anchors.

The Count de Tourville, misled by the flapping sails, did not at first appreciate what had been done. As a result, the French vessels, drifting with the tide, moved steadily farther away from the stationary Dutch and English ships. Before the French fleet could come to anchor, it was out of cannon range.

During the night, a breeze sprang up, and Torrington got his fleet under way. A number of dismasted ships were taken in tow. The French followed, gradually closing the gap. Fearing the results of another engagement, the English admiral set his disabled ships on fire and cast them loose. He then retreated eastward through the Channel and took refuge in the Thames, pulling up all the channel buoys to keep the French from following him in.

The battle off Beachy Head had been an undoubted French victory. Counting the disabled ships fired and abandoned, the Earl of Torrington had lost nine vessels, most of them from the Dutch division of his fleet. The French had not lost a ship and had established at least partial control of the Channel. On the other hand, the English-Dutch fleet still existed in sufficient strength to make the cross-Channel invasion a risk which Louis XIV dared not assume.

Fortunately for English morale, word of King William's victory on the Boyne arrived close upon the heels of the discouraging naval news. As a result, people tended to talk about the victory on land and to disregard the defeat at sea.

Not King William, though! No sooner was he back in England than the startled Earl of Torrington found himself the subject of a full-fledged court-martial. Somehow, the king could not avoid the suspicion that his English admiral had deliberately sacrificed his good Dutch sailors while personally staying out of danger. As a Dutchman born and bred, the king was sickened by the thought. The Earl spoke eloquently in his own behalf and managed to convince the court that he had acted blamelessly and in the best interests of the country. He was acquitted. The king, however, would not be mollified. Never again was the Earl of Torrington entrusted with a command.

12.

For the English and the Dutch, 1691 was a year of building and strengthening. For the French, it was a year of successfully wielding the advantage gained at Beachy Head.

It was the urbane and likeable Comte de Tourville who directed the naval fortunes of France during this magnificent year which saw no battle. The French navy was everywhere, yet nowhere. It convoyed and protected French commerce. It raided English and Dutch shipping, creating despair in London and in Amsterdam. It carried troops and agents to and from Ireland. Where the enemy was weak, it was sure to appear. Where the enemy was strong, there was not a sign of a French vessel. By early summer, the English and Dutch had built up greater naval power than the French, but it did them little good. They swept the seas in vain, searching for the will-o'-the-wisp Comte and his ships of war. As Mahan expressed it: "The year 1691 was distinguished by only one great maritime event. This was ever afterward known in France as Tourville's 'deep-sea' or 'offshore' cruise, and the memory of it, as a brilliant strategy and tactical display, remains to this day in the French navy."

Ex-King James had not yet given up hope of retaking England. With his powerful host, Louis XIV, he gathered an army of 30,000 men and numerous boats on the shore of the bay known as La Hogue. With the help of the French fleet, James was certain that this force would cross the narrow Channel and take England. So sure was he of success that he issued a Declaration, condemning his enemies in England and reaffirming his own unvarying rightness.

The Declaration was a mistake. Queen Mary—who was once more in charge during her husband's absence in Holland—had it reprinted and widely published. Its greatest impact was upon the officers of the English fleet, which James had once commanded. Many an officer who had somewhat favored the cause of his old commander and former king was affronted by the arrogance of the Declaration. Admiral Russell spoke for many when he rebuffed James's emissary with the words: "He takes the wrong way with us. Do not think that I will let the French triumph over us in our own sea. Understand this, that if I meet them, I fight them, aye, though His Majesty himself should be on board."

13.

The Comte de Tourville, meanwhile, was having his troubles trying to assemble the French fleet at its point of rendezvous—the island of Ushant, off the tip of the Brittany Peninsula. The Mediterranean squadron ran into westerly gales which prevented it from passing through the Strait of Gibraltar; two great ships were wrecked in the attempt. These same gales kept the Brest squadron pinned in port. Finally King Louis XIV, in a childish fit of impatience, sent his Grand Admiral unmistakable orders: "You are to engage the enemy, whether they be strong or weak, wherever you can find them."

Tourville knew that it was folly to obey the orders, for without his two missing squadrons he had but forty-four ships with which to oppose more than twice as many warships in the enemy's combined fleet. He protested, and was told: "It is not for you to discuss the orders of the King! It belongs to you to execute them and to enter the Channel." The Grand Admiral shrugged. After the Battle of Beachy Head he had been criticized for timidity. He would not be so criticized again!

About the middle of May, the combined English-Dutch fleet, ninety-nine vessels strong, sailed eastward from the Thames. Off Barfleur, they encountered Tourville and his forty-four. Surely, with odds of 9 to 4 against them, the Frenchmen would flee. Instead, they bore up bravely to the attack, to the consternation of the Dutch, who began to suspect that there might be something to these rumors of collusion within the English fleet. At this point, there was nothing to do but to fight hard and hope for the best. Dutch Admiral Van Almonde led his ships into position at the head of the allied line.

Actually, Admiral Van Almonde had no cause for worry. The English officers, stung by the implication of disloyalty in James's Declaration and the subsequent rumors, were determined to fight brilliantly to erase the stain. Russell had issued a most unusual order to his crews: "If your commanders play false, overboard with them! And with myself, the first!"

Considering the odds against him, Tourville fought a brilliant battle. His plan of action was much like that which Torrington had tried and failed to carry out at Beachy Head—to thin out his van and keep it largely disengaged at long range while massing the greater part of his fleet against the rear of the allied line. The wind being in his favor, he was able to open the action exactly as he had planned.

Soon after the firing began, the wind died out, thus largely freezing the two fleets into position. At this point, the Dutch had been trying to close with the spaced-out French van with the thought of doubling around it. They were foiled and had to content themselves with long-range cannonading. At the rear of the English line, Vice-Admiral Ashby had succeeded in cutting off the last five French ships and had them in full flight when the calm stopped him on the far side of the French line. In the rear, as in the van, the dying of the wind brought virtually a cessation of hostilities.

In the center, it was quite the other way. Here, the two fleets had come to rest only about half a musket shot apart, within easy cannon range. Though the ships could not move, the calm sea provided steady gun platforms from which the gunners were able to deal out frightful punishment.

In the midst of the heaviest fighting lay two of France's greatest ships: Tourville's flagship *Soleil Royal* (104 guns) and the *Ambitieux* (90). These were two of the most gaudily decorated sailing ships ever to take to sea; today, they were demonstrating that they carried guns as well as sculptured figures, elaborate carvings, and gold paint. They fought magnificently.

Admiral Russell had succeeded in massing a number of his best ships, including his flagship *Britannia* (100), against these two French titans. At one point, the *Soleil Royal* and the *Ambitieux* found themselves exchanging broadsides with nine English vessels, two of which presently went down under the heavy French cannonading. In time, the situation eased. Other French ships came drifting up on the slack waters, drawing the English fire and enabling Tourville to launch boats with which to tow his blood-soaked and badly damaged flagship out of action.

About three o'clock in the afternoon, after four hours of heavy action, a fog closed in, hiding the rival battle lines and making effective cannon fire impossible. Both fleets promptly dropped anchor where they were. During the next two hours, the only action revolved around the ships of Vice-Admiral Ashby, who was worried by his detached position on the far side of the French fleet and attempted the difficult and dangerous feat of drifting through the enemy's line in order to return to his proper position. This resulted in a series of furious brief actions in the fog, as one of Ashby's ships would suddenly drift into sight of one of the anchored French vessels, exchange broadsides with it, then drift quietly on and be lost to sight. Eventually, the lost squadron succeeded in getting through, though with the loss of one ship-of-the-line, eight fireships, and large numbers of men.

We should pause at this point to pay tribute to Ashby's second-in-command, Rear Admiral Richard Carter, for a display of two very different types of heroism. Of all the high English naval officers, he was the most suspected and the most frequently and bitterly accused of disloyalty, for it was well known that he had attended meetings of Jacobites planning the return of James to the throne. He had borne the accusations with what many regarded as "a guilty silence." Now, as his ship exchanged shots with a fog-shrouded French vessel, he fell to the deck, mortally wounded. He refused to be carried below—refused, even, to relax his grip upon his sword. His last words were: "Fight the ship! Fight the ship as long as she can swim!"

Long after his death, the truth about Rear Admiral Carter was revealed. Far from being disloyal, he had served as a martyr for the cause of William and Mary. It was at King William's suggestion that he had wormed himself into the Jacobite group, attending the meetings so that his king could learn who was loyal and what was afoot. This was a secret which he could not share with anyone. He must have believed that it would die with him.

After two hours of fog, a breeze sprang up from the east, clearing the air and giving the English-Dutch fleet the weather gauge. At this, Tourville ordered a general retirement, his ships making for the shelter of the Cotentin Peninsula and the Bay of La Hogue, where Louis and James and their armies were still awaiting the opportunity to launch their invasion. The English and Dutch tried to close, and there was more furious fighting. Several attempts to board the shattered *Soleil Royal* were beaten off, though Tourville was at last forced to transfer his flag to the less-damaged *Ambitieux*.

The fog rolled in again in the early evening, once more putting an end to the fighting. In this first day of the Battle of La Hogue, the French had more than held their own. They had sunk three English ships-of-the-line and had lost none of their own, though a number had been badly damaged. Losses in manpower had been heavy on both sides, though only the English had lost an officer of flag rank. Had the battle ended at this point, it would certainly have been regarded as a French victory.

The Comte de Tourville had done his utmost against tremendous odds. His problem now was to save his fleet from destruction. With this in mind, he signaled a general retirement to the protected harbors of Brest and St. Malo. The English and the Dutch, stung by their earlier rebuff, now pressed hard in pursuit, seeking to destroy King Louis' fleet.

Despite adverse winds and tides, inopportune calms, and the efforts of the pursuers, seven French ships managed to round the Cotentin Peninsula and its fringe of offshore islands and escaped to Brest. Twenty-five ships were herded into the shallow bay on which stood the unprotected little port of Cherbourg. Three of these, including the battered *Soleil Royal,* ran aground and were subsequently burned by the English. The other twenty-two escaped through a daring feat of seamanship. Guided by a skilled French pilot, Hervé Riel, they passed through the swirling currents of the treacherous and rock-studded Race of Alderney and escaped to St. Malo. Neither threats nor the offering of huge rewards could tempt a single English or Dutch captain to venture into that dreaded graveyard of ships in pursuit.

The remaining twelve ships of Tourville's fleet, including his new flagship *Ambitieux,* found themselves cornered in the large bay of La Hogue, where the armed forces of Louis and James covered the shore. These ships were beached in front of two French forts, whose heavy guns were counted upon to protect them from all harm.

Sir George Rooke, who had broken the boom at Londonderry, was now given an even more daring assignment. With a flotilla of ketches, ships' boats, and fireships, he led a raid on the six ships beached before one of the forts. Disregarding the inaccurate fire from the fort and sweeping away a flotilla of small French boats which came out to meet him, he pressed to the attack. There was heavy fighting on the decks of the grounded ships and on the beaches. At one point, English sailors armed with boathooks found themselves assailed by saber-wielding French cavalry. To their joy, they found that a boathook is ideally suited for pulling a horseman from his mount. The six grounded warships were burned.

The next morning, Rooke and his raiders were back. It was much the same story, varied only by more effective fire from the second French fort. The English sailors managed to train the guns of some of the grounded French ships on the fort, blast its cannons into silence, then burn the ships and escape.

It is said that King James, watching this struggle which doomed his hopes of invading England, could not resist crying out: "See my brave English sailors! How they fight!" The reaction of King Louis to this outburst has not been recorded, but can well be imagined.

As a classic example of locking the barn door after the horse had been stolen, Louis XIV subsequently saw to it that Cherbourg was fortified and shielded by a seawall. Had this been done before the Battle of La Hogue, he would not have lost his ships.

14.

King Louis XIV was remarkably philosophical about the disaster which his fleet had suffered. When next he met the Comte de Tourville, at Versailles, he exclaimed: "I was so happy to hear that with forty-four of my warships you fought for a whole day against ninety-nine of my enemies' ships that I feel no unhappiness over the loss I have experienced." Apparently, he meant it, too. Within a few months, Tourville was honored by being made a Marshal of France. In a more practical field, Louis set his shipyards to work to rebuild the weakened fleet.

The Comte de Tourville put his refurbished fleet to very effective use in June of 1693. Lying in wait in the Bay of Lagos, near Cape St. Vincent, he intercepted a rich fleet of four hundred English and Dutch merchant ships being convoyed from Smyrna by Sir George Rooke, commanding twenty-three ships-of-the-line. When Rooke realized that he was facing ninety major French warships, he ordered his convoy to scatter while he did his best to protect them with his comparatively feeble force. His best was not good enough. After losing three warships, he ceased his efforts and fled. The French pursued the merchant vessels, capturing forty and sinking fifty more that tried to resist. The loss to England from this one raid was placed at a million pounds, sterling.

Now that he had achieved success upon the sea, Louis XIV lost interest and permitted his great fleet to go to pieces. The warships were used in small groups for raiding commerce. In this, they were aided and abetted by a picturesque band of privateers, working out of the ports of St. Malo, Dunkirk, Calais, Dieppe, and Le Havre. Among the most famous and successful of these semipiratical naval heroes were Jean Bart, Baron Pointis, and Rene Duguay-Trouin. Against their lightning-like raids, the naval might of England and the Netherlands could do little.

The logical antidote for the privateer raids was the destruction of the ports from which the raiders sailed. In November, 1693, Commodore Sir John Benbow appeared off the waterfront of St. Malo with a fleet consisting of twelve ships-of-the-line, four special mortar ships, ten smaller warships, and a specially equipped vessel of shallow draft called a galiot. This was much like the "Hell-burners" which had so terrified the Spaniards at Antwerp. Its hold was loaded with one hundred barrels of gunpowder, around which were packed chunks of iron, pieces of chain, stones, and other objects calculated to spread destruction.

The galiot was held in reserve for three days, while the cannons and mortars of the warships hammered at the town. When at last it was sent in, the plans went wrong. Instead of lodging against the sea wall, it ran on a rock some distance from both the sea wall and the town. At closer range, the explosion might have been devastating. As it was, it blew down part of the wall, wrecked a number of houses, and killed some citizens. From a military or naval point of view, it accomplished nothing.

A year later, a similar attempt was made to destroy Dunkirk. This time, the fleet brought in by Sir Cloudesley Shovell and Sir John Benbow contained not one but seventeen "Hell-burners." Some of these were laden with explosives. Others—the so-called smoak boats—were soaked with chemicals which, when burned, produced a choking and poisonous smog. Though these devices proved inconvenient to the inhabitants of the town and to certain of the English seamen who happened to get downwind, they were not very successful.

The same sort of activity was attempted against both Dunkirk and St. Malo in 1695, with similar results.

The only other noteworthy naval activities of the war consisted of a raid by Baron Pointis on Cartagena, in South America, and of the use of French warships to blockade Barcelona, Spain, during its siege by the French army. Though both endeavors were successful—the Cartagena raid netting the French nine million pounds in Spanish gold—neither was a notable achievement in naval warfare.

Though the war sputtered out upon the sea, it continued to be fought with vigor on the land, as the army of William III struggled to prevent the superior French forces from sweeping over the Netherlands. In the end, William was successful. By the terms of the Treaty of Ryswick, signed in 1697, all of the French conquests were restored except for a few small towns along the fringes of the Netherlands. Louis also agreed to drop his support of James and to acknowledge William's right to the English throne, despite the death of Queen Mary from smallpox in 1694.

The French King's expensive bid for empire and glory had netted him neither.

15.

King William died in March, 1702, having outlived his arch-rival, James, by less than six months. His successor had already been chosen, for in 1701 Parliament had passed the Act of Settlement to straighten out the dynastic tangle caused by the death of Queen Mary without children. By the terms of this law, William was to be followed on the throne by Queen Mary's sister Anne—the other of James's Protestant daughters. Should Queen Anne die childless, the throne was to go to her cousin, Princess Sophia of Hanover, and/or to her descendants.

The death of King William added further complications to an already explosive situation in Europe. King Charles II of Spain had died without children, leaving his throne to Philip of Anjou, who happened to be a grandson of Louis XIV. The thought of one all-powerful royal family holding the thrones of both France and Spain proved alarming in the extreme to the statesmen of all other European nations. Austria, Prussia, and the Holy Roman Empire were groping toward an agreement for concerted resistance. Now Louis helped them solve their problem by announcing his support of Prince James—Catholic son of James II—as next ruler of England. Almost at once, England and the Netherlands joined the other opponents of France, and the War of the Spanish Succession began. In the American colonies, it became known as Queen Anne's War.

Nominally, Queen Anne's husband, Prince George of Denmark, was Lord High Admiral of the English fleet. Actually, Sir George Rooke exercised direct control. The revised edition of *Fighting Instructions* which he issued must have proved satisfactory, for it remained in use with no basic change for almost one hundred years.

Though the War of the Spanish Succession involved much land action, there was little fighting on the sea. We shall, as usual, confine ourselves to the naval aspects alone.

On August 19, 1702, Vice-Admiral John Benbow, commanding a squadron of ten English ships-of-the-line in the Caribbean, sighted a squadron of ten large French warships under the command of Admiral Jean Baptiste Ducassé. The French fled, with Benbow's fleet in pursuit. On that day and the next, there was some desultory fighting at long range, but it was not until two o'clock of the morning of the 24th that the leading English ship, Benbow's flagship *Breda* (70), drew close enough to the last ship in the French formation to make an attempt at capture. Without waiting for daylight or for his other ships, Benbow launched an all-out attack.

Admiral Benbow was a rough, tough fighting man, as disdainful of the enemy as he was of the feelings of those who served under him. It was a bad combination. Having riddled and crippled the lagging French ship, he tried to lead a boarding assault, only to be repelled with a bullet in his face. Once more he tried to board, this time being wounded in the arm. Despite his wounds, he made a third attempt. This time, a chain shot smashed his right leg. Even so, he would not relinquish his command, but continued to give orders while lying on the deck.

Dawn revealed the other ships of the French squadron returning to the rescue of their companion. This was bad, but far worse was the sight of the other English vessels drawing away to avoid action. Admiral Benbow's signals to engage the enemy were ignored. The French arrived, bombarded the *Breda* mercilessly, then sailed away, towing the disabled vessel which Benbow had so nearly captured. Not until they were safely out of range did the other English vessels return.

Though mortally wounded, Admiral Benbow still wished to pursue and attack the enemy. His captains, whom he summoned to his side, flatly refused, saying that from what had already taken place he should be able to see that nothing could be done against so strong an enemy. They made no mention of their own insubordination. The unhappy admiral was compelled to give up the pursuit.

As he lay dying in Jamaica, Admiral Benbow received a most unusual communication from his late enemy:

Sir:
I had little hopes on Monday last but to have supped in your cabin [as your prisoner], but it pleased God to order it otherwise. I am thankful for it. As for those cowardly captains who deserted you, hang them up, for by God they deserve it!

Yours,
DUCASSÉ

Vice-Admiral John Benbow did not live to "hang them up," but in due time the English Admiralty took care of the situation. The four captains chiefly responsible for the insubordination were summoned to stand court-martial. One died before the court convened, one was cashiered out of the service, and two were shot.

16.

While Admiral Benbow was meeting discouragement and death in the Caribbean, Sir George Rooke was commanding an expedition of 150 ships and 15,000 troops against Cadiz. The great Spanish port city proved too tough a nut to crack. Rooke was unhappily contemplating the results of failure when news arrived which gave him the best of excuses to abandon the siege.

The French fleet against which Benbow had fought in vain had been sighted off the Spanish coast, escorting a rich convoy toward Vigo. At once, Admiral Rooke dropped his siege operations and embarked, sailing northward in the hope of intercepting the convoy at sea. He was too late. When he reached Vigo, the French ships were already in the harbor, which was closed by a boom of floating logs protected by the guns of five anchored ships-of-the-line.

Sir George Rooke was in no mood to face the consequences of a second failure. A special squadron was created, consisting of twenty-five of his best warships plus assorted fireships and bomb ketches. Headed by the ship-of-the-line *Torbay,* the warships headed for the harbor under full sail. Under the impact of the *Torbay*'s heavy bow, the boom parted, and the English warships poured through the gap. At once, a flaming battle spread to all parts of Vigo Harbor.

Rooke's foresight presently paid off. While the ships had been attacking the harbor mouth, a landing force had been quietly going ashore near Vigo and advancing toward the town. On the piers, Spanish soldiers and stevedores were frantically unloading the cargo of twenty million pieces-of-eight, to prevent their capture when the inevitable English naval victory should be complete. They should not have worked so hard. Six million coins still remained in the treasure ship when the battle reached it, and it was burned and sunk. These six million were all that the Spaniards ever recovered. The fourteen million which they had labored so mightily to unload were captured by the English landing force and were borne away as spoils of war.

The taking of Vigo was a genuine triumph for the English navy and for Admiral Sir George Rooke. Of the seventeen French warships in the harbor, seven were sunk and ten captured. Three Spanish warships were also destroyed. Four Spanish galleons, including the treasure ship, were sunk, and nine were taken with their cargoes intact.

17.

In December, 1703, England signed a trade treaty with Portugal. Besides providing good markets for both English and Portuguese goods, this treaty also made the Portuguese seaports available as bases from which the English fleet could operate. Admiral Rooke immediately took advantage of the situation by taking his fleet to Lisbon for supplies and refitting.

Having erased his failure at Cadiz by his victory at Vigo, Rooke sailed early in 1704 for the purpose of taking Barcelona. Besides his naval force, he took with him a corps of 5,000 German troops under the command of the Prince of Hesse-Darmstadt.

Barcelona, like Cadiz, resisted all English and Hessian efforts. Admitting failure, Admiral Rooke lifted the siege early in the summer and sailed westward toward Lisbon, smarting under the realization that once more he had a defeat on his record which had to be erased.

To leave the Mediterranean, it was necessary to pass the strategically located Spanish stronghold of Gibraltar. Luck was with Admiral Rooke, for there was only a single small warship in the harbor, and the fort was undermanned, being garrisoned by only fifty-six Spanish soldiers and about one hundred militiamen, under Admiral Diego de Salinas. Here was a prize worth taking! After consultation with his chief subordinates, Sir Cloudesley Shovell, Admiral George Byng, and Dutch Admiral Van der Dussen, Rooke sent his fleet in against the defenses of Gibraltar.

For three days, the English and Dutch vessels pounded the shore batteries and the forts. The softening up was effective. When the Hessian soldiers went ashore, there was little resistance. On July 24, 1704, the Spanish flag was hauled down at Gibraltar. Though the conquest was made in the name of "King Charles of Spain," meaning Archduke Charles of Austria, whom the English were supporting for the Spanish throne, it was, in effect, an English conquest. "King Charles" never ruled, and England kept "the Rock." No other conquest in her history has done more for England's power and prestige.

Rooke's campaigning along the Spanish coasts had been greatly facilitated by the inconsistent policy of King Louis XIV. Faced with an economic pinch, the French king had decided to forgo needed repairs and replacements in his fleet in order to concentrate on building up powerful land forces with which to meet those of the English Duke of Marlborough. The fleet had suffered and had remained largely inactive.

The seizure of Gibraltar brought home to Louis the short-sightedness of his position. This was serious! England was now in a position to block off the strait and keep the French fleets based at Brest and Toulon from uniting for concerted action. Early in August he sent out his Toulon squadron of about fifty ships-of-the-line, plus some smaller auxiliaries, under the command of the Count of Toulouse, one of his numerous illegitimate sons.

On August 13, 1704, the French fleet encountered Rooke's squadron off Malaga. The two fleets were of almost exactly equal strength. Rooke, being a Formalist, resolved to make this a classic battle in the Formalist tradition of a rigidly maintained battle line. Since the two fleets were sailing in parallel columns, with the English to windward, he ordered his ships to turn in unison and close with the French.

The maneuver of closing proved very trying to the English captains. Each had to turn directly toward the French line, thus exposing his ship to raking fire while his own guns would not bear. The French, meanwhile, were firing their broadsides, then wearing away, thus upsetting the English calculations and doing considerable damage. For hours, this type of maneuvering and countermaneuvering continued between the two fleets, without the loss of a single ship, though casualties were severe, especially on Rooke's battered vessels. When, toward nightfall, the wind shifted in favor of the French, the Count of Toulouse made off with his fleet and returned to Toulon.

Each side claimed the victory, which neither fleet had clearly won. Actually, all that the Battle off Malaga proved was that when two opposing fleets follow the strict Formalist line, neither is likely to win a decisive victory.

18.

Nothing of note happened on the sea for two and a half years after the drawn battle off Malaga. On the land, though, the English did well. On the very day when Rooke and the Count of Toulouse were exchanging broadsides, the army led by the Duke of Marlborough and

Prince Eugene of Savoy smashed the French at Blenheim. Barcelona was taken in October, 1705, by Lord Peterborough. The following May, Marlborough scored another victory at Ramillies. The glory and the conquests of which Louis XIV was perpetually dreaming seemed constantly to recede from his clutching fingers.

Sir Cloudesley Shovell had now succeeded Sir George Rooke in command of the British[1] fleet in the Mediterranean. In July, 1707, the French naval base of Toulon was under siege by the army led by Prince Eugene of Savoy. Sir Cloudesley Shovell closed the ring by bringing up his fleet and attacking from the sea. Toulon failed to yield. As the garrison continued its fierce resistance, and as rumors spread of a strong French army coming to its relief, the British fleet and army ceased their efforts and went away.

Heading home for England and a furlough, Sir Cloudesley Shovell had the misfortune to run into a severe storm off the Scilly Islands. His flagship, the *Association,* ripped her bottom out on the rocks and went down in four minutes, with the loss of all hands. The *Eagle* and the *Romney,* other ships-of-the-line, suffered the same fate. In Admiral Shovell, Great Britain had lost one of her most able leaders.

The war, meanwhile, had spread to the American colonies, where it mainly manifested itself through terrifying but unimportant Indian raids. On only two occasions was there any naval activity.

Port Royal was considered to be the strongest and most important base in the French colony of Acadia. In September, 1710, a fleet of six regular British men-of-war, supplemented by thirty smaller ships from the New England colonies, set out to reduce the stronghold. The result was an anticlimax. The French, short of food and even shorter of spirit, would not resist. They eagerly snatched at the first terms of surrender offered them and tottered out, asking only to be fed. In honor of the Queen, Port Royal was renamed Annapolis. Acadia also received a new name—Nova Scotia.

---

[1] Thus far, we have used the terms "England" and "English," because the events described took place before May, 1707. In that month, the Act of Union was passed by the English and Scottish governments, uniting the countries of England and Scotland into the single country of Great Britain. From this point on, we shall speak of "Great Britain" and use the adjective "British" unless referring to something that happened before May of 1707 or unless speaking of something that applies only to that part of Great Britain known as England.

19.

Sir Francis Nicholson, who had conducted the successful invasion of Acadia, now became convinced that he could conquer all of Canada. With all possible speed, he traveled to England, where he succeeded in winning the members of Parliament to his views. Back he came, having been voted supplies, men, arms, and permission to use them for an invasion of Canada.

In July, 1711, an army under Nicholson started north from Albany. At about the same time, a fleet of fifteen ships-of-the-line and forty transports left Boston and sailed northeast under the command of Sir Hovenden Walker. After some delays off the Gaspé Peninsula, the ships at last entered the mouth of the St. Lawrence and started upstream toward Quebec.

The French never had to raise a hand in their own defense. During the night of August 22, a dense fog rolled in, borne by an easterly gale. In the blindness and confusion, eight ships lost their way and were crushed upon the rocks, with a loss of nearly 900 men. Shocked and discouraged, Walker turned his remaining ships around and left the river.

On his way home, the British admiral managed to rationalize his disaster into a fortunate accident. "Had we arrived safely in Quebec," he wrote in his report, "ten or twelve thousand men must have been left to perish of cold and hunger. By the loss of a part, Providence saved all the rest." To his surprise, nobody else was able to see the advantages of such an expedition.

The war finally came to an end in 1713, with the signing of the Treaty of Utrecht. The terms clearly favored Great Britain, who received from France the Hudson's Bay Territory, the island of St. Kitts, Newfoundland, and Acadia, and from Spain Gibraltar and the island of Minorca. In addition, France had to agree to destroy the fortifications of the pirates' nest at Dunkirk, and Spain had to grant to the British Royal African Company the right to supply Negro slaves for thirty years to the Spanish colonies in America. Finally, Philip of Anjou was permitted to occupy the Spanish throne, on the understanding that no one ruler was ever to govern both France and Spain. In return, Louis XIV agreed to recognize Queen Anne as the rightful ruler of Great Britain.

There was one more result of the War of the Spanish Succession. To quote Mahan: "England was *the* sea power; there was no second."

20.

After a reign of seventy-two years, King Louis XIV died in 1715. He had outlived his son and his grandson. As he lay dying, he called his five-year-old great-grandson to his bedside. "My child," he said, "you are going to be a great king. Do not imitate me in my taste for building, nor in my love of war. Strive, on the contrary, to live at peace with your neighbors. . . . Make it your endeavor to ease the burden of your people, which I, unhappily, have not been able to do."

The advice was excellent, but it was a clear-cut case of "too little and too late." The child who would be Louis XV was too little to profit by it, and it was far too late for any such second thoughts to help the gaudy old spendthrift of Versailles. By his luxuries, his wars, and his quest for glory he had driven France to the verge of bankruptcy. He had spilled the blood and tears of a continent. The gains for which such a price had been paid were small indeed.

7 BRITANNIA RULES THE WAVES

⚓

1.

Queen Anne died in 1714. As cousin Sophia was already dead, the British crown went to Sophia's son George, of the German house of Hanover, in accordance with the terms of the Act of Settlement.

King George I never became an Englishman—never learned to speak English and never came to regard his British kingdom as more important than his little German state of Hanover. Handicapped by his inability to communicate with his English-speaking subjects, King George played little active part in politics and depended heavily upon his ministers to conduct the affairs of the country. Particularly did he depend upon Sir Robert Walpole, the leader of the dominant Whig party. As the most influential minister in the king's cabinet, Walpole became known as the first, or prime, minister—the first Prime Minister in British history.

George I died in 1727, after a dull but peaceful reign. During his thirteen years on the throne, Britain had traded and prospered and gained in strength.

King George II, who followed his father into power, was also a German at heart. He, too, neglected the government, with the result that Walpole and the prime ministers who followed him gained a stronger and stronger hold on the conduct of affairs. In time, the Prime Minister was to become the leading political figure in Great Britain.

2.

Though Sir Robert Walpole believed that Great Britain's best interests would be served by peaceful trade and the expansion of her commercial interests, he was unable to cope successfully with a growing clamor for war against Spain. The story back of this little war, which refused to remain little, makes an interesting study in mass hysteria.

Basically, the cause of the war was commercial jealousy between Spain and Great Britain. Spain had a rich empire in the warm lands of the Americas, an empire from which flowed an apparently inexhaustible supply of gold and silver. Trade with this empire was regulated by stringent laws. British merchants, smarting at their exclusion from so rich a market, did not hesitate to smuggle goods to the Spanish settlers overseas. The Spanish authorities, for their part, cracked down hard whenever they could catch a smuggler in the act. From these causes came the predisposition for war.

The excuse was furnished by a British ship captain named Jenkins. He appeared in a British seaport with one of his ears missing from the side of his head but present in his pocket. To all who would listen, Jenkins explained that the Spaniards had captured him and had sliced off one of his ears, bidding him take it to his king and to deliver the message that the same thing would have happened to King George himself, had he been present. The story spread throughout Britain, causing anger and excitement everywhere.

The Spaniards, too, had their atrocity story. An unnamed Spanish nobleman was said to have been captured by the British, who forced him to cut off his own nose and swallow it. A demand for revenge against the cruel British swept through Spain.

Prime Minister Walpole did his best to avert the war. Evidence was produced that Jenkins had actually lost his ear in England, as a punishment for thievery. "The Fable of Jenkins' Ear" was discussed in Parliament. It did no good. The public preferred to believe the atrocity stories. War was declared against Spain in October, 1739.

The War of Jenkins' Ear began badly for Great Britain. A zealous minister named José Patino had built the Spanish fleet into a powerful fighting force. At once it took to sea and began to capture British vessels in enormous numbers. A British fleet under Admiral Edward Vernon took Porto Bello, Panama, with great fanfare, but profited only to the extent of three small vessels captured and about $3000 in loot. Going after larger game, Vernon tried to take Cartagena, but was driven off with very heavy losses. An attempt to take Cuba also failed, after costing 1,800 casualties.

Commodore George Anson, meanwhile, was coasting along the Chilean shore with a small squadron of third- and fourth-raters. He took, looted, and burned the small Spanish town of Payta. Later, off Panama, he captured a richly laden galleon, from which he took about

$1,500,000 in treasure. By this time, the *Centurion* (60) was the only seaworthy ship in his squadron. In her, he completed his return voyage westward, around the world—the first such circumnavigation since Drake did it in 1577–1580 to escape the Spaniards.

Even counting Anson's one rich capture, the British gains from the War of Jenkins' Ear seem insignificant when compared to British losses of 20,000 men and 407 ships, mostly merchant vessels, during two years of fighting against the Spaniards.

3 .

While Great Britain and Spain were damaging each other in their little war, Frederick the Great was eyeing some lands belonging to neighboring Austria. Emperor Charles VI of Austria had died, leaving his throne to his daughter, Maria Theresa. It should be easy to take land away from this mere girl! First, Frederick tried peaceful means, offering to help the queen defend her territories against all comers if she would give him her province of Silesia. When she refused, Frederick's Prussian armies moved into Silesia. At the same time, French, Spanish, and Bavarian armies also attacked, hoping to win rich parts of "defenseless" Austria.

Since Great Britain was already fighting against Spain, the Spanish attack on Austria automatically brought Great Britain into this larger war as an ally of the Austrians. The War of the Austrian Succession (1740–48) was on. In the American colonies, it became known as King George's War.

The War of the Austrian Succession was principally fought upon the land by Austrian troops who defended their native soil with unexpected vigor and success. Some British troops saw limited action on the Continent, under the personal leadership of King George II. The victory which this able royal general won over the French at Dettingen in 1745 is notable as the last battle in which a King of Great Britain personally led his armed forces in the field.

The campaigns on the sea had little effect on the outcome of the war and exerted little impact on affairs in landlocked and embattled Austria.

In February, 1744, Admiral Thomas Matthews was cruising in the western Mediterranean with a British squadron consisting of twenty-eight large ships-of-the-line and a number of smaller vessels. Off Toulon, he sighted a combined Spanish and French fleet, also of twenty-eight ships, under French Admiral La Bruyère de Court and Spanish

Admiral Don Jose Navarro. The French-Spanish allies fled, with the British squadron in pursuit.

After two days of vain pursuit in light and tricky winds, Admiral Matthews was able to bring his van and center opposite the center and rear of the allied squadron. In the uncertain wind, he was able to gain no more. At last, in desperation, he hoisted the signal to engage and swung his van in against the center of the enemy's line. The British center engaged the allies' rear. The British rear, having not yet come up opposite any part of the enemy line, had no one to engage, but swung in nevertheless, thus going through the motions.

For about three hours, the engaged portions of the fleets battled indecisively, with the French van and the British rear completely disengaged from any enemy. Then, as Admiral Matthews detected what he thought was a doubling maneuver in the French van to enclose the head of his line, he broke off action and retired, having captured one Spanish ship.

Later, back in England, Admiral Matthews brought charges against Vice-Admiral Lestock, who had commanded the British rear division. It was Matthews' contention that Lestock should have hoisted all sails on his ships and moved forward to help the embattled divisions ahead of him, instead of continuing uselessly in line. Lestock answered that he could not do this, since the admiral's flagship was flying not only the signal to engage but also the signal to maintain the line ahead. He pointed out, moreover, that the current edition of *Fighting Instructions* emphasized the necessity for maintaining a single line unless otherwise specifically directed. He won acquittal. As a matter of fact, the charges backfired. It was Admiral Matthews who found himself cashiered out of the service.

4.

Following the loss of Acadia, the French had built for themselves a tremendous fortified base at Louisburg, on Cape Breton Island. Based on plans originally drawn up by the great Marquis de Vauban, this new "Gibraltar of the West" was a masterpiece of defensive ingenuity. So much French money was poured into its construction that King Louis XV pettishly exclaimed that he momentarily expected to see the tops of its walls appear over the horizon.

Louisburg quickly proved to be a thorn in the side of the British colonies. From its ample harbor, French ships fanned out on commerce-raiding expeditions which threatened the complete paralysis of colonial sea-borne trade. Petitions were sent to London for an expedition to attack Louisburg. His Majesty's government, pondering the thirty-foot-thick walls and the fort's reputation as the strongest spot in North America, declined to act.

The capture and destruction of the fishing village of Canseau (Canso) on the north shore of Nova Scotia by an expedition from Louisburg finally triggered some action. If Great Britain would not knock down this hornets' nest, the colonists would! An army of 3,250 men was enlisted from the New England colonies and New York, and a fleet of thirteen small, armed ships was put together, ten of them having been contributed by Massachusetts. With this little force, the volunteers sailed north in March, 1745, under the command of William Pepperrell of Maine. Neither "General" Pepperrell nor any of his men had had any experience at all in the conducting of a military expedition.

As a matter of fact, the expedition against Louisburg was not quite so foolhardy as it appeared. Prisoners released from there on parole had reported the defenses in bad repair, the food supplies inadequate, and the morale of the garrison low. Pepperrell and his men were counting on these conditions.

During most of April, the little squadron of colonial warships contented itself with blockading Louisburg. A few inbound French vessels were taken, and on April 18 the French frigate *Renommée* (36) was turned back in a blazing gun battle, her captain disconcerted by the number of little vessels which swarmed about him and by the boldness of their crews. Unable to enter the harbor and deliver her supplies, reinforcements, and dispatches, *Renommée* returned to France and gave King Louis his first news of the siege of Louisburg.

The British government, meanwhile, found its hand forced. Pepperrell's bold move, made without British aid or sanction, must not be permitted to fail. Word was rushed to Commodore Peter Warren to move his three ships north from the West Indies and cooperate with the expedition. On the way, the ship bearing the message encountered a fourth British warship, the frigate *Eltham* (40), escorting a merchant convoy. The frigate was detached and sent north to join the blockaders. The day after her arrival, Warren himself appeared, with the ship-of-the-line *Superbe* (60) and the two forty-gun frigates *Launceston* and *Mermaid*. With these powerful additions, the cork of the blockade was twisted in tight.

On April 30, General Pepperrell and his troops went ashore and began the formal, close-in siege. There was some sharp fighting in the taking of key outposts, but no general assault was attempted. It became a question of endurance—whether the defenders or the attackers could longer endure the privation and discomfort of the conditions under which they lived and fought. The safe arrival of a single ship bearing supplies, munitions, and reinforcements might well insure victory for the French defenders.

On May 19, Warren's four British warships more than proved their value. The French ship-of-the-line *Vigilant* (64), trying to get through to Louisburg, encountered the Massachusetts snow *Shirley* (20), and promptly attacked this lesser craft. *Shirley,* being no match for the monster, fled and led her pursuer to the *Mermaid.* Together, the frigate and the snow undertook a running fight against the *Vigilant,* which carried more and heavier guns than both of them. The sound of the cannonading attracted the *Superbe* and the *Eltham,* which joined in the fight. Surrounded by enemies, the *Vigilant* fought against odds for an hour, then surrendered. The supplies and munitions which were to have strengthened Louisburg went instead to the camp of the attackers.

The siege was prosecuted with vigor and imagination, and on June 17 the discouraged inhabitants of "the Gibraltar of the West" surrendered to the army of amateurs who had dared to move against their mighty walls. One may well wonder, though, how much success General Pepperrell and his New Englanders would have enjoyed without the timely, though reluctant, infusion of British sea power.

Leaving at Louisburg a strong though reluctant garrison—most of whom subsequently died there of disease and privation—Pepperrell sailed home by way of the island of St. John's, which he captured without difficulty. For his part in the endeavor, he was made a baronet. Captain Warren was promoted to the rank of Rear Admiral.

The success at Louisburg led to a plan to attack Quebec once again. Scarcely had the preparations gotten under way, early in 1746, when word was received of a fleet of forty French ships-of-the-line, heading westward for an invasion of the British colonies. At once, offensive preparations were discarded in favor of defense. The attack was awaited with the greatest of apprehension, but weeks went by and no French fleet appeared.

Not until after the war did the British colonists learn what had happened. The fleet had sailed all right, under the Duke d'Anville. From the start, it had been an unfortunate expedition. Fever had raged, killing many of the men, including the admiral. A great storm had scattered the ships, and some vessels had turned back. In October, fewer than half the ships, seaworn and undermanned, reached the coast of Nova Scotia. It was agreed by the captains that they could not take Louisburg, but they agreed to move against Annapolis—a decision which caused the new commanding officer, Vice-Admiral D'Estournel, to kill himself in despair. Under Admiral La Jonquière, the expedition approached Annapolis, only to turn back when it was learned that there were British warships in the harbor. Actually, there were only two, the third-rater *Chester* (54) and the Massachusetts snow *Shirley* (20). Discomfited by such a tiny force, the ill-starred French armada returned home, having accomplished nothing.

If these facts had been known in the spring and summer of 1746, there would have been far less wear and tear on the nerves of the seacoast inhabitants of North America.

5.

In the late fall of 1747, there occurred an event which should have served as a warning of things to come. Unfortunately for Great Britain, it was not evaluated at its true worth.

A British squadron, under Commodore Sir Charles Knowles, lay in Boston harbor. Additional crewmen were needed, so press gangs were sent ashore to round up able-bodied Boston citizens. This was accepted procedure in England, but in Boston, Massachusetts, it caused a tremendous furor.

Scarcely had the boats put off from the shore, bearing the kidnapped men, when an angry mob began to gather. A group of British naval officers, ashore seeing the town, was seized and held as hostages. Seeking to put down the disturbance, the Governor called out the militia. Far from attacking the rioters, the militiamen refused even to defend the Governor, who was forced to take refuge in a fortified building. Even when Commodore Knowles threatened to bombard the town, the mob stubbornly refused to release the hostages.

In the end, peace was restored through the holding of a town meeting. The British officers were released unharmed, but not until the newly impressed seamen had been brought ashore and set free. Commodore Knowles's squadron was forced to get along without the reluctant Bostonians.

For the first time, Boston had openly defied British authority and had gotten away with it.

6.

The French had not given up the idea of sending a strong expedition to the North American coast. In the spring of 1747, they assembled a large fleet of transports in which to carry troops for the reconquest of Louisburg. To guard this convoy, French Admiral La Jonquière had two ships-of-the-line and twelve frigates.

The British heard about the preparations in ample time. A fleet of twelve ships-of-the-line and a few smaller vessels was sent out under Admiral George Anson to intercept the French. Anson took a position off Cape Finisterre and waited. The time was not allowed to go to waste. As his fleet lay off the coast, Admiral Anson insisted that his captains and crews practice, over and over again, all of the maneuvers which they might be called upon to use in battle. This valuable activity, so self-evident to modern eyes, was regarded then as one of Anson's brilliant innovations.

On May 3, Admiral La Jonquière appeared, with his warships and transports. At the end of a running fight which lasted for about three hours, all but one of the French warships and six of the laden transports had been captured. Among the prisoners was no less a person than Admiral La Jonquière himself. Upon interrogation, it was learned that he was not only the commanding officer of the squadron but was also the newly appointed Governor-General of the French colonies in America. An important catch, indeed!

Careful training had paid a quick dividend. It paid another, shortly, when Admiral Anson became Lord Anson, Baron of Soberton.

7.

In October, 1747, French Commodore Des Herbieres de l'Etenduère set out from Toulon with nine ships-of-the-line and a few frigates to convoy a tremendous fleet of 250 merchant vessels, headed for the West Indies. Off Belle Isle, he was sighted by Rear Admiral Edward Hawke, commanding a British squadron of fourteen ships and some frigates. Despite the disparity in numbers, Commodore de l'Etenduère interposed his warships between the British and the convoy, ready to fight to the end and to sacrifice his squadron to insure the safety of his charges.

In the battle which followed, the victory went to Hawke, but most of the honor went to l'Etenduère. So fiercely did the French resist, and so savagely did they maul the British squadron, that the great convoy escaped intact, still guarded by the frigates. When at last the smoke clouds cleared, one French ship-of-the-line had been sunk and six had been captured. Two had escaped, including the French flagship *Tonnant* (80), which limped out of action without interference when Captain Thomas Fox of the *Kent* (64) misinterpreted signal flags directing him to pursue and take her. This was understandable in view of Admiral Hawke's *melee* tactics, which developed as a result of his initial signals for a general chase.

Melees produce victories, but they also produce confusion.

8.

The last important naval battle of the war took place in October, 1748, off Havana, Cuba. Rear Admiral Charles Knowles, in his flagship *Cornwall* (80), was leading a seven-ship British squadron when he encountered seven Spanish ships under Vice-Admiral Reggio. As in the case of the battle off Toulon, the British engaged before the head of their line had overtaken the lead ship of the Spanish line. As a result, the battle opened with two British ships not engaged. Though they eventually managed to join the action, the early stages of the fighting were conducted with the British at a distinct disadvantage.

At the very start, the *Cornwall* and the Spanish flagship *Africa* (74) became heavily engaged at close range. Both were badly damaged, the *Cornwall* so seriously that she had to drop out of the line for repairs. For some reason, Admiral Knowles chose to stay with his inactive flagship, rather than shift his flag to some less damaged vessel. While repairs were in process, the disabled Spanish *Conquistador* (64) came drifting by. Knowles was in no position to use his broadside guns against his damaged enemy, but he was not without resources. He had on board some 4.6-inch mortars, of a type developed by Baron van Coehoorn of the Netherlands for the discharge of explosive shells. Though the Coehoorn mortars were intended solely for the use of landing forces, Admiral Knowles tried the experiment of using them against the *Conquistador*. They were extremely effective. The Spanish ship was set on fire, and eventually she was forced to surrender.

After six hours of action, the Spanish squadron retired to Havana, leaving the *Conquistador* in British hands and the *Africa* burning and abandoned on the surface of the sea. It was a British victory, but not a very decisive one. Perhaps its most important result was the knowledge gained concerning the use of explosive shells against wooden warships.

The war came to an end in the same month as the battle off Havana. Of all the nations involved, only Prussia profited materially by the terms of the Treaty of Aix-la-Chapelle. Silesia was granted to Frederick the Great, who had taken it at the very beginning of the war. All other conquests made in the war were restored to their original owners. This included Louisburg, much to the disgust of the New England colonists. Maria Theresa was acknowledged the rightful ruler of Austria.

9.

The first three of the great wars for colonial possessions broke out in Europe and later spread to the American colonies. The fourth and greatest started in North America and soon spread throughout most of the world. In the American colonies, it was called the French and Indian War (1754–63). In Europe, where war was formally declared two years later, it was called the Seven Years' War (1756–63).

The immediate cause of the war was a dispute over the strategically important Ohio Valley, which was claimed by France as a part of the Louisiana Territory and by Great Britain on the basis that the Virginia colony's charter granted it lands "from sea to sea." Fighting broke out when the French built a string of forts in the valley and a Virginia real-estate company, the Ohio Company, tried to force the French to move. The British commander in the first little skirmishes of the war was a young Virginian named George Washington.

Since the end of the War of the Austrian Succession, Europe had been in a turmoil of shifting alliances as Maria Theresa sought to get friends who would help her regain Silesia from Frederick the Great. The strongest link in this chain of promises and half-promises was a secret treaty between Austria and Russia, directed against Prussia. Now, as word of the fighting in North America was received, Great Britain and France joined in the scramble for allies.

King George II of Great Britain first asked Maria Theresa of Austria to sign another treaty of alliance. She refused, for she felt that Britain's power, which was chiefly naval, had been of little use to her in the last war and would probably be no more useful in the next. The

British king then promptly turned about and suggested an alliance with his former enemy, Frederick the Great of Prussia, who was happy to agree.

King Louis XV of France had been counting on renewing his alliance with Frederick, and he was much distressed to learn that Frederick had joined his British enemies. In desperation, the French king then made an alliance with Maria Theresa of Austria. Thus Great Britain and France traded partners for this new war, in what is sometimes called the Diplomatic Revolution.

10.

It is amazing how much fighting went on between the British and the French before war was formally declared. The little battles among the colonists stimulated the French into sending a fleet of warships to the St. Lawrence, bringing troops and supplies to strengthen the garrisons in Canada. The British, to counter this move, sent out Vice-Admiral Edward Boscawen with a squadron of twenty-four ships-of-the-line. Boscawen failed to find the main body of the French expedition, but he stumbled upon four ships-of-the-line which had become separated. In a sharp action, two of these were captured. Two escaped and managed to reach the St. Lawrence. At about the same time, Admiral Hawke managed to intercept a rich convoy off Cape Finisterre. No less than 300 French merchant ships, laden with goods from the colonies, fell into his hands.

The French, meanwhile, were carrying on activities of their own. From Toulon in April, 1756, went out a fleet of twelve ships-of-the-line under the Marquis de la Galissonière, convoying 150 transports loaded with 16,000 troops. The objective was the British base of Minorca, defended by a small garrison under Lieutenant-General William Blakeney.

Great Britain moved at once to defend Minorca and to strengthen Gibraltar. Admiral Sir John Byng was sent out with ten ships-of-the-line. At Gibraltar, he picked up three more, then sailed for Minorca, hoping that he was not too late to save the garrison.

Admiral Byng was not too late. As his ships approached Minorca, he could see the British flag still flying over Fort St. Philip at Port Mahon. Bad luck, however, attended him. A calm area in the lee of the island prevented his immediate approach. Before the wind shifted, Galissonière's fleet appeared. Evidently, the French warships would have to be disposed of before Blakeney's garrison could be relieved.

It was noon the next day (May 18, 1756) before Byng managed to work out of the calm area and maneuver himself into the windward position he wanted. In forming his battle line, he detached his smallest ship, the *Deptford* (50), to lie to windward with his frigates and other auxiliaries and relay signals from his flagship, so that all ships might know at once what had been signaled. With this done, each battle line contained twelve ships.

Unfortunately, there were no signals to convey exactly what Admiral Byng had in mind, nor did the *Fighting Instructions* cover the case. It was his intention to slant his battle line toward the French, thus bringing on close action without exposing any ship to the raking fire invited by a bow-on approach. As his ships came about to approach, the division of six ships under his immediate command became the rear division, with the six ships under Rear Admiral Temple West serving as the van. West, not understanding what Byng intended, turned his division toward the French line and executed the bow-on approach, with all of its disadvantages of raking fire received and no fire at all given out. Byng's rear division, on the other hand, came slanting in toward the French, as he had wanted his whole fleet to do.

Everything went wrong. The *Intrepid,* last ship in West's division, lost her foremast and went out of control, swinging around squarely into the midst of Byng's second division. At once, the neat order of the slanted approach was broken up, as the ships veered out of line to prevent collision. While West's division went plowing doggedly on, taking its damage and its heavy casualties, Byng's second division was frantically maneuvering in an attempt to regain formation. Some of the Admiral's officers urged him to lead what ships he could into the action and disregard the rest. This he refused to do, for he had sat on the court which had found Admiral Matthews guilty of letting his ships straggle into action, and he had no desire to be found guilty of the same offense.

While Admiral Byng was still wrestling with the organization of his division, Galissonière withdrew his fleet to Port Mahon, leaving West's division badly battered and with heavy casualties on every ship. For two days, the British squadron hovered outside Port Mahon, hoping that the French would come out again. The French were not that foolish. They stayed safely in port and lent their weight to the attack on Fort St. Philip. At last, needing dockyard facilities to repair his six damaged ships, Admiral Byng sailed for Gibraltar, leaving Blakeney's garrison to its fate. By the time Admiral Hawke could come out to supersede Byng, it was too late to save Minorca.

Poor Admiral Byng soon found that he had stepped from the frying pan into the fire. In order to avoid a court-martial for a minor offense, he had brought on one for something far more serious. Though his brother officers cleared him of a charge of cowardice, he was found guilty of "not having done his utmost." The sentence was death! The unfortunate admiral was made to kneel on the quarter-deck of the ship *Monarch,* where a marine firing squad carried out the sentence of the court.

All of the battles described above took place while France and Great Britain were technically at peace. On June 16, 1756, war was formally declared between the two nations.

11.

The war, which had begun in the woodlands of western Pennsylvania, soon spread more widely than any previous conflict. Some historians, in fact, refer to it as the first of the true world wars. It was fought in North America, where the British tried to pry loose the French hold on Canada and the Mississippi Valley. It was fought in Europe, where a combination of nations tried in vain to snatch Silesia from the grasp of Frederick the Great. It was fought in India, where a young genius named Robert Clive contended first with the French, then with the ruler of Bengal and succeeded in adding "the brightest jewel to Britain's crown." And it was fought upon the seas, where Great Britain's ever-present naval power provided a decisive margin.

In the beginning, the Seven Years' War was a series of disasters for the British. Besides Byng's defeat and the loss of Minorca, there was bad news from other theaters of action. A strong British force under General Edward Braddock, advancing toward Fort Duquesne (where Pittsburgh, Pennsylvania, now stands), was ambushed by French and Indians and was annihilated. Soon afterward, the French took Oswego, on Lake Ontario, and Fort William Henry, near Lake George. In India, the British post at Calcutta was taken by the Bengalese, who locked a large number of captive Englishmen in a small room, where most of them died of suffocation—the infamous "black hole of Calcutta."

An able man was needed to give intelligent direction to the war. One was available in the person of William Pitt, the Elder. Though King George II disliked Pitt and prevented him from replacing the Duke of Newcastle as Prime Minister, he permitted him to become Secretary of State in charge of the War.

William Pitt the Elder put planning and intelligence into the British war effort. Though few troops were sent into Germany to help Frederick the Great, the Prussian leader was supplied with funds to hold his own well-trained forces together. Able British officers were promoted over their incompetent seniors in all areas of action. Plans were made to strike at the principal enemy, France, at the key points upon which her strength depended.

12.

One of William Pitt's pet projects was what he called "conjunct expeditions." Today, we would call them combined operations, or amphibious assaults. The new techniques involved had to be worked out experimentally, while the commanders learned by doing. An expedition in September, 1757, failed to take Rochefort, on the Bay of Biscay, though it did capture the island of Aix and added mightily to the experience and education of a number of young officers, including Captain Richard Howe of the Royal Navy and Lieutenant-Colonel James Wolfe of the British Army. In June, 1758, a conjunct expedition failed to take St. Malo, though the French lost more than one hundred privateer ships in the harbor. Two months later, Cherbourg was taken, looted, dismantled, and abandoned. A second expedition against St. Malo failed, resulting in a Dunkirk-type evacuation under strong French attack. All of these early applications of Pitt's new method were frankly experimental.

It was on the western side of the Atlantic that the "conjunct expeditions" really paid off. Louisburg had again become a menace to British shipping and to British safety in America. The garrison was now ten times as strong as it had been in 1745. This time it was no reasonable target for a small colonial expedition. A regular British army of 14,000 men was sent in transports convoyed by twenty-three ships-of-the-line and eighteen frigates under the command of Admiral Edward Boscawen. The lessons of the earlier expeditions were intelligently applied. Following a heavy barrage from the big guns of the ships, the soldiers went ashore in three perfectly timed landing operations directed at carefully selected spots. Though French fire and the boiling surf took well over one hundred men, the troops went ashore so quickly and forcefully that a large group of French defenders was cut off from Louisburg and captured. A formal, unhurried siege followed, carried on in perfect confidence that the Royal Navy would permit no French relief or reinforcements to arrive. Louisburg surrendered on July 27, 1758, after seven weeks of siege.

Though Lord Jeffrey Amherst had conducted the siege of Louisburg flawlessly, it was his second-in-command, Brigadier General James Wolfe, who had captured the attention of Pitt and the other British leaders. His bravery, coolness, and resourcefulness had been outstanding. Promoted to the rank of Major General, Wolfe was placed in charge of the far more important expedition against Quebec.

The Quebec expedition started with the worst possible stroke of misfortune. A French warship captured a small British vessel bearing the complete plans for the expedition. Thus French General Louis Joseph de Montcalm knew in advance that Major General James Wolfe would come up the St. Lawrence with 8,500 men in transports convoyed by twenty-three ships-of-the-line and thirteen frigates under the command of Admiral Charles Saunders. He also knew that a larger force under Lord Jeffrey Amherst was to come north through the Champlain Valley, taking Ticonderoga and Crown Point, was to bluff an attack at Montreal in order to draw defenders from Quebec, and was then to join Wolfe's army. Finally, he knew that a third force under General John Prideaux was to take Niagara and approach Quebec across Lake Ontario and down the St. Lawrence. It was a good plan of campaign, but the French knowledge of it made it most unlikely to succeed.

As a matter of fact, General Montcalm did not have to do a thing in order to stop two of the three attacks. Lord Jeffrey Amherst, advancing according to plan, easily took Ticonderoga and Crown Point and was then held up by the nonappearance of promised transport vessels. General Prideaux took Niagara without opposition and was then killed by the explosion of one of his own cannons. None of his subordinates were capable of carrying on. Only the force led by General Wolfe even managed to reach Quebec.

Wolfe found "the Gibraltar of North America" to be even stronger than he had expected. The fortified part of the city stood at the top of 300-foot cliffs extending along the river. On the cliffs above the few beaches where landings might be made, General Montcalm had dug entrenchments and had stationed troops. An attempt to duplicate the Louisburg attack against these beaches resulted in a bloody repulse and the loss of more than 500 men.

After nearly a complete summer of fruitless siege operations, Wolfe appeared to have failed. Quebec seemed invulnerable. There was only one trick left in the bag, and he played it. Using the sailors and the ships of the fleet to mislead Montcalm into expecting another attack below the city, he slipped ashore under cover of darkness with the pick of his troops at the foot of a narrow crevice leading up the cliff. Advanced scouts climbed up and killed the French sentries without a sound. To the amazement of General Montcalm, morning revealed a British army atop the cliff on the Plains of Abraham, before Quebec.

Flustered, the French general rushed into battle without even gathering his full forces. In a few crashing volleys, the French lines were withered. A bayonet charge swept them back. Quebec was lost to the French.

Neither Wolfe nor Montcalm lived to see the fall of Quebec. Both had been killed in the battle.

The taking of Quebec, which led directly to the conquest of Canada, is generally regarded as a military operation. In a strict sense, it was. Yet it was the British navy which made it possible—transporting troops and supplies to North America, sealing off the French from reinforcement, landing the soldiers at precisely chosen points of attack, and even providing supporting gunfire and the illusion of diversionary attack.

In another brilliant "conjunct expedition" in 1759, a British squadron under Commodore John Moore and an expeditionary force under Colonel John Barrington succeeded in taking the West Indies Island of Martinique from superior French forces. In this, it must be said that Colonel Barrington played his part better than Commodore Moore. After carrying the soldiers safely to Martinique and covering their landing, the Commodore took his eleven ships out to intercept a French squadron of nine ships under Commodore Bompart. The French got by him undetected (a specialty of Bompart's) but it did them little good. During the absence of the main units of the fleet, Colonel Barrington had organized the frigates and armed transports into an effective covering force and had exhausted and discouraged the French by landing forces far in their rear. Before Bompart's arrival,

Martinique had already fallen. After indulging in a little ill-natured cannonading, the elusive Frenchman sailed away, still a jump or two ahead of Commodore Moore's superior squadron.

13.

Suffering from many reverses across the ocean, the French revived their old plan of conquering Great Britain itself. If only they could control the Channel for a few hours, they felt sure that they could pour such strong armies onto British soil that conquest would be inevitable.

To gain control of the Channel, it was necessary to unite the French fleets based at Toulon and Brest. This would not be easy, as Admiral Edward Boscawen was patrolling the Strait of Gibraltar, and Admiral Edward Hawke was blockading Brest. It would take a fortunate series of circumstances, combined with some fast action, to bring the two French squadrons together.

In mid-August, French Admiral Sabran de la Clue thought he saw his chance to escape from Toulon and reach Brest undetected. Information reached him that Boscawen's squadron had put into Gibraltar for refitting and careening. Accordingly, he set sail with twelve ships-of-the-line and three frigates and headed westward, hoping that the easterly winds and low visibility would see him through. He had not counted on the thoroughness of his opponent. In the strait, a British frigate on picket duty sent up a rocket, and the secret was out. Within two and a half hours, the British squadron in Gibraltar had pulled itself together and had put to sea.

When once through the strait, Admiral De la Clue felt growing hopefulness. The visibility had steadily grown worse. It was now so bad that he could not even see all the other ships of his own squadron. Presently, five ships-of-the-line and three frigates lost touch and disappeared. Surely, they would not be far away when the weather cleared!

Sunrise revealed clear weather and eight sails on the horizon to windward. De la Clue lay to and waited for his eight lost vessels to rejoin him. They were close upon him before he discovered that these were not French ships at all but eight British ships-of-the-line, bearing down under full sail with their gun ports open and their guns run out. With all haste, the French admiral hoisted sail and bore away, hoping to avoid an engagement with this superior foe.

It soon became evident to Admiral Boscawen that he would never overtake the French if he maintained the rigid formation prescribed by the *Fighting Instructions*. Accordingly, he risked a court-martial by ordering a general chase before the enemy had been defeated and driven in flight. This caused the British formation to lengthen and separate, as the fastest ships drew ahead of their slower sisters.

Early in the afternoon, the leading British ships began to draw into range of the slowest French vessel, the *Centaur* (74). It was Boscawen's hope that a single one of his ships would drop out to dispose of the *Centaur,* leaving the others free to pursue the remaining French vessels—a somewhat irregular maneuver which had been devised and advocated by Admiral Hawke for use in just this situation. Lacking official signals to impart his wish, Boscawen had the frustration of seeing all of his leading ships cease the chase in order to concentrate their fire on the French laggard, while the remaining French ships drove steadily on toward possible escape.

In the *Centaur,* Boscawen's leading ships caught a Tartar. Knowing that his ship was doomed, the *Centaur*'s captain, De Sabran, directed his fire at the masts and rigging of his assailants. As a result, few British sailors died, but five ships-of-the-line were badly crippled aloft and were unable to join effectively in further pursuit. At the sacrifice of his life, Captain De Sabran had given his admiral and his fellow captains precious hours. Darkness intervened with the French fleet still in flight.

Darkness did not save the French. With the first light of day, Admiral De la Clue could see the English fleet still grimly pursuing. Two of his own ships, damaged and limping, had disappeared in the night. Clearly, the game was up. Not far to the east lay the coast of neutral Portugal. Perhaps there would be sanctuary there. In any event, there would be rocks upon which his ships could be run, in order to keep them out of British hands. The admiral set his course for the coast.

Only the admiral had the courage of his convictions. Under his orders, his flagship *Ocean* drove at full speed into the reefs of Lagos Bay, crushing her hull and sending her masts overboard from the force of the impact. Badly wounded, Admiral De la Clue was carried ashore, there to witness the timid behavior of his captains, who anchored their three ships off the shore in the apparent belief that neutrality would protect them. It did not. Disregarding the halfhearted fire of a nearby Portuguese fort, Boscawen brought his ships in close and fired systematically into the three anchored vessels until their colors were hauled down in surrender. Thus was the Toulon squadron eliminated from the French plans for mounting an invasion.

14.

The elimination of the Toulon squadron forced a considerable modification in the French plans for invading Great Britain. The plans were not, however, given up entirely. Instructions were issued to French Admiral Compte Hubert de Conflans to take his fleet from Brest at the earliest opportunity and use it to carry the army of the Duke d'Aiguillon to Scotland, whence a land invasion of England could be made.

It seems self-evident that any opportunity to cross the Channel without interference by the British fleet would be of short duration and would have to be snatched with the greatest of speed. The obvious move was for D'Aiguillon to march his army to Brest and have it ready to go aboard the ships at a moment's notice. This he refused to do, as a result of interservice jealousy. At Vannes, where his troops were stationed, he was the ranking officer. At Brest, he would be subordinate to Conflans. He therefore refused to travel by land but insisted that Conflans bring the fleet to him!

In mid-November, a storm forced Admiral Hawke to relax the tight blockade he had been maintaining at Brest. Leaving four frigates to watch the port, he crossed the Channel to Torbay. Almost at once, Conflans came out with his entire fleet—twenty-one ships-of-the-line. It is conceivable that he might have gotten through to Scotland had he gone that way at once, but he first had to turn south to pick up the troops at Vannes. Brushing the four British frigates aside, he sailed south along the coast. Off Vannes, which lies on a branch of Quiberon Bay, was a small squadron of British frigates, which Conflans planned to surprise and destroy on his way in to pick up the troops.

Scarcely had the French sails disappeared over the southern horizon when Hawke was back off Brest with his blockading fleet. Learning what had happened, he started in pursuit, hoping to arrive at Quiberon Bay in time to save the frigates and prevent the loading of the troops.

For five days, light and shifting winds impeded pursuer and pursued alike. During all this time, Hawke caught no sight of the ships he was so doggedly following. Then he had a stroke of luck. Ahead of him,

Conflans had to shorten sail in order not to arrive in the dangerous and reef-strewn area of Quiberon Bay at night. Hawke drove on, the distance steadily shrinking during the hours of darkness.

In the morning, the two fleets were in sight. So intent was Admiral Conflans on surprising the British frigates and trapping them in the bay that it was some time before he became aware of the approach of twenty-three ships-of-the-line behind him. A cannon shot from the leading British vessel alerted the French and the frigate squadron at the same time. While the frigates got under way and escaped, Conflans made frantic efforts to form his ships into line, while at the same time crowding on all sail and making for the entrance to Quiberon Bay.

As the chase developed, the wind and sea rose rapidly into a full-scale storm. This presented to Admiral Conflans the hope of escape, for he knew the channels among the dangerous reefs, and he felt sure that the British would never dare to send their ships in among the reefs in such dirty weather. He reckoned without Admiral Hawke, who was willing to take almost any risk, rather than let the elusive foe escape. Signaling a general chase, Hawke let his fastest ships draw up on the rear of the French line so that his steersmen could take advantage of the French knowledge and follow them closely through the gaps in the foaming reefs. "Where a French ship can go, an English ship can follow!"

Just outside Quiberon Bay, the British van caught the French rear. Wisely, Hawke chose the leeward position. As his ships heeled far over in the wind, all three gun decks were rolled up above the waves. The French ships, on the other hand, had their lowest gun decks on the engaged side rolled far down. As the opening shots were fired, one French 74 opened her lowest row of gun ports and promptly foundered, carrying down more than 800 men.

Panic swept the French fleet. Through the gaps in the reef dashed the fleeing ships, with the British close behind. Periodically, the shrieking wind was drowned out by crashing broadsides. One of the French ships tried to exchange fire with Hawke's flagship *Royal George* (100) and was ripped to pieces. The French never had a chance to organize a battle line. The seven vessels of the French van managed to escape through another channel and to reach Rochefort. Conflans deliberately drove his flagship upon the rocks. Six other ships, frantically jettisoning guns, anchors, and material of all sorts, managed to ride a high tide into the Vilaine River, where they remained stranded for more than a year.

The French navy had been eliminated as a fighting force. Much of it had been destroyed, the rest scattered. The majority of the ships which remained intact were now interned in neutral ports. There was no question now that Britannia ruled the waves.

15.

The French Secretary of State, the Duke of Choiseul, still felt that he had a high trump card to play. Neutral Spain had a respectable fleet of fifty-six ships-of-the-line and a mounting anger against Great Britain for repeated violations of Spanish rights and property. Quietly and skilfully, Choiseul played upon the Spanish feelings.

Through the fall of 1761, the Spanish court turned a smiling face toward Lord Bristol, the British ambassador. He was completely deceived. On September 21, he cheerfully reported to London that the greater part of the Spanish treasure fleet from Panama and Mexico had safely arrived at Cadiz. On November 2, he reported: "Two ships have lately arrived at Cadiz with very extraordinary rich cargoes from the West Indies, so that all the wealth that was expected from Spanish America is now safe in Old Spain."

Lord Bristol's next report was very different. With the arrival of the last two treasure ships, the smiles had disappeared from Spanish faces. Now there were sneers, demands, ultimatums. Spain had gathered her resources and was ready for war. The formal declaration was made on January 4, 1762.

Little Portugal was the first to feel the impact of the new alliance. A combined French and Spanish note demanded that the Portuguese join in the war against the British. Portugal refused and called for help, meanwhile vainly struggling to keep out Spanish and French invaders who came pouring across her borders. At once, a British expeditionary force was sent out under the command of the Count of Lippe-Buckenburg. Soon after the Count and his soldiers landed, the French and Spaniards were driven out of Portugal.

To William Pitt, the Spanish declaration of war was no blow at all. He had little regard for Spanish naval power and some lofty ambitions concerning Spanish territories. In the spring of 1762, two expeditions set out, one bound for Havana, the other for Manila.

The Havana expedition consisted of nineteen ships-of-the-line and eighteen smaller vessels, under Admiral George Pocock, convoying a large group of transports bearing an army of 12,000 men under the Earl of Albemarle. Surprise was achieved by approaching along the northern coast of Cuba, following a dangerous and little-used route. As a result, the Spaniards heard no tidings of the fleet before it suddenly appeared off the Havana waterfront.

The Spaniards resisted as best they could. Though they did not move fast enough to check Albemarle's amphibious assault at the beaches, they did offer determined resistance at Morro Castle, the city's main fortification. After two months of formal siege, Albemarle's sappers exploded a mine under the castle wall, opening a great gap in the defenses. The garrison quickly surrendered. Ten days later, on August 14, Havana itself was occupied.

The capture of Havana brought rich spoils into the British coffers. The treasure and merchandise seized amounted to fully $15,000,000. In addition, fourteen ships-of-the-line and four frigates were taken in the harbor. Officially, it is listed as the richest haul ever made from a single British conquest.

In the meantime, the Manila expedition was making good progress. From Madras, in India, had sailed a fleet of eight ships-of-the-line and a few frigates under Vice-Admiral Samuel Cornish, convoying the transports of a military expedition headed by Brigadier General William Draper. In the main, these were not regular British soldiers but members of the private army maintained by the British East India Company. In a deal with the company, William Pitt had chartered part of its army for a specific purpose.

Though the Spaniards tried to resist the landing at Manila, they could not cope with the heavy covering fire laid down by the British warships. The red-coated soldiers went ashore, where they quickly routed an army of Spaniards and loyal Filipinos. After twelve days of siege, Manila surrendered, yielding $4,000,000 in ransom for private property seized. This amount was further boosted by the activities of Admiral Cornish's ships, which presently captured the galleon *Santissima Trinidad,* laden with cargo valued at $3,000,000.

Halfway around the world, off Cape St. Vincent, a roving British squadron picked up the galleon *Santa Hermione,* a treasure ship from Peru, bearing gold and silver worth $5,000,000.

By the end of 1762, the ruling powers in Madrid had come to rue their accepted role as cat's-paw for the government of France.

16.

The Treaty of Paris was signed on February 10, 1763. By its terms, Great Britain gained Canada, all French lands in North America east of the Mississippi except the city of New Orleans, a number of the West Indies islands, Florida, Minorca, part of Senegal, and various minor possessions. Havana and Manila were returned to Spain and Belle Isle to France. Hanover received the island of Goree, off the African coast. Prussia gained nothing except acknowledgment of her rights to Silesia, which she had already had for more than twenty years. France and Spain were the big losers.

The British Empire now bestrode the world like a giant. The flag flew on every continent. For the first time, it could truly be said that the sun never set on the British flag.

In the establishment of the Empire and in its protection, the British navy was all-important.

8 THE BIRTH OF THE AMERICAN NAVY

⚓

1.

The first naval battle in American history took place on April 23, 1635, between "fleets" representing the English colonies of Virginia and Maryland. The forces engaged were not impressive, but men were killed, and it was unquestionably a battle.

The cause of the conflict was a dispute over the ownership of Kent Island, in Chesapeake Bay. According to Maryland's charter, the island clearly lay within the borders of this new colony. Kent Island, however, contained a settlement which had been founded by a Virginian named William Claiborne. A citizen represented the settlement in meetings of the Virginia House of Burgesses. To Virginians in general, and to William Claiborne in particular, these facts were proof of ownership. Rival petitions were submitted to King Charles I.

Before the king could settle the question, direct action was taken. A Virginia ship was seized for trading in Maryland waters without a license. In a rage, Claiborne sent out an armed sloop, the *Cockatrice,* under Lieutenant Warren, to take whatever Maryland vessels could be found. The sloop's armament consisted of a single light cannon, mounted in the bow.

Governor Leonard Calvert of Maryland was quick to counter Claiborne's move. Two Maryland pinnaces were sent out to hunt down the *Cockatrice.* Neither vessel was armed with a cannon, but both were packed with angry settlers grasping muskets, fowling pieces, blunderbusses, and assorted other weapons.

The rival forces came together in the Pocomoke River. Disregarding the greater range and heavier impact of the *Cockatrice*'s weapon, the Maryland pinnaces parted and approached their quarry from different bearings. Soon Lieutenant Warren found himself in the embarrassing position of having only one weapon with which to counter two enemies. Though he dealt out some punishment, and succeeded in killing one Marylander and in wounding several, his crew suffered more. He himself was killed, as were four members of his crew. The survivors on the *Cockatrice* were forced to surrender. Kent Island became a possession of Maryland.

2.

The very next year after the Kent Island fracas, there was another little "naval battle" in the colonies. A Rhode Island trader named John Gallop was sailing in his small sloop along the northern shore of Long Island Sound when he saw a pinnace lying at anchor not far from the shore. It looked like the boat of a trader who had mysteriously disappeared several weeks before. Alerting his little crew of two men and two boys, Gallop swung in to examine the pinnace.

The pinnace was anything but deserted. Fourteen Indians lay on the deck. As the sloop approached they arose and seized various weapons, one of them opening fire with a blunderbuss. At the same time, one of the Indians cut the anchor cable, permitting the pinnace to drift toward the breakers of the lee shore.

Fortunately for Gallop and his little crew, each of the five had a fowling piece aboard. A brisk fire was opened. The Indians then dove down the hatch to the comparative safety of the cabin. Against odds of fourteen to five, Gallop dared not board, and he could see little virtue in wasting powder in an aimless bombardment. Ramming supplied the answer. Beating to windward, he swung his sloop about and drove it before the wind against the side of the pinnace. As the boats crashed together, the Indians rushed up onto the deck, and six of them leaped overboard and were drowned. The others retreated once more to the cabin.

Once more, Gallop beat to windward. This time, he fastened his iron anchor to his bow, providing a metal ram not unlike those of the ancient galleys. Down he came again, the fluke of the anchor penetrating the planking of the pinnace. No Indians appeared on deck, even when he and his crew fired through the planking into the cabin. With some effort, he then succeeded in disengaging the boats and in drawing off for another ramming maneuver.

As the sloop bore down for its third assault, four more Indians rushed from the cabin and threw themselves into the water. Two more appeared on deck and made signs of submission. One was taken aboard the sloop and bound; the other, somewhat illogically, was thrown overboard to drown.

In the cabin of the pinnace, Gallop and his crew found the decomposing body of the missing trader. They also discovered that the remaining two Indians had retreated through a small hatchway into the hold, where it would be extremely dangerous to follow them. Accordingly, Gallop ordered his crew back aboard the sloop and abandoned the pinnace. It presently drifted onto a shoal and broke up, carrying down with it the last two of the fourteen who had taken it from its owner.

3.

During the four Intercolonial Wars, the fortunes and activities of the seagoing colonists were largely merged with and subordinate to the fortunes and activities of the British and French navies. While certain campaigns, notably the expeditions led by Phips against Port Royal and by Pepperrell against Louisburg, were predominantly colonial, most of the naval endeavors lend themselves better to treatment in connection with the major struggle between England and France, and have been so treated in an earlier chapter.

Two naval events of King George's War, however, were so basically American that they deserve treatment in this chapter. The first of the two, in fact, may well be regarded as the first truly American naval victory.

On June 25, 1744, the Massachusetts snow, *Prince of Orange,* was cruising south of Nova Scotia on the lookout for French privateers or warships slow enough for her to catch and weak enough for her to capture. This was an unlikely combination. The *Prince of Orange* had originally been a none-too-sprightly merchant ship. She had been converted into a warship by the simple expedient of cutting gun ports to accommodate twenty small cannons—nine 9-pounders on each beam with two 9-pounder chasers in the bow.

Captain Edward Tyng, his ship, and his crew were all from Massachusetts. Their voyage was being made in accordance with the orders and instructions issued by Governor William Shirley and the Massachusetts General Court. Though the *Prince of Orange* flew the flag of Great Britain, her activities were in no way directed by the lords of the British Admiralty.

About 9:00 A.M., a sail was sighted on the northern horizon. Captain Tyng lowered his flag, ran in his guns, closed his gun ports, and headed south in imitation of a panic-stricken merchant vessel trying to escape. *Prince of Orange* sailed slowly, letting her pursuer overtake her from astern. As the distance between the vessels closed, Captain Tyng was able to discover that his prospective opponent was a French sloop-of-war armed with sixteen guns. Eight were light swivels, but the other eight were long 18-pounders, capable of outranging his own light carriage guns and of delivering far harder blows. If the French captain kept his head and utilized his advantages to the full, he should have little difficulty in defeating and capturing the Massachusetts snow.

This being so, the evident thing to do was to startle the Frenchman into panic. The simulated flight was continued until the sloop-of-war was very close, well within the range of the snow's 9-pounders. Then, at a command from Tyng, the *Prince of Orange* came about fast. At the same time, all twenty gun ports swung open and all twenty guns were run out, in an attempt to make the little snow look as much like a ship-of-the-line as possible. The trick worked. Momentarily startled into believing he had come much too close to a warship more powerful than his own, the French captain swung his ship around in flight. The pursuer became the pursued, a happy circumstance for Captain Tyng, who was able to use his two chasers against the sloop's unarmed and unprotected stern.

It soon became evident that the French sloop-of-war was a bit faster beating upwind than the Massachusetts snow. Slowly, the distance widened. Tyng's gunners tried desperately to cripple the enemy's ship before she could pull out of range. Their shooting was good, their luck bad. Nine hits were scored by the chasers, but not one of them brought down a mast or otherwise slowed the quarry. When the range became too great, the chasers fell silent.

It was at this point that the wind failed. *Prince of Orange* was equipped with five long sweeps on either beam, and these were immediately pressed into use. The sloop-of-war also put out sweeps, and the chase continued. Under oars as under sail, the French vessel was faster. Tyng's action in sending out longboats to tow was of no avail, for the French captain did likewise and continued to gain. By late afternoon, the sloop-of-war, though still in sight, was far ahead.

At dusk, the Frenchman made the serious mistake of lighting three lanterns. Very evidently, he felt that he had lost his pursuer. Tyng, taking his cue from this, swung his ship off to starboard as though giving up the pursuit and hoisted a single lantern to his gaffhead.

As soon as night concealed him, the Yankee skipper ordered his men once more to the sweeps and resumed his laborious course toward the three distant points of light that marked the enemy's position. At the same time, he had one of his men lower his own lantern slowly, a few inches at a time. When at last the lantern reached the deck, it was put out, leaving the ship in complete darkness. The trick worked. Those aboard the French vessel had seen their pursuer turn aside just at nightfall. Now, as they watched, they could see the single point of light dip lower and lower and at last disappear completely, apparently over the horizon. Vastly relieved, the French captain permitted his men to cease rowing. The sloop-of-war drifted to a stop.

Not until long after midnight did the *Prince of Orange* draw near to her quarry. During the late stages of the approach, the men rowed slowly and as quietly as possible. Each gun was fully manned. The ships were within a hundred yards of one another before a French crewman discerned the enemy ship in the darkness. His cry of warning was drowned out by the thunder of a broadside, followed at once by the sound of crashing timbers and the cries of injured men.

Caught unawares and badly hurt by the first broadside, the sloop-of-war fought at a disadvantage. Some of her heavy guns got into action, doing damage and inflicting casualties, but Tyng's gunners fired faster and more accurately. As a last resort, the Frenchmen manned their sweeps and tried to board. As they swung to port toward the *Prince of Orange,* the snow's crewmen turned more tightly to starboard on an inside course and greeted the oncoming sloop with a broadside from the hitherto-unused port battery. That ended the affair. The French surrendered.

The French captain was brought aboard the snow. He identified himself as Captain Delebroix and his ship as the sloop-of-war *Succès* which had served as flagship during the French surprise attack on Canso that had given the British colonists their first indication that their mother country was at war with France. He was anything but pleased to see the little 9-pounders on the deck of the *Prince of Orange* and to realize that he had had it in his power to remain out of range of these guns and use his own heavier artillery to batter the snow to pieces.

Nearly a year later, on June 15, 1745, a little squadron of three colonial ships, headed by Captain Daniel Fones in the Rhode Island sloop *Tartar,* sailed through the Gut of Canso between Nova Scotia and Cape Breton Island and surprised a large army of Indians and French irregulars trying to cross onto the island to aid the defenders of Louisburg. The French squadron, consisting of two sloops, two schooners, a shallop, and fifty canoes, was unaware of the approach of the three warships until cannon balls began to plunge into the water among their own overladen craft. No real battle developed. Many French and Indians were killed, and the army of liberation was dispersed. Two days later, the Louisburg garrison surrendered to Pepperrell and his amateur army.

On land and on sea, Americans were learning to be resourceful fighters.

4.

King George II of Great Britain died in 1760, while the fourth of the Intercolonial Wars—called the Seven Years' War in Europe and the French and Indian War in America—was still in progress. He was followed on the throne by his twenty-two-year-old grandson, King George III.

George III had been raised by his mother to be just the kind of king which Great Britain could ill afford at this point in her history. The mother, Princess Augusta of Hanover, was doubly unhappy. She had seen her husband die in 1751 without ever becoming king, and she had helplessly observed the manner in which her husband's grandfather and father, George I and George II, had let the power of government slip from their hands into the hands of their ministers. Her son must redeem this error and become a ruling as well as a reigning monarch! The boy was brought up to the tune of an oft-repeated motto: "George, be a *king!*"

George tried hard to be a king. Not quite daring to defy Parliament openly, he nevertheless attempted to control that body by other means. He used all of his influence to secure the election of members who would do his bidding. His ministers were selected on the same basis. Unlike the earlier Georges, he sided with the Tory party. So strong was this alliance that presently the members of the Tory group became known as "the King's friends." Naturally, the Whigs became the king's opponents. A terrific struggle was waged between the two parties, with the issue of royal rule or Parliamentary rule involved in almost every point of difference.

The struggle for supremacy was not confined to Great Britain, but spilled over into the British colonies in North America. For more than a century and a half, the colonists along the Atlantic coast had been contending with hostile Indians and Frenchmen, with forest-grown and rock-strewn fields, and with the other hardships of life in an undeveloped land. To succeed—indeed, to survive at all—had required great resourcefulness and boldness of action. When emergencies threatened, one could scarcely wait for help from a distant mother country. The mother country, moreover, had shown little desire either to interfere or to help. Prime Minister Walpole had set the pattern with his "Policy of Salutary Neglect," well described by his motto: "Let sleeping dogs lie." As a result, the British colonists in America had developed into an independent breed of people, used to making their own decisions and to governing themselves.

Before 1763, the menace of the French in nearby Canada had served to keep the colonists somewhat dependent upon the mother country for protection. With the signing of the Treaty of Paris, the danger was removed, and with it the incentive to cling to Britain's skirts.

Now, suddenly, under King George III, the British government was belatedly trying to run the affairs of the American colonies, which it had so long neglected. It was the king's intention to knit the empire more closely together, under the control of the central British government, and to use the colonies as a source of money to help pay some of the enormous debts that had been piled up during the recent wars. George III was also much impressed with a new economic theory called mercantilism, which maintained, among other things, that colonies should be used primarily for the benefit of the mother country.

By a series of ill-considered acts, spread over the twelve-year period from 1763 to 1775, King George III and his ministers succeeded in transforming the loyal British subjects in America into armed and hostile opponents, willing to resist to the utmost any encroachment upon their rights.

5.

One of the most important causes of the American Revolution was taxation, and one of the most onerous forms of taxation was the levying of tariffs, or duties, on goods shipped into the colonies. The colonists were well conditioned to circumvent and to resist any such restrictions on their trade. For over a century, the British government had had on the books various Navigation Acts, forbidding trade in certain commodities between British colonies and the colonies of such other nations as France and the Netherlands. The laws were not realistic, for such needed commodities as sugar, molasses, and rum were not available in sufficient quantities from Britain's West Indies possessions. Hence, the laws were not enforced, and smuggling became both necessary and accepted. Indeed, the British government, through the practice of Salutary Neglect, seemed to give tacit approval to the practice. It is not surprising that many Americans came to feel that they had an acknowledged right to smuggle. Such revered patriots as Sam Adams and John Hancock were influenced toward their acts of resistance by large vested interests in stocks of smuggled goods.

Whenever a British official undertook to enforce the laws against smuggling, he aroused a storm of protest among the colonists. One such official was Lieutenant William Dudington, in command of His Majesty's armed schooner *Gaspee,* stationed off the mouth of Narragansett Bay. The lieutenant was ardent and industrious in the stopping and searching of suspected smuggling vessels and was responsible for the confiscation of a number of ships and cargoes and the arrest of a good many Rhode Island citizens. It is not surprising that he was extremely unpopular in Providence, Newport, and other nearby towns.

On June 10, 1772, the *Gaspee* sighted a small ship slipping into Narragansett Bay. At once, guns were run out and a chase was commenced. The quarry was elusive and was also of very shallow draft. It passed gracefully over a mud bar on which the *Gaspee* grounded solidly. As the tide went out, the armed schooner canted over into a position of growing helplessness. Not before the next high tide, shortly after midnight, would there be much hope of freeing her.

The plight of the stranded *Gaspee* formed a fascinating topic of conversation in the bars of Providence. To one Abraham Whipple, the situation seemed to present some exciting possibilities. Whipple had gained a considerable reputation during the French and Indian War as commander of the privateer *Game Cock*. When he spoke, men listened with interest and respect.

After darkness fell, Abraham Whipple and a number of other determined colonists put out from the Providence waterfront in eight small boats. Though they rowed silently, they were discovered as they approached the *Gaspee*. Lieutenant Dudington himself called out, "Who comes there?"

To gain time, Whipple tried to identify himself as the Sheriff of Kent County. Dudington did not believe him and demanded that the boats withdraw. At once, shots rang out. The British lieutenant fell to the deck with one bullet in his leg and another in his groin. There was no more resistance. Whipple and his men swarmed aboard the *Gaspee*, forced the crew to take to their open boats, then burned the hated schooner. No one died, though Lieutenant Dudington was long incapacitated by his wounds.

British anger ran high over this "atrocious offence." The names of the raiders were well known, but somehow witnesses could never be produced who would incriminate them. Abraham Whipple and his companions went free. An added wedge had been driven between Great Britain and her American colonies.

6.

When the American Revolution broke out in April of 1775, the United States had literally no navy at all. The mother country of Great Britain was the acknowledged Queen of the Seas, with well over 500 effective first-line war vessels, ranging upward from brigs, schooners, and sloops-of-war to powerful frigates and majestic ships-of-the-line. It is doubtful if ever a major struggle was undertaken with a greater disparity of force upon the sea.

Though the Continental Congress at first boggled at the prospect of naval warfare, the patriots of certain of the colonies did not.

In May, 1775, British General Gage sent two sloops and the armed schooner *Margaretta* from Boston to Machias, Maine, for a cargo of lumber, needed for building barracks for the troops. Word of the fighting at Lexington and Concord had reached the people of Machias, most of whom strongly sympathized with their fellow citizens of Massachusetts. A plot was formed to seize the schooner.

Somehow, Midshipman Moore, the commander of the *Margaretta*, became aware of the plot while he and his fellow officers were attending a church service in Machias on Sunday, June 12. In the midst of the service, they rushed from the church and down to the waterfront, with a mob of armed citizens in close pursuit. The officers were able to reach the *Margaretta* when a member of the crew fired a shot from one of the schooner's swivel guns over the heads of the crowd, causing a brief hesitation. Quickly, the *Margaretta* stood out to sea.

Jeremiah O'Brien, of Machias, was unwilling to let the king's ship escape. He and a number of followers seized the *Unity,* one of the lumber sloops, and set out in hot pursuit, in blithe disregard of the fact that they had only small arms with which to oppose the seven cannons on the *Margaretta.* An accident to the schooner's rigging permitted the sloop to come within range. The battle, which Midshipman Moore had done his best to avoid, was now inevitable.

The *Margaretta* opened the firing with a broadside, which killed one of O'Brien's men. At that, the men on the sloop opened up with their hunting rifles and killed the schooner's steersman. Firing became general as the vessels drifted together. Several attempts to board the *Margaretta* were beaten off by the British crew. When Midshipman Moore fell dead with a bullet through his brain, the fight went out of his men. The next boarding attempt carried the *Margaretta.* The colonists had won the first naval battle of the Revolution.

The taste of victory was sweet to Jeremiah O'Brien. The schooner's armament was transferred to the *Unity,* which immediately sailed in search of British prizes. Two were quickly taken.

To the British authorities, this taking of prizes without the formality of a commission or even a letter of marque was simple piracy. Since they were unable to capture O'Brien, they vented their displeasure on his fellow citizens by sending a naval expedition to Falmouth, Maine, and burning the town. This, of course, resulted in a wave of anti-British feeling from Maine to Georgia.

Word of O'Brien's successful endeavor brought out a swarm of privateers, most of which were officially sanctioned by the colonies from whose ports they sailed. Much unguarded British shipping fell into the hands of the eager colonial captains, some of whom made considerable fortunes from the cargoes which they seized.

7.

In Philadelphia, where the Second Continental Congress was sitting, a long and heated debate was going on over the question of naval activity against Great Britain. George Washington, John Adams, and a few other farseeing statesmen clearly understood that forceful resistance to British power would be impossible if control of the waterways were surrendered without a struggle. A majority of the members, shrinking from the role of David, pointed to the prohibitive odds against any naval success. This group had every prospect of carrying the day when word of the burning of Falmouth reached Congress and tipped the scales.

On October 13, 1775, Congress officially voted to create an American navy and to build and equip "a swift sailing vessel to carry ten guns, for intercepting such transports as may be laden with warlike stores for the enemy." From this tiny seed has grown the navy of the United States of America.

The first navy department—the so-called Marine Committee—consisted of three members: John Langdon, of New Hampshire; Silas Deane, of Connecticut; and, most important of all, John Adams, of Massachusetts, who is usually regarded as the Father of the American Navy. Before the end of the year, four more members were added to the Marine Committee and $100,000 was appropriated with which to transform merchant vessels into warships.

The fleet, as assembled in December of 1775, consisted of the flagship *Alfred* (30), the *Columbus* (28), the *Andrew Doria* (16), the *Cabot* (14), and three little craft, the *Wasp,* the *Hornet,* and the *Fly,* armed with a few pieces of light ordnance. Esek Hopkins, a retired merchant skipper, was selected as commander-in-chief, with the rank of Commodore.

The entire American navy, as of the end of 1775, was not equal in weight of broadside to one standard British ship-of-the-line!

8.

The Marine Committee was soon given an excellent opportunity to use its new little navy. In Williamsburg, Governor Dunmore of Virginia showed himself a staunch foe of any who would oppose British rule. As part of his preparations for dealing with local patriots, the Governor fitted out a fleet of small warships for use on the James River and adjoining waterways. Commodore Esek Hopkins was ordered to take his ships to Virginia and destroy Dunmore's squadron. He was then to sail to Rhode Island and "attack, take, and destroy" whatever British naval forces he could find there.

Esek Hopkins soon showed that he had only the most casual regard for orders. Although his instructions reached him on January 5, 1776, it was February 18 before he put to sea from his base in Philadelphia.

A collision off the Virginia capes disabled the *Hornet* and the *Fly* and convinced the Commodore that Virginia, at this season, was not a good place for naval activity. Accordingly, he discarded his orders and swung out to sea toward the Bahamas, with the thought of capturing Forts Nassau and Montague and bringing back their large supplies of powder for use by General Washington's armies.

The attack on Fort Montague was a success, thanks largely to the energy and initiative of Lieutenant John Paul Jones, second-in-command of the *Alfred,* under Captain Dudley Saltonstall. It was Jones himself, seated high up in the crosstrees of the *Alfred,* who spied out the channels and guided the little squadron through the dangerous shallows to the fort. The storming of the bastions was largely the work of 200 United States Marines, who received the Corps' first baptism of fire on a note of victory.

Characteristically, Commodore Hopkins made the mistake of delaying the assault on Fort Nassau until the next day. When at last the attack was launched, the Marines had an easy time of it, but American jubilation was short-lived. The great stores of powder were not there. During the intervening night, they had been loaded upon a ship and spirited safely away. Hopkins had to be satisfied with what other supplies he could take.

The Commodore now elected to reconsult his orders. As a result, he sailed north toward Rhode Island. Off Block Island, the squadron encountered two small British warships convoying two merchant ships laden with liquor. The vessels were taken, and all hands proceeded to get royally drunk. They were still under the weather when they came upon H. M. S. *Glasgow* (20), which should not have been a fair match for either the *Alfred* or the *Columbus* alone. The American crews, still suffering from hangovers, were not at their best. At the end of three hours, the *Glasgow* got away, leaving the American squadron in bad shape. All of the ships were seriously damaged except the *Columbus,* which had been handled so ineptly that she had never gotten into the action at all.

The cruise of the squadron brought a court-martial and resultant censure to Commodore Esek Hopkins. It also brought some recognition of the ability of two younger officers—Nicholas Biddle and John Paul Jones.

What of Governor Dunmore? Without help from Commodore Hopkins and the American fleet, the Virginia patriots drove him out of his ornate palace at Williamsburg and forced him to take refuge on one of the ships of his Tory navy. After some fighting along the coast, including a bombardment of Norfolk by the Governor's ships, Dunmore was at last compelled to flee from Virginia. He never returned.

9.

Fortunately for American morale, some of the minor naval units fought with determination and success during the unhappy year of 1776.

John Barry, an experienced merchant captain, was given command of the sloop-of-war *Lexington* (16). In April, 1776, he took his newly commissioned ship down Delaware Bay and there encountered the British sloop *Edward* (8). Despite the difference in firepower, the *Edward*'s captain elected to slug it out with Barry's ship. After a few close-range broadsides, the British flag was hauled down, and the regular American navy had recorded its first official capture of a commissioned enemy warship.

In Boston, the command of the tiny armed ship *Franklin* (4) was entrusted to twenty-six-year-old James Mugford, another merchant skipper, who had been briefly impressed for service aboard a British warship and while there had learned of the impending sailing of a British ammunition ship bringing supplies to "His Majesty's troops in the colonies." For some reason, the Marine Committee saw fit to rescind the appointment and dispatched a messenger to Boston with new orders. Mugford sailed before the messenger arrived.

Far out in Massachusetts Bay, James Mugford found the ship he was seeking, the 300-ton transport *Hope* (6). In plain sight on the horizon was a squadron of British warships. Despite the danger and the odds, Mugford sailed boldly and skilfully to the attack. To his amazement, he met no resistance. Swinging his ship adroitly across the *Hope*'s stern, he personally led a boarding party onto the deck. There he found the British captain shouting orders for the topsail halyards and ties to be cut, so that the ship would be crippled and might easily be recaptured by the British squadron, which could be seen getting under way in the middle distance.

Drawing his pistol, Mugford pointed it at the captain's head, shouting, "If a knife is touched to those ropes, not a man of this crew shall live." Not a rope was cut. Side by side, the *Franklin* and the *Hope* fled to Boston, with Banks's squadron close behind. It proved to be a most fortunate capture, for the *Hope*'s hold contained 1,500 barrels of powder, 1,000 carbines, and other items of military equipment badly needed by Washington's army.

Within a week, Mugford and the *Franklin* were at sea again. This time, his luck was bad. In trying to avoid the British blockaders he ran hard aground and was quickly spotted by the enemy. Knowing that he would be attacked, Captain Mugford rigged boarding nets and moved all four of his guns to the seaward side of his ship. After dark, thirteen barges approached and there was a desperate fight, some of it hand to hand, with pikes and cutlasses. Mugford himself was mortally wounded by a musket ball. His dying words were, "Do not give up the vessel. You will be able to beat them off."

The vessel was not given up, and the British were beaten off. After repeated attempts to board, they rowed away, having suffered seventy casualties. Captain Mugford was the only American killed.

10.

An important part of the British strategy of 1776 involved the capture of leading American cities. New York was taken without much difficulty by means of a combined naval and military campaign. George Washington's army was too small and too inexperienced to be able to check the British veterans under General Howe. The only resistance to the British fleet, commanded by Admiral Richard Howe, came from a Connecticut genius named David Bushnell.

To Bushnell must go the credit for designing and building the first successful submarine. The *American Turtle* had a hull of oak. Her shape was much like that of a peach pit, floating upright in the water. She was taller than she was long. The operator sat inside, looking out through a glass port set in a little conning tower at the top. A hand-operated screw permitted him to inch the *Turtle* forward; another permitted him to move her up or down. An auger, ingeniously set in the top, could be turned from inside, thus permitting the operator to engage the auger's threaded tip in the bottom on an enemy vessel. The auger and an attached powder charge, with a clockwork detonating mechanism, could then be left attached to the enemy vessel while the *Turtle* made good her escape.

As Howe's British fleet lay in New York Harbor, Bushnell's *Turtle* was quietly slipped into the water. Into her clambered her "crew"—a sergeant named Ezra Lee. Straining mightily at his crank, Sergeant

Lee slowly made his way toward H. M. S. *Eagle* (64), the nearest anchored ship-of-the-line. As he neared the towering sides of his enemy, Sergeant Lee let water into his ballast tank and turned his vertical propeller. Obediently, the *Turtle* slipped under the surface and slid along the *Eagle*'s bottom. Thus far, everything had worked to perfection.

Trouble came when Lee tried to dig the auger into the enemy's underwater planking. The *Eagle*'s bottom was copper-sheathed! The auger broke off. Casting off his explosive charge, the sergeant strained to get back to the surface and to Manhattan Island. He made it safely. As for the explosive, it went off with a thunderous roar some distance away from the *Eagle,* startling the crew of that mighty ship and bringing angry shouts from the Lords of the British Admiralty, in far-off London. The tenor of the complaint was that such sneaky attacks were anything but sporting.

Even if Bushnell's attack on the *Eagle* had succeeded, New York could not have been held. Admiral Howe's fleet, cooperating with his brother's army, would have made Manhattan Island untenable by the Americans, even if a single 64 lay shattered on the bottom of the harbor. Washington was forced to evacuate the city and to begin that long retreat across New Jersey that was to culminate in the amazing American victories at Trenton and Princeton, far beyond the reach of naval aid. The main interest in Busnell's endeavor lies in the fact that it was the first attempt to sink a warship by submarine attack.

11.

In that same summer of 1776, the British sent an amphibious expedition to capture Charleston, South Carolina. Four frigates and six lesser warships, under Rear Admiral Sir Peter Parker, were given the task of convoying thirty transports to Charleston, reducing the city's defenses, and clearing the way for a landing force of 2,000 British regulars under General Sir John Clinton. It looked like an easy assignment, for the only defense of Charleston was a little fort of soft palmetto logs, which had been hastily constructed on an island near the harbor mouth. Colonel William Moultrie had the unenviable assignment of keeping the British out.

The garrison in the little log fort made no move as the ten warships slid by, blasting with their heavy guns. It was only after the vessels had made stationary targets of themselves by dropping anchor that

Colonel Moultrie gave the order to fire. Almost at once, hits were scored. To Admiral Parker's chagrin, his ships seemed to be taking more punishment than they were giving. The contemptible little fort seemed to be able to absorb heavy cannon fire without any sign of harm!

As a matter of fact, the little wooden fort *was* able to take a surprising amount of punishment. Cannon balls penetrated deep into the spongy wood but did not go through and hurled no splinters. Colonel Moultrie's men had built better than they knew!

After ten hours of cannonading, the garrison of the palmetto fort was as full of fight as ever. The same could not be said for Parker's squadron. All ten of his warships had been roughly used. The flagship *Bristol* had been raked when one of her cables had parted and her stern had swung toward the fort. As a result, her captain and forty of her crew were dead, and the admiral himself had a painful and embarrassing wound. The frigate *Actaeon,* badly battered, was firmly aground. The other vessels had suffered in lesser degrees. At dusk, Admiral Parker raised anchor and sailed away, leaving *Actaeon* in flames. British casualties were 225 men. Two Americans had been killed and twenty-one wounded.

We should note two examples of unusual heroism. Early in the attack on the palmetto fort, a British cannon ball carried away the flagstaff of the fort, dropping the flag onto the beach. Without hesitation, Sergeant William Jasper left the fort, ran along the shell-swept beach, rescued the flag, fastened it to a cannon ramrod, and restored it to the top of the wall. Against all probability, he was never touched by the storm of projectiles through which he passed.

Later, as the British were abandoning the attack, a group from the fort rowed out to the burning *Actaeon,* fired her guns at the retiring warships, loaded three boats with needed stores, and got away before the fire reached her magazines and blew her sky-high.

Admiral Parker and General Clinton did not come back. The attack on Charleston was abandoned.

12.

The most significant naval battle of 1776 took place on Lake Champlain, far from the waters of the ocean. To give it its proper perspective, we must go back a year, to the fall of 1775.

A two-pronged American invasion of Canada had been launched in

September. Richard Montgomery had led one force north through the Champlain Valley and had succeeded in taking Montreal. Benedict Arnold had led a second force through northern New England to Quebec. Together, Montgomery and Arnold had instituted a forlorn siege of the strongest fortress in North America—a siege which had had to be abandoned in April, 1776, when a British squadron under Captain Charles Douglas sailed up the St. Lawrence bearing troops and supplies for the strengthening of the garrison. Now, in the fall of 1776, the Americans were in full retreat south through the Champlain Valley. Montgomery was dead. Arnold was in command.

Among the supplies brought from England by Captain Douglas were timbers and rigging for ships. These were taken along by the pursuing British army. Advancing slowly in the wake of the retreating Americans, Sir Guy Carlton paused at the northern end of Lake Champlain long enough to build and launch a fleet of twenty-five vessels. Most were small, but one, the *Inflexible,* was ship-rigged and mounted eighteen 12-pounders and four smaller guns. In October, this flotilla started south through the lake, carrying Carlton's army of 13,000 regular troops.

In the course of his retreat, Benedict Arnold had picked up, at the head of Lake Champlain, the former British schooner *Royal Savage.* Armed with twelve small guns—6-pounders and 4-pounders—she became the nucleus of a new fleet. Fourteen more little ships were built by the Americans at Crown Point. Eight of these were "gundalows" (gondolas)—single-masted small craft mounting one 12-pounder at the bow and two 9-pounders amidships. Four were galleys, equipped with two lateen sails and with supplementary sweeps for action in calm weather. Each galley mounted ten guns, ranging from a single 18-pounder down to six 6-pounders. The two smallest were a schooner and a sloop, equipped with 3- and 4-pounder guns. It was a pathetic little squadron with which to meet the twenty-five British ships commanded by Commodore Thomas Pringle. The British firepower surpassed that of the Americans in the ratio of 17 to 10.

Unimpressed by the odds, Benedict Arnold took his squadron north and found a strategic anchorage west of Valcour Island. On October 11, the British came down the lake, bowling along before a stiff breeze from the north. They were well past Valcour Island before they discovered Arnold's ships. At once, they came about and started to beat upwind toward Arnold's anchorage.

The *Royal Savage* was the first American ship to be engaged. Ineptly handled, she had drifted to leeward, and was thus the first to be reached by the British. The firing began at 11 A.M. Long before noon, the *Royal Savage* was out of action, crippled and driven ashore on the tip of Valcour Island. Her men escaped to the land.

For four and a half hours, from 12:30 until 5:00, a hot general action was fought between the fleets. The British had all the best of it, both because of better ships and equipment and because of men better trained for warfare afloat. Aboard the American galley *Congress,* General Arnold himself was the only one who knew how to lay and fire a gun; he did so with conspicuous success during the entire battle. The American ships were badly mauled, suffering heavy casualties, much damage, and, toward the end, an acute shortage of ammunition.

With a complete triumph in his hands, Commodore Pringle broke off the close action and retired to the mouth of the channel, whence he kept up a distant cannonading until darkness obscured all targets. It was one of those inexplicable "wait until tomorrow" moves through which the British, both ashore and afloat, frequently lost the fruits of their victories during the Revolution.

Arnold, hemmed in behind Valcour Island, was bloody but unbowed. His fleet was crippled, and his ammunition was almost gone, but his defiance was as strong as ever. One ship, the gundalow *Philadelphia,* sank shortly after the British had retired. The *New York,* badly damaged, had lost every one of her officers except her captain. The *Royal Savage* was a wreck upon the shore. Not a single vessel was in shape to endure more action. A renewal of the struggle on the morrow would be disastrous. Yet surrender was unthinkable. Escape, impossible as it looked, was the only answer.

During the night, Arnold's battered vessels quietly moved from their anchorage. It is not known whether they passed around the northern end of Valcour Island or slipped through or around the British squadron in the darkness. With the dawn, Pringle found only an empty stretch of water between the island and the shore. The Americans were gone, making as much speed as possible southward through the lake.

The British pursued vigorously, gaining on October 12 while the Americans stopped briefly at Sullivan's Island to make necessary repairs. At noon on the 13th, the galley *Washington* was overtaken and smashed into helplessness. Her captain resisted as long as he could, then ran her ashore and blew her up. The *Congress,* next to be caught, put up a running fight for two hours, then was beached and burned. Arnold and the surviving crew members escaped into the woods. The pattern was set. A few of the American ships got away; most of them were run ashore and destroyed.

Commodore Pringle had won a victory. He had eliminated the American fleet on Lake Champlain. What had he really accomplished? His own ships were so badly damaged that he dared go no farther with them. Back to the northern end of the lake he sailed, taking Carlton's soldiers with him. Before the fleet was usable again, winter was at hand. It was now too late to stage an invasion. Benedict Arnold had lost a battle but had won a campaign.

13.

In view of the discrepancy in naval power between the Americans and the British, large fleet actions were out of the question. At no time during the war, or for decades afterward, did the United States possess even a single activated and commissioned ship-of-the-line. In the main, the war at sea consisted of actions between individual ships, up to and including the frigate class, and in raids on commerce. Of these activities, the latter was by far the more important.

The raids on British commerce started early in the war, as early as the summer of 1775. Oddly enough, they were at first carried on by the army, since Congress had not yet gotten around to creating the Marine Committee or any official naval organization. Members of Colonel Glover's Marblehead regiment—mostly Grand Banks fishermen—made up the crews. Their assignment was to take needed supplies from British merchant vessels and transports.

The small schooner *Hannah,* built in Marblehead and fitted out at Beverly, Massachusetts, was the first of George Washington's "mosquito fleet." She was, therefore, the first official American warship. On September 5, 1775, she set out from Beverly under Captain Nicholas Broughton. Two days later, she was back, escorting two captured British supply vessels.

In the weeks which followed, the *Hannah* was joined by thirteen other little-armed ships, under the over-all command of Commodore John Manley. The hunting was good. Thirty-five prizes were taken, the most important being the brigantine *Nancy* taken by Manley himself in the armed schooner *Lee* (8). The *Nancy*'s cargo included

2,000 muskets, 100,000 flints, 31 tons of musket bullets, much gun-powder, and a 13-inch brass mortar. It has been said that if George Washington had sat down to write out a requisition for the things he needed most, his list would have corresponded almost exactly to the *Nancy*'s cargo manifest.

It will not be possible to treat the activities of all of the American commerce raiders. A few of the more important—both regular navy and privateer—will be mentioned in order to give the flavor and something of the importance of their deeds upon the sea. Some of the most active characters are hard to pinpoint, since they sometimes served as commanders of commissioned American warships and sometimes as the captains of privateers.

Early in the summer of 1776, the United States brig *Reprisal* (16) sailed for Martinique to pick up ammunition and supplies, quietly fur-nished to the American cause by the still-neutral French government. On the way, she took a number of British prizes, which she sent back to American ports under prize crews.

Not far from Martinique, the *Reprisal* encountered H. M. S. *Shark* (16). The two ships were equal in armament and similar in design. The *Shark,* however, possessed one great advantage, for she was fully manned, whereas the *Reprisal* was short eighty crew members. Never-theless, Captain Lambert Wickes accepted the *Shark*'s challenge to do battle. A few minutes of brisk cannonading convinced the British cap-tain that he had caught a Tartar. With his ship damaged, he hauled out of action, leaving the *Reprisal* to continue on her original assign-ment.

Upon her return home with the French supplies, the *Reprisal* was sent eastward to convey Benjamin Franklin to France, where he was to serve as American minister. The little brig was thus the first Ameri-can warship to appear in European waters. The voyage was not lim-ited to Mr. Franklin's passage. Three prizes were taken on the way over and a number of others soon afterward in the Bay of Biscay.

A few weeks after her arrival in European waters, the *Reprisal* was joined by the brigantine *Lexington* (16) and the cutter *Dolphin* (10). Together, the three small ships cruised the English Channel and the Irish Sea, taking prizes within sight of the shores of mighty Britain, much to the indignation of the local populace. As Silas Deane wrote to Robert Morris: "Captain Wickes has most effectively alarmed Eng-land, prevented the great fair at Chester, occasioned insurance to rise, and even deterred the English merchants from shipping goods in English bottoms at any rate; so that in a few weeks forty sail of French ships were loading in the Thames on freight; an instance never before known."

Neither the brig *Reprisal* nor the brigantine *Lexington* was destined to return home in triumph. On the way westward across the Atlantic, the *Reprisal* was caught in a furious storm. She was in no condition to withstand a battering. Not long before, she had escaped from a far stronger British warship by the desperate expedient of jettisoning guns, cargo, and even some of her heavy beams. Now, under the hammering of the waves, her weakened hull gave way and she foundered. There was only one survivor, the ship's cook, who clung to a piece of wreckage for three days until picked up by a passing ship.

The *Lexington,* too, came to a sad end. Raiding in the English Channel, she encountered the British cutter *Alert* (10). Captain Henry Johnson knew that his *Lexington* was short of ammunition, but he never dreamed that the smaller British ship would cause him trouble. She did. The *Alert* bore in bravely and gave him shot for shot. Soon Captain Johnson found himself opposing ten loaded guns with sixteen empty ones. He tried to flee, but the *Alert* overhauled him and forced him to surrender.

Another famous raider, Gustavus Conyngham, sailed from Dunkirk in May, 1777, in command of the lugger *Surprise* (10). Though the *Surprise* took only two prizes, one was a richly laden British mail packet from Harwich. Also included in the loot which he brought back to Dunkirk were the Lieutenant and the Garrison Adjutant of the British island of Guernsey, taken during a daring raid. So vehemently did the British government protest that Conyngham was imprisoned by the French authorities at Dunkirk. He was soon allowed to escape and was supplied with the cutter *Revenge* (14), in place of the confiscated *Surprise.*

Taking advantage of the extreme speed of his new ship, Conyngham now made himself a troublesome and most embarrassing raider, taking no fewer than sixty ships in European waters. It was not until he returned to America early in 1779 that his luck deserted him. The *Revenge* was cornered by the British frigate *Galatea,* and Conyngham was imprisoned in the strongly guarded Old Mill Prison in England. He did not stay imprisoned for long. In November, 1779, he burrowed out, escaping with sixty companions, most of whom reached the safety of the Netherlands with him.

Among the most daring, ingenious, and picturesque of the commerce raiders was Abraham Whipple, designated by one biographer as "America's damndest naval hero." This was the same Abraham Whipple who had carved such a swath as captain of the *Game Cock* and had aroused British fury by his destruction of the *Gaspee* off Providence. Now, sometimes as a privateer and sometimes as a regular naval commander, he was twisting the lion's tail with a vengeance. It is recorded that in one six-month period he took no fewer than twenty-six British ships as prizes.

Typical of Whipple's maneuvers was his escape through the British blockade of Narragansett Bay, carrying vital dispatches addressed to Benjamin Franklin in France. Fifteen British warships had the various channels out of Narragansett Bay plugged tight, every one of the blockaders being more powerful than Whipple's frigate, *Providence* (28). Under cover of darkness he sailed down the West Channel toward the frigate *Lark* (40) and the *razee Renown* (50). The quarters were too close for him to hope to get by both guardians undetected. Instead, he boldly sailed across the *Lark*'s stern, delivered a raking broadside which paralyzed the enemy long enough for him to get by, then sailed boldly toward the *Renown,* on which boatswain's pipes could be heard twittering as the crew was called to battle stations. Further surprise was now out of the question. Captain Whipple raised his voice and shouted orders to the steersman: "Pass her to starboard, on the Narragansett side." Those words were for British ears. Quietly he added: "Now, luff ship and pass her close to *larboard.*" All along the *Renown*'s starboard side, gun ports were opened, guns run out, and the crews made ready. Whipple's attack was from the other side —the unprotected larboard. His broadside unshipped *Renown*'s rudder and caused much other damage. Out to sea he went, free, fast, and virtually undamaged.

The most famous of Whipple's many feats was his raid on a huge British convoy in the summer of 1779. Three American ships were involved—Whipple's *Providence,* the frigate *Queen of France* (28), and the brig *Ranger* (18). On July 24, they sighted a convoy of more than a hundred armed merchantmen, guarded by the ship-of-the-line *Holderness* (74) and eight frigates. Boldly, Whipple had the British colors hoisted on his three ships and joined the convoy, as though to furnish added protection.

During the next two days, the three bogus British warships reaped a rich harvest in prizes. Captains were invited aboard for dinner; when they accepted, they and their ships were taken. At night, vessels were lured away by masthead lights duplicating those of the flagship *Holderness*. Ships were edged out into fogbanks and taken. By ones and twos, richly laden members of the convoy were separated from their powerful but unsuspecting guardians and sent on westward toward the American coast under prize crews. Only a lack of manpower to furnish more such crews stopped the toll at eleven. Of these, eight safely ran the blockade, the other three being retaken by the British. It was a record haul, and for sheer impunity it was a feat unmatched in the annals of the sea.

Some of the other Yankee captains were Joshua Barney, Timothy Boardman, John Peck Rathburne, Isaiah Robinson, among others. And, of course, John Paul Jones, who deserves separate treatment.

14.

One of the best things that ever happened to the American Navy was an erroneous charge of murder brought by the British government against a Scottish merchant marine officer named John Paul. Paul was cleared of the charge, but his situation was precarious. It became far worse when he actually did kill a man while helping to suppress a mutiny. Rather than take a chance with an Admiralty Court, he quietly left the West Indies for the American mainland, where anti-British feeling was simmering toward the boiling point during this year of 1773. To make it more difficult for the British authorities to find him, the fugitive changed his name, adding the very common surname Jones to the two names which he already had.

When hostilities began in 1775, experienced officers were scarce in the American colonies. The Marine Committee, casting about, offered John Paul Jones the command of the sloop *Providence*. He declined, modestly stating that he needed more experience. Instead, he signed on as First Lieutenant of the little American flagship *Alfred* (24), serving under Captain Dudley Saltonstall. While holding this position, he had the honor of raising a thirteen-striped American flag aboard a warship for the first time.

To his vast disappointment, John Paul Jones was able to learn little from bumbling old Dudley Saltonstall or from the stodgy commander-in-chief, Esek Hopkins. Had they wished, both of these men could have learned much from him. During the cruise of the squadron to the Bahamas and back to Rhode Island, the young officer gained in confidence and came to appreciate his own abilities as compared with those of his nominally superior officers. He now felt himself ready to assume command of a ship of his own.

"I wish to have no connection with any ship that does not sail fast," said John Paul Jones, "for I intend to go in harm's way." Given the little twelve-gun sloop *Providence,* he promptly reduced her armament by half in order to increase her speed.

While Esek Hopkins and his squadron gathered moss in Newport, John Paul Jones and his *Providence* were usefully cruising the seas, outsailing and taking lesser ships and outsailing and escaping from those too big for him to take or to fight. The frigates *Cerberus* and *Solebay* found the little *Providence* adept at striking and escaping. The captain of the frigate *Milford* had even more reason for anguish. For eight hours, he thought he had the little raider, which limped along just within cannon range like a mother bird dragging a wing to decoy a fox. Time after time, *Milford*'s captain had his ship swung round to bring his broadside guns to bear. Always, as he swung, the elusive sloop seemed to put on a burst of speed, so that the salvos fell just short. Every time, the thunder of the British cannons was answered by the spiteful crack of a single musket, fired by a marine on the afterdeck of the *Providence*. After almost a solid day of frigate-baiting and after causing the British captain to waste scores of rounds of big-gun ammunition, Jones showed how fast his little sloop really was. Away he sped over the horizon, to take a dozen prizes on the Canadian fishing banks.

In October, 1776, Jones sailed from Newport in the *Alfred* to release American prisoners being held on Cape Breton Island. With him went the brigantine *Hampden* (14) under Captain Hoysted Hacker, a political appointee. At the very outset, Hacker ripped the *Hampden*'s bottom on a reef, necessitating a return to port. It was November before the expedition could sail again, this time with Hacker in command of the *Providence*. Two prizes, the brigantine *Active* and the big British transport *Mellish,* were taken before a storm blew up which frightened Hacker into deserting the expedition and running for home.

In anger and disgust, John Paul Jones carried on with the *Alfred*. Ice prevented him from reaching the prison camp where the prisoners were confined, but he made the most of his opportunities and took five prizes on the way home, one of them a ten-gun British warship. Then disaster threatened in the form of his old enemy, the frigate *Milford*.

Darkness was falling. Jones hoisted a lantern to his masthead and once more played decoy to *Milford*'s fox while his prizes scattered and got away safely. For more than five hours, the *Milford* hopefully followed the will-o'-the-wisp lantern before John Paul Jones put it out and headed for Boston to rejoin his prize ships.

On the basis of performance, John Paul Jones had clearly demonstrated that he stood Number One among American naval commanders. In making appointments, however, Congress and the Marine Committee found it necessary to pay heed to politics and outside influence. Jones was listed eighteenth. It was precisely the sort of treatment that had been handed to that other energetic genius of the war, Benedict Arnold. The principal difference between these very similar men was that under the press of injustice John Paul Jones remained loyal to the American cause, and Benedict Arnold did not.

On the beach, while lesser men received commands, John Paul Jones sat down and did a lot of writing. Some of it was in the form of letters—angry letters condemning Congress, the Marine Committee, and the minor mariners who had been preferred. Not all of the letters were destructively critical. Among them was one outlining the qualifications desirable in an officer of the United States Navy. It included the following: "It is by no means enough that an officer of the Navy should be a capable mariner. He should be as well a gentleman of liberal education, refined manners, punctilious courtesy, and the nicest sense of personal honor. When a commander has by tact, patience, justice, and firmness, each exercised in its proper turn, produced such an impression on those under his orders in a ship of war, he has only to await the appearance of his enemy's topsails upon the horizon. When this moment does come, he may be sure of victory over an equal or somewhat superior force, or honorable defeat by one greatly superior."

This sage observation has served ever since as a guiding star in the training of officers in the navy of the United States.[1]

Jones's letter-writing restored him to favor and raised him in the list. In June, 1777, he was given command of the new sloop *Ranger* (18). Here, again, he was able to score a "first" in connection with

---

[1] It is entirely possible that John Paul Jones was not the author of this famous letter, long and widely attributed to him. Samuel Eliot Morison, for one, avers that it was probably the invention of A. C. Buell, one of Jones's earlier biographers.

the American flag. The flag which he had raised in 1775 aboard the *Alfred* had had thirteen stripes and a British Union Jack. The flag which he now raised for the first time on any ship had thirteen stripes and a circle of thirteen stars on a field of blue. This flag—the first version of the Stars and Stripes—had been officially adopted by Congress on June 14, 1777, the same day on which Jones received his appointment to the *Ranger*.

Wrote John Paul Jones: "That flag and I are twins born in the same hour from the same womb of destiny. We cannot be parted in life or death. So long as we can float, we shall float together. If we must sink, we shall go down as one."

On November 1, 1777, John Paul Jones and the *Ranger* departed for France, bearing vital news. British General Burgoyne had surrendered at Saratoga, with his entire army! Here was information which Benjamin Franklin could use to good advantage in encouraging France to come into the war against Great Britain. The *Ranger* arrived in France on December 2, a very fast crossing, especially when one takes into consideration the delays involved in chasing and taking two British prizes en route.

Soon afterward, in the harbor of Brest, Jones scored still another "first" with the flag. A squadron of French warships lay at Brest, under the command of Admiral Picquet. The French had never before seen the flag of stars and stripes which floated from the *Ranger*'s masthead. Nevertheless, at Jones's request, they fired a formal salute of nine guns—the first official salute to the American flag in foreign waters. This amounted almost to a formal recognition by France of the independence of the United States. It did much to increase tension and to bring France and Great Britain nearer to the brink of open war.

15.

There have been few naval commanders who could match John Paul Jones in daring. Britain's mighty fleet controlled the sea, but that did not keep Jones and his men out of British waters. It did not even keep them out of Britain herself. After taking several prizes in the Irish Sea, Jones determined to carry the war directly to the enemy. The port of Whitehaven was selected. This town was not far from Jones's birthplace, and he knew it well. There he directed the *Ranger*. Jones himself led thirty volunteers in two boats, taking the forts, spiking the guns, and setting fire to some of the piers, warehouses, and ships in reprisal for the British burning of Falmouth. The actual damage was not great, but the effect on British morale and British insurance rates was catastrophic.

Across Solway Firth from Whitehaven lies St. Mary's Isle, which was then owned by the Earl of Selkirk. Jones intended to seize the Earl and hold him as hostage, in order to insure better treatment of American prisoners in Great Britain. Storming into the Earl's house, the Americans found only women and servants. The Earl was in London. With utmost politeness, John Paul Jones calmed the ladies' fears and withdrew his men, leaving all unharmed. Later, discovering that some of his crew had taken the Selkirk silverware, he sent it back to Lady Selkirk with a note saying, "I wage no war with the fair."

He did, however, wage war with the British navy. In Carrickfergus, Ireland, lay the British sloop *Drake* (20). Without showing any flag, *Ranger* hove to in the harbor mouth, with her stern toward the British ship. *Drake* sent a boat to investigate the newcomer; Jones captured it as it came alongside. Then *Drake* hoisted canvas and came out. When within shouting distance, her captain hailed, "What ship is that?"

Jones shouted, "The American Continental ship *Ranger!*" As his voice rang out, the Stars and Stripes went up to the masthead.

At the very outset, John Paul Jones gained the advantage. His stern was toward the bow of the *Drake,* which was still slowly breasting the incoming tide. As the range closed to pistol-shot distance, Jones swung about and delivered a raking broadside which swept the British deck from bow to stern. *Drake* never recovered. Though she battled furiously for an hour and four minutes before striking, she had no chance. Forty-two of her men, including her captain, were dead. Jones lost two men.

John Paul Jones had his enemies, and these set about discrediting him as soon as he arrived in France with the *Drake* as prize. One was Lieutenant Thomas Simpson, a jealous and almost mutinous officer who had served aboard the *Ranger.* Another, far more dangerous, was Mr. Arthur Lee, one of the American representatives in France. Together, these and others, disregarding his accomplishments, removed him from command of the *Ranger,* which was turned over to Simpson. Only Benjamin Franklin stood by Jones.

16.

Not until after France had come into the war was Franklin able to get another command for John Paul Jones. And what a command! She was an ancient and condemned French merchant ship, the *Duras,* suffering from rot and from a host of other ailments. The guns which Jones managed to hunt down for her were little better, a miscellaneous assortment of rejected cannons no longer considered good enough for any use by the French. Ah, well, she was a ship! Jones renamed her the *Bonhomme Richard,* in honor of Franklin's *Almanack,* and set about fitting her for sea.

On August 14, 1779, Jones sailed in the *Bonhomme Richard* (32) in company with four French ships, *Alliance* (32), *Pallas* (32), *Cerf* (18), and *Vengeance* (12). No one was in over-all command, an arrangement certain to make for confusion. Jones wanted to raid enemy shipping off Scotland, but the French captains voted him down. Without notice, the *Cerf* turned about and headed for home. Captain Pierre Landais of the *Alliance* tried to assume the command. When that failed, he adopted an uncooperative attitude. From the start, it appeared to be an ill-starred venture.

Before dawn on the morning of September 23, off Flamborough Head, the little squadron sighted a fleet of forty British merchantmen escorted by the big new frigate *Serapis* (50) and the *Countess of Scarborough* (20). John Paul Jones signaled for his ships to form line of battle. Only the *Pallas* did so. The *Vengeance* veered away and made for the merchant vessels, which scattered like a covey of quail. *Alliance* held off and made no move at all.

Jones might not be able to command his squadron, but he had control of his own ship. Boldly, the creaking old *Richard* made for the far newer and stronger *Serapis,* while the *Pallas* bore up to attack the *Countess of Scarborough.* The proposed fleet action became two individual duels between single ships.

In the same split second, *Serapis* and *Richard* fired their opening broadsides. The result was frightful for the American ship. The solid shot from the *Serapis* ripped through the rotten sides, spreading death and destruction; below decks two of the *Richard's* main guns blew up, slaughtering their crews, smashing boards and timbers, and setting fires. The screaming of the wounded had scarcely begun when a second British broadside smashed through the main gun deck.

John Paul Jones was rapidly losing his gun battle with the British frigate. Within a matter of minutes, most of his guns were out of action, while those of the *Serapis* continued to thunder. He tried to grapple, and failed. Again he tried. This time the bowsprit of the *Serapis* rammed through the shrouds of the *Richard*'s mizzenmast and became firmly entangled. Heavy hawsers completed the entrapment of the two antagonists. Maneuvering was now out of the question. The battle had become a slugging match—infighting of the most vicious sort.

The battle went on—guns firing at little more than arms' length. The *Bonhomme Richard* was a slowly sinking wreck, yet she continued to flail away with the three small cannons on the upper deck which could still be fired. Loaded with grape and cannister, these caused heavy casualties among the British. Still, the battle was too one-sided. It seemed certain that *Richard* must soon sink or surrender. So, apparently, believed Jones's master gunner, who rushed along the deck crying, "We surrender! Quarter! Give us quarter!"

Promptly, John Paul Jones wheeled and hurled a pistol at the man, knocking him down and stilling his cries. The voice, however, had been heard aboard the British ship. Called Captain Pearson of the *Serapis,* "Have you struck your colors?"

"No!" roared John Paul Jones. "I have not yet begun to fight!"

The battle was resumed in all its fury. While the great guns roared below, marksmen in the tops blazed away with muskets. Here the Americans gained an advantage. Slowly, the British sharpshooters were eliminated. The way was now clear for daring hands to work out along the *Richard*'s spars and into the rigging of the *Serapis.*

Out along a spar a sailor named Hamilton edged his way, with a bucket of grenades. Below him yawned an open hatch, leading down to the *Serapis'* main gun deck. One of his grenades went down the hatch and exploded. At once, there was a series of explosions as the powder supplies beside the guns went off, one after another. Fire and death swept the gun deck. *Serapis* began to suffer some of the agony with which her opponent was now so familiar.

Now, at last, *Alliance* made her move, sweeping in toward the embattled warships. Though the sun had not yet risen, there was a full moon, supplying plenty of light. To make sure there could be no mistake, John Paul Jones had hung three lanterns on the *Richard*'s disengaged side—a prearranged signal. Surely, Captain Landais knew which ship was which. If he did, his next act was betrayal of the worst sort, for he fired a broadside into the *Richard*'s stern! Dozens of Americans died under the impact of the French cannon balls, killed by their own allies!

Twice more *Alliance* fired her broadside guns, each time doing frightful damage to the *Richard* and her crew. The *Serapis* suffered, too, for some of the French balls went completely through the *Richard* and into the British hull. John Paul Jones fought on with undiminished ardor.

It was the British who cracked first, overcome as much by the terrible tenacity of the American crew as by the damage they had received. Captain Pearson himself hauled down the flag in surrender.

Pallas, meanwhile, had taken *Countess of Scarborough.* Together, the four ships started a halting voyage toward the coast of Holland. Only three arrived. The *Bonhomme Richard,* shattered and mauled, could not be kept afloat. She went down at sea, her flag still flying, while Jones and his crew transferred to the *Serapis.*

When at last Captain Pearson was exchanged, he had to stand a court-martial in Great Britain. In his statement to the court, he gave eloquent testimony to the character of John Paul Jones. "Long before the close of the action," he testified, "it became apparent that the American ship was dominated by a commanding will of a most unalterable resolution, and there can be no doubt that the intention of her commander was, if he could not conquer, to sink alongside."

Pierre Landais had not finished his mischief-making. With the help of Mr. Arthur Lee, he had the hero of the action beached while he himself continued in command of the *Alliance*. While Jones was languishing in France—a hero to everyone but Lee and the Marine Committee—Landais was crossing the ocean to the United States. When he arrived, it was found that he had gone completely insane and had had to be imprisoned by his own crew. That did much to explain his actions during the battle, but it did little indeed to place a keel under America's ablest naval officer.

17.

In spite of the individual brilliance of John Paul Jones and a few other able American sea captains, it was inevitable that Britain's powerful fleet would sweep the tiny navy of the United States from the seas. One by one—and sometimes in far greater numbers—America's warships were eliminated.

In June, 1777, the new American frigate *Hancock* (32) and the light frigate *Boston* (24) set out in company on a raiding expedition. The two captains disliked one another and could agree on nothing, to the great misfortune of both. Captain John Manley of the *Hancock,* the senior officer, was austere and overbearing. Captain Hector Mc-Neil of the *Boston* was timid. It was a bad combination.

Off the Newfoundland fishing banks, *Hancock* and *Boston* managed to converge on the new British frigate *Fox* (28). Attacked from both sides at once, the *Fox* was able to resist but briefly. *Boston* fired a broadside into her, and *Hancock* raked her from stern to bow. Fox surrendered.

Since the area to the north, around Nova Scotia, was well patrolled by British warships, McNeil wanted to go south to the West Indies. Manley overruled him. North went the two frigates. Sailing in a fog, they blundered into the midst of a British squadron consisting of the frigates *Rainbow* (48) and *Flora* (32) and the brig *Viper* (10). Mc-Neil, in the *Boston,* briefly engaged the *Flora,* then fled, leaving his opponent free to recapture the *Fox. Hancock* also fled, but was overtaken after a three-day chase. Cornered, she turned to fight her two antagonists. It was a vicious battle, but a short one. *Hancock*'s foremast was shot down, crippling her for either flight or maneuver. With the *Rainbow* thundering broadsides and the *Viper* sliding in to rake, there was no point in further resistance. The American colors came down. When next the *Hancock* sailed the sea, she had a new name and a new flag. She had become H. M. S. *Iris.*

18.

In the late summer of 1777, a strong British squadron appeared in Delaware Bay under Lord Richard Howe. The evident intention of the expedition was to sail up the Delaware River and take Philadelphia. This proved to be no easy task. The river below the capital city was protected by strong forts at Red Bank and on Mud and Fort islands and by underwater barriers in the river itself. Still, the British ships had considerable firepower, and they did not hesitate to launch a bold attack.

On October 22, the British ship-of-the-line *Augusta* (64), followed by two frigates and three sloops, moved in to bombard the fort on Mud Island. At the same time, a strong force of Hessian soldiers went overland to outflank the Red Bank defenses. The result was disastrous. The Hessians were driven back with heavy casualties. The ships were hammered hard by the guns in the fort. To make matters worse, *Augusta* and the sloop *Merlin* (16) went hard aground. Having stationary targets, the American gunners redoubled their efforts and succeeded in setting the *Augusta* on fire. Fearful of the explosion when her magazines should go, Lord Howe ordered the *Merlin* burned and fell back down the river.

In less than three weeks, the British squadron was back, reinforced by the *razee Isis* (50) and the frigate *Hammond*. Admiral William Cornwallis was in command. This time, the attack was made against Fort Mifflin, on Fort Island. The fort resisted well, with the help of some galleys sent by the Pennsylvania state government. The odds, however, proved too great. Fort Mifflin was evacuated after five days of bombardment, and the way to Philadelphia was open.

The passing of the river defenses was a disaster to the American navy. One ship was lost when the British captured the grounded frigate *Delaware* (24), stuck fast on a mud bar. Six small vessels—the *Andrea Doria, Racehorse, Surprise, Repulse, Champion,* and *Fly*—tried to escape upstream. They were pursued by the captured *Delaware* and by some smaller British vessels and had to be abandoned and burned to keep them from falling into the enemy's hands. Even worse, the American frigates *Washington* and *Effingham,* under construction at Philadelphia, had to be destroyed. An American squadron of nine ships had been lost.

19.

At sea, the new American frigate *Raleigh* (32) was sailing eastward in company with the *Alfred* (30). Captain Thomas Thompson of the *Raleigh*—senior officer of the expedition—was cursed with timidity that amounted almost to cowardice. Captain Elisha Hinman of the *Alfred* was a born fighter.

On September 2, 1777, *Raleigh* and *Alfred* captured a small merchant ship bound for England. From her captain, they learned that she was a straggler from a large convoy, traveling from the West Indies under the protection of the corvettes *Camel, Druid, Weazel,* and *Grasshopper*. At once, the American frigates clapped on sail and started out in pursuit.

The convoy was sighted late in the afternoon of September 4. As the two frigates bore down with guns out and colors flying, the nearest of the corvettes H. M. S. *Druid* (22), cleared for action and stood out boldly toward the *Raleigh,* which was sailing far ahead of the slower

Alfred. For nearly an hour the two ships blasted away, the smaller corvette giving as much as she received. Such spunky opposition took the zeal out of Captain Thompson, who presently veered away and swung back to rejoin the *Alfred.* The convoy made a clean escape.

Returning empty-handed in March, 1778, the poorly matched companions encountered further trouble, in the form of the British sloops *Ariadne* and *Ceres.* Two frigates should have made quick work of two sloops, but these did not. *Alfred* sailed boldly in to the attack, but timid Captain Thompson swung the *Raleigh* away and fled, leaving the *Alfred* to be battered to pieces by enemies who attacked from two sides at once. Having finished the first frigate, the two sloops pursued the *Raleigh* halfway across the Atlantic, finally giving up the chase when Captain Thompson jettisoned guns and other gear in order to lighten ship. This disgraceful performance earned Thomas Thompson a court-martial and dismissal from the service.

Very different was the story of the beautiful new frigate *Randolph* (32), commanded by able and peppery Nicholas Biddle. On March 7, 1778, *Randolph* was sailing near the island of Barbados, accompanied by three little vessels of the South Carolina state navy and by the South Carolina sloop *General Moultrie* (18). Suddenly, out of the fog, loomed the bulk of H. M. S. *Yarmouth* (64), a British ship-of-the-line. In the excitement, the *General Moultrie* fired a broadside which struck the *Randolph* rather than the *Yarmouth.* Then the little state ships scattered, leaving *Randolph* to contend with an enemy which outgunned her sixty-four to thirty-two and outweighed her by an even greater margin.

Undeterred, Captain Nicholas Biddle came into the action with all guns blazing. For an hour, the two unequal opponents blasted away at point-blank range, a welterweight against a heavyweight, a lynx against a lion. Early in the action, Captain Biddle was so badly wounded that he could not stand, but he insisted on directing the action from a chair. The *Yarmouth* was not escaping without blood and damage. In fact, she seemed to be getting somewhat the worst of the struggle until a British cannon ball struck the *Randolph*'s magazine. With a sudden burst of flame and a thunderclap of sound, the American frigate was gone, together with Captain Biddle and all but one of her crew. The sole survivor, picked up from a piece of floating wreckage five days later, supplied the story of the battle as seen by the men of the *Randolph.*

Raleigh, having returned in disgrace from her unfortunate cruise with the *Alfred,* received a new captain with a more daring spirit. He was John Barry, famous for his capture of the *Alfred* early in the war. On September 25, 1779, the unfortunate frigate found game too big for her to handle—H. M. S. *Experiment* (50) and the sloop *Unicorn* (22). Since thirty-two guns were no match for seventy-two, Barry fled northeastward, hotly pursued. On the afternoon of the 27th, *Unicorn* drew up into range and opened fire. By a combination of accuracy and luck, the British gunners managed to damage the *Raleigh*'s fore- and mizzenmasts, making her almost unmanageable and cutting down her speed, so that the heavier *Experiment* was able to catch up and join in the attack.

Outgunned, outmaneuvered, and outlucked, Barry resolved to destroy his ship, rather than have it fall into British hands. He rammed her hard on a rocky island, some thirty-five miles off the coast of Maine. Even then he did not surrender, but continued to trade broadsides with both British ships until darkness brought a temporary end to the struggle.

Under cover of night, John Barry landed his men on the rocky island and instituted a small-boat ferry service to the distant mainland. Before leaving the *Raleigh,* he laid powder trains and issued orders that Midshipman Jesse Jacocks was to light the trains before leaving the ship. Jacocks disobeyed orders. Instead of lighting the trains, he merely darkened the ship, remaining aboard. As a result, the British were able to take the *Raleigh* in the morning, and by midafternoon had her afloat again. They also captured 140 American seamen still on the island. Barry and 85 of his men had managed to escape to the mainland.

20.

The worst disaster of all was the American expedition against the forts at the mouth of the Penobscot River, in Maine. Captain Dudley Saltonstall was in command. Under him were twenty-two transports, laden with 3,000 soldiers, and nineteen warships—U. S. frigate *Warren* (32), U. S. brigs *Providence* and *Diligent,* three Massachusetts brigs, one New Hampshire brig, and twelve privateers. It was a force more than ample to take the little forts and to capture or destroy the three British sloops guarding the river mouth.

Since Britain controlled the seas, common sense dictated a quick, incisive move. Saltonstall, however, was in no hurry. He anchored his fleet and proceeded to waste two valuable weeks, doing nothing. As might have been expected, the enemy put to good use the time which the American commander wasted.

On August 13, 1779, seven British warships appeared—H. M. S. *Raisonable* (64), two frigates, three sloops, and a brig. Despite the presence of one ship-of-the-line, the American firepower outweighed that of the British nearly four to one. Nevertheless, Captain Saltonstall and his forty-one ships fled from the seven Britishers, seeking safety in the shallower waters upriver.

There was no battle, as such. Trapped by the pursuing enemy, the *Warren* and one or two of the other ships fired a few shots to betoken resistance. It was a poor token indeed. As the enemy came within effective range, Captain Saltonstall ordered his ships to be run aground and burned. While forty-one American vessels went up in flames, Saltonstall and most of his men escaped inland. About 500 American soldiers were captured.

So disgraceful was the Penobscot fiasco that it was studiously omitted from American history books for well over a century!

Another unhappy occasion was the loss of the frigates *Providence, Queen of France,* and *Boston* and the sloop *Ranger* when the British captured Charleston in February, 1780. Profiting by their unhappy experience of 1776, the British this time sent ships-of-the-line instead of frigates against the Charleston defenses. The forts were passed, and H. M. S. *Renown, Roebuck,* and *Romulus* forced their way into the harbor. The fire must have burned out in Captain Abraham Whipple's soul. Although he had boldly faced even greater odds in the past, he made no effort to oppose the British battleships. The four American vessels were ignominiously surrendered.

To all intents and purposes, the fall of Charleston liquidated the last of the United States Navy. Things looked black, but help was on the way. Benjamin Franklin's diplomacy had prevailed, and France was in the war as America's ally. The task of waging the war upon the sea now devolved upon the French Navy, assisted in some measure by the omnipresent American privateers.

9 FRANCE CARRIES THE LOAD

⚓

1.

France, Spain, and the Netherlands looked on with undisguised satisfaction as Great Britain encountered defiance and resistance in her American colonies. All three nations had been defeated by the British and had been relieved of colonies and of maritime supremacy. Anything that these raw Americans could do to embarrass Britain and to lessen her power would be more than welcome.

To the amazement of the world, the American Revolution was not quickly suppressed. The colonists resisted with surprising vigor, and the British generals, who had been selected in the most haphazard of ways, mismanaged the war from the beginning. Lord North, the British Prime Minister, summed it up admirably when he said, "I don't know whether our generals frighten the enemy, but they certainly frighten me."

After the American Declaration of Independence, in 1776, the European nations began to look with increasing hope upon the efforts of the Americans to gain their freedom and thus to deal a real blow to the British Empire. In the court of France, resourceful old Benjamin Franklin was hard at work trying to convince the ministers of King Louis XVI that there was now a golden opportunity to weaken the ancient enemy. Gradually, his views were accepted. Secret aid was sent to the Americans through a dummy trading concern, Hortalies & Cie., oganized by Pierre A. C. de Beaumarchais. After General John Burgoyne's British army became entrapped in the woods of northern New York and was forced to surrender at Saratoga, the mask was thrown off. On July 10, 1778, France came openly into the war. Spain followed suit the next year, and the Netherlands in 1780.

Had the British navy been put to more efficient use, the entry of the three European nations into the war might not have made a tremendous difference. Great Britain had 150 ships-of-the-line, as opposed to 80 French and 60 Spanish. The Dutch navy at this time was insignificant and the American fleet almost nonexistent. What is more, the ships of the hostile nations were scattered in various bases and could be brought together only with the greatest of difficulty. All that Great Britain had to do was to blockade the coasts of the hostile countries, thus keeping the segments of the fleets from uniting, cutting off all aid to the Americans, and blocking all moves against the British Isles. Instead, she weakened her home fleet in order to scatter her ships widely in small squadrons to protect all of the distant parts of the Empire. Against opponents less inept, this might have been a fatal mistake.

The French and Spanish navies, however, were nothing if not inept. Both services were riddled with corruption. Commissions and commands were granted on a basis of wealth and social standing, without regard for experience and ability. Both fleets were guided by a tradition of fighting on the defensive and never risking a squadron in order to gain a victory. If Britain had to make mistakes, these were the opponents against whom it would be safest to make them.

2.

With war impending but not yet declared, Admiral Augustus Keppel found himself in command of His Majesty's home fleet, of which only ten ships-of-the-line were fit for sea. Frantically, he pushed the work of building and repair and managed to add another ten. With this small fleet, he set out in mid-June, 1778, and promptly encountered two French frigates. Though Great Britain and France were still technically at peace, he captured both ships in order to keep them from carrying home word of the weakness of his force. From papers found aboard, he discovered that the French squadron across the Channel at Brest included thirty-two ships-of-the-line and numerous auxiliary vessels. In something approaching panic, Keppel rushed his preparations. Ten more ships were added before war was declared.

On July 23, Keppel and his thirty British ships sighted the thirty-two ships of the French squadron under the Comte d'Orvilliers. Keppel tried to close, but the French line bore away, avoiding battle. When darkness fell, D'Orvilliers changed course and continued to retire. Two of his ships-of-the-line missed the signals and became separated from the main body. Daylight revealed these two to Keppel, who moved to cut them off, feeling sure that the French would come back to rescue two warships as important as these.

Keppel was right. The French fleet did come back. There followed four days of maneuvering, with the British fleet interposed between D'Orvilliers and the two fugitive ships, which had escaped to the northwest. At last, late in the morning of July 27, the two fleets came within cannon range. The French had the weather gauge, but Keppel had managed to get his squadron between the French and their home port of Brest. As the battle lines passed in opposite directions, both fleets cannonaded furiously, the French aiming high to destroy masts and rigging, the British aiming low to damage ships and kill men. Keppel himself held back the fire of his flagship, the *Victory* (100), until he had passed the first six ships of the French line and had come opposite the French flagship *Bretagne* (110), into whose hull he discharged his first broadside. Thereafter, his gunners continued to fire at the passing French ships as rapidly as they could reload their guns.

Just as the two fleets cleared one another, the wind swung around to give Keppel the weather gauge. For a few brief minutes, he thought that victory was his. Joyfully, he ordered his ships about to form a line in pursuit of the French. To his dismay, he saw that five of his ships had been dismasted and were drifting helplessly out of line. To make matters worse, the rear division, headed by Vice-Admiral Hugh Palliser, was not following his signals but was continuing straight on, away from the enemy.

Admiral D'Orvilliers saw the confusion in the British formation and took steps to come about and attack. Fortunately for Keppel, the Comte's orders were followed slowly and with great lack of precision. By the time the French line was re-formed, the British had begun to bring order out of their chaos. Palliser's division had finally come about and was rejoining, and Keppel was leading his still-active ships back for further action. Seeing this, D'Orvilliers sheered off and took advantage of the fact that he now had a clear route to Brest. Though no ships had been sunk or captured by either fleet, he felt, with some justification, that he had won a victory of sorts. He felt even better a week later when his two missing ships sailed safely into Brest and rejoined his fleet.

There was great dissatisfaction in Great Britain over the outcome of this indecisive battle off Ushant. Admiral Keppel was a Whig, and as such he was automatically under suspicion of favoring the cause of America and her allies. Two ardent Tories, the Earl of Sandwich and Vice-Admiral Palliser, forced him to stand a court-martial. Four charges were leveled at him, each involving a possible sentence of death.

When the facts were examined, most navy men tended to side with Admiral Keppel. His luck had been bad in losing the services of his five disabled ships and in having his signals to Palliser's division obscured by smoke and haze. (No one ventured to bring up the possibility that the vice-admiral's failure to cooperate might have been intentional, though it certainly must have crossed the minds of some of those sitting on the court.) Keppel's orders—some of which did, indeed, violate the doctrines laid down by the hallowed *Fighting Instructions*—were shown to have been intelligently conceived. He himself had shown great zeal for attacking the enemy. Common sense prevailed. Admiral Keppel was acquitted on all counts.

With this decision, the unquiet ghost of Admiral Byng ceased to haunt the officers of the British navy. The dead albatross of the *Fighting Instructions* slipped from around their necks. For the first time in well over a century, it became relatively safe for the commanding officers of the Royal Navy to exercise their own judgment and initiative.

3.

News of the French alliance caused great consternation among the British in America. Now the American troops under General Washington would be supplemented by French troops. Far worse would be the presence of French naval units. The British forces in the Delaware Bay region were especially vulnerable. With all speed, British Admiral Lord Richard Howe removed his ships from that natural trap and departed for New York, where he would be safer. Soon afterward, General Clinton abandoned Philadelphia and took his British army overland toward New York. On the way, he was ambushed at Monmouth, New Jersey, by Washington's American army. Thanks to the incompetence or worse of American General Charles Lee, the battle was a draw. Had Lee not thrown away the chance for victory and had Admiral Howe not carried all of Clinton's baggage and equipment by sea, thus permitting the army to travel light, the British general might well have suffered the same fate as General Burgoyne.

Early in July, 1778, French Admiral Charles le Comte d'Estaing arrived at the entrance to Delaware Bay with twelve large ships-of-the-line and four frigates from the naval base at Toulon. With the exception of the British frigate *Mermaid,* left for picket duty, the birds had flown. Pursued by the French warships, the *Mermaid* was run ashore. Finding nothing more to do in Delaware Bay, D'Estaing sailed north in Admiral Howe's wake.

Admiral Howe, meanwhile, was having some bad moments. British picket frigates at Gibraltar, though unable to stop the Toulon squadron, had given an accurate report of its strength. To oppose the twelve first-line French ships, he had only nine ships of inferior size, three being merely *razees.* The odds were too great to risk an all-out naval engagement. Accordingly, Howe took his fleet into lower New York Bay and set about blocking the channels with sunken hulks.

Arriving off Sandy Hook, D'Estaing could see Howe's fleet lying at anchor just beyond the low, narrow spit of land. It seemed self-evident that the British squadron would soon be crushed and Clinton tightly bottled up in New York. This cheerful prospect was presently dispelled by American pilots, brought aboard the flagship *Languedoc* (90). Though Howe had not succeeded in blocking the channels very effectively, Nature had. The depth of water over the bars was not sufficient to permit the passage of the eight largest French warships. Although wind and tide were in his favor, D'Estaing dared not risk his big ships in shoal water. He sent out sounding crews in small boats, who substantiated the pilots' findings. With a last look at Howe's fleet —so near and yet so far, so helpless and yet so safe—the French admiral sailed eastward toward Narragansett Bay, where the American army had been trying in vain to rout the British from a strong base at Newport.

4 .

The arrival of D'Estaing's squadron off Newport caused an immediate panic among the British, who felt sure that the town would soon be taken. In the harbor lay the frigates *Cerberus, Flora,* and *Juno,* and thirteen transports. Acting with too much haste, the British naval commander at Newport burned all sixteen vessels to prevent their capture. While their smoke still darkened the sky, Admiral Howe's British fleet, now reinforced by four more ships-of-the-line, was seen at the entrance to the bay.

Learning of Howe's approach, D'Estaing promptly brought out his fleet for battle. For all of one day, August 11, the two fleets maneuvered for position, amid steadily increasing winds and seas. The next day, the weather was worse. Late in the afternoon, D'Estaing was just leading his line on an overtaking course toward the British rear when a hurricane broke in all its fury. There could be no battle now. Both fleets were scattered. On every ship, the sole question was one of survival.

After two days, the "great French storm"—the worst in fifty years —blew itself out. Neither squadron had lost any ships, though many had been badly damaged. As the individual vessels sought the others of their scattered groups, there were numerous two-ship actions in passing. D'Estaing's flagship *Languedoc,* completely dismasted and barely able to crawl under a jury rig, encountered H. M. S. *Renown* (50), still intact after riding out the storm. Despite the *Renown*'s ability to choose positions and to rake her larger but crippled opponent at will, the British ship was unable either to take or to destroy the *Languedoc,* though the execution among the French crew was dreadful. In the end, the vessels parted, and the *Languedoc* managed to rejoin her squadron.

Pulling his battered squadron together, Admiral D'Estaing now sailed for Boston, abandoning the American army besieging Newport and leaving that important base in British hands. To the disappointed American patriots, it appeared a cowardly and disgraceful move. Boston mobs insulted the French allies, leading D'Estaing to quit the American coast and head for the West Indies, where he hoped to do more good for France and more harm to Britain than he had yet managed.

5.

It is easy to understand D'Estaing's eagerness to quit the unprofitable and inhospitable American coast for a campaign in the West Indies. It was here that France hoped to gain her chief rewards from the war. The raw materials and the harbors of these tropical islands were well worth fighting for.

As Admiral D'Estaing's French fleet entered West Indian waters, the British were just in the act of capturing the French island of St. Lucia. In the harbor lay the transports which had brought the British troops to the island. They were protected by five British ships-of-the-line and a few smaller vessels under the command of Rear Admiral Samuel Barrington.

Hearing of the approach of D'Estaing's more powerful squadron,

Barrington stretched his little line of ships across the entrance to St. Lucia Harbor and prepared to die defending the transports and the troops ashore. It proved to be unnecessary. As at Sandy Hook, D'Estaing found that he could not get at this snugly placed enemy fleet. In the end—being at heart a soldier rather than an admiral—he landed his men elsewhere on the island and attempted to drive the British out by a land attack. This failed, too. St. Lucia was left in British hands.

Reinforcements now arrived from France, raising D'Estaing's squadron to twenty ships-of-the-line. With this added strength, he managed to capture the islands of St. Vincent and Grenada without much difficulty. He also took some thirty richly laden merchant vessels flying the British flag among the islands.

It was not, of course, any part of the British plan to permit the West Indies to be lost by default. Out from Great Britain came a squadron of twenty-two ships-of-the-line, under the command of Vice-Admiral John Byron, whose mission was to find and destroy D'Estaing's squadron and retake the islands. To aid in these objectives, he had 9,000 troops in convoyed transports.

Byron found the French squadron lying at anchor in St. George Harbor, Grenada. Seeing the enemy apparently unprepared for action, the British admiral immediately ordered an attack and hoisted the signal for a general chase. As a result, his own squadron rushed into action in rather poor order, without taking the time to firm up a line of battle.

D'Estaing was not so unprepared as Byron had assumed. Before the British came within range, the French ships got under way and managed to form a line. In effect, D'Estaing "crossed the T" of the approaching British column, whose leading ships were subjected to heavy raking fire before they were able to swing into a parallel course. During this part of the fighting, four British ships were disabled by the usual high-aimed French fire. Two others were badly damaged.

After nearly six hours of furious fighting, there was a lull. This was abruptly ended when Byron saw the French line coming about to approach his crippled British ships. He himself made all haste to go to their rescue, but veered away when he found the danger not so great as expected. Instead of trying to capture the dismasted ships, as a British admiral would certainly have done, D'Estaing merely sailed by them and mauled them with broadsides as he passed. Both fleets then withdrew, the French to St. George Harbor, the British to St. Kitts.

D'Estaing had won a battle, but he had missed the obvious move of pursuing and destroying his defeated enemy. After a long delay, he sailed for St. Kitts, where he found Byron's fleet lying at anchor, still in bad repair. Instead of going into the harbor to complete his work, the French admiral merely sailed back and forth in sight of the enemy, inviting them to come out. When they did not do so, he sailed away.

6.

The absence of D'Estaing's squadron from the Atlantic coast had permitted the British to launch a sea-borne invasion of the southern states. Chief among the places taken was Savannah, Georgia. To aid in recapturing Savannah, D'Estaing's squadron appeared off the Georgia coast on September 1, 1779, bearing 6,000 French troops to cooperate with the American forces under General Benjamin Lincoln.

The siege of Savannah was a complete failure. British General Augustine Prevost defended the town with vigor and intelligence and succeeded in inflicting very heavy casualties on the French and American attackers. At the end of two fruitless months, D'Estaing took his ships and returned to France, and General Lincoln marched his troops north to Charleston. There, in his turn, he was besieged by the British and was eventually forced to surrender the town, his army, himself, and the four American warships in the harbor.

Throughout the United States, there was a tendency to condemn D'Estaing for an utterly useless naval campaign. So bitter was the feeling on both sides of the Atlantic that it was felt necessary to send Washington's friend, the Marquis de Lafayette, to France to smooth over relations.

Actually, the campaign had many good results for the American cause. The knowledge of D'Estaing's approach had forced the British to evacuate Philadelphia, and the fear that he might return to Narragansett Bay later caused them to leave Newport. The French operation in the West Indies had drawn many British warships away from the Atlantic seaboard, making it easier for American privateers to slip in and out and lessening British naval support of military operations. France also profited from the capture of St. Vincent and Grenada.

In considering the case of Admiral D'Estaing, the French government took into account the fact that he was, by choice, a military man and that he acted with the greatest of heroism whenever he found his feet on solid ground. It was only on the unfamiliar sea that he showed timidity. He was relieved of his command, being replaced by the more experienced Comte de Guichen, but he was not otherwise penalized. One of his associates, Admiral Pierre Suffren, summed it up well with the words, "If only he were as much a sailor as he is a hero!"

7.

We should pause here to note the work of a layman—John Clerk, of Elgin, Scotland. Clerk was neither a military nor a naval man, which perhaps accounts for the fact that he was able to apply a clear, intelligent, unindoctrinated view to the naval practices of his day. Studying the *Fighting Instructions,* he came to the conclusion that any admiral who followed them to the letter could never win decisive victories. Only by engaging the enemy closely, breaking the line, and attacking boldly ship-to-ship could one fleet annihilate another. The *Instructions,* stressing orthodoxy and discouraging the taking of risks, could lead only to routine endeavor and modest successes. These views and others of like nature were expressed in a privately printed pamphlet, *An Essay on Naval Tactics,* first issued in 1780.

Clerk and his friends made certain that copies of the *Essay* were sent to all prominent British naval officers. Many of the recipients derisively repudiated this brash amateur who presumed to tell them how they should carry on their professional activities. Most of the others chose to pretend that they had never seen the pamphlet nor heard of its author. A few, including Captain Horatio Nelson, had the honesty to acknowledge the rightness of some of Clerk's heretical contentions. One gets the impression that Clerk's *Essay* exerted almost no impact at all on British naval circles.

If so, we must recognize a strange coincidence. From the year of the *Essay*'s issuance, the maneuvers which it recommended began to appear with increasing frequency wherever the British navy was active. Even those officers who most loudly derided Clerk, even those who looked blank and denied that they had ever heard of him, began to follow his advice.

Can it be that the British navy owes John Clerk a greater debt than it will ever acknowledge?

8.

Spain's entry into the war in June, 1779, was followed by a comic-opera attempt to invade England. The plan had been worked out long before. The French and Spanish fleets would join forces, sweep aside British naval resistance, and land troops on the always vulnerable Isle of Wight and at Portsmouth. It was a good plan, and it had an excellent chance of success if intelligently carried out.

The current commander of Britain's home-based Grand Fleet was Admiral Sir Charles Hardy, an austere, timid man who has been described as being "old beyond his years." His were scarcely the shoulders upon which one would expect the mantle of Drake to fall.

Because of the scattering of British naval power to distant areas, Admiral Hardy had only thirty-five ships-of-the-line with which to oppose the sixty-eight allied ships available to French Admiral D'Orvilliers. As though these odds were not sufficiently favorable for the invaders, Hardy took his little squadron westward beyond the Scilly Islands, leaving the seas between France and England free of defenders. He did not even send out scout frigates, perhaps because he was afraid that the enemy might follow one of them back to his main fleet.

How did the French and Spaniards seize their glowing opportunity? First, they wasted more than a month in ironing out minor matters of protocol between Admirals D'Orvilliers and Cordoba and in completing Spanish preparations that were supposed to have been attended to long before. When at last they reached the Channel, in mid-August, they wasted more time in searching for the missing British fleet, rather than in taking advantage of its absence. While all this was going on, Admiral Hardy was peacefully cruising his little section of sea off the Scillies in complete ignorance of the enemy's movements. Not until the allied fleet appeared off the Plymouth waterfront, and there captured a stray British sixty-four-gun ship, was an alarm given. Suddenly, and with good reason, Britain was swept from apathy into panic.

The French naval authorities chose this unlikely time to change the plans. D'Orvilliers received word that he was to make his landing at Falmouth Bay, in Cornwall. Here he would have no protection, no safe anchorage for his fleet. Indignantly, he rushed back counterarguments, meanwhile wasting precious days doing nothing in the Channel. Poor D'Orvilliers was in the unhappy position of a man holding a hot soup tureen while members of his family debate endlessly about where he shall put it down.

At last the French admiral found out, in some manner, where the

British fleet was located. Here was something constructive which he could do—eliminate the enemy's sea power, while Paris and Madrid were making up their minds concerning the details of the invasion. Westward he sailed, looking for Hardy's squadron.

All things considered, Admiral Hardy was a lucky man. The enemy, which had been between him and his harbors, passed him in the night. When daylight revealed the two fleets to one another, the French and Spaniards were on Hardy's western horizon. At once they came about, intent on battle. Hardy, having been given a head start, did not relinquish it. Thanks largely to the recently adopted British practice of sheathing the bottoms of warships with copper, his ships were not impeded by the luxuriant marine growth that held back his enemies. The British squadron showed a clean pair of heels, dashing safely into port as the allied squadron fell farther and farther behind.

Though the way to invasion was still open, Admiral D'Orvilliers had had enough. His ships were low on food and water, his crews decimated by disease. With a Gallic shrug, he returned to Brest, where he resigned his commission and retired to private life.

Thus was Britain saved, without a battle and with remarkably little glory.

9 .

It was a good thing for Great Britain that she began to find able naval leaders among her seamen, for in the years 1779 and 1780 her situation became increasingly desperate. Spain and France together still held a predominance of sea power in European waters, and the Netherlands government was preparing to throw its little navy onto the heavy side of the scales. Farther east, a combination of three unfriendly powers—Russia, Sweden, and Denmark—was carrying on a sort of cold-war activity by supplying Britain's enemies with needed equipment. Spain was blockading Gibraltar and threatening Minorca. Even the despised Americans, with ships borrowed from the French, were burning or capturing vessels and raiding towns on the very shores of Great Britain.

Vice-Admiral George Darby, vigorous and intelligent, took over the command of the Grand Fleet, thus placing Britain's defenses in firm hands. Sir George Brydges Rodney, a fighter in the old tradition, replaced Byron in charge of the West Indies squadron. He was willing and anxious to assume the offensive in this important area or, it soon developed, anywhere else.

Admiral Rodney was sent to the West Indies by a most unusual route. Borrowing some of Darby's ships, he set sail with twenty-two of the line to convoy some transports and supply ships to Gibraltar and Minorca. Off Cape Finisterre, on January 8, 1780, he came upon a fleet of Spanish merchant ships under the protection of a 64 and six frigates. The whole lot were quickly rounded up. From the captured officers, who evidently talked too much, he learned of a strong Spanish squadron waiting off Cape St. Vincent to intercept any Gibraltar-bound convoys. Counting on his own strength to get him out again, Rodney planned to fall neatly into the Spanish trap.

The information proved to be accurate. Off Cape St. Vincent were eleven Spanish ships-of-the-line, commanded by Admiral Juan de Langera in the *Phoenix* (80). The Spaniards took one look at the British force bearing down upon them and promptly took off in the direction of Cadiz. Admiral Rodney clapped on all sails and pursued.

Up to the masthead of Rodney's flagship *Sandwich* (90) went two flags, one signaling a general chase, the other "Keep to leeward." The well-trained subordinates followed instructions to the letter, gradually overhauling the Spanish vessels and at the same time sliding in between them and the Spanish coast. Just at sundown, the leading British ships came within range and opened a twilight action which presently became a full-fledged night engagement lighted only by the moon, the blinding glare of broadsides, and the flames of burning ships.

The battle lasted for a full nine hours. Of all the British ships engaged, the *Bienfaisant* (64) had the most success.[1] She early found herself exchanging broadsides with the *San Domingo* (70). Suddenly, there was a tremendous explosion, and the *San Domingo* was gone, leaving only some scattered wreckage and a single survivor. Later, the *Bienfaisant* received the surrender of the Spanish flagship *Phoenix*. Since there was smallpox aboard the British ship, the crew of the *Phoenix* were paroled on their own vessel, rather than being taken aboard. The sole exception was Admiral De Langera, who became the guest of Rodney aboard the *Sandwich*. It is interesting to note that the paroled Spanish crew dutifully and honorably lived up to their

[1] The presence of this French-sounding ship in a British squadron, and of other foreign-sounding ships in the squadrons of various nations, comes about from the custom of incorporating captured vessels into the fleets of their captors without changing their names. The purpose was to build morale through the constant reminder of the victories in which the ships had been captured.

pledged word and turned themselves in as prisoners of war and their ship as a lawful prize.

The morning's total showed that four of the Spanish ships and two frigates had escaped in the darkness. One had been blown up. Six had been captured, though two of these were in such damaged condition that they subsequently sank. It was a most worthwhile victory, and a badly needed brace for British morale.

Following his victory off Cape St. Vincent, Rodney proceeded to reinforce and supply Gibraltar, without any interference from a strong squadron of twenty-four allied ships lying at Cadiz under Don Luiz Cordova. He then sent back to England the ships which he had borrowed from Darby and proceeded to the West Indies with the smaller part of the squadron with which he had left home.

10.

The new French admiral in the West Indies, the Comte de Guichen, was able but was neither energetic nor aggressive. Since his fleet greatly outnumbered both the British squadron in the West Indies and Rodney's relieving squadron, the obvious move would have been to destroy each separately before they could be joined. He made no move to do this, leaving his fleet of twenty-two ships quietly at anchor in the harbor of Fort Royal, Martinique, while Rodney sailed unopposed to St. Lucia and took command of what was left of Byron's West Indies squadron. All together, the British admiral still had two fewer ships than his French opponent.

Rodney was a fighting admiral. As soon as he reached the West Indies, he dispatched frigates to watch the French anchorage. When one of these brought him news, on April 15, 1780, that the French fleet was coming out, he sailed at once to intercept it. Contact was made just before sundown the next day. Besides his warships, De Guichen had a large number of laden merchantmen, which he was escorting on the first leg of their journey to France, and a group of transports loaded with troops for the proposed conquest of the British-held island of Barbados.

The next morning, the French fleet was still doggedly butting its way eastward through the channel between Martinique and Dominica, and had passed the point of Cape St. Martin. Noting that De Guichen's twenty-two warships were spread out into a straggling line twelve miles in length, Rodney bunched his twenty into a close-knit line of only five miles, with the intention of concentrating all twenty of his ships against the last ten in the French formation.

Realizing his danger, Admiral De Guichen brought all of his ships about simultaneously and made haste to close up his line. Rodney waited until his flagship was opposite the French flagship, then brought his ships about to resume the parallel course. A signal was then hoisted to close with the enemy, with each ship to engage the enemy ship opposite its position.

There followed one of those misunderstandings which so often seem to rob naval commanders of the fruits of victory. What Rodney intended was for the entire British line to concentrate on the segment of the French line which was opposite—each ship, that is, to engage the French ship which was then immediately abreast of it. Captain Robert Carkett of the leading British ship, *Stirling Castle,* chose to believe that he was to engage the first ship in the French formation. Accordingly, he made all possible sail in order to catch up with the French leader, still far ahead. He was followed by all the other ships of the British van, including the flagship of Admiral Sir Hyde Parker, in command of the van division. This stretched the British formation out and lost the advantage of concentration.

Under the circumstances, no decisive victory could be achieved. Rodney brought his flagship *Sandwich* within a cable's length of the French battle line and hammered away furiously, supported in this close action by only four other ships. The others of the British line contented themselves with cannonading at long range, except for the four leading ships, which never drew close enough to the enemy for any effective action. After more than three hours of battle, the French turned away. Rodney could not pursue them, for many of his ships had been crippled aloft by the usual high French fire.

In a sense, the battle off Cape St. Martin was a standoff. The French had done more material damage, but had received far more casualties. The merchant convoy had managed to get through safely on its way to France. On the other hand, the proposed French invasion of Barbados had had to be abandoned.

To Admiral Rodney, the whole affair was heartbreaking. Seeing the overextended French battle line, he had felt sure of an overwhelming victory, one upon which he could build a reputation for greatness. Afterward, he felt that he had been robbed by the failure of his subordinates. He told them so in no uncertain words and later saw to it that two of them were court-martialed. One, Captain Bateman of the *Yarmouth,* was subsequently dismissed from the service.

In mid-May, admirals Rodney and De Guichen met again, this time off St. Lucia. Several days of maneuvering, sparring, and intermittent, indecisive battle followed, strangely characterized by Rodney's quietly leaving his flagship, with his flag still flying on it, to conduct the battle at long range from the frigate *Venus.* This by-no-means-effective procedure placed a heavy responsibility on the shoulders of Captain Middleton of the *Sandwich,* who not only had to perform his own duties in the heat of the action but many of the admiral's duties as well. Though the British fleet suffered three badly damaged ships and eventually had to break off contact to keep them from sinking, Admiral Rodney was really very lucky to have escaped a severe beating.

Fall arrived without further action. The French, always mindful of the preservation of their fleet, issued orders to De Guichen to return his ships to France before the hurricane season. He did so. Rodney, not quite so forehanded, took half of his fleet to New York. A tropical hurricane caught those which he left at St. Lucia, sinking two ships-of-the-line and some frigates and dismasting the rest. It was a severe blow to British sea power in western waters.

11.

To his discredit, Admiral Rodney now permitted his personal affairs to interfere with his naval efficiency. Like many a naval man, he was having difficulty making both ends meet. He was engaged in refitting his shattered fleet at Barbados when word arrived, in January, 1781, that the Netherlands had entered the war. Leaving the refitting chore in the hands of Rear Admiral Sir Samuel Hood, who had come out from England with eight ships-of-the-line to replace Parker, Rodney at once took off with a small squadron to capture the Dutch islands of St. Eustatius and Curacao and the mainland colony of Surinam.

St. Eustatius fell without resistance. To his delight, Admiral Rodney found that it was wealthy beyond belief, having served as a valuable shipping and receiving point for goods traded between the Dutch and the Americans. So rich were the pickings, personal and official, that Rodney stayed on, industriously feathering his nest and neglecting not only Curacao and Surinam but also his main fleet at Barbados.

While Rodney and Hood were thus employed, a large French convoy sailed from Brest, escorted by twenty-six ships-of-the-line under the command of the Comte de Grasse. Five of the warships, under Commodore Pierre Suffren, subsequently parted company with the main body and went on an expedition of their own into the Indian Ocean. The remainder steered for the West Indies.

Hood was making a routine patrol off Martinique with seventeen ships-of-the-line when suddenly De Grasse appeared on the horizon with twenty-one warships and a large convoy. Despite the difference in numbers, Hood attacked at once. Driving in boldly, the three lead ships of the British line were subjected to heavy raking fire. Thereupon, Hood sheered off, and for two hours the fleets sailed parallel at a respectful distance and cannonaded one another ineffectively. Hood at last broke off the action because his three damaged vessels were taking in water faster than their pumps could handle it. De Grasse, having protected his convoy and brought his own fleet undamaged through the fray, held his course to Fort Royal without making any attempt to pursue his damaged enemy.

News of the arrival of De Grasse shook Admiral Rodney out of his complacency. Back to Barbados he came to take charge of his fleet. There, he learned that De Grasse had not been idle. A French attempt to take St. Lucia had been thwarted by the crews of three British frigates, who had gone ashore and had vigorously employed the guns of the island's defenses. Tobago, though, had fallen and was now in French hands.

Once more, Admiral Rodney tasted frustration. On June 5, 1781, he caught up with the French fleet off the Grenadine Islands. Conditions were excellent for an attack except for one factor: somewhere near at hand were dangerous, current-whipped reefs not clearly indicated on his charts. He dared not send his ships through the perilous waters between him and the French. De Grasse was permitted to escape unscathed—a fact which was destined to have most fateful consequences for the British Empire.

12.

Meanwhile, on the mainland of North America, some significant developments were taking place. Having occupied Savannah and Charleston, Cornwallis led his army north. Despite some setbacks, he advanced steadily across the Carolinas into Virginia, where he met a small but well-trained American army under the Marquis de Lafayette. At first, Lafayette retreated; then, receiving reinforcements, he stood his ground. Cornwallis, meeting resistance, thought to play safe by occupying Yorktown, on the peninsula between the James and the York rivers. This snug seaport seemed to offer him the opportunity of advancing later by land or of boarding the first squadron of British warships which came along and going north by sea.

George Washington was quick to see the possibilities of the situation. After bluffing a land attack on New York, to keep British General Clinton on the defensive, he quickly and quietly led his army south to reinforce Lafayette. With him came French troops under the Comte de Rochambeau. Escape by land was now denied the British. If only there were some way to control the sea approaches!

There was. As Washington's troops moved south, the French frigate *Concorde* was on its way from Boston to the West Indies, bearing a letter from Rochambeau to Admiral De Grasse. The letter contained no orders, but it did give the admiral a complete picture of the situation. Seeing the same possibilities that Washington had, De Grasse took his fleet north toward Chesapeake Bay.

The British were completely fooled. In the West Indies, Admiral Rodney jumped to the conclusion that De Grasse would take at least half of his ships to France for the winter, sending only about a dozen north for action along the American coast. There would be no serious threat in this. Accordingly, he took a number of his ships that needed refitting and sailed for England, where his reputation and his finances were in need of bolstering. Sir Samuel Hood, with fourteen ships of the West Indies squadron, was sent to keep track of De Grasse's American expedition. In New York, Lord Thomas Graves did nothing with his six ships-of-the-line, leaving them at anchor as a passive counter to eight French ships under De Barras, stationed at Newport.

Admiral De Grasse took his twenty-eight ships on an indirect route to avoid detection. While doing so, he was passed unseen by Hood's fourteen ships, which sped on in the hope of overtaking him. It was Hood's hope that he could find and defeat the French on the open sea before he had to join forces with Graves, who was his senior and would thus assume command.

Reaching the mouth of Chesapeake Bay on August 25, Admiral Hood looked in vain for the French fleet, which had not yet arrived. Then on he went to New York, where he regretfully relinquished the top command of his squadron to Graves. Five days later, on August 30, De Grasse reached Chesapeake Bay, sailed in, and effectively bot-

1. An English Warship of the Early Thirteenth Century

2. The Fleet of King Henry V of England is Blessed Before It Sails
   Against the French, 1415 *From Ellis and Horne, The Story of the Greatest Nations*

Painting by Allen, after Holbein; National Maritime Museum, London

3. King Henry VIII of England Departs for France aboard his Tremendous and
Topheavy Warship, *Henri Grâce à Dieu*—the "Great Harry"

4. A Spanish Galleon in Heavy Weather, Early Sixteenth Century

5. Magellan's Flagship *Victoria* Threads its Way through the
Strait of Magellan toward the Pacific Ocean, 1520

From Ellis and Horne, The Story of the Greatest Nations

6. British Warships Attack the Spanish Armada, 1588

8. Sir Richard Grenville's *Revenge* Battles an Entire
   Spanish Squadron, August, 1591

7. The English Galleon *Revenge,* Most Famous of the Ships
   which Fought against the Spaniards, 1577–1591

Painting by Storck, National Maritime Museum, London

9. De Ruyter's Dutch Fleet Defeats the English under the Duke of Albemarle, in the Four Days' Battle, June, 1666

10. Hawke's British Squadron Defeats the French under Conflans in Quiberon Bay, November, 1759

Painting by Pocock, National Maritime Museum, London

11. John Paul Jones, America's First Great Naval Leader

12. The *Alliance* Fires on the *Bon Homme Richard,*
during the Battle with the *Serapis*

Painting by Paton; Official U.S. Navy Photograph

13. Admiral Graves' British Squadron Engages the French under De Grasse off Chesapeake Bay, September 5, 1781

14. Rodney's British Fleet Defeats the French under De Grasse in the Battle of the Saints' Passage, April 8, 1782

Painting by Pocock; National Maritime Museum, London

15. H.M.S. *Goliath* Rounds the End of the Anchored French Column to Begin
the Action in the Battle of Aboukir, or the Nile, August 1, 1798

16. Warship Types of the Late 1700's.
A 100-Gun British Ship-of-the-Line and
an American 44-Gun Frigate Pass off Gibraltar

18. U.S.S. *Constitution*—"Old Ironsides"—the Most Famous of Joshua Humphreys' Frigates

17. U.S.S. *Constellation* Defeats the French
Frigate *Insurgente*, February 9, 1799

19. The Frigate *Constitution* Leads the American Squadron against the
Pirate Gunboat Flotilla in Tripoli Harbor, August 3, 1814

21. Nelson's British Fleet Smashes French and Spanish Sea Power
in the Great Battle off Cape Trafalgar, October 20, 1805

22. Caught in a Calm, U.S.S. *Constitution* Narrowly Escapes a Pursuing
British Squadron off the New Jersey Coast, July 18, 1812

Painting by Pocock; National Maritime Museum, London

20. Nelson's British Squadron Defeats the Danes at Copenhagen, April 2, 1801

Painting by Dwight Shepler; Official U.S. Navy Photograph

23. U.S.S. *Enterprise* Defeats H.M.S. *Boxer* in a Battle in which both Captains were Killed, off the Coast of Maine, September 5, 1813

25. From the Deck of a British Warship, Francis Scott Key Watches the Bombardment of Fort McHenry and Receives the Inspiration for "The Star-Spangled Banner"

Drawing by W. G. Powell; Official U.S. Navy Photograph

G. Powell

24. Commodore Perry, in the *Niagara*, Breaks the British Line in the Battle of Lake Erie, September 10, 1813

26. Admiral Exmouth's British Squadron Bombards Algiers,
    August 27, 1816

27. British, French, and Russian Squadrons, under Admiral Codrington,
    Destroy the Turkish-Egyptian Fleet at Navarino, October 20, 1827

tled up Cornwallis' British army, which was still at Yorktown. The 3,300 French troops which the fleet had brought from the West Indies formed a welcome addition to the besieging forces.

Admiral Graves received word on August 31 that the small French squadron at Newport had put to sea, presumably headed for the Chesapeake. Accordingly, he himself sailed with the twenty ships of his own and Hood's squadrons, hoping to intercept the eight French vessels. He had no idea of the much larger fleet of twenty-eight French warships already lying off Yorktown.

The first contact brought mutual surprise. The British were amazed to find a French fleet far stronger than their own. The French, for their part, were caught with many of their men ashore and with many of their ships in the process of unloading supplies. Had Graves acted quickly, he might have succeeded in destroying the French fleet by making an attack upon them as they lay at a disadvantage or, failing that, by destroying them piecemeal as they emerged from Chesapeake Bay. Though he had the weather gauge, the inadequate signal system still in use made it impossible for him to act in time. He fell back to the open sea. Before he could organize his fleet for effective action the French ships came straggling out.

There was still a chance for Admiral Graves to win a victory. The French fleet was badly disorganized—divided into three widely separated groups of ships. Hoisting signals that he hoped would lead each of his own three groups to attack the French ships opposite them, Graves swung his van in at a long slant toward the French van and attacked. His subordinates did not do as he had hoped. They doggedly maintained a line ahead, too far from the enemy for effective action. Hood, in command of the rear division, never brought his ships into action at all. The suspicion has never died that he intentionally misunderstood Graves's signals in order to embarrass his superior officer.

As the fighting waxed hot between the van sections, there was a memorable bit of personal heroism. Aboard the French ship *Auguste,* an important rigging line was shot away. Two men who went up to repair it were quickly killed by British sharpshooters. At this, Vice-Admiral Antoine Bougainville cried out, offering his purse to anyone who would repair the line. A daring young sailor clambered aloft and repaired the damage amid a storm of shot. Returning unwounded to the deck, he brushed aside the proffered reward with the words, "You need not pay me for doing my duty, Admiral."

After nearly two hours of action, De Grasse bore away in the growing darkness. As usual, the British ships were too badly damaged aloft to prevent the ending of the battle. They followed doggedly, the two fleets forging eastward within sight of one another for five days, the British intent upon further fighting, the French trying to keep the British far enough from Chesapeake Bay to ensure the safe arrival of De Barras' Newport squadron. When this had been achieved, De Grasse reversed course and returned to Yorktown, where he now had thirty-six ships—more than enough to repulse any British attack. Completely frustrated, Graves returned to New York, abandoning Cornwallis, who surrendered on October 19, 1781.

Effectively, the surrender of Cornwallis brought an end to the American part of the war. The United States had won their independence. Though peace could not be made at once, because of the treaty of alliance with France, the American armed forces became inactive. France, Spain, and the Netherlands were left to carry on the war as best they could in the West Indies and elsewhere.

13.

At this point, we shall digress to consider the brief and minor part played in the war by the Netherlands.

Despite the reviving trade rivalry with Great Britain, the people of the Netherlands did not want war. Particularly opposed was the *Stadtholder,* William V, whose family of Orange still felt, at this time, a dual loyalty to the British and Dutch governments. It was generally felt that a war with Great Britain would accomplish nothing good for the country, and it was widely recognized that the armed forces were in no condition for a major struggle.

The British, on the other hand, seemed determined to provoke hostilities. They had some minor grievances, including the granting of asylum at Texel to the American squadron of John Paul Jones and the steady increase in Dutch trade with the Americans, who were seriously in need of the goods brought in through St. Eustatius Island by neutral Dutch ships. More important were the prizes—the wealth piled up on the piers of St. Eustatius, the weakly defended Dutch colonies, and the cancellation of the favorable trade provisions which had been granted to the Dutch by the Treaty of Utrecht in 1713.

Regarding herself as Mistress of the Seas, by right and by might, Britain began a systematic harrying of Dutch trade. Though the two nations were not at war, Dutch ships were consistently stopped and searched. The cargoes of some were seized. This campaign reached its height in January, 1780, when a strong British squadron under Commodore Fielding overtook a large Dutch convoy, protected by three ships-of-the-line and some frigates, under the command of Rear Admiral Bylandt. Depending on the rights of neutrals, the Dutch admiral refused to permit the searching of the ships in his care. The British thereupon opened fire. Faced with destruction, Bylandt did not resist, but struck his flag as though surrendering during a state of war. Escorted into a British harbor, he and his men continued to regard themselves as prisoners illegally held in an undeclared war.

The attack on Bylandt's squadron did much to dispel the insistence on peace among the Netherlanders. Work was rushed on the building of new ships-of-war and on the strengthening of the coast defenses. As Benjamin Franklin wrote home from Paris in June, 1780, "Holland, offended by fresh insults from England, is arming vigorously. That nation has madly brought itself into the greatest distress, and has not a friend in the world."

Actually, Franklin's statement was a slight exaggeration. Great Britain did have a friend—the *Stadtholder* of the Netherlands, who continued to cling to the olive branch despite the insults to his country. His influence steadily declined as that of the Patriot party in the States-General increased.

Hoping to benefit from the growth of war fever in the Netherlands, an American diplomat named William Lee sought out a group of Dutch Patriots and drew up an unofficial treaty between the United States and the Netherlands. Before even submitting his paper to the Dutch government, Lee entrusted a copy of it to Henry Laurens, the United States Minister to the Netherlands, who was to take it to Congress for consideration. Laurens' ship was stopped on the high seas by a British warship. In a panic, Laurens tore up the treaty and threw the scraps overboard. The bits of white paper were seen fluttering through the air, and British boats were sent out to collect them before they could sink. The treaty draft, pieced together and submitted to Parliament, led to the long imprisonment of Henry Laurens in the Tower of London and to a hasty declaration of war by Great Britain against the Netherlands.

Aside from the prompt capture of St. Eustatius by money-hungry Admiral Rodney, the chief result of the new declaration of war was a minor naval battle fought near Dogger Bank in the North Sea in August, 1781.

The Battle of Dogger Bank was strongly reminiscent of the earlier bloody battles of the Anglo-Dutch wars. A squadron of seven British ships-of-the-line and six frigates, under Sir Hyde Parker, happened to encounter a Dutch fleet of exactly the same size under Rear Admiral Johan Zoutman. Each squadron was convoying merchant vessels. Parker, having the wind, led his ships in to the attack, hoping to scatter the Dutch and capture the convoy. Zoutman stood up to him, with somewhat the same ends in view. Unlike the recent British battles with the French, this was a fight between two aggressive sluggers rather than between a slugger and a defensive boxer.

After some hundred minutes of hammer-and-tongs cannonading, the British sheered off with all of their ships intact but with 471 dead or wounded. The Dutch had lost a few more men, but their fleet, too, was still in fighting condition. Neither convoy had been harmed. There followed more than two hours of maneuvering, as each admiral sought a chance to resume advantageously. Then a storm came up, and the fleets lost contact. It is hard to score it as a victory for either fleet.

A curious footnote to the Battle of Dogger Bank is the comment made by the *Stadtholder* when informed that his fleet had engaged in battle with the British. Said he, "I hope the British have sustained no loss." Under such circumstances, it is a wonder that the Dutch did as well as they did in the war.

14.

French Admiral De Grasse, fresh from his successful naval campaign off the Virginia capes, sailed for the West Indies late in 1781 with the intention of converting the British colonies there into colonies of France. In his fleet, he had thirty-one ships-of-the-line, plus various auxiliaries. He was closely followed by an anxious Admiral Hood, with twenty-two ships, plus auxiliaries.

The islands of Nevis and St. Kitts were the first targets selected by De Grasse. Nevis, being undefended, fell without resistance. St. Kitts, however, had a garrison. Landing troops at the town of Basse Terre, De Grasse quickly drove out the British soldiers, who retired to a more defensible position on Brimstone Hill, above the town. Strongly entrenched there, British General Shirley turned a deaf ear toward all French demands for his surrender.

Hood, meanwhile, was kept informed of the developments. He knew that the French fleet was snugly ensconced in Frigate Bay, whence it would be difficult to evict them with an inferior fleet, such as his. Guile must take the place of force.

Admiral Hood's application of guile to this situation has been much praised by naval men. Apparently he had not one good plan to use, but two—the second in case unforseen circumstances should render the first impractical, as indeed they did. He had, moreover, thoroughly indoctrinated his officers with the details of both procedures, by means of a series of planning conferences.

Hood's first plan envisioned surprising the French and destroying their fleet while it was still at anchor in Frigate Bay. This became impossible when his own fleet was delayed by the accidental collision of a frigate with the leading ship of his line. By the time the confusion had been dispelled and the damage repaired, word had reached De Grasse that a British fleet was on the way.

Admiral De Grasse was busily preparing his ships for action when the British squadron rounded a distant headland and appeared off the entrance to Frigate Bay. The French admiral must have been tremendously cheered by the very evident signs of consternation among the enemy—the disorganized milling about of ships, the hurried raising of signal flags, the rushing about on the decks, and the tendency of ships to veer away and flee in a southerly direction. It was clear to De Grasse that Hood had not expected to blunder upon a French fleet so much stronger than his own. Here was a chance to eliminate a troublesome foe. At once, the French ships hoisted anchor and sails and set out in disorganized pursuit, obeying their admiral's signal for a general chase. As darkness fell, the French ships were hot upon the trail of a British squadron which seemed unable to draw away but somehow managed to keep just out of cannon range.

Dawn revealed the British ships sailing in perfect formation, their synthetic confusion having served its purpose and having been discarded. They now came about, sweeping wide of the French formation, and bore northward at a far greater speed than the French vessels could muster. Once again, the use of coppered bottoms to discourage marine growth paid off. The French were left far behind. When De Grasse got back to St. Kitts, there were the twenty-two British ships lying at anchor in Frigate Bay. They had displaced the French without the firing of a shot.

Hood's ships were anchored in an unusual formation. The leading ship had its bow so close to the shore that the enemy could not pass inside it. The next fifteen ships extended westward in a straight line. The final six extended northward, giving the entire formation an L shape. It was not the soundest of arrangements for defense, since many of the ships were masked from using their broadside guns and since the northern end of the L was subject to attack and to raking fire by an enemy enterprising enough to pass inside the angle of the L. Even the use of springs on the anchor cables, to permit the individual ships to swing about, did not entirely remove these weaknesses. Against the type of attack employed by De Grasse, it proved sound enough.

The French admiral could think of nothing more effective to do than to bring his ships along the English line, cannonading as he passed. This, to a large extent, threw away his advantages of mobility and of greater numbers. During the morning, he made one pass of this type, without dealing out any more damage than he received. In the afternoon, he tried again, with no better results. Then he gave up, anchored his ships outside the bay, and waited for time to play its part.

Time, it so happened, was working for both sides. While the fleets lay stalemated, the French besiegers of Brimstone Hill were slowly gaining the upper hand over General Shirley and his British defenders, who at last surrendered, giving the French control of St. Kitts. At the same time, a squadron of twelve British ships-of-the-line was steadily sailing westward under Admiral Rodney. Should these arrive with Hood's fleet still intact, the balance of naval power in the West Indies would swing back into the hands of Great Britain.

Now that St. Kitts had been lost, Hood's problem became one of escape from De Grasse and his blockading squadron. Through his telescope, he could plainly see the victorious French troops setting up artillery where it could blast his vessels with impunity. Somehow, he must escape.

In slipping out of Frigate Bay undetected, Admiral Hood borrowed and adapted a trick which his late enemy, George Washington, had used effectively against Lord Cornwallis some five years before. Instead of blazing campfires, Hood left behind him buoys bearing lights. One after another, his ships cut their anchor cables and slipped away, leaving the lighted buoys bobbing on the waves of the bay. De Grasse did not know that the British were gone until the first light of dawn revealed an empty anchorage.

15.

Although Admiral De Grasse did not yet know it, the timidity which had kept him from making an all-out assault on Hood's inferior fleet and on the strategically located British naval base of St. Lucia had lost him the campaign and had lost France the war. The tide had now begun to flow strongly in the opposite direction.

Numerous factors were involved. One was the approach of Rodney's squadron, which would give Great Britain a slight but significant edge in ships and guns in the West Indies area. Another, of still greater importance, was the new British series of improvements in guns and gunnery. In addition to their usual long guns, Rodney's ships were equipped with carronades—short-barreled guns of heavy caliber, able to deliver devastating blows at short range. These "smashers," as they were sometimes called, vastly increased the power of the British broadsides. Sir Charles Douglas, Rodney's "flag captain," was responsible for significant improvements in the mounting and servicing of guns, enabling each piece to be fired at more than three times the former speed and permitting each to be trained through a wider arc of fire. Still another improvement was a better system of signals, which had been worked out by Admiral Sir Richard Kempenfelt. The presence of a copy of Clerk's *Essay* in Rodney's cabin may possibly have been another important factor in this series of unpleasant surprises awaiting the French.

From St. Lucia, Rodney, with his thirty-eight ships-of-the-line, was able to keep excellent track of all moves made by Admiral De Grasse, whose squadron of thirty-six vessels was based at Fort Royal, in nearby Martinique. So close were the two bases that when De Grasse sallied forth on April 8, 1782, sharp-eyed British observers on the peaks of St. Lucia saw the glint of sunlight on sails and immediately reported the matter to Admiral Rodney. Almost at once, the British fleet put to sea in pursuit.

De Grasse had a double purpose in sailing. He had in his care more than one hundred French merchant vessels, which must be sent safely on their way to France. Once these were free and clear, he intended to double back with his fleet in order to invade the British colony of Jamaica. To assist in this purpose, he had aboard his warships some 5,400 French troops.

His first move was eastward, to launch his convoy on its way. Together, merchant ships and warships beat their way slowly againt the trade winds through the Saints' Passage, between Dominica and Guadeloupe. In hard pursuit came the British, led by a van division under Hood that steadily drew away from the main British force and closed with the French rear.

Now that his convoy was safely on its way, entrusted to the protection of two 50-gun ships, Admiral De Grasse cast a speculative eye back toward his British pursuers. Hood's nine van ships, sailing far ahead of their sisters, offered him an opportunity to attack a part of the British fleet with the entire French force and, by destroying it, to restore preponderance to the French. A bold attack would probably have accomplished this purpose. French naval tradition, however, was not based on boldness. De Grasse contented himself with sending back part of his force to exchange long-range cannon fire with Hood. The result was more damage to the French than to the British. One 64-gun French ship was forced to drop out of line and run for Guadeloupe, and several others received damage that would later cause consternation.

Turning once more to retreat upwind, De Grasse began to experience troubles. Two of his 74-gun ships, damaged by cannon fire, lost masts and fell behind and to leeward of the main body. One of these, the *Zélé*, was so seriously crippled that it became necessary to detach a frigate to take it in tow for Guadeloupe. This activity, in turn, drew Rodney to send warships to capture the cripples.

Much as he wished to avoid conflict with a superior British fleet, De Grasse could not honorably abandon his damaged ships. Back he came before the wind, ready to do battle if necessary but hoping that this engagement, like so many others, would resolve itself into an indecisive formalist cannonade.

At about 8:00 A.M., April 12, 1782, the fleets drew within range, each in line ahead, sailing slowly on opposite courses. The range was short and the cannonading heavy. The French were dismayed at the tremendous volume of fire from the *Duke* (98) and the eleven other British ships that had recently been equipped with improved artillery. The dreadful execution was increased by the presence of troops on the decks of the French ships, men helpless to strike a blow in return. Their blood and their death served only to increase the despair of the crews of the French warships.

Just as the two battle lines drew even, head to tail, Nature dealt the

French an additional blow. The wind, which had been favoring De Grasse, veered sharply, turning, each of the French ships from its broadside position toward the British line. Confusion reigned. Wide gaps appeared in the already ragged French formation. Rodney, whose flagship *Formidable* (98) was fifteenth in the British line, swung his ship to starboard and passed through a gap in the French formation, followed by five other vessels. The *Duke,* immediately ahead of the *Formidable,* swung through another gap. Astern, the *Bedford* also broke through, followed by Hood's entire rear division. In a matter of minutes, the formal battle degenerated into three distinct *melees* as the separated groups of French ships struggled to get away.

Though the French were badly beaten, most of them managed to escape. Admiral Rodney seemed content to take the ships nearest at hand, so there was no hot pursuit of the many that managed to break clear and flee downwind. Five were trapped, including the French flagship *Ville de Paris* (110). Around this monstrous ship the battle raged for many hours. At last, in the early evening, Admiral De Grasse surrendered. On his ship there were only three living men without a wound.

There can be no question that Admiral Rodney's disregard of the formalist *Fighting Instructions*—his unorthodox breaking of the enemy line—was responsible for the winning of the victory. There is much question about his reason for doing so. Was it his own idea? Was the move taken against Rodney's better judgment, at the insistence of Sir Charles Douglas, as Douglas stoutly maintained in later years? Can the inspiration be credited to Clerk's *Essay,* which Rodney possessed but said he had never read? Or did it just happen naturally, as a whim of the shifting wind? The definitive answer to these questions have never been given.

After the battle, there was much recrimination. Sir Charles Douglas and Sir Samuel Hood both claimed that a far greater victory could and should have been won. If only Rodney had pursued the beaten French, he could have shattered their sea power. Said Hood: "Had I had the honor of commanding His Majesty's noble fleet on the 12th., I may, without much imputation of vanity, say the flag of England should now have graced the sterns of upwards of twenty sail of the enemy's ships-of-the-line."

The British people and their Parliament, though, seemed well content. Both Rodney and Hood were granted peerages. Later, a monument was erected in Westminster Abbey, dedicated to the 243 British seamen who died in the action. A victory, after all, was a victory!

16.

Spain's entry into the war had been chiefly for the purpose of recovering her erstwhile possessions of Gibraltar and Minorca. Accordingly, siege lines were established on the landward side of the Gibraltar peninsula in 1779, soon after the declaration of war, and a low-pressure siege was instituted. It continued, without much result, for the better part of two years.

In June, 1781, the pressure to weaken Britain's hold on the Mediterranean was stepped up enormously. A French-Spanish fleet of forty-nine ships-of-the-line, carrying 8,000 French soldiers under the Duc de Crillon, appeared off Minorca. The small British garrison, under Sir James Murray, was unable to prevent a landing and soon retired to Fort St. Philip, there to be tightly besieged. After nearly eight months of privation and disease, which laid low nearly 80 per cent of the defenders, the few effectives who survived were forced to surrender. Spain had recovered her island.

Pressure was now increased on Gibraltar. The allied fleet which had been blockading Minorca appeared off the Rock, while at the same time the land forces, vastly increased by reinforcements under Crillon, stepped up their attack. British General George A. Eliott, with only 7,000 men, faced a difficult task in repelling 40,000 attackers on the land and a formidable allied fleet.

In mounting his attack, the Duc de Crillon placed heavy dependence upon a new and secret weapon—the floating battery. There were ten of these, each built on the hull of a large converted merchant vessel. On the side which would face the British defenses, each was protected by a sloping wooden casemate, five feet in thickness, covered with hides which were kept wet by an ingenious system of water tanks and pipes. Crillon felt that his batteries were indestructible and that the heavy volume of fire which they could deal out would soon silence the defenses of Gibraltar. The attack was launched by land and by sea at dawn, September 13, 1782.

General Eliott, in charge of the defenses of Gibraltar, was not a man to give up easily. Realizing that the whole key to the situation lay in silencing the floating batteries, he wisely disregarded the massed Spanish artillery on the shore and concentrated on Crillon's creations.

Repeated hits by solid shots failed to damage the casemates but did disrupt the tank-and-pipe systems, permitting the protective hides to dry out. British soldiers, in the meantime, were stoking up special furnaces and were heating shot to an incandescent glow. After six hours of standard cannonading, the glowing cannon balls were put to use. At first, there was no evident effect. The firing continued. During the afternoon, smoke was seen to be rising from several of the casemates. As darkness fell, flames became evident. Two of the batteries were burning. The light of the flames illuminated the other batteries, permitting the British to continue their glowing barrage. Soon there were more fires to light up the harbor. By noon the next day, eight of the batteries had been destroyed and two were briskly burning. Crillon's secret weapon had failed.

Despite the destruction of his floating batteries, the Duc de Crillon continued his efforts through standard siege methods, making full use of his land-based batteries, his strong French-Spanish fleet, and his massed manpower. The danger was far from over.

To the rescue came Admiral Richard Howe with thirty-four ships-of-the-line escorting numerous transports laden with troops and supplies. Fearful lest General Eliott should give up before his arrival, Howe dispatched a fast vessel on ahead to bear tidings of his approach. By a daring feat of seamanship, the messenger managed to thread its way through the great blockading squadron and to bring cheer to the defenders, who, it developed, had had no thought of surrendering.

By sheer bad luck, Admiral Howe reached the Strait of Gibraltar on October 11, 1782, in the midst of a howling westward gale. His ships passed through without mishap but were unable to reach Gibraltar, being blown for some distance into the Mediterranean. Spanish Admiral Cordoba promptly brought out forty-four ships to capture or destroy the British squadron. Failing this, he planned to keep Howe from reaching the Gibraltar garrison with aid.

There followed a game of sea-borne chess, as Cordoba maneuvered to bring about a battle and Howe, just as stubbornly, maneuvered to avoid one until his troops and supplies should have been safely delivered. After a week of dodging the Spaniard's moves, Howe at last succeeded in slipping by the blockading fleet and in bringing his convoy safely into Gibraltar Harbor. The ships were unloaded, and the Gibraltar stronghold was rendered safe.

Lord Howe was now free to take his ships out and accept the battle he had so long been forced to avoid. On October 20, he sailed westward through the strait and formed a battle line, confident that the allies would leap at the opportunity to engage, since they now had forty-seven ships to his thirty-four. To the admiral's disgust, the French and Spaniards proved to be timid. There was some distant cannonading, with little result, but every attempt which he made to close was countered by an allied retreat. At last, the French and Spanish ships clapped on sail and made for Cadiz, while Lord Howe disconsolately set off for England. He had done a great work in relieving Gibraltar, but he had not won the glorious victory which he so much desired.

General Eliott, too, had done a great work. For his part in saving the Gibraltar stronghold he was granted a peerage, becoming the first Baron Heathfield.

17.

It was unfortunate for France that her ablest naval officer stood too far down the scale of social prominence and influence to be given an important assignment. Had the able and aggressive Admiral Pierre de Suffren been in charge of some of the major fleets sent out by his country, it seems likely that the naval history of the war would have had a very different outcome.

We last saw Suffren parting company early in 1781 with the fleet which the Comte de Grasse was taking westward to the New World. Of the twenty-six warships in the group, De Grasse took twenty-one for his campaign in the West Indies. Suffren was allotted five of the smaller ones with which to convoy troop transports to the Dutch colony at the Cape of Good Hope. The entry of the Netherlands into the war had created the likelihood of a British attack upon this important outpost.

Arriving at the Cape Verde Islands, Suffren was startled to find a British squadron at anchor in the harbor of Porto Praya. The presence of warships and transports confirmed his suspicion that this might indeed be the much-feared expedition to conquer the Cape. At once, the French admiral attacked. The British, still at anchor, answered his fire. After some time, seeing that he was unable to defeat his securely placed enemy, Suffren led his fleet out of the harbor and proceeded toward South Africa. The British commander, Commodore George Johnston, completed his refurbishing before setting out in the Frenchman's wake.

The contest for the Cape of Good Hope proved to be a race, rather than a battle. Suffren got there before Johnston. The French supplies and soldiers which he unloaded made the defenses of the Cape so strong that Johnston judged an attack would now be foolhardy. After a two-month delay, Suffren took his five warships eastward toward India.

At the island of Mauritius, Suffren's little squadron joined the larger squadron of his fellow countryman, the Comte d'Orves. There were now twelve French warships instead of five. For a time, D'Orves commanded the combined squadron, but his time was short, for he was a dying man. On the ninth of February, 1782, he died, having handed over the command to Suffren.

Affairs in India, meanwhile, had been going badly for the French and for their allies. A new British commander, Lord George Macartney, had brought word of his country's declaration of war against the Netherlands and had set busily to work to capture as many Dutch and French bases as he could. Already, Pondicherry, Madras, Pulicat, Negapatam, Fort Ostenburg, and the important naval base of Trincomalee had fallen to Lord Macartney's land forces and to a British naval squadron under Sir Edward Hughes. It appeared to be but a matter of time—and brief time, at that—before the entire Indian Ocean area would be in British hands.

Somehow, Admiral Suffren had acquired the mistaken idea that the base at Madras was still in the hands of the French. Confidently, he stood in toward the port, his warships escorting some loaded transports and some prizes which he had taken in the Indian Ocean. In the harbor he found the British squadron of Admiral Hughes. Being in no condition to fight, Suffren turned and ran for Pondicherry, which he also assumed to be under the French flag. Hughes pursued him, picking off some of the convoyed ships as the two fleets swept southward.

On February 17, after two days of flight, Suffren turned to offer battle. His plan was a good one, to split his force into two groups of six and enfold the British, but his subordinates were deficient in daring and understanding. Four of them missed their assignments, and the plan was bungled. After an hour of indecisive struggle, the French drew off. Hughes's ships had been too badly battered to continue the pursuit.

It was nearly two months before the squadrons met again. Hughes, in the meantime, had received two more ships-of-the-line from home, bringing his total up to eleven. Suffren still had his same twelve ships, but he now had a base from which to work. Troops landed from his transports had taken Cuddalore from the British.

Fearing that Suffren might follow his capture of Cuddalore by an attack on Trincomalee, Hughes started for the great Ceylonese base in April with reinforcements and supplies. On April 12 (while Rodney was fighting De Grasse in the Saints' Passage, half a world away), Suffren's squadron overhauled the British and swept into action. Eleven of his ships were to attack from windward and one from leeward, giving a progressive concentration of two on one from the rear of the British line. Again, his subordinates bungled it. While nine of the French ships stood off and bombarded ineffectually at long range, three—the flagship *Heros,* the *Brilliant,* and the *Orient*—bore the brunt of the British fire. Both fleets suffered heavy damage, though neither lost a ship. Each, by a strange coincidence, had 137 men killed. Once more, the battle had been a draw.

18.

During the next twelve weeks, Admiral Suffren used his time well by making an alliance with a native ruler named Hyder Ali, who agreed to lead his land forces against the British while Suffren fought them on the sea.

On July 5, Suffren appeared off Negapatam, where Hughes's squadron lay at anchor. An injury to one of the French ships had brought the two groups to equality, at eleven apiece. As planned, Hughes came out in pursuit and followed the French southward, thus leaving his base at the very time when the native troops under Hyder Ali were converging on it for an attack. It was an outstanding piece of cooperation, even though the native assault proved unsuccessful.

Hughes overtook Suffren, and the two fleets hammered each other from parallel courses for some ninety minutes. During this time, one French ship was disabled and forced to drop out of formation; all British ships stayed in line, though several were severely damaged. Then a shift of the wind forced all ships to change course. Most bore away from the enemy, but two French ships and four British turned inward and presently found themselves in a furious *melee* in which the French vessels, being outnumbered, were badly battered. The captain of the *Sévère,* losing his nerve, hauled down his flag, whereupon his under-officers quickly raised it again and compelled the gunners to continue firing. The ship was thus saved and continued in action until

Admiral Suffren was able to re-form his line and come back to the assistance of his embattled pair of warships. In the end, it was Hughes who broke away and retired to Negapatam.

That evening an English boat came under a flag of truce, bearing a message for Admiral Suffren. Sir Edward Hughes demanded possession of the *Sévère,* which had been seen to strike her flag briefly in the midst of the battle. Suffren, who had not yet heard of the incident, replied that no French ships had surrendered. "But," he added, "if Sir Edward Hughes thinks that one of these ships belongs to him, let him come in person and try to get it." Sir Edward did not appear.

There followed another eight weeks of refitting and preparation, during which Admiral Suffren received two more ships from home and Hughes received one, making the odds fourteen to twelve in favor of the French. As usual, the energetic Frenchman did not let the time go to waste. Late in August, his fleet traveled south to Ceylon, where he captured Trincomalee in a six-day campaign of which Hughes remained in complete ignorance.

On September 2, Admiral Hughes appeared off Trincomalee and was amazed to find the French fleet at anchor in a base which he thought was British. Suffren, never one to dodge a fight, came out with all speed, whereupon Hughes retired downwind, drawing the French away from the port. The French fleet gradually drew up on the British in order to engage at point-blank range, but again Suffren's subordinates spoiled everything. The opening shots were fired at long range before the French ships were in the planned enveloping position. The result was another draw, in which both fleets were damaged but neither was defeated.

The coming of the winter monsoon made further operations for 1782 impracticable. Hughes took his fleet to Bombay, where he was presently reinforced by six additional ships. Suffren went to Sumatra. India was left temporarily at peace.

19.

Admiral Hughes returned first in the spring of 1783, bringing his fleet to the eastern shore of India to cooperate with British land forces besieging Cuddalore. Soon afterward, Suffren appeared, having stopped at Trincomalee on the way from Sumatra. The French admiral ran the British blockade and entered Cuddalore Harbor, where he took aboard some of the town's defenders to help the thinned-out crews of his ships. He did not remain long, but soon came out again, looking for a fight.

For three hours on the afternoon of June 20, the two battle lines engaged in a formalist, line-of-battle engagement, blasting each other with everything they had, killing about a hundred men in each fleet, but neither sinking nor taking a ship. It was by now becoming clear that the art of shipbuilding had so far surpassed the art of gunnery that no ship could sink a ship-of-the-line by artillery fire. In the early evening, Admiral Hughes broke off action, leaving Suffren in possession of the scene of battle and in a fine position to harry the British besiegers of Cuddalore.

In the face of many hardships, Admiral Suffren had broken even in four battles against the British and had won the fifth, against odds of eighteen to fourteen. It was a record unmatched by any other French naval commander of the time. What he could have done had he been placed in charge of a major fleet, with good subordinates, makes intriguing speculation. He might well have been the outstanding hero of the war.

20.

Though Admiral Suffren and Admiral Hughes did not know it, their final battle was fought nearly half a year after the war had ended. On January 20, 1783, the war had at last been terminated by the signing of the Treaty of Paris.[1]

The chief gainer from the Treaty of Paris was the newly independent United States of America. By the terms of the treaty, the United States obtained her freedom and all land between Canada on the north and Florida on the South, between the Atlantic Ocean on the east and the Mississippi on the west, except for the city of New Orleans and a little surrounding territory. Spain gained back Minorca and Florida, though she had to give up all claim to Gibraltar, Jamaica, and the Bahama Islands, which remained British possessions. The Netherlands lost St. Eustatius Island to Great Britain. France and Great Britain restored to each other all lands taken during the war, including the conquests made by Admiral Suffren in India and Ceylon.

Thus ended the War of the American Revolution which, in its eight years of struggle, had spread far from the little village green at Lexington where it had begun.

[1] Not to be confused with the earlier Treaty of Paris, which had brought an end to the Seven Years' War in 1763.

10 GREAT BRITAIN
AND THE FRENCH REVOLUTION

⚓

1.

From the French point of view, intervention in the American Revolution proved to have been a colossal blunder.

The heritage of debt left to France by the costly wars and the vast building enterprises of Louis XIV had severely strained the French economy. Things had become worse during the extravagant reign of Louis XV, who had also waged costly and unproductive wars. A regime of economy and reform was badly needed. Instead, Louis XVI, at the urging of his gay young queen, continued the spendthrift ways of his predecessors. He also allowed himself to be persuaded that it would help France if she should side with the American colonies in their rebellion against Great Britain. The war which followed helped the American colonies, but it ruined France.

The French Revolution followed inevitably. In 1789, the absolute monarchy of France was followed by a constitutional monarchy, with Louis XVI still on the throne but with the chief power of government in the hands of a conservative National Assembly. In 1791, a new constitution further limited the king's powers and gave authority to the liberal Legislative Assembly. By the fall of 1792, the radical Jacobins had control of France. The monarchy was abolished and a republic created. In January, 1793, King Louis XVI was condemned to lose his head under the guillotine.

The leaders of the other European monarchies looked on in horror as the rabble of France tore down their government and killed their king. Even those who had favored the earlier and milder phases of the revolution could not stomach this. Such things must not be!

The French, too, knew that war would be the result. Danton screeched defiance to the world when he cried, "To the coalized kings of Europe we throw, as gage of battle, the head of a king!"

Eleven days after the execution of the king, the new Republic of France was at war with Great Britain, Spain, and the Netherlands. Sardinia was already in the fight. Soon the coalition—the brainchild of William Pitt the younger—was joined by various states of the Holy Roman Empire. Revolutionary France found herself at war with most of Europe!

2.

The French navy did not prosper under the Revolution. Most of the officers had been aristocrats, and now the aristocrats were gone, many of them dead, their places taken by landlubbers who knew little of the sea and nothing of naval warfare. The ships themselves were neglected in favor of land armaments. The great naval bases at Brest and Toulon were permitted to fall into disrepair.

Toulon became the scene of some of the earliest naval action of the war. This city and Marseilles were centers of moderate feeling, their people being opposed to the Jacobin excesses of 1793. When a British fleet under Admiral Samuel Hood appeared off the coast late in August, there were many in Toulon who were willing to deal with the enemy. Under cover of darkness six British ships-of-the-line and twenty-five frigates slipped into the harbor, where they were later joined by seventeen Spanish ships. The British and the Spaniards got along badly and quarreled constantly, but for the time being they held Toulon. Within the harbor, tied up to the city's piers, were thirty-two of the largest French ships-of-the-line.

The Jacobins were quick to send a Revolutionary army against Toulon. In the assault on the outer defenses, there was heavy land fighting, in the course of which British General Charles O'Hara was wounded and was captured by the French. During a session of adroit questioning, he unwarily revealed important information to an eager young captain of artillery named Napoleon Bonaparte. As a result, the French were able to take some key positions and to ring Toulon with batteries which rendered the great base untenable.

Faced with the closing ring of French armies and with unmistakable signs of an autumn storm which might trap his fleet in the harbor, Admiral Hood put prize crews on five French ships which were fitted for sea. Then he called to his assistance a brilliant but erratic character named William Sidney Smith, a naval freebooter who had served in many fleets, including the British. As the Revolutionary armies entered the town, Smith conducted a raid into the inner harbor, where lay some of the choicest of the French vessels. With the enemy actually swarming on the piers, this bold raider touched off a fireship in the midst of the crowded French shipping. Flames shot skyward from ships, piers, and warehouses. The glare of thirteen burning French ships-of-the-line lighted Admiral Hood on his way out of Toulon.

3.

Like many a revolutionary regime, the new-born French Republic amazed its enemies by its vigor and its ardor. Under the leadership of such generals as Lazare Carnot, the French troops beat back those of the coalition arrayed against them. Austria, Russia, and Prussia suddenly found it more interesting and far more profitable to slice up defenseless Poland than to butt heads with France. Spain and the Netherlands found the going hard and lost their will to fight. Great Britain suddenly found herself practically alone against the French.

France, though seemingly victorious, was hungry. Most of her soldiers had come from the farms. One cannot fight and raise crops at the same time. The harvest of 1793 was subnormal. Grain was desperately needed. From the seaports of the New World, a vast convoy of 130 loaded grain ships began its precarious voyage eastward toward the empty stomachs of France.

Rear Admiral Louis Thomas Villaret-Joyeuse, of the French Republican Navy, was handed the assignment of meeting the grain convoy and of seeing that it safely reached port in France. His was no enviable position. Orders from the great Robespierre himself spelled out what must be done and what would happen if it were not. There must be no battle with the British, except for the purpose of saving the grain fleet. Should the convoy be taken, or should the French fleet be destroyed, Villaret-Joyeuse would pay with his head. Nor would there be any disguising of what took place. An ardent government official, the Deputy Saint-André, was installed on the flagship. Also installed was a small-sized guillotine for the deputy's use.

Word reached London that the convoy was on its way. Out went Admiral Richard Howe, with instructions to intercept the grain and to destroy the French fleet from Brest which would try to shepherd the convoy safely into the ports of France. These assignments were complicated by the added duty of safely escorting a group of British merchant vessels seaward.

Checking at Brest, Howe found that the French fleet was still in port. Relieved by this, he sailed westward with his convoy, which he eventually sent on its way with a guard of eight warships, six of which were to return to him after the merchant ships had gotten off to a safe start. Then back he went to Brest, where he learned, to his dismay, that the French fleet had put to sea two days before and had slipped by him undetected. There was nothing to do now but to patrol the Atlantic approaches to France in the hope of encountering the convoy or the French fleet.

Villaret-Joyeuse, meanwhile, was making the most of his opportunities. Nobody knew better than he how much the men under him, from midshipmen to captains, needed training. He himself had been jumped all the way from lieutenant to rear admiral when the revolution had stripped the fleet of its trained officers. The captains under him were a nondescript lot, many having recently been common seamen, and the crews were almost hopeless. As he cruised back and forth, scanning the horizon for his convoy, he carried out on every one of his twenty-six ships-of-the-line an intensive training program. In the brief space of eleven days he succeeded in working a minor miracle.

On the morning of May 28, 1794, Villaret-Joyeuse thought for a few happy moments that he had found his convoy. As the sails mounted higher on the western horizon, he discovered that he was wrong. What was bearing down on him was Howe's squadron of twenty-five British ships-of-the-line. At all costs, the enemy must be decoyed away from the waters through which the grain convoy would soon be passing. Using the newly gained skill of his crews, the French admiral formed his ships into something resembling a line of battle and set a course eastward.

Not knowing where the grain convoy was, and not wishing to let the French fleet escape again, Howe followed the Frenchman's lead. This took him first to the east; then, on a wide circle, to the north and west. Five French ships, unable to keep up with the others of the line, began to lag astern. To overtake and capture them, Howe detached six fast 74's as a "flying squadron." Villaret-Joyeuse saw the danger. Back he swept in a great circle, losing precious miles but restoring his lagging five to the comparative safety of his battle line.

The "flying squadron," robbed of its prey, nevertheless pressed the pursuit of the French rear. By late afternoon, *Bellerophon* (74) was in range of the last French ship, the *Revolutionnaire* (110). In the cannonading which followed, *Bellerophon* found that she had more than met her match. Damaged and partly dismasted, with many of her crew dead, she staggered out of action. Her five sisters took her place, mauling the *Revolutionnaire* and being mauled in return. As darkness fell, the great French three-decker was a helpless hulk. So was the British *Audacious*. Five other British 74's, including *Bellerophon,* had suffered severely. Except for the *Revolutionnaire,* the French fleet had escaped without damage.

With the dawn, both the *Audacious* and the *Revolutionnaire* were out of sight, each feebly striving under jury rig to reach a friendly port. Both eventually made it. The British ship was not replaced, but a French ship-of-the-line, returning from a mission, happened upon the action and joined the French formation.

In spite of the relative increase in French strength, Admiral Howe moved in boldly in an attempt to close. As the lines passed in opposite directions, he first signaled a swing toward the enemy, then quickly canceled the order. One British ship, the *Queen,* failed to see the cancellation and drove in alone, being shattered by the broadsides of all twenty-six of the French ships as she passed along their line. Seeing a chance to take the helpless British ship, Villaret-Joyeuse swung his entire force around to close with the *Queen.* This maneuver brought the French down wind and closed the distances between the fleets.

Howe thought that he saw the opportunity for a crushing victory, somewhat on the pattern of the one which Rodney had fashioned in the Saints' Passage. He, too, swung his fleet around, to parallel the French line, but on an opposite course. Signals were hoisted to break through the center of the French formation, thus splitting the line in two and forcing a *melee,* with its subsequent decisive outcome.

Captain A. J. P. Molloy, whose ship *Caesar* (80) led the British line, either lost his nerve or failed to understand. He continued parallel to the French line, firing at long range and studiously ignoring a tempting gap between the fourteenth and fifteenth French ships. The twelve British captains immediately behind Molloy, torn between the tradition of keeping the battle line intact and their understanding of their admiral's intent, played safe and followed the *Caesar,* thus honoring the letter of the *Fighting Instructions.* Howe's flagship *Queen Charlotte* (100) was the first to swing through the gap, raking the French *Montagne* (120) and *Jacobin* (80) as she went through. She was followed by only two other British ships, *Bellerophon* (74) and *Leviathan* (74).

During the frantic cannonading which accompanied and followed the breakthrough, one of the French ships ran out of grapeshot, which are highly effective for destroying rigging and killing men on crowded decks. Aboard the ship were some sacks of gold coins. In the emergency, the French captain had some of the guns loaded with coins and discharged at the British ship nearest at hand. A number of these strange and expensive missiles were later found embedded in the *Leviathan's* hull, to the vast delight of the Portsmouth dockyard workers.

Three ships are not enough to separate fourteen from twelve. Although Howe and his two loyal followers dealt out heavy punishment to the French vessels which surrounded them, they were fortunate indeed to be able to fight their way free and escape to the now-distant British battle line. Behind them they left three French ships so badly crippled that they could not move at all without frigates to tow them. One of these stayed with the fleet, under tow; the other two were towed out of action and toward the French coast under cover of night. With them went an undamaged French ship, whose captain had decided on his own to escort the cripples. Upon the arrival of the ships at Brest, his decision cost him his head.

Came a two-day fog, through which Admiral Howe and his fleet groped blindly for an elusive enemy that stayed just out of reach and drew the British watchdogs farther and farther from the sea lanes where the grain convoy must pass. Then, on the first day of June, 1794, the weather cleared and the two fleets were again in sight of one another. To Howe's joy, he had the weather gauge. The decision to close or not to close rested with him.

Admiral Richard Howe had a plan which, if carried out as conceived, would force a close-in fight to a decision. Each of his ships was to bear directly down on the French line, pass astern of the French ship in the corresponding position, rake while passing, then engage heavily from leeward. French ships crippled in the engagement would thus drift downwind into the British formation, where they could be further hammered and taken.

As before, the *Caesar,* first ship in the British formation, spoiled the plan. Captain Molloy continued parallel to the French line, signaling that he was unable to comply with the orders because of a damaged rudder. This caused a faltering in the execution of the maneuver and exposed the other British ships longer than necessary to raking fire as they wore around and headed for the French line. It brought particular hardship on the *Bellerophon,* second in line, which now had to contend with both the first and second French vessels. Only the *Queen Charlotte* and five others managed to break through. The others were forced to turn short and engage from the windward side.

For nearly three hours there was a furious *melee.* The greatest violence of all occurred when the *Brunswick* (74) fouled the *Vengeur du Peuple* (74) and became so tightly locked to her French opponent's hull that the lower gun ports of neither vessel could be opened. In the restricted quarters, the French gunners were unable to serve their main batteries. The British, through the use of newly devised flexible ramrods, managed to use their heavy artillery, beginning the engagement by blasting open the covers of their own gun ports, then continuing to smash solid shots through the *Vengeur's* hull. On the upper decks, the French gained the upper hand, serving their carronades so well that the British upperworks were swept clean of living men. At last, the mutual agony ended when the ships drifted apart just as the fleets were breaking off action. *Brunswick,* badly battered, had lost more than a quarter of her men, but *Vengeur's* hurts were deeper and more serious. Not long after disengaging, she heeled over and went down, carrying more than half of her crew with her.

As the cannonading died down, the two fleets drifted slowly apart. To the east—leeward—the least-damaged French ships were striving to form a new battle line behind their flagship *Montagne,* either for flight or for renewal. The British ships, damaged in varying degrees, floated in a strung-out mass, without formation. Upwind lay ten badly hurt French warships, drifting very slowly because all were entirely without masts. The ten became nine when the riddled *Jacobin* went down before the eyes of both fleets.

Lord Howe, sixty-eight years old and so exhausted he could scarcely stand, looked about him. Plainly, he had won a victory, though how great a victory was yet to be determined. The French might come back, either to fight on or to rescue their cripples. If they did not, it might still be possible to pursue them and take them all, thus smashing French sea power. The thought of added hours or days on the quarterdeck appalled the old sea dog. To the dismay of his younger officers, he ordered the British fleet to beat upwind and take the prizes.

Villaret-Joyeuse seized the opportunity to escape with his surviving ships. Three of the dismasted cripples also managed to get away, being taken in tow after dark by daring French frigates. The other six were captured and eventually found their way into the British navy.

Even though His Lordship had chosen the lesser though easier prize, his victory was well received at home. There were celebrations, and the affair as a whole became known as "the Glorious First of June." Captain Molloy was court-martialed and dismissed from the service.

Back in Brest, Rear Admiral Villaret-Joyeuse did not fare badly. The grain fleet had slipped through safely while the battle raged, and he had managed to bring home all but eight of his warships. In a sense he, too, had won a victory. He was promoted to vice-admiral.

Deputy Saint André, though a landlubber, had found the whole experience most enlightening. Before the battle, he had decried the need of special training and elaborate maneuvers, predicting that the brave sailors of the Republic would simply "resort to the boarding tactics in which the French were always victorious, and thus astonish the world by new prodigies of valor." Watching the battle, he had learned that it is not that simple to win a naval victory. Said he, afterward, "If they had added to their courage a little training, the day might have been ours."

4.

Among the ship captains serving under Rear Admiral Samuel Hood in the Mediterranean was a daring and unorthodox character named Horatio Nelson, captain of the *Agamemnon* (64). He was a man of vivid contrasts: a naval hero much given to severe seasickness, a brilliant seaman whose first fame was won on land, a national idol whose private life made conservative Britons shudder.

We first see Nelson directing the sieges of two Corsican cities in 1794. Though the main British force consisted of well-trained navy men from the *Agamemnon,* both of these operations were fought on land. By clever placement of artillery and by resolution in attack, Nelson and 1,200 British sailors and marines took Bastia from 4,000 defenders. Soon afterward, he and his men took Calvi. In this battle, an enemy shell struck the ground near Horatio Nelson, driving sand into his right eye and destroying its sight.

Technically, it was not Captain Nelson of the Royal Navy who won these victories but Brigadier General Nelson, operating under a temporary and irregular commission granted by the army.

5.

Late in 1794, Admiral Hood was replaced as commander of British forces in the Mediterranean by Vice-Admiral William Hotham. The new commanding officer lacked both energy and initiative.

On March 13, 1795, fourteen British ships of the line under Hotham encountered fifteen French ships under Admiral Pierre Martin. At the moment of sighting, the British were at a decided disadvantage, for four of their ships were widely separated from the other ten. While the ten ships of Hotham's main group were forming a battle line, in spite of a brisk wind and a rising sea, the French admiral was trying to cut off the four British laggards and capture them. The attempt failed. The four ships managed to skirt the French formation and join their sisters in the battle line. By the time this was accomplished, the two fleets were equal in numbers, for a French vessel had lost her masts in the storm.

It was Admiral Martin's misfortune, and also Napoleon's, that the attempt to capture the four British vessels failed. One of them was the *Agamemnon,* commanded by Horatio Nelson.

Having failed to take the four, Admiral Martin belatedly strove to organize his fleet for battle. While this was being done, two of his 80's, the *Ça Ira* and the *Victoire,* collided. Both suffered damage aloft, the *Ça Ira* being especially handicapped. She was at once taken in tow by a frigate, and two other ships were detailed to keep her from being cut off. Nevertheless, Nelson in the *Agamemnon* managed to keep close to her stern, veering from time to time in order to rake her. Eventually, he succeeded in dismasting her completely. This brought back Martin with the French battle line and forced Nelson to rejoin his own formation, as darkness ended the conflict.

The next morning, the crippled *Ça Ira* was seen to be in tow of the *Censeur* (74), both ships lagging somewhat behind Martin's squadron. At once, Hotham ordered his battle line forward to cut off the cripples, while Martin hoisted signals to bring his own line back to their rescue. Hotham's signals were observed; Martin's were misinterpreted. As a result, the French squadron bore away for Toulon while the British were gobbling up the *Ça Ira* and the *Censeur.*

At this, Admiral Hotham called it a day. He had taken two prizes, and four of his own ships were badly in need of repairs. Though the French line was still in sight and might conceivably be headed off, no general chase was signaled.

Angry and incredulous, brash Captain Nelson stormed aboard his admiral's flagship to make a personal protest. He was blandly brushed off. "We must be contented," said Admiral Hotham, soothingly. "We have done very well."

Nelson sputtered, but he knew better than to press his luck too far. Later, in his dispatches, he wrote: "Had we taken ten sail, and allowed the eleventh to escape, when it had been possible to have got at her, I could never have called it well done. . . . We should have had such a day as, I believe, the annals of England never produced. . . . Sure I am, had I commanded on the 14th., that either the whole French fleet would have graced my triumph or I should have been in a confounded scrape."

When the two captured French ships were later examined at Gibraltar, it was found that both were armed with secret weapons—with furnaces for the heating of red-hot shot and with inflammatory projectiles, much like the old Greek Fire. Either these weapons had not been used in the battle or they had been found ineffective. Nobody in the British fleet was even aware of them until afterward.

6.

Early in June, 1795, Admiral Martin once more emerged from Toulon, this time with nineteen ships-of-the-line. It was basically a training cruise. For a full month he sailed the Mediterranean without sight of a British sail. Early in July, he stumbled upon a little squadron of five British ships, including Nelson's *Agamemnon*. The British ships fled toward Hotham's anchorage off northern Corsica, with the French in pursuit. Off San Fiorenzo Bay, the chase was reversed. Martin saw Hotham emerging from the anchorage with twenty-three of the line. It was now his turn to come about and sprint for home.

After five days of pursuit, Hotham's British squadron overtook the French. The pursuers were just closing in on their prey when a calm paralyzed both fleets. A little long-range gunnery was all that was possible. This time, the French tried to use their new weapons. The sole result was the destruction of one of their own ships, *L'Alcide* (74), whose store of combustibles went off with a mighty flash, incinerating all but 200 of her crewmen.

With the return of the wind, the *Agamemnon* and the *Cumberland* quickly got under way to attack the French. To the disgust of both captains, Hotham's flagship blossomed out with signals recalling all ships to line. Martin and his eighteen surviving ships were permitted to escape.

The battle of July 13, 1795, marked the end of the line for both Martin and Hotham. The former was removed by the new and conservative Directory of France, which thought him too adventuresome. He was replaced by Rear Admiral François Brueys. Hotham, on the other hand, was removed for not being adventuresome enough. He was replaced by Admiral Sir John Jervis.

7.

When the war against the First Coalition had begun, early in 1793, France had been in a desperate condition—friendless, alone, fighting an apparently hopeless battle against the massed military and naval might of Europe and at the same time trying to contend with those of her own people who opposed the Revolution. Four years later, it was France who had power on land and sea, and it was Great Britain who had her back to the wall. What had happened in the brief space of forty-eight months to bring about such a complete reversal of positions?

First of all, the Revolution had passed its peak of blood and terror. Danton had sickened of the executions and had tried to moderate them. For this, he himself had been condemned by Robespierre and had gone under the guillotine. Less than four months later (July 27, 1794), Robespierre himself had been condemned by his jealous colleagues and had been guillotined—face up, so that he could see the knife descend. This had effectively ended the so-called Reign of Terror. The fanatical Commune had been replaced by the more moderate Directory, in which foreign governments felt that they could afford some confidence.

No less important, the armies of France had been spectacularly successful. As has often happened during revolutionary movements, the despised common people had shown that they would fight far better for a government which they felt was theirs than for the arbitrary government of an hereditary king. A French army under General Jourdan had defeated the Austrians at Fleurus and had driven them out of Belgium. General Pichegru had crossed the Rhine during the winter of 1794–95 and had conquered the Netherlands. Another French army, under Generals Dugommier and Perignon, had crossed the Pyrenees and had defeated the Spaniards. A British invasion at

Quiberon Bay to aid a local French revolt had been broken up by General Hoche. Spain, Prussia, Saxony, Hanover, and Hesse-Cassel had dropped out of the war against France in 1795, and Baden, Wurttemburg, and Bavaria in 1796. Presently, Spain and the Netherlands had come into the war again, this time on the side of France.

As 1797 dawned, only Great Britain, Portugal, and Austria remained of the original First Coalition, and Austria was sagging on the ropes, on the verge of being knocked out.

8.

We should note one significant military-naval incident of General Pichegru's conquest of the Netherlands.

The winter of 1794–95 was the most severe in more than a century. This was of great help to the French invaders. Rivers which normally remained open all the year were iced over, thus facilitating the passage of armies. Even the salty waters of the Zuider Zee were frozen, effectively trapping the Dutch fleet and preventing its flight to Britain. Out over the frozen waters rode Pichegru's cavalry, deploying so as to approach the immobilized warships from bow and stern, where the broadside guns would not bear. Artillery was dragged out onto the ice and placed for deliberate raking fire. At this point, the flags came fluttering down, and the Dutch fleet belonged to France.

We should also note the rise, during this period, of one of the great "children of Destiny." At the siege of Toulon, Napoleon Bonaparte had been a mere captain of artillery. His brilliance in this action had led a grateful Robespierre to jump him to the rank of brigadier general. When a Paris mob demonstrated against the Directory in 1795, General Bonaparte gained still more fame by killing about one hundred of the Parisians and dispersing the rest with what he called "a whiff of grapeshot." The Directors reciprocated with another promotion and an assignment as commander of the Army of the Interior. Still rising, he married the influential widow, Josephine de Beauharnais, in 1796, and with her help gained command of the army in Italy. Here, as 1797 dawned, he was hard at work transforming what had been a losing campaign against the Austrians into one of brilliant victory.

Against the rising star of Napoleonic France, Great Britain stood virtually alone.

9.

The ancient French dream of conquering Great Britain never seemed more likely to succeed than during the closing weeks of 1796 and the opening weeks of 1797. Control of the sea no longer lay with the British. Against them were three of the great sea powers of Europe—Spain on the south, the Netherlands (then known as the Batavian Republic) on the north, and France in between. Should these three fleets unite under competent leadership, control of the Channel would fall into the hands of the allies, and Britain would be wide open to invasion by the seemingly ever victorious armies of the French Republic.

The Mediterranean was growing too hot to be held. Sir John Jervis, stern martinet and master of discipline, did his best, but it was not good enough. He had only twenty-one ships-of-the-line, all in poor condition and all short of supplies. Even worse, he had a lily-livered subordinate in the person of Rear Admiral Robert Mann.

Hoping to hold Corsica, Admiral Jervis sent Mann with seven ships to take aboard supplies at Gibraltar and then return to the British base at San Fiorenzo Bay, where he himself remained with the other fourteen ships. As he entered the Strait, Mann was horrified to see a Spanish fleet of nineteen ships, proceeding eastward. In wild alarm, he dashed into Gibraltar Harbor, allowing the Spaniards to pass unopposed. Then, despite his orders to return to Corsica, he took his seven vessels to England, leaving Jervis to face the consequences.

While vainly awaiting the return of Rear Admiral Mann to Corsica, Jervis received a series of unpleasant surprises. The first was an attack from behind, delivered by none other than young General Bonaparte. French troops, quietly ferried over from Italy, began a systematic reconquest of Corsica. There were too many of them. The island could not be held. To Horatio Nelson fell the task of evacuating the British positions before they should be overrun. Some men were lost, but the greater part of the evacuation was successfully accomplished.

The next surprise came by sea. Instead of Mann with his seven ships, Jervis beheld Spanish Admiral Juan de Langara with thirty-eight. The Spaniard had an excellent opportunity to eliminate Jervis and his little force, but he did not take it. Instead, he contented himself with sailing contemptuously past the British anchorage, checking on the numbers and condition of his enemies. Then he sailed westward to Toulon, leaving for another day the elimination of the little squadron.

Admiral Jervis must have heaved a large sigh of relief as the Spanish sails vanished over the western horizon. He did not need the receipt of orders from home—which he nevertheless received—to convince him of the necessity of the move which he now took with all speed. As quickly as he could, he gathered his ships and set sail for the Strait of Gibraltar and the comparative safety of Lisbon Harbor.

The Mediterranean was left in the sole possession of France and her allies.

10.

Early in February, 1797, a Spanish fleet of twenty-four ships-of-the-line and twelve frigates under the command of Admiral Don José de Cordova passed westward through the Strait of Gibraltar, borne by a strong easterly wind. Don José's orders were to stop in at Cadiz, then to sail north to Brest to join forces with the French for the projected invasion of the British Isles. It was felt likely that the small British squadron under Admiral Jervis would try to keep the Spaniards from Brest, but could be brushed aside without much difficulty.

The easterly wind blew Cordova's fleet farther west than anticipated, right past Jervis' squadron. There was nothing now to prevent an easy run to Brest. Don José, however, was not a flexible commander. He had intended to stop at Cadiz and would do so. His course was set eastward, with the help of an accommodating wind that had providentially swung around to blow from the west.

Admiral Sir John Jervis was at sea off Cape St. Vincent with his little squadron of fifteen ships, plus a few frigates. His ships might be few, but his men were well trained and had learned to take individual responsibility. Accordingly, when one of his frigates brought him news of a Spanish fleet to the southwest, heading for Cadiz, he did not flinch despite the odds but set a southerly course to intercept. Calling his captains aboard his flagship *Victory* (110), he proposed a toast: "To victory over the Dons in the battle they cannot escape tomorrow!" In a more serious vein, he told his men: "A victory is very essential to England at this hour." Indeed, it was!

Daylight and a lifting fog on February 14 revealed the Spanish fleet. Seventeen ships were sailing closely bunched, in three parallel columns. A mile or so ahead were five other ships, under Admiral

Juan Joaquin Moreno, who had accidentally drawn ahead of the main body during the night. To the south, beyond and between the two bodies, were two 74's which had been detached to scout for the British fleet. They had been searching in the wrong direction.

Admiral Jervis formed his fleet into a single, closely knit line of battle and set a course for the gap between Moreno's five ships and the main Spanish body. This gap was rapidly narrowing, for Moreno had swung his ships around and was beating upwind to rejoin Cordova, if possible. The two scouts, meanwhile, were hastening to join Moreno's group.

Seeing that the British ships would reach the gap before it could be closed, Admiral Cordova swung his main body to the north to pass Jervis' line in the opposite direction. As the swing was made, the Spanish formation degenerated into a mass, in which some of the ships masked the fire of others. Almost at the same moment as the swing, the leading British ship, the *Culloden* (74), opened fire at long range.

To Captain Troubridge of the *Culloden,* it was evident that Admiral Jervis must soon give the signal for the British ships to tack in order, so as to engage the Spaniards on a parallel course. The signal was long in coming. *Culloden* was actually abreast of the last of the Spanish ships before the desired flags were seen fluttering from the flagship *Victory.* At that, the captain brought his ship about so quickly that Admiral Jervis cried in admiration: "Look at Troubridge! He handles his ship as if the eyes of all England were on him!"

As the British ships came about in turn, to follow the Spanish main body, Moreno's seven detached ships hurled themselves at the point where the turn was being made. Without breaking formation, *Irresistible, Victory, Britannia,* and *Egmont* blasted the seven Spaniards and hurled them back, badly battered. At this, Moreno gave up his attack and turned north, setting a course to rejoin Cordova's main body at a point some miles behind the rear of the British formation.

Captain Horatio Nelson was aboard his ship *Captain* (74), third from the rear of the British line. As his ship drove south toward the "knuckle," or turning point, he saw that the northerly courses set by Cordova's main body and by Moreno's seven ships would converge before the British line, on its present course, could intercept. With great personal daring, he ordered the *Captain* out of line, to wear around to the north and to meet the head of the Spanish main body. Seeing this, Admiral Jervis signaled Captain Cuthbert Collingwood of the *Excellent* (74), last ship in line, to follow Nelson and support him.

Nelson's *Captain* sailed into the main body of the Spanish fleet in a blaze of cannon fire, a mere 74 swapping broadsides with such monsters as the *San Nicholas* (80), the *San Josef* (112), and the mighty flagship *Santissima Trinidad* (130). Heavily damaged in the uneven exchange, the *Captain* veered away, being saved by the timely arrival of Collingwood, who sent his *Excellent* in between the Spaniards and Nelson's ship. Collingwood's crew had been especially trained in rapid, accurate gunnery. In the exchange which followed, they gave far more than they received.

Damage repaired, back came Nelson. He saw before him two great Spanish ships locked close together, with rigging tangled. Skilfully bringing the *Captain* against the stern of the *San Nicholas,* he first raked the Spanish monster with a broadside, then ordered boarders through the shattered windows and ports of the Spaniard's stern. He himself climbed aboard, cutlass in hand, and led his marines onto the enemy's deck. After a few minutes of hot fighting, what was left of the Spanish crew surrendered.

Alongside towered the still greater *San Josef,* from whose decks Spanish soldiers were pouring a heavy fire of musketry down upon the British boarders. Once more, it was "Boarders away!" Nelson led the way up the side of the Spanish giant, followed by his men. The Spanish crew, massing along the rail to resist, found themselves unexpectedly assailed from behind. The British *Prince George* (98), sailing by, fired a broadside that swept the decks. The fight went out of the remaining Spaniards. They quickly surrendered to Captain Nelson.

The *Prince George,* arriving so providentially, had been a part of the main British battle line. The attack launched by Nelson and Collingwood had slowed the Spaniards, allowing the British line to overtake the Spanish rear and to turn the battle into a *melee*. Now it was every ship for itself.

In the very heart of the fighting, the *Santissima Trinidad,* largest warship in the world, found herself taking such grievous hurts that Admiral Cordova not only hauled down the Spanish flag but also hoisted the British colors, in order to stay the attack. At this point, the bold Moreno succeeded at last in reaching the main body of the Spanish fleet and in interposing his seven vessels between the British and Cordova's flagship. At once, the admiral again changed colors, as his crippled ship limped out of action.

As the fleets parted, Admiral Jervis found himself in possession of four Spanish prizes, including the two which Nelson had taken by boarding. He had lost no British ships, though a number were badly battered. The Spaniards had had 404 killed and 1,089 wounded; the British, 73 and 227. Neither fleet was in a condition to renew the battle.

Though Admiral Sir John Jervis did not at first realize it, the Battle of Cape Vincent had been a resounding British victory. The Spanish fleet, badly knocked about, had been eliminated as a factor in the proposed invasion of the British Isles. The French and Dutch still remained as threats, but the danger had been greatly lessened. Later, as a reward for a job well done, Sir John Jervis was made the Earl of St. Vincent. His two vice-admirals, Thompson and Waldegrave, were made baronets. Nelson, for his bold part in the affair, was made a Knight of the Bath and promoted to the rank of rear admiral.

Nelson's successful departure from the line, on his own initiative, dealt the last blow to the steadily weakening hold of the *Fighting Instructions* on the minds of British naval leaders. Poor Admiral Byng had been executed for a much milder breach of doctrine. Jervis, however, was a man who appreciated daring and originality. When one of the British captains complained to the admiral that Nelson's move had been completely unauthorized, Admiral Jervis smiled and said: "It certainly was, and if ever *you* commit such a breach of your orders I will forgive you, too."

11.

For the "enlisted men" of the British navy, life in the eighteenth century was no bed of roses. To begin with, only a small percentage of the men had actually enlisted; the others had been forcibly taken from merchant vessels, picked up by "press gangs," released from prisons, sentenced to naval service by judges, or drafted to fill county quotas. Few of those upon the ships actually wanted to be there.

The pay was pitifully small—only a shilling a day—and it was often withheld for long periods. Married men received no more, but they had the privilege of having half of their pay issued directly to their families. The food varied from not very good to extremely bad.

The quarters were cramped and uncomfortable. The discipline was rigid, involving the frequent use of the "cat," with which a man's back could be laid open to the bone. Under ordinary conditions, there was no shore leave. Only the frequent issue of grog made life even bearable.

There were, in the service, a few humane officers who tried to modify the cruel rigidity of the system by applications of fairness and common decency. Admiral Lord Richard Howe became known as "Black Dick, the Sailors' Friend"—a nickname which gave him much pleasure. Jervis and Nelson treated their men as well as the system allowed. But for each such exception among the officers there were dozens of martinets, glorying in their power over their fellow men.

Into this unfair and unbalanced system, the ideas of the egalitarian French Revolution fell like a shower of sparks into a powder barrel. The first explosion was mild enough. A number of sailors, more literate than their shipmates, drew up written petitions for higher pay, better food, and a little liberty in port. Mild as this activity was, it was an unheard-of step to be taken by sailors in the British navy. Only the fact that most of the petitions were sent to "Black Dick" Howe saved them from instant rejection and their perpetrators from severe retribution.

Admiral Howe read the petitions carefully and sympathetically and took constructive action. An appeal was sent to Parliament, and the Channel Fleet, under Lord Bridport, was ordered to the British base at Spithead. While the sailors waited impatiently for news, Parliament did nothing for two weeks, then ordered the Channel Fleet out again. The sailors refused to go. After a week of quiet disobedience—more of a strike than a mutiny—Parliament gave in and granted most of the demands. The better conditions so gained applied not only to the Spithead mutineers but to all enlisted men in the British navy.

On May 12, 1797—three days before Parliament granted the new terms—the disaffection spread to Vice-Admiral Adam Duncan's North Sea Fleet, a collection of ancient ships which had been resurrected to check the menace of Dutch sea power. The first signs of mutiny appeared on a group of Duncan's ships which were anchored off the Nore, a sandbank near the mouth of the Thames. The admiral took forthright steps to check the malady. A personal appeal was all that was needed to gain the cooperation of the crew of his flagship, the *Venerable* (74). He next went to the *razee Adamant* (50), where he found the crew defiant. A huge sailor appeared to be the ringleader.

He was no match for Duncan, who was nearly seven feet tall and powerfully built. The admiral quelled the mutiny on the *Adamant* by picking up the sailor, holding him out over the ship's rail, and shaking him into a state of semiconsciousness. Then he set him down with the remark, "Look, my lads, at this pretty fellow who wants to take command of my fleet!"

With the exception of a single frigate, no other ships at the Nore could be won over. Their crews hoisted the sails and departed for Sheerness, where a radical named Richard Parker had taken over part of the fleet and had organized it into what he called "the Floating Republic."

12.

Vice-Admiral Adam Duncan was not a man to be balked by the disappearance of most of his fleet. Taking the *Venerable,* the *Adamant,* and the loyal frigate, he sailed for Texel to fulfill his orders of blockading Admiral De Winter's Dutch fleet. If no one else would follow him, he and his gallant few would go and would die alone!

Admiral De Winter was thoroughly puzzled by what followed. His fleet of sixteen ships-of-the-line, plus assorted smaller craft, lay in the shelter of Texel Island. Outside the channel, a British 74 and a *razee* prowled on patrol. Some miles out toward the horizon was a single frigate, steadily holding station. From time to time, the British 74 was observed to make signals, which were immediately repeated by the frigate, presumably for the benefit of someone farther out at sea. The British were not being very subtle about their trap. He, Jan de Winter, would not be so foolish as to venture out into the power of that great fleet lying in wait just over the horizon.

Thus did Admiral Duncan, with but two ships and a frigate, hold the Dutch navy paralyzed while British officialdom was dealing with the mutiny. By June 14, De Winter's great opportunity was gone forever. Parker and twenty-eight of the mutineers were dangling from the gibbet. The ships and men of the Channel and North Sea fleets were ready to resume the defense of their islands and their fully implemented blockade of the Dutch coast.

13.

The infection of mutiny, like that of smallpox, travels far and fast. The ship-of-the-line *Marlborough* (74), having taken part in the original Spithead rebellion, suffered a recurrence of mutineering fever while on her way to join the Mediterranean Fleet. The officers were openly defied, and effective discipline aboard became impossible.

The Earl of St. Vincent (Admiral Jervis), in command of the Mediterranean Fleet, heard of the trouble as soon as the *Marlborough* arrived. Such behavior must be rooted out, once and for all! The affected 74 was ordered to pull in her guns and close her gun ports. At once, she was surrounded by small boats, each armed with a carronade. Behind these loomed the great ships of the Mediterranean Fleet, with guns bearing.

The name of the mutinous ringleader was known. The *Marlborough*'s crew was ordered to seize him and to string him up to the yardarm. Any refusal, any hesitation, would lead to the immediate destruction of the ship and its crew. There was no refusal, no hesitation, no sign of further disobedience. Within a matter of minutes, the terrified mutineer was jerking and kicking in mid-air. The surgery had been complete and effective.

The prompt, positive action of the Earl of St. Vincent provided the British Admiralty with a new and effective cure for mutiny. From that time on, the mere threat to "send them to Jervis" was enough!

14.

Despite its name, the Mediterranean Fleet of the Earl of St. Vincent was not in the Mediterranean in the summer of 1797 and had not been since February, when the combination of French and Spanish naval might had made that body of water too perilous for British warships. The Earl and his men, however, were by no means idle. They lay off the Spanish port of Cadiz, blockading it, and at the same time kept a watchful eye on the Strait of Gibraltar.

Sir Horatio Nelson now flew his rear admiral's flag from the *Theseus* (74). He was in command of the inner squadron, detailed to keep a close eye on what went on in Cadiz Harbor and to interfere as much as possible with any interesting Spanish maneuvers. It was an assignment with possibilities for adventure and excitement.

Early in July, Rear Admiral Nelson himself led a night attack in small boats, aimed at the destruction of some Spanish warships in the harbor. The raiders were discovered, and the Spaniards came boiling out in a fleet of small boats and cutters. On the dark waters of the harbor, Nelson's boat, containing only thirteen men, was attacked by an armed launch manned by twenty-seven Spaniards. It was the fiercest kind of fighting, hand to hand, with cutlasses and dirks. It is recorded that Nelson swung his blade with the best of them, cutting down more than one Spaniard and being himself saved from probable death by his loyal coxswain Sykes, who took upon his own head a slash aimed at his admiral. After eighteen Spaniards had been killed, the rest surrendered.

Such bold adventures might amply prove the courage of British seamen and their leaders, but they could do little to harm the French-Spanish-Dutch cause or even the fleet within Cadiz, which was proving itself too strong to be taken. Some more practical form of activity was needed.

Less than two weeks later, word was received that the Spanish Viceroy of Mexico had brought the heavily laden plate fleet into the harbor of Santa Cruz on Teneriffe Island, in the Canaries. Here was a chance to strike a blow at Spain and, at the same time, to add to the fortunes of Great Britain and of certain members of her fleet. Rear Admiral Nelson was placed in charge of the expedition.

Well-defended Santa Cruz had been taken only once, by Blake in 1657. That had been an epic expedition, famed for careful planning, daring execution, and great good luck. Nelson, studying the story of the raid, decided that it would be unrealistic to count on that much luck a second time. He would not try to send his fleet into that forbidding entrance but would lead his men ashore in small boats and storm the waterfront on foot.

Nelson's luck was bad on all counts. To begin with, there was no Spanish treasure fleet at Santa Cruz, merely a single merchant vessel from the Philippines. His first attempt, on July 22, was foiled by adverse winds and currents. Two nights later, he tried again, with 1,100 men in a large fleet of small boats. Only nine of the boats, including the admiral's, reached the mole. Just as Nelson stepped out of his boat, he was struck in the right elbow by a musket ball, which mangled the joint and cut some arteries. His stepson, Josiah Nisbet, caught him as he fell, helped him back into his boat, and stayed the blood with a rough tourniquet. Nelson was rowed back to his ship, where the surgeon botched his job so badly that the entire right arm had to be amputated.

In the admiral's absence, the attack went badly. A group of 340 armed British seamen, led by Captain Troubridge, managed to reach the town, where daylight found them surrounded by several thousand

Spaniards. Capture was averted by the most audacious of bluffs. Troubridge sent word, under a flag of truce, that he would burn the town unless his men were permitted to depart in peace. Spanish Governor Gutierrez, knowing the spreading damage that a few well-placed torches could create in crowded Santa Cruz, readily agreed, on the understanding that the British squadron would go away and would not again attack the Canary Islands. On this humane note, the fighting ceased, and the British survivors returned sadly to their ships.

As soon as he could, Rear Admiral Horatio Nelson scrawled a left-handed letter to the Earl of St. Vincent: "I am become a burthen to my friends and useless to my country. . . . When I leave your command, I become dead to the world. 'I go hence, and am no more seen.' "

It was an understandable thing to write, but a most inaccurate bit of prophecy.

15.

Dutch Admiral De Winter had "missed the boat" by not conducting his invasion while the British fleet was immobilized by the strike-mutiny of May and June, 1797. Now, in October, he rather illogically decided to come out and settle the question of control of the North Sea. Admiral Adam Duncan was more than willing to cooperate in the settling of this question.

Old and decrepit as were Duncan's ships, they were not so bad as De Winter's. The Dutch fleet was in a rundown condition, and it suffered the further disability of small size and shallow draft which the shoal waters of the Netherlands' coast imposed upon all Dutch vessels.

On October 8, 1797, De Winter came out from Texel with a squadron of fifteen ships-of-the line and eight frigates and headed in a southwesterly direction toward Brest. A British brig, the *Speculator,* which had been keeping watch on Texel, rushed to Yarmouth to inform Admiral Duncan that the enemy were out. The next day, two British ships, *Russell* (74) and *Adamant* (64), sighted the Dutch squadron and began to shadow it, staying within sight in spite of several attempts by De Winter to close with them. Through the 9th and the 10th, the course toward Brest was followed.

Early in the morning of October 11, Duncan's British squadron was seen coming in from the west. At once, De Winter reversed course and sailed northeast, back toward Texel, forming a battle line as he sailed. Duncan set a converging course and closed as rapidly as the squally wind conditions permitted.

In numbers, there was not much choice between the fleets. Including the *Russell* and the *Adamant,* picked up at the scene, Duncan had sixteen ships-of-the-line as opposed to De Winter's fifteen, and four frigates as opposed to De Winter's eight. The British ships, however, were larger, seven of them being 74's, whereas only four of the Dutch ships carried that many guns.

By mid-morning, Admiral Duncan had overtaken the Dutch off the little town of Camperdown and had also gained the wind gauge. His fleet advanced downwind toward the enemy in two irregular columns, the left one under his personal command from the *Venerable* (74), the right one under Vice-Admiral Richard Onslow in the *Monarch* (74).

During the approach, it became painfully evident to Admiral Duncan that his captains had little knowledge of or regard for signals. It was his plan to approach the Dutch in a long, even line abreast, taking what damage was necessary from raking fire in order to close quickly. He hoisted the proper signals, but the only result was an irregular bunching of the two British columns. Despairing at last of accomplishing the formation he had ordered, Duncan hoisted new signals, directing his own column to attack the Dutch center while Onslow's column was to attack the rear. All ships were further ordered to pass through the Dutch line and attack from leeward, thus preventing the escape of injured Dutch vessels into the shoal waters to the eastward. This, it will be recognized, was an application of Lord Howe's plan for the Battle of the First of June, 1794.

Again, the signals were not understood. Typical was the reaction of Scottish Captain John Inglis of the *Belliqueux* (64), who threw his signal book to the deck, snapped shut his telescope, and cried out to his helmsman: "Damn it, Jock! Up with the hellum, and gang recht into the middle o't."

Venerable, following Duncan's plan, broke through the Dutch line immediately astern of De Winter's flagship *Vrijheid* (74), which he raked as he went through. To leeward of her was the *Staten-General* (74), which he also raked. Toward the rear of the Dutch formation, *Monarch* passed similarly astern of the Dutch *Jupiter* (74), raking her in passing. The other fourteen ships of Duncan's squadron followed Inglis' example and attacked at close range from windward.

The battle, thus begun, quickly degenerated into a point-blank *melee* of the most vicious sort. There was none of the French technique of aiming for the rigging. Both the Dutch and the British were born fighters, and they laid their guns to destroy ships and to kill men. The muffing of the signals turned out to be fortunate for the British, for the two ships which had broken through were able to co-operate with the battle line to windward in doubling up on one Dutch ship after another. In this way, *Vrijheid* and *Jupiter,* attacked from both sides at once, were quickly battered into helplessness and forced to surrender. Others were taken in turn, after the hardest kind of fighting. At the end of two and a half hours, nine Dutch ships and two frigates had been taken; the others had made good their escape. It is worth noting that none of these Dutch vessels had been surrendered before receiving such grievous wounds that they could not subsequently be repaired. The British had lost no ships, but they had 202 dead and 622 wounded, representing casualties of more than 10 per cent of their entire complement. The Dutch losses were even higher.

As a result of the Battle of Camperdown, the Dutch navy was removed as a threat to the British Isles. Admiral Duncan was rewarded by being made Viscount of Camperdown. Admiral Onslow was made a baronet. Bungled as it may have been in execution, Camperdown was nevertheless a hard-fought and most important British victory. The rewards were well merited.

The defeated Dutch admiral, Jan de Winter, did not fare so well. Wounded during the battle, he was captured and taken aboard the *Venerable.* There he made light of his wounds and challenged Admiral Duncan to a game of whist. Duncan won, leading De Winter to comment, "It is a hard thing to be beaten by the same man twice in one day." Later, in London, De Winter's wounds proved to be far more serious than he had assumed. He died of them.

16.

General Napoleon Bonaparte, having defeated the Austrians in Italy and having forced upon them the unfavorable Treaty of Campo Formio in October, 1797, spent much of the winter which followed in the intensive study of books stripped from the great Ambrosian Library of Milan. All of the books selected dealt with the Near East. The passages which he marked all dealt with Egypt.

The defeat of the Spanish navy at Cape St. Vincent and of the Dutch at Camperdown had considerably reduced the chances of a successful invasion of the British Isles. Never mind! The brilliant general had a better plan in mind—a blow at Britain's Asiatic empire through the conquest of India. The first step in such a campaign would be the invasion of Egypt. Napoleon would follow in the footsteps of Alexander the Great!

It would not do for the British to get wind of the great endeavor. Accordingly, the French invasion forces continued to occupy the Channel coast, where an increasing number of barges was accumulating. Boasts were made about the impending invasion of the British Isles. Napoleon and the French Directors were confident that these evident preparations would lead Parliament to recall every available warship for the defense of the homeland, leaving the way clear for the great Eastern adventure.

As a matter of fact, this decoying operation was not very successful. The British were far too curious about the intriguing reports out of Leghorn and Naples concerning the frantic new activities being carried on in Toulon, Genoa, and other places under French control. Something was cooking in the Mediterranean—something big! An urgent message was sent to the Earl of St. Vincent: "The appearance of a British fleet in the Mediterranean is a condition on which the fate of Europe may be said to depend."

Contrary to his prediction, Rear Admiral Horatio Nelson had not gone hence, to be no more seen, in spite of the loss of an eye and an arm. Early in 1798, he was back with St. Vincent's fleet off Cadiz. Such was his reputation that he was the first choice not only of the Earl of St. Vincent but also of King George III himself to preside at the re-entry of the British fleet into the Mediterranean.

St. Vincent was faced by no easy problem. His fleet off Cadiz consisted of only eighteen ships-of-the-line, plus a few frigates, with which to bottle up a Spanish fleet which had now been rebuilt to a strength of more than thirty. All he could spare for Nelson were three 74's—the flagship *Vanguard,* the *Orion,* and the *Alexander*—and four frigates. With this inadequate force, he sent the expedition out "to proceed on quest." Where the quest would lead, no one could be sure. Naples, Sicily, Portugal, Ireland, Jamaica, and the Black Sea region all seemed possible. Egypt was never even considered.

17.

Nelson sailed on May 9, and a few days later passed Toulon at a respectful distance. On the 17th, he captured a small French ship, from whose captain he learned that there were nineteen French ships-of-the-line in Toulon Harbor, and that troops were going aboard innumerable transports. Evidently, the French move, whatever it was, would be made soon.

Two nights later, misfortune struck. Out of the northwest came a sudden gale. The *Vanguard*'s masts went by the board, leaving the flagship a helpless wreck, drifting before the wind toward the French-held coast. Fortunately, the *Alexander* was able to take her in tow and to get her to a little group of islands south of Sardinia, where repairs could be made. The *Orion* stood by, but there was no sign of the frigates, which had become separated in the storm and which subsequently deserted Nelson and returned all the way to England.

It was not until May 27 that Nelson managed to get his damage repaired and to set out for the vicinity of Toulon. On the way, he met an American merchant ship, whose captain gave him shocking news. The French expedition had sailed on the 19th, with thirteen ships-of-the-line and no fewer than 400 laden transports. The destination was completely unknown.

The only clue was that northwest wind, which had dismasted the *Vanguard* and had supplied Napoleon with what he must have considered a favorable wind for reaching his mysterious destination. No one would try to beat upwind against a gale like that. The French fleet must have sailed east or south or southeast. At once, the name of Egypt leaped into Nelson's mind.

Still hoping to rendezvous with his frigates, Nelson encountered instead a fleet of ten British ships-of-the-line, a 50-gunner, and a brig. St. Vincent had been reinforced, and in return had reinforced his rear admiral. Now there was a respectable British fighting force in the Mediterranean. If only there were some frigates to serve as eyes for the fleet.

There was also a message from St. Vincent: "You are perfectly justifiable in pursuing the French squadron to any part of the Mediterranean, Adriatic, Morea, or even into the Black Sea; on falling in with the said armament, you are to use your utmost endeavours to take, sink, burn, or destroy it." These were orders to gladden the heart of a fighting admiral!

On June 7, the day after the arrival of his reinforcements, Rear Admiral Nelson set out on a frustrating voyage—the search for the vanished French fleet. Learning that Napoleon was to be joined by more ships from Genoa, he set sail for the Italian coast in an attempt to interrupt the rendezvous. Here he learned that the French fleet had sailed for Malta. Proceeding under full sail for Malta, he met a ship off Sicily whose captain told him that the French had taken Malta but had already left, headed eastward. Egypt! Nelson set a straight course for Alexandria, sure that he would find the French expedition there. There were no French ships at Alexandria, and nobody had seen any.

Frantic—certain now that he had made a terrible mistake—Nelson sailed north for Asia Minor, westward to Sicily, eastward to the islands off Greece, southward to Crete. A month went by, without a sign of his quarry! On July 28, he sailed again for Egypt.

Where were the French? What had they been doing?

As Nelson knew, the great French flotilla had left Toulon on May 19. It had picked up the ships from Genoa at a rendezvous off Elba and had sailed directly to Malta, taking the island from the Knights of St. John. It had left Malta on June 19, sailing due east toward Crete on a hunch of Napoleon's. That night the French fleet, sailing east, and Nelson's fleet, sailing southeast toward Egypt, had passed through the same water at about the same time, undetected in the darkness. Nelson, following the more direct route, had reached Alexandria first, but had departed immediately on his wild goose chase. Two days later, Napoleon had arrived.

The Mamelukes of Egypt were unable to offer much opposition to the great General Bonaparte and his 38,000 veteran French soldiers. Alexandria was surrendered after a siege of a few hours. Near Cairo, the invaders met resistance at Embabeh. Pointing to the pyramids, Napoleon inspired his soldiers with the words: "Soldiers of France! From yonder pyramids, forty centuries of history look down on you." The Mameluke cavalry charged; the French hollow squares stood firm; Egyptian resistance ceased.

Meanwhile, Nelson was still groping across the Mediterranean, severely handicapped by the lack of small, fast ships for scouts. "Were I to die," he wrote, " 'want of frigates' would be found written on my heart." Nelson, however, wasted no time as the search went on. Frequent conferences were held aboard the flagship with his officers—his "band of brothers"—to discuss all possible contingencies. As a result, every captain knew exactly what would be expected of him under all possible conditions. It was an excellent example of indoctrination, as defined by Mahan: "the formation of a similar habit of thought."

18.

Vice-Admiral François Paul Brueys of the French navy had performed a difficult task in bringing the French expedition unscathed across the Mediterranean, despite the bloodhound tactics of Nelson's British fleet and the constant interference of the great General Bonaparte. Now that the French invaders had been landed and the conquest of Egypt had begun, Brueys found himself faced with the further task of keeping the fleet on hand in Egyptian waters, ready for whatever further use might occur to the general. Alexandria Harbor, silted and neglected through the centuries, was completely unsuitable. Aboukir Bay, some fifteen miles to the east at the Rosetta mouth of the Nile, was selected as the best place for a safe anchorage.

As a young officer, Brueys had been with De Grasse during the attack on Hood's anchored fleet at St. Kitts. How difficult it had been to attack that fleet, lying at anchor with the lead ship too near shore to permit the passage of the French battle line! All that had been possible was a passing cannonade. He would use the same technique!

Aboukir Bay is shielded on the west by jutting Aboukir Point, off which lies a large area of shoal water. To the north, off the point, lies Becquieres Island, surrounded by shoal waters. Brueys' fleet would be anchored just east of the point, with the leading ship, *Guerrier,* at the five-fathom line, adjoining water too shallow to be traversed by a large ship. This would keep an attacking force from sliding in between his battle line and the shore. Very good! Only the starboard guns, those facing the open water to the east, need be ready for action. The baggage which had been clogging the gun decks dangerously could all be moved to port, where it would not be in the way because the port guns would not be needed. To help in defense, some small batteries were mounted on the point and on the island.

Had Vice-Admiral Brueys been a thorough man, he would have checked the positions of his ships and would have discovered that the captain of the *Guerrier* had disregarded orders and had anchored in seven rather than five fathoms of water. Brueys was not a thorough man.

Nelson's fleet, driving south with the help of a northwesterly wind, sighted the French line about four in the afternoon of August 1, 1798, and at once pressed forward to attack. The two fleets were approximately even in numbers—fourteen British ships and a brig against thirteen French ships and four frigates. The most powerful ship involved was the French flagship, *L'Orient* (120). Two other French ships, *Franklin* and *Tonnant,* were 80's. The British *Leander* was a 50. All of the others, in both fleets, were 74's.

At six o'clock in the evening, just before sundown, the British line, headed by *Goliath,* rounded Becquieres Island and stood in toward the anchored French fleet. At once, possibilities began to occur to Nelson's well-indoctrinated captains. Captain Foley of the *Goliath* thought he saw enough open water between the *Guerrier* and the shore to permit his ship to pass. He took the chance and went through safely, raking *Guerrier* with a broadside as he crossed her bow, then dropping a stern anchor which brought his ship to rest opposite the unprepared port side of *Conquerant,* the second ship in the French line. *Zealous, Orion,* and *Theseus* followed *Goliath* around the head of the column, and *Audacious,* living up to her name, passed between *Guerrier* and *Conquerant,* raking both as she went through. All five took up positions on the "blind" sides of leading French ships, whence they cannonaded unmercifully. Meanwhile, the remainder of the British squadron slid down the starboard side of the French formation, shelling as they went and eventually dropping stern anchors to hold them in position for further battering of the enemy. All but Troubridge's *Culloden,* that is! Cutting too close to Becquieres Island, she had gone aground. She was out of action all that night, while her captain watched the fireworks and ate his heart out.

The French found themselves in a desperate situation. The first eight ships in their column were being battered from both sides at once by thirteen British ships, while the five French ships at the tail of the column had to remain out of the fighting because of the strong northwest wind blowing directly over their bows. With such a situation, only one end was possible.

Against overwhelming odds, the French fought with gallant desperation. Young Captain DuPetit-Thouars of the *Tonnant,* with both legs and an arm shot off, had his officers place him upright in a tub of bran, from which position he continued to give orders until he died from loss of blood. Admiral Brueys and Captain Casabianca, on *L'Orient,* beat off the attack of *Bellerophon* and succeeded in dismasting the British ship and putting her out of action. Attacked now by the

Alexander and the *Swiftsure,* the French flagship took a terrible beating. Admiral Brueys was horribly wounded, but proclaimed that a French admiral ought to die on his quarterdeck, and did so. Captain Casabianca was also killed. As the ship began to burn, the captain's ten-year-old son refused to leave the place where his father had stationed him. He, too, perished.[1]

Aboard the *Vanguard,* Admiral Nelson was struck in the head by a flying splinter, which laid open his scalp and temporarily drowned out the sight from his good eye. He was carried below but refused to accept medical attention ahead of his turn. Later, discovering that the wound was not so serious as he had supposed, he resumed his place on the quarterdeck.

At about ten in the evening, the blazing flagship *L'Orient* blew up, with a terrific concussion and a mountainous column of flame. The shock immediately stilled the firing on both sides. It was fully five minutes before the gunners of the *Leander,* recovering from their daze, resumed action. The firing spread. The battle of blinding flashes and inky darkness lasted all night.

As dawn broke, the three undamaged ships at the rear of the French line cut their cables, hoisted sails, and began to edge away to the eastward. Two undamaged frigates accompanied them. *Timoleon* went aground and was burned by her captain, but *Guilliame Tell, Généreux,* and the frigates managed to get away. Nelson signaled the *Zealous* and the *Audacious* to intercept the fugitives, but when the captain of *Audacious* missed the signal and made no move, he recalled the *Zealous.* The odds of one ship against two ships and two frigates were too great, and no other British vessels were in position and condition to act.

The French fleet that had brought Napoleon to Egypt was no more. Of the thirteen ships-of-the-line, nine had been taken and two destroyed. One of the four frigates had been taken and one sunk. More than 3,200 Frenchmen had been killed or wounded and 2,000 captured. The French army that had conquered Egypt had been cut off from home by the long arm of British sea power.

19.

It was important that word of the Nile victory reach the Admiralty as quickly as possible. Accordingly, Admiral Nelson dispatched his

---

[1] This is the event described in the poem "Casabianca," by Felicia Hemans, which opens with the well-known words: "The boy stood on the burning deck."

fastest ship, the 50-gun *Leander,* to bear the news. Off Crete, *Leander* encountered the French 74-gun *Généreux,* one of the two French ships-of-the-line which had escaped from the Nile debacle. There was every reason for *Leander* to avoid action. She was eighty men short of her usual complement. She was outgunned, approximately three to two. She was carrying important dispatches. Being a lighter, handier ship, she could easily have pulled away in the light breezes then prevailing. Apparently, the thought of flight never entered the mind of Captain Thomas Thompson. With supreme confidence, he shortened sail and waited for the larger *Généreux* to come up.

Considering the difference in the sizes of the ships, the battle was not so one-sided as one might have thought. For six and a half hours, the two vessels hammered each other at close range, with frightful effect. At the end of that time, *Généreux* had been badly hurt, but *Leander* had been reduced to a hulk, with all three masts gone, her steering gear disabled, and most of her guns out of action. Not until all hope was gone did Captain Thompson surrender. He, his surviving crewmen, and his ship were taken to Corfu and held there by the French.

Word of the Nile victory had to reach the Admiralty through other means.

After seven months on Corfu, *Leander* and her men were returned to the British navy when a Russian-Turkish force captured the island from the French. Captain Thompson was court-martialed for the loss of his ship, but was honorably acquitted by his judges and was enthusiastically cheered by the crews of all nearby British warships when the verdict became known. British naval personnel have always appreciated valor far more than prudence.

20.

Nelson's victory at the Nile had tremendous repercussions. Russia, which had been quietly cooperating with Great Britain in the Baltic, was encouraged to come openly into the war against France. Soon a Russian army appeared in Italy, and part of Russia's Black Sea fleet, under Admiral Feodor Ushakov, undertook the patrol of the Adriatic. Turkey, incensed at Napoleon's invasion of her tributary state of Egypt, declared war against the French. Austria and Naples, too, joined the anti-French alliance. Once more, the pendulum had begun to swing.

Napoleon, casting about for an effective countermove, decided to lead his splendid army northward along the eastern end of the Mediterranean, conquering Turkish lands as he went. With Constantinople in his hands, he would be able to dictate favorable terms to these presumptuous enemies who were massing against his country.

There was one enemy on whom Napoleon Bonaparte failed to count. This was Sir William Sidney Smith, whom we last saw leading the desperate fireship raid in the harbor of Toulon. Smith had a real grudge against the French. He had been captured in 1796 during a raid on Le Havre and had been held as a criminal rather than as a prisoner of war, subject to exchange. Escaping, with the help of a bribed jailor, he had made his way to London, where he had managed to win an appointment as Minister Plenipotentiary to the Sublime Porte—Turkey, that is. One of the appurtenances of his new office was a little fleet of two British ships-of-the-line, the *Tigre* (80) and the *Theseus* (74).

Turning the southeastern corner of the Mediterranean, Napoleon Bonaparte found before him the ancient fortified city of St. Jean d'Acre, garrisoned with some 3,000 Turkish troops. Under ordinary conditions, this would not have been a formidable obstacle; walled cities fall easy prey to heavy artillery. The French army, however, lacked artillery. To avoid dragging the guns through the desert sands, Napoleon had sent them on ahead in a flotilla of small sailing barges. Barges, guns, and all had disappeared.

Sir William Sidney Smith was responsible. Leaving Constantinople with the *Tigre* and the *Theseus,* he had appeared off Acre in time to intercept the French flotilla. The captured guns had been added to the defenses of Acre, along with several hundred British sailors and marines. *Tigre* and *Theseus,* with some smaller auxiliary craft, had been carefully anchored off the waterfront in such positions that their guns could sweep the approaches to the walls. Acre was now ready for Napoleon's attack.

The siege which followed was the first important defeat in Napoleon Bonaparte's career. From March 18 to May 20, 1799, the French army kept steady pressure on the ancient city. It availed them little. Time after time, the attackers were hurled back by the defenders on the walls and by the withering volleys of cannon fire from the anchored warships. In a frenzy of frustration, great General Bonaparte cried out, "The whole fate of the East lies in that one miserable little town!"

Napoleon was right. The fate of the East did lie in Acre. In a broader sense, the fate of the East—the fate of the world—lay in those two grim ships-of-the-line anchored off the waterfront, and in the naval might of Britain which they represented.

After the loss of more than 5,000 men, Napoleon Bonaparte gave up the fruitless attack on Acre and led his army back into Egypt. The conquest of Turkey, like that of India, would have to wait.

21.

The armies of France did not do well during Napoleon's absence. While he and his men remained inactive in Egypt, other French generals were losing battles. Northern Italy—which Napoleon had secured by the Treaty of Campo Formio—was now gone again. Russia, Austria, Naples, Portugal, and Turkey had joined Britain in the formation of a Second Coalition, which threatened to sweep all before it. The one winning general must be brought home from Egypt to save France from her enemies.

To bring Napoleon and his army back from Egypt, it was necessary for France and her allies to obtain naval control of the Mediterranean, at least briefly. The solving of this problem was entrusted to the Minister of Marine, Vice-Admiral Eustache Bruix. At once, he rushed to Brest, under strict orders to fit out the French fleet there and get it to the Mediterranean without fighting a battle.

On April 26, 1799, the Gods of the Sea smiled on Admiral Bruix. A strong onshore wind sprang up, endangering the ships of Lord Bridport's blockading squadron off Brest. Seizing his opportunity, Bruix at once put to sea with twenty-four ships-of-the-line and ten frigates, and set sail to the south, toward the Strait of Gibraltar.

When word reached Lord Bridport that the fleet from Brest had sailed, he at once jumped to the conclusion that a French invasion of Ireland was under way. Accordingly, he took his squadron westward to block the entrance to St. George's Channel. While he was faithfully but uselessly patrolling there, Bruix sailed serenely on his way.

Off Cadiz lay a British blockading squadron of fifteen ships, temporarily commanded by Vice-Admiral Baron Keith (George Keith Elphinstone), during the illness of the Earl of St. Vincent. This was a nerve-wracking assignment at best, for the Spanish fleet being blockaded had three more ships-of-the-line than the British who were blockading them. On the morning of May 4, the western horizon was suddenly fringed with sails—twenty-four French ships-of-the-line and ten frigates, all of them upwind from Keith's vessels. His squadron was fairly caught, sandwiched in between enemy forces which outnumbered him forty-two ships to fifteen!

To the amazement of Admiral Keith, the French sailed peacefully by. They knew where he was, all right, and they knew of his weakness. Bruix, however, had definite orders to avoid a battle, and avoid it he did, though at the expense of leaving intact an important segment of the British navy which he might easily have destroyed or taken. On he went, through the Strait of Gibraltar and into the harbor of Toulon, which he reached on May 13.

Two necessary ingredients of any realistic attempt to rescue the army in Egypt would be speed and surprise. Bruix wasted both. He spent weeks in running errands for French generals in Italy, while Napoleon and his soldiers settled steadily from discouragement into despair.

The British were not much better. The Earl of St. Vincent, still too ill for active command, permitted his fleet of thirty-three ships to remain divided between the squadron off Spain, under Keith, and the squadron off Naples, under Nelson, who was pleasantly recovering from his latest wound as the guest of Sir William Hamilton, British Ambassador to the Kingdom of the Two Sicilies. To be more precise, Admiral Nelson was the guest of the young and charming Lady Emma Hamilton, a hero-worshipping female who presently became his mistress, in flagrant disregard of the feelings of her husband, of Nelson's wife, and of society in general. From this point on, "dearest Emma" was a person who had to be taken into account as far as the operations of much of the British navy were concerned.

22.

Early in June, 1799, Admiral Keith, weary of shilly-shallying and inaction, followed Bruix' fleet into the Gulf of Genoa and was straining for a sight of French topsails on the horizon when he was overtaken by a dispatch boat, bearing definite instructions that he was to go to Minorca at once and confer with the Earl of St. Vincent. With a last, frustrated peek at the horizon ahead, he turned sadly about and obeyed his orders.

Arriving at the sickbed, Admiral Keith was informed that the Spanish fleet under Don José de Mazarredo had shifted its base from Cadiz to Cartagena, to simplify the problem of uniting with Bruix' squadron.

This was vital information, but it was hardly vital enough to have occasioned the "drop everything and come" orders which had been rushed to Keith. Had the admiral been granted even one more day of uninterrupted activity, there might well have been no French squadron for the Spaniards to join.

Having mismanaged the show from his bed in Minorca, the Earl of St. Vincent presently relinquished his Mediterranean command and returned home to Britain, leaving Keith in command. At once Keith set out for the Gulf of Genoa, hoping to find that Bruix had waited for him. Of course, he had not. All that now sailed the Gulf of Genoa under the French tricolor was a pathetic little squadron of three frigates and two brigs. These the British admiral quickly gobbled up, though they scarcely served as an appetizer.

Returning to Minorca, Admiral Keith learned that the worst had happened. While he had been searching for Bruix off Genoa, the Frenchman had taken his fleet to Cartagena and had united with the Spaniards. There was now a unified French-Spanish fleet of forty-two ships to oppose his divided fleet of thirty-seven—nineteen under his personal command at Minorca and eighteen under Nelson at Naples. A frantic call was sent to Baron Nelson of the Nile to bring his ships westward and close ranks.

Baron Nelson declined. Excellent reasons were given. At first, he maintained that it was necessary to support the government of the Two Sicilies against mounting French pressure. Later, when French land forces had taken Naples, he declared that it was necessary to blockade the port to prevent the French from using it. When Admiral Caracciolo of the Neapolitan navy started cooperating with the French, it became necessary to capture him, try him, and execute him. There was a new title, Duke of Brontë, to be accepted by the British rear admiral in the interests of international solidarity. The real reason was never mentioned. While Admiral Keith chafed and swore and the French-Spanish fleet slipped out of Cartagena and sailed unopposed to Brest, Horatio Nelson dallied with Emma Hamilton to their mutual hearts' delight.

The ghost of Admiral Byng must have wailed aloud!

23.

The departure of the allied fleet from Cartagena sealed the fate of the French army in Egypt. The ships were to have been used to bring supplies and assistance to the soldiers of the expedition and to cooperate with them in their campaign. The diversion to Brest meant that new plans had been made for the use of the ships and that the army in Egypt was being cast adrift to fend for itself.

The responsible person was Napoleon Bonaparte. In August, 1799, Napoleon, seeing little future for the Egyptian campaign, had abandoned his soldiers, had slipped across the Mediterranean on a fast warship, and had landed in southern France without having caught a glimpse of a British sail. Arriving in France, he was hailed as a hero! The victories over the Mamelukes in Egypt were magnified all out of proportion. The defeat in the Nile was laid to Admiral Brueys' failure to obey orders. Acre was dismissed as a mere reconnaissance mission. The ever-victorious Napoleon Bonaparte had returned!

What of the betrayed army in Egypt? For nearly two years it carried on, under French Generals Kleber, Menou, and Friant. Attacks by Turkish and British expeditions were successfully beaten off. At last, in the summer of 1801, the weary and disillusioned army succumbed to a perfectly organized amphibious attack, conducted by Vice-Admiral Lord George Keith, Major General Sir John Moore, and that perpetual gadfly, Sir William Sidney Smith.

Admiral Nelson? He lingered at Naples while Sir William Hamilton held his post there, making occasional expeditions on his own initiative. These were not without value to the British cause. In February, 1800, while on a cruise toward Malta, he encountered a French squadron made up of frigates and of the ship-of-the-line *Généreux* (74), one of the two which had escaped him at the Nile. The *Généreux* and one frigate were taken. Later, he encountered the other fugitive, *Guillaume Tell* (80), and took her, too. "What a pleasure," wrote Lord Nelson, "what happiness, to have the Nile fleet all taken, under my orders and regulations!"

There was, quite understandably, bad blood between Vice-Admiral Keith and Rear Admiral Nelson. There was also an unfortunate series of misunderstandings between Nelson and Sir William Sidney Smith. These factors led to a request for reassignment, which was granted by the Admiralty. Not entirely by coincidence, the transfer came through at the same time when Sir William Hamilton was superseded as Ambassador to the Two Sicilies. Together the three—Sir William and Emma Hamilton and Admiral Horatio Nelson—traveled northward by land through Austria and Germany. They reached England in November, 1800.

In England, Admiral Nelson received a mixed reception. He was given a hero's welcome by the public, was snubbed by the king and by most of the nobility, and was tearfully reproached by his wife because of his infamous attachment to Lady Hamilton. When it became known that Lady Hamilton was bearing Nelson's child—a daughter named Horatia—Lord and Lady Nelson obtained a permanent legal separation.

11 THE AMERICAN NAVY REVIVED

⚓

1.

With the end of the American Revolution in 1783, the United States officially got rid of the last remnants of the navy that had almost ceased to exist during the war. A navy, thought Congress, was too expensive a luxury to be maintained in times of peace. The two remaining commissioned warships—the frigates *Alliance* and *Hague*—were sold. The ship-of-the-line *America* (74), the first battleship built for the United States Navy, was completed but never commissioned. Instead, she was presented to France to replace the *Magnifique* (74), which had been lost in a storm off the Massachusetts coast. The United States was without power on the sea.

Even at the point of lowest ebb, it was recognized that some day conditions might justify a rebirth of American sea power. At Philadelphia, in 1787, the framers of the Constitution included among the rights of Congress "to provide and maintain a navy." When the War Department was officially created in 1789, the Secretary of War was made responsible for naval as well as military forces. This provision was, at the time, purely academic. There were no naval forces.

2.

Not long after the close of hostilities with the Mother Country in 1783, American shippers and seamen began to realize some rather unpleasant facts of international life. While the thirteen states had been colonies of Great Britain, their ships had flown the British flag. This had meant to all and sundry upon the sea that the power of the British Navy stood behind these ships. The new flag of stars and stripes had no such meaning. Where were the warships to protect the merchant vessels of this new, weak, and no-doubt transitory country?

The trouble began as early as 1785. In that year, the American merchant ship *Dauphin,* proceeding peacefully through the Mediterranean, was pursued and overtaken by an armed ship belonging to the Dey of Algiers. Resistance was impossible. The *Dauphin* was forced to haul down her flag and follow her captor to Algiers. Ship and cargo were confiscated. Passengers and crew were held for ransom. Those who had no wealthy family or friends to buy their freedom were sold into slavery.

At about the same time, the same thing happened to the American schooner *Maria.* An intolerable pattern was being set.

Congress protested, but in vain. The Dey did express willingness to release the Americans and to refrain from further seizures provided his price for such "protection" were met. The new government of the United States could not afford the extravagant terms mentioned. The Americans remained in slavery, and further seizures were made. The situation grew much worse in 1793 when Portugal made a treaty with the Barbary states of North Africa, recognizing the right of their ships to pass through the Strait of Gibraltar and operate in the ocean waters off the Portuguese coast. The Barbary pirates of Algiers and Tripoli were not slow to take advantage of this. Within a month of the signing of the treaty, no fewer than eleven American ships were seized.

In 1795, the United States gave in and agreed to meet the demands of the Dey of Algiers. The release of the enslaved Americans required nearly a million dollars in cash and presents, and the protection was set at an annual cost exceeding $20,000. Like most acts of appeasement, it accomplished little. The Dey began to make additional demands and to take for his own whatever American property he fancied. He thought nothing, for example, of demanding an ornate mirror belonging to the American Consul, William Eaton, and Eaton had to give it to him. Far worse was the upsurge in demands among the other Barbary rulers. All along the southern shore of the Mediterranean, assorted Deys, Beys, and Bashaws loudly demanded the same fine treatment being accorded the Dey of Algiers.

Peace-loving Americans, including many members of Congress, began to get hot under the collar. Though the pirates were temporarily out of reach, they need not necessarily remain so. A bill was passed calling for the creation of six frigates—four 44's and two 36's. To placate the more money-minded members, a provision was included stating that "if a peace should take place between the United States and the regency of Algiers, no further proceedings shall be had under this act." Fortunately for American naval power, the situation did not arise.

Joshua Humphreys, of Philadelphia, was given the contract of building one of the 44's, the frigate *Constitution*. He drew his plans with care and forethought, hoping to produce a ship which would have the advantages not only of the light, fast frigates of the past but also of the heavier and harder-hitting *razees,* which were now beginning to appear in some numbers in the navy of France.

The *Constitution,* as designed by Humphreys, would be large, strong, and seaworthy, with more guns than the frigates of her day customarily carried. She would not, however, have the logy dead-weight of a *razee,* but would be built from scratch to handle well and gracefully, even in light winds. To accomplish this maneuverability, Humphreys designed a sleek hull strongly but lightly braced by a system of trusses of his own invention. Her sides were of live oak, far stronger than the usual fir and pine planking. Though she was no ship-of-the-line, she was admirably created to overtake and defeat anything in her own class and to show her heels to anything stronger.

So favorably regarded were Humphreys' plans for the *Constitution* that they were adopted for the other five frigates as well. Construction of the six was started in various shipyards along the Atlantic coast.

In Algiers, William Eaton was protesting an unscheduled hike in the Dey's rates for protection. "When," he asked, "are these extortionate demands to end?"

The Dey sneered. "Never."

Had the Dey been able to see the activity in American shipyards, he might have realized that his answer was highly optimistic.

3.

The new navy was not destined to have its first trial of fire against the Barbary pirates but against quite another power, one which had long been regarded as a friend of the United States.

Hard feeling had developed between the governments of France and America. The French Directors took umbrage at America's refusal to permit French warships to bring their prizes into American seaports; at America's insistence that the French minister, Citizen Genet, be recalled by his government for various unacceptable activities; and at the action of President John Adams in replacing the popular American Minister to France, James Monroe, with the less popular C. C. Pinckney.

To settle the differences, Mr. Pinckney was joined in France by John Marshall and Elbridge Gerry. These three men sat down with three French representatives in order to discuss the problems and reach a settlement. Somewhat naively, Mr. Marshall held the belief that all that was needed was a friendly discussion and a meeting of minds. One of the French representatives presently upset that idea. "Gentlemen," he said, "you do not speak to the point. It is money. It is expected that you will offer money."

"How much money?" asked Mr. Pinckney.

He was told that the Directory would be happy to discuss the questions at issue if the five members should be presented with 1,200,000 gold pounds (*livres d'or*) as a gift, and if France were granted an American loan of 32,000,000 Dutch florins.

To this bald-faced demand for bribery, C. C. Pinckney gave his answer: "No, and no again! Not a sixpence!"

The French representatives shrugged. In that case, they said, it would be necessary for the French navy to take steps. If the American government would not produce the required amount, American merchant vessels would.

When Pinckney, Marshall, and Gerry made their report to Congress, the names of the three French representatives were withheld. They were referred to merely as "Monsieur X, Monsieur Y, and Monsieur Z." From this, the episode became known as "the XYZ Affair."

Congress and the American public were angry and aghast. Pinckney's quiet reply to the three Frenchmen was widely misquoted as "Millions for defence, but not one cent for tribute!" No war was declared, but work on the new American warships was rushed toward completion. A Navy Department was created, with Benjamin Stoddert as its first Secretary. If the French Navy should come raiding into American waters, it would find something besides helpless merchantmen awaiting it!

4.

The first move of the French was to turn loose upon the American coast a swarm of privateers. These crossed the ocean with high hopes of easy wealth. No sooner had their raiding begun than it was spoiled by the appearance of patrolling warships of the United States Navy.

On July 7, 1798, the French privateer *Croyable* (14) was cruising off Egg Harbor, New Jersey, in search of easy victims. Her captain was happy to see a sail on the horizon, then unhappy to learn that it belonged to the U. S. corvette *Delaware* (20). *Croyable* fled but was overtaken. After a brief exchange of cannon fire, the French captain surrendered. *Croyable* became the American armed schooner *Retaliation*.

Four months later, *Retaliation* was cruising off the island of Guadeloupe, in company with the United States brigs *Montezuma* (20) and *Norfolk* (18). As day broke, two large ships were seen, flying no flags. *Retaliation* dropped back to investigate. Her captain, Lieutenant William Bainbridge, imprudently sailed too close and found himself under fire from the heavy artillery of the French *razee Voluntaire* (50) and the frigate *Insurgente* (36). With fourteen guns, he could not hope to oppose eighty-six! Bainbridge quickly surrendered, and *Retaliation* once more displayed the tricolor flag of France.

Montezuma and *Norfolk,* meanwhile, had taken flight, with *Insurgente* hot after them. She was the fastest frigate in the French navy and was rapidly overhauling her prey when the flagship *Voluntaire* hoisted a signal recalling her. Lieutenant Bainbridge was responsible. Held captive on the deck of the *razee,* he had casually let slip the information that the two fleeing American ships mounted far heavier guns than, in fact, they did. The French commodore had a sudden vision of the *Insurgente* becoming so badly damaged that she would fall an easy victim to the first British ship she should meet. Captain Barreault of the *Insurgente* was anything but pleased at having to give up two victims who were practically within his grasp. Nothing, he swore, should prevent him from taking the next American ship he should encounter.

Captain Barreault had his chance on February 9, 1799. Off Nevis Island, a frigate was sighted, flying the stars and stripes of the United States. It was the *Constellation* (44), under Captain Thomas Truxtun, the fastest frigate of the new American navy. In all probability, *Insurgente* was a bit faster, but this advantage was lost as the ships closed toward maximum gun range. A sudden squall carried away one of the spars from *Insurgente*'s mainmast.

The French fired first, directing heavy cannon fire at the masts and rigging of the approaching *Constellation*. It was the old French technique of crippling first, before the kill. Through the storm of shot, which did only minor damage, *Constellation* came on, in grim silence. Not until the two ships were parallel, at pistol-shot range, did Truxtun give the command to fire. The broadside which followed spread death, destruction, and consternation throughout the French frigate. The cannonading continued, and the damage increased. Little by little, *Constellation* forged ahead. With a sudden turn of the wheel, Truxton brought her across the Frenchman's bow, delivering devastating raking fire. Another turn, and Truxton was hammering the *Insurgente*'s other side. He was just swinging around her stern, to deliver more raking fire, when the tricolor came fluttering down.

5.

Among the new American warships were two little schooner-rigged Baltimore clippers, the *Experiment* and the *Enterprise*. They were lightly armed, carrying only 12 guns each, but they were among the fastest and most maneuverable ships upon the sea.

Experiment, commanded by Lieutenant Charles Stewart, saw relatively little action. The first use of her guns against hostile forces came on New Year's Day, 1800. The wind had died completely, leaving the little vessel becalmed near the coast of Haiti. Out from shore came twelve large barges, each mounting a single swivel-gun and manned by from fifty to seventy picaroons—guerrilla-pirates—armed with muskets. Lieutenant David Porter, second in command, directed the *Experiment*'s gunnery. Simulating a defenseless merchant ship, he had his gun ports kept closed until the galleys were close by, then opened a sudden fire with grape shot. Despite very heavy losses, the picaroons kept attacking, throwing their dead overboard and replacing them with fresh men from the shore, who seemed to be present in infinite numbers. Only after Porter changed to solid shot and quickly smashed three of the barges into kindling did the attackers cease their efforts. No Americans were killed. Porter, with a bullet in his shoulder, was the only casualty, but it was a battle which had gained nothing for anybody.

Later, *Experiment* made three captures. The first, which involved a brisk but short action, was the French privateer *Deux Amis* (8). Later, Stewart's ship was chased by a 16-gun French brig and the privateer *Diana* (8). He fled, but when he saw the pursuers abandon the chase and separate, he circled back and took the *Diana* after a short fight. The third, met at night, fought for four hours before surrendering. Only then was it discovered that she was the British armed schooner *Louisa Bridger*. She was released with profuse apologies and red faces.

Enterprise, under Lieutenant John Shaw, began her career with a bit of bad fortune. Like her sister, she met a ship in the night, and presently she found herself under fire. Both ships were badly damaged before it was discovered that the "enemy" was an 18-gun Spanish brig from Havana—a neutral ship. Together, the two vessels limped into St. Thomas for repairs.

With the bad luck out of the way, *Enterprise* went on to win for herself a new and happy nickname: "lucky little *Enterprise.*" In quick succession, she overpowered and captured the French privateers *Le Cygne* (4), *Citoyenne* (6), and *L'Aigle* (10), the last of which put up a desperate struggle before being taken.

In July, 1800, *Enterprise* was caught in a calm by the French brig *Flambeau* (18), which outgunned her in a ratio of three to two. A freak of weather gave the French vessel wind, which was denied to the clipper. At first, Shaw pulled in his guns and closed his ports, hoping to escape notice as an unimportant merchant vessel of unknown nationality. A sudden breeze changed his plans. With wind for her sails, *Enterprise* could outmaneuver any brig afloat. The flag went up, the guns ran out, and the clipper whisked into action. For twenty minutes, the two ships traded broadsides, before the Frenchman's fore-topmast went overboard, taking six crewmen with it. Without losing all headway, Shaw managed to launch a manned lifeboat with which to save the six, while he continued to blast away at their companions. By the time the struggling Frenchmen had been pulled from the water, *Flambeau* had struck her colors.

Early in the next year, "lucky little *Enterprise*" returned from her cruise with a record of eighteen French vessels and 300 prisoners taken.

As far as the larger ships were concerned, this was *Constellation*'s war. She alone seemed able to find worthy opponents. On February 1, 1800, Captain Truxton sighted a large ship and gave chase. It proved to be the French frigate *Vengeance* (52), larger and more heavily armed than any American ship. Being loaded with a valuable cargo of specie, *Vengeance* took to her sails to avoid contact.

After more than twenty-four hours of pursuit, *Constellation* drew within cannon range of her opponent. In the opening exchanges, both ships suffered heavily aloft. Maneuvering was soon out of the question. Side by side, at pistol-shot range, the two frigates wallowed along, blasting each other with everything they had. It was a frightful ordeal for both. *Vengeance* hit harder, with a greater weight of metal, but *Constellation* showed greater accuracy. For five hours, each ship was a floating hell. Twice, the French captain hauled down his colors in surrender, but both times the gesture was hidden by the smoke, and the flag was presently raised again. The fighting continued. Toward the end, the American crewmen were dividing their attention between the enemy and their own mainmast, badly weakened and completely devoid of shrouds. Suddenly it went, hurling to his death Midshipman James Jarvis, who had refused to abandon his precarious perch. As the heavy mast dragged overside, *Constellation* lost all power not only to maneuver but even to hold a course.

Taking advantage of her enemy's helplessness, *Vengeance* turned to flee. She was a dying ship, her rigging ruined, her hull a sieve, more than half of her crew dead or seriously wounded. Just short of the entrance to Curacao harbor she sank in shallow water. *Constellation,* under jury rigging, made Jamaica with heavy damage and with thirty-nine casualties, but clearly the victor.

At the very end of the undeclared war, another American frigate managed to see some action. She was the *Boston* (28), a light frigate which had been donated by the patriotic citizens of the Massachusetts capital. Under Captain George Little, she went cruising among the West Indies in October, 1800. Without much difficulty, she managed to overtake and overawe the French brig *Deux Anges* (20) on October 12. Shortly thereafter, she found a slightly larger and far more spunky opponent in the corvette *Berceau* (24). At first, *Berceau* tried to flee, but when overtaken she opened a rapid and well-aimed fire, mainly directed at the *Boston*'s rigging. After an hour, the frigate's upperworks were so badly damaged that she could not match her opponent's speed. *Berceau* drew out of range, as *Boston*'s crew went aloft to make repairs. They worked so fast and so efficiently that before long they had their ship under way again. Darkness had fallen when the ships were again in range, but Little reopened the battle regardless of the poor visibility. This time, the American fire, too, was directed at the upperworks. Within an hour, all three of *Berceau*'s masts were gone, and she was helpless. Her captain prudently surrendered.

Napoleon Bonaparte, as First Consul, was now virtually in control of France. To him, this foolish naval war against the United States represented a drain of power desperately needed for his major struggle, that against implacable Britain. In two and a half years, these upstart Americans had taken no fewer than eighty-four armed French vessels. At his urgent request, a treaty was negotiated, and the fighting stopped.

Messieurs X, Y, and Z had received an answer which they and all their countrymen could understand.

6.

During the naval war with France, the United States had not been free to employ its growing naval might against the Barbary pirates. As a result, the rulers of the Mohammedan states had grown increasingly arrogant, and their demands for tribute had risen steadily.

In May, 1800, Captain William Bainbridge was sent in the frigate *George Washington* to deliver the annual tribute to the Dey of Algiers. Not knowing what was in store, he entered the harbor and dropped anchor directly before the most powerful fort on the waterfront. The Dey accepted the tribute, but would not let Bainbridge go, insisting that the American commander must use his ship as a messenger boat to carry an Algerian ambassador to the Turkish court at Constantinople. Naturally, Bainbridge protested. The Dey looked meaningfully at the frowning guns of the fort, bearing on the frigate, then announced: "You pay me tribute, by which you become my slaves. I have therefore the right to order you as I may think proper."

Though completely outraged, Bainbridge had to comply. Later, in his official report, he described the Dey as "a huge, shabby beast, sitting on his rump upon a low bench with his hind legs gathered up like a tailor or a bear, who extended his forepaw as if to receive something to eat. . . . I hope I may never again be sent to Algiers with tribute, unless I am authorized to deliver it from the mouth of our cannon."

The end came when the Bashaw of Tripoli, blinded by greed, overreached the bounds of reason. He had increased his own demands to $20,000 a year, a bonus of $250,000, and an American frigate as an outright gift. When the American consul objected, the Bashaw chopped down the consular flagpole and brought the stars and stripes crashing to the earth.

Thomas Jefferson, peace-loving and intelligent, was the newly elected President of the United States. Feeling that great military forces were the weapons of tyranny, he nevertheless could appreciate that a navy presented no such dangers. "Naval force can never undermine our liberties," he declared. "Tribute or war is the usual alternative of these Barbary pirates. Why not build a navy and decide on war? We cannot begin in a better cause or against a better foe."

7.

On July 1, 1801, the American frigates *President, Philadelphia,* and *Essex* sailed majestically into Gibraltar harbor. Present also was a British squadron, including the flagship of Admiral Lord Nelson. From the quarterdeck of the *Victory,* Nelson watched with approval as the three sleek warships moved smartly to their positions and dropped anchor. Said he, prophetically, "There is in the handling of those transatlantic ships a nucleus of trouble for the navy of Great Britain."

A fourth warship, the clipper *Enterprise,* had been detached from the American squadron off Gibraltar and sent eastward through the Mediterranean to scout out the situation and give protection to American commerce. Off Malta she encountered the Tripolitan warship *Tripoli* (14). Without awaiting a hail or a signal, the *Tripoli* opened fire. Lieutenant Andrew Sterett, commander of the *Enterprise,* promptly followed suit. For three hours the two little ships blazed away at one another, most of the hits being scored by the American gunners. Twice during that time, Rais Mahomet Rous of the *Tripoli* hauled down his flag in apparent surrender, only to reopen fire when he thought he had the American ship at a disadvantage. The third time, he really meant it. Twenty Mohammedan crewmen were dead, and thirty more were wounded. Aboard the *Enterprise,* there was not a single casualty. Since Sterett's orders did not permit him to take prizes, he stripped the *Tripoli* of all armament, ammunition, and supplies, chopped down her masts, and sent her limping home a chastened wreck under a jury rig.

The rest of 1801 and all of 1802 were devoid of action. Commodore Richard Dale, in charge of the Mediterranean squadron, tried in vain to negotiate a peace treaty with Tripoli. His successor, Commodore Richard V. Morris, maintained an irregular blockade, which had little result. He was succeeded in August, 1803, by Commodore Edward Preble, a genuine fighting seaman.

8.

Preble's tour of duty began badly. Capture of a Moroccan ship with American prisoners aboard took him and most of his squadron to Tangier, where he succeeded in convincing the Emperor of Morocco of the folly of antagonizing the United States. Behind him at Tripoli he left the frigate *Philadelphia,* to maintain the blockade of the port. On October 31, 1803, the frigate detected a small Tripolitan ship attempting to slip into the harbor. The quarry fled, with the *Philadelphia* in pursuit. Inaccurate charts proved the frigate's undoing. She grounded hard upon an uncharted reef.

The crew of the *Philadelphia* made a desperate effort to free their vessel. The sails were backed, ballast was pumped, and many of the forward guns were jettisoned in an effort to struggle free. As a last expedient, the foremast was cut away, without avail. Meanwhile, a swarm of Tripolitan gunboats had issued from the harbor and was closing in on the helpless warship. As the tide fell, the *Philadelphia* heeled slowly over, placing her gun deck at such a slant that not a single piece would bear. There was now no chance to return the fire of the assailants. Captain William Bainbridge was forced to surrender. He and his crew were thrust into Tripolitan dungeons while his ship was hauled clear of the reef and towed in triumph into Tripoli harbor.

Commodore Preble was dismayed at the loss of his frigate and at its addition to the Tripolitan fleet. Here was a situation which demanded immediate rectifying. A volunteer crew was selected, headed by Lieutenant Stephen Decatur and including 83 picked men from the crews of the *Constitution* and the *Enterprise.* Not the least important member of the party was the little vessel in which the expedition set sail on February 16, 1804. She was a Mediterranean-rigged ketch which the Americans had captured and had renamed *Intrepid.* Her steersman was a Sicilian seaman who knew Tripoli harbor and could speak the local language like a native.

Under cover of the night, *Intrepid* stole into Tripoli harbor. The shore was lined with forts and batteries, and the water was covered with pirate warcraft. From the *Philadelphia,* a menacing black bulk against the sky, came a peremptory challenge.

"We are a blockade-runner and have lost our anchors," called the Sicilian steersman. "May we tie up alongside?"

Permission was granted.

Scarcely had the ships touched sides when Decatur and his men were swarming aboard the frigate, swinging cutlasses with deadly effect. Those of the pirate crew who were not cut down were driven over the rail. At once, torches were applied to the captive warship. Flames swept along the decks and up the rigging. Two cannons, fired down through open hatches, blew gaping holes in the bottom planking. Not until destruction was certain did the volunteers go over the side and return to the *Intrepid*. They had not lost a man.

As Decatur and his men guided their little vessel out of the harbor amid a storm of poorly aimed cannon fire, the *Philadelphia* blew up with a horrendous roar. The Bashaw had lost his beautiful new warship!

When the news reached Gibraltar, Admiral Horatio Nelson opened his eyes wide. He, of all men, knew a masterly coup when he saw it. "This," he said, "is the most bold and daring act of the age."

9.

Though the *Philadelphia* had been destroyed, Captain Bainbridge and his men were still prisoners, with assorted other Americans, in the Bashaw's dungeons. A ransom price of $1,000 each had been placed on them. The release of these people was one of the major problems facing Commodore Preble.

During the spring and early summer of 1804, the situation remained a stalemate. The American warships blockaded Tripoli, but Preble had neither sufficient artillery nor sufficient manpower to silence the defenses and to take the city.

One of the most formidable defenses of Tripoli was the large fleet of Tripolitan gunboats which lay in the shelter of the harbor forts. On August 3, daredevil Stephen Decatur led a raid of small American gunboats against this flotilla. According to the plan, the frigate *Constitution* was to bombard the Tripolitan squadron and the forts, providing a barrage for the protection of Decatur and his men.

The *Constitution*'s part in the engagement was anything but successful. No sooner had the Americans appeared than the pirate vessels came swarming out, surrounding Decatur's gunboats so closely that effective cannon fire from the frigate was impossible. As many Americans as pirates would have been killed.

The American gunboats, however, had ample opportunity for action. At the very outset, Decatur and his crew singled out, boarded, and took a pirate gunboat in short order, using cutlasses to strike down all but five of the pirate crew. The men in the other American gunboats were similarly busy.

Stephen Decatur's brother James was the commanding officer of one of the smaller American gunboats. As his vessel came alongside a pirate craft, the pirate captain struck his colors in apparent surrender. It was a trick. As James leaped aboard, the Tripolitan drew a pistol and shot him dead.

At news of his brother's death, Stephen Decatur went berserk. Forgetting all else, he set out in pursuit of the man who had killed James. The fleeing pirate craft was overtaken and boarded. Cutlass in hand, Decatur attacked the pirate captain. A swing of the captain's scimitar broke Decatur's blade, and the two men grappled, rolling on the deck. Another pirate rushed up, swinging his heavy, curved blade. Stephen Decatur would have died there and then had it not been for the self-sacrifice of a wounded member of his crew, who threw himself before the assailant and took the blow himself. At the same time, Decatur managed to reach his pistol and to kill the pirate captain.

Surely, the man who had saved Decatur's life at the cost of his own deserves mention. Who was he? Accounts differ. He is variously spoken of as Seaman Reuben James, Seaman Daniel Frazer, and Marine Daniel Frazier. Whoever he was, his bravery and his devotion to his captain cannot be questioned.

The raid, as such, could hardly be called a success. Besides the two Tripolitan gunboats taken by Decatur, only one other was captured. This one was boarded by Lieutenant John Trippe and ten men who, by hard fighting, managed to overcome her crew of thirty-six pirates. The Bashaw's gunboat fleet continued to exist, minus only three vessels. Commodore Preble was bitterly disappointed in the results.

The Bashaw, too, was becoming increasingly unhappy. Though his city remained untaken, he did not enjoy the constant blockade and the intermittent bombardment that marked the summer of 1804. His fortifications still stood, but some of his batteries had been silenced by the big guns on the ships. The minaret of the mosque had been brought crashing down, to the consternation of the faithful. His own palace had been damaged by cannon fire. Worse yet, the blockade was bad for the buccaneering business.

Perhaps these Americans would be tempted by a bargain. The ransom of the prisoners was cut in two, reduced to $500 each. There were no takers.

10.

On September 4, *Intrepid* saw action once again. Her purpose this time was to destroy the entire Tripolitan gunboat squadron at a single blow. She was packed from keel to deck with explosives and was manned by thirteen daring volunteers under the command of Lieutenant Richard Somers. Under cover of night, she was to creep in among the tightly packed vessels in the anchorage. When she was as far in as she could get, her crew was to take to her small boat and escape, leaving a slow-burning fuse to set off the thunders of destruction.

The Tripolitans had become more watchful since the burning of the *Philadelphia*. Despite the darkness, *Intrepid* was seen as she neared the harbor entrance. Two big rowing galleys converged on her. It was impossible now to reach the crowded anchorage and equally impossible to escape. Somers waited until the two galleys drew alongside, then threw a torch down the hatchway. All three vessels disappeared in a thundering detonation. *Intrepid* and her daring crew had failed in their mission but had exacted a high price from the enemy.

On September 10, 1804, the frigates *President, Constellation, Essex,* and *Congress* joined the little fleet before Tripoli. *Constitution* was ordered home, and Preble with her. He had done well and hated to leave. Still, orders were orders. Captain Samuel Barron became the new Commodore.

Commodore Preble had been a hard commanding officer—austere and demanding. When, for example, Stephen Decatur had returned from his raid, sick at his brother's death and shaken at his own close call, Preble had demanded in a fury why he had taken only three of the enemy's gunboats. The commodore had, nevertheless, been respected and even loved. He had shaped the inexperienced officers under him into the nucleus of a well-trained naval force. "Preble's Boys," as they were called, were destined to contribute much that was good to the subsequent history of the United States Navy.

After Preble's departure, the war against the Tripoli pirates bogged down. Barron had not his predecessor's driving force, and he was further hampered by the presence of a Congressional appeaser named Tobias Lear. The officers whom Preble had trained wanted to fight to a finish and then hang the Bashaw for piracy. This now seemed possible, for a strange army of adventurers was making its way westward from Egypt to join forces with the American naval expedition. The leader was American Consul William Eaton. A key member of the group was the Bashaw's exiled brother, who had a good claim to the throne. When this group should arrive, the Bashaw might very well be through.

Tobias Lear spoiled this clear-cut decision. He wanted to bargain, and bargain he did. The result was a compromise. The Bashaw reduced the ransom to $300 per man. Congress paid it, and the American squadron was forced to end hostilities. To many who knew the true worth of appeasement, it was evident that the whole thing would have to be done over again before very long.

The fleet sailed for home amid general feelings of disgust.

11.

The police action in the Mediterranean was followed by another cutback of the American navy. President Thomas Jefferson might recognize the fact that a naval force offered no threat to American liberty, but he deplored the expense of maintaining the fleet on a full-time basis. The Democratic-Republican party, moreover, was opposed to powerful armed forces. The shores of the United States must be defended, but there was no excuse for building war equipment which could carry the American flag across the oceans.

The result was an expensive mistake. Many of the large American warships were decommissioned and were replaced by tiny gunboats.

Gunboats, as such, have their uses. The American forces in the Mediterranean had suffered from a lack of such light-draft vessels, suitable for use in shoal waters and for action in and around harbors. It made good sense to build fifteen "Jeffersonian gunboats," each about fifty feet in length, mounting a single gun in the bow, driven by a single lateen sail supplemented by eighteen long oars, or sweeps. But it made no sense at all to expand the gunboat fleet, in 1806 and 1807, from 15 to 238. It was a most expensive and inefficient way to maintain firepower afloat. Mahan points out that, gun-for-gun and pound-of-shot for pound-of-shot, gunboat firepower cost fully three times as much as frigate firepower.

Once more, the United States Navy languished, suffering from neglect. The pious hope was that there would never be another war.

12 NAPOLEON'S QUEST FOR POWER

⚓

1.

On November 9, 1799, a small group of plotters overthrew the government of France. The five Directors were persuaded to resign in favor of three Consuls. The upper legislative body agreed. When the lower body objected, soldiers were brought in, and the members were driven from the chamber with bayonets. There was no more resistance.

Although the three Consuls were supposed to share responsibility, the new Constitution was so phrased that the actual power all lay in the hands of the First Consul. Consuls Two and Three were mere figureheads.

It is said that when the Constitution was officially proclaimed and was read aloud to the people of Paris, two old women stood together in the crowd. One was deaf.

"I cannot hear," she said to her companion. "What do you see in this new Constitution?"

Her friend replied, "I see Bonaparte in it."

It was a shrewd observation, for Napoleon Bonaparte was the new First Consul—the new Master of France.

2.

Occasionally, great naval powers lose the ability to distinguish between control of the seas and outright ownership. Such a lapse by Great Britain in 1800 provided the astute Napoleon Bonaparte with an opportunity to drive a wedge between the British government and a number of allied and neutral governments of northern Europe.

Antagonized by short-sighted British policy and subtly wooed by Napoleon, Russia, Sweden, and Prussia formed in December, 1800, a

League of Armed Neutrality, for the purposes of protecting their neutral rights upon the sea and of keeping the British fleet out of the Baltic. Denmark was invited to join and did so regretfully, fearing to antagonize her powerful near neighbor, Czar Paul of Russia.

Great Britain reacted promptly. Under French influence, the League of Armed Neutrality represented a tremendous danger to the British Empire. A fleet was dispatched to the Baltic under the command of Admiral Hyde Parker, who was noted for his restraint and his diplomatic finesse. Second in command was Rear Admiral Horatio Nelson, noted for his energy, his resourcefulness, and his fighting ability. It was felt that if Parker's qualities failed to avert hostilities, Nelson's qualities might be turned to very good account.

Denmark is the sentinel which guards the entrance to the Baltic. The Danes would then be the first potential enemies to be faced. Nelson wanted to bypass them, for he felt that the aggressive Russians were the key to the whole League. If the British fleet could get by the Danes without a fight, it would be possible to keep the powerful Russian and Swedish fleets from uniting. If necessary, they could be beaten separately. If, on the other hand, the British fleet should expend itself against the Danes, there might not be enough left to face the greater enemies.

Sir Hyde Parker was horrified. To him, entering the Baltic without first defeating the Danes was equivalent to walking into a trap. A beaten British fleet, or even a victorious one which had been badly battered, could never fight its way out past the fresh and undamaged Danes. As the higher ranking officer, he vetoed the plan of his brilliant assistant.

On March 19, 1801, the British fleet anchored in the Kattegat, north of the Danish capital of Copenhagen. A messenger was sent to the Danes with a demand that they leave the League of Armed Neutrality within forty-eight hours or suffer the consequences. The Danes refused and intensified their already-vigorous efforts to make Copenhagen unassailable.

Now that a battle was inevitable, Sir Hyde Parker generously yielded precedence to Rear Admiral Nelson and granted him a large measure of liberty in planning the attack. Copenhagen would not be an easy city to subdue. It is located on the eastern shore of Zealand Island, overlooking the narrow channel between Denmark and Sweden. Off the waterfront lie extensive areas of shoal water, creased by a single narrow channel through which ships can reach the city docks. The main international waterway is divided, directly opposite the city, by the extensive Middle Ground Shoal. It is a difficult area in which to conduct a naval operation involving large, deep-draft warships.

Though the Danes had only four ships rigged for sea, they had available a number of armed hulks, ranging all the way from brigs, sloops, and frigates up to 74-gun ships-of-the-line. Off the city's waterfront, just beyond the shoal water, eighteen ships and hulks were anchored in a long line, ready to fight though not to maneuver. At the northern end of this line, beside the narrow channel to the city, stood the powerful Trekroner Fort, mounting 68 heavy guns. The city channel, behind the fort, was barred by three anchored 74's and a 70. The anchored flotilla was backed up by heavy batteries on the shore, including those in the formidable Copenhagen citadel.

On March 30, the British squadron took advantage of a wind from the northwest and moved southward toward Copenhagen. When batteries on the Danish shore opened fire, the ships veered to the eastward and ran down along the Swedish coast out of range. The Swedish guns remained silent, so the ships arrived unharmed at an anchorage north of the Middle Ground Shoal.

Because of the extensive shoal areas and the tricky channels near the city, it was deemed best to hold the largest ships out where the water was deep. Accordingly, Nelson shifted his flag from *St. George* (98) to *Elephant* (74). Leaving eight of the largest ships with Sir Hyde Parker at the anchorage, he conducted twelve third-rate ships-of-the-line (74's, 64's, and 50's) and six frigates southward along the outer channel east of the Middle Ground Shoal. His purpose was to approach the line of Danish ships from the south, where he would be least expected and would be farthest from the powerful guns of the Trekroner Fort.

From his position south of the city, Admiral Nelson kept a nervous watch for a shift in the wind which would permit him to approach the Danish line. He also kept an apprehensive eye to the south for any sign of approaching Russian and/or Swedish warships, coming to the rescue of the Danish ally.

Early in the morning of April 2, the hoped-for shift in the wind occurred, and Nelson's squadron moved to the attack. Most of it, that is, moved to the attack. The *Agamemnon* (64), *Russell* (74), and *Bellona* (74) fouled on the Middle Ground and were put out of the action before it even began. With the remaining nine ships and assorted smaller craft, the admiral went on.

Edgar (74), the first ship of the British line, passed the four southernmost Danish ships, mauling them with her broadsides as she did so. She then dropped anchor opposite the fifth and set to work methodically with her guns. The other eight ships of the British line chose advantageous positions and anchored, Nelson's *Elephant* coming to rest opposite the *Dannebrog* (62), flagship of Danish Commodore Olfert Fischer. The toughest assignment went to the little frigates, under Captain Riou. Because of the unexpected grounding of the three ships-of-the-line, the frigates had to fill the gap and engage the northernmost Danish ships and also the heavy guns of the Trekroner Fort.

The Danes aboard the anchored warships showed unexpected fire and ability. Their guns were served fast and accurately, and presently they began to score damaging hits. Unlike many a sea fight of maneuver and passing cannonade, this was a toe-to-toe slugging match in which victory would go to the side which could deal out the most death and destruction in the shortest time. Said Nelson, to his flag captain, "This is warm work, and it may be the last for any of us at any moment."

Admiral Hyde Parker, from his anchorage north of the Middle Ground Shoal, watched the action in an agony of worry and uncertainty. He had intended to bring his big ships in as close as possible to lend support, but the southeasterly wind which had carried Nelson into action kept Parker out of it. He could see that the nearest ships to him, the four northernmost frigates, had been badly mauled and had been forced out of action. Word reached him that gallant Captain Riou had been cut in two by a cannon ball. The assumption was that the larger British vessels were little better off. At 1:30 P.M., three and a half hours after the beginning of the action, he hoisted Signal 39, to break off action and withdraw.

Aboard the *Elephant,* Nelson was enjoying the hot, close action. His "feel" of the battle was far better than Parker's. Knowing well the damage being done to his own squadron, he could see that the Danes were suffering even more. A number of the anchored blockships were briskly burning and were out of action. The *Dannebrog,* for example, now had but three of her 62 guns still in action. Commodore Fischer had been forced to leave her and transfer to the *Holstein* (60), then to transfer again to the Trekroner Fort, when his new flagship was shattered and he himself was wounded. A hard-earned victory was in sight.

At this crucial moment, Nelson was informed that Parker's flagship was flying Signal 39. To his flag captain, he exploded: "Leave off action? Now, damn me if I do!" He hesitated, then added, with a grim smile, "You know, Foley, I have only one eye. I have a right to be blind sometimes." Carefully, he raised his telescope to his blinded eye and turned it in the direction of Parker's flagship. "I really do not see the signal. Keep our flags for close action flying."

The battle went on. Presently, a strange thing became evident. Danish ships would strike their colors in surrender, then later resume firing as boatloads of volunteers rowed out from the city to reman the guns. A number of British boarding parties were destroyed by this unorthodox maneuver. At last, to check it, Nelson sent ashore a flag of truce with a message that if resistance continued he would feel justified in using fireships against the anchored hulks and would destroy both them and their crews.

The Danes had had enough. The firing stopped, and negotiating began. Nelson offered every opportunity for peaceful conciliation, hailing the Danes as brothers of the British, with whom they should never be at war and offering to spare Denmark and Copenhagen any further trouble as soon as peace should be agreed upon. As the Danes showed willingness to listen, Nelson seized the opportunity to tow away some of the anchored blockships as prizes and to remove his squadron from the dangerous neighborhood of the Trekroner Fort.

For a few days, the situation remained ticklish. The Danes, for their part, did not wish to fight the British, but even less did they want to antagonize their powerful neighbor, mad Czar Paul of Russia. The British, knowing that their fleet was now in no condition to meet the combined Russian and Swedish squadrons, nervously dickered for time and for supplies. In the end, a fourteen-week truce was agreed upon, during which period Denmark would furnish equipment needed to refurbish the British fighting ships.

Scarcely had the agreement been made when a Russian ship appeared from the east, bearing word that Czar Paul had been assassinated and that the League of Armed Neutrality was now a thing of the past.

The Battle of Copenhagen, for all its brilliance, its bravery, and its masterly execution, had been completely unnecessary. Some 350 British and more than twice as many Danes had died in vain.

3.

Act One of the naval war between Britain and France petered out in a series of little incidents.

Late in June, 1801, three French ships-of-the-line and a frigate left the Toulon naval base and headed westward under the command of Rear Admiral Charles Linois, who was under orders to pass through the Strait of Gibraltar and add his ships to the French-Spanish squadron at Cadiz. It was not believed that Linois would have much trouble, for reports indicated that Cadiz was being watched by nothing more formidable than a handful of British frigates.

Linois reached the Strait without difficulty and put in at the port of Algeciras—directly across from Britain's base of Gibraltar—for water and supplies. There he learned that the frigate squadron off Cadiz had been reinforced by seven ships-of-the-line under Sir James Saumarez. His easy assignment would now be difficult, if not imposble.

The French arrival at Algeciras had not gone unnoticed by the British at Gibraltar. Presently, a frigate put out into the Strait, bearing word to Saumarez of the presence of Linois and his squadron. Knowing that the enemy would soon be upon him, Admiral Linois anchored his three ships just off the shoal water before the seaport. *Formidable* (80) was at the northern end of the line, with *Desaix* (74) and *Indomptable* (74) immediately astern. The frigate was moored at the southern end of the compact formation, partly protected by a small island.

As anticipated, Saumarez sailed immediately to the attack. Besides his flagship *Caesar* (80), he had five 74's, giving him approximately a two-to-one advantage over Linois. Probably, therefore, he was overconfident. His attack showed anything but careful planning.

The *Pompée,* first of the British formation, sailed along the anchored French line and came to rest opposite the *Formidable.* Even before she started swapping punches with this largest of the French ships, she had already been badly damaged by the broadsides of the other anchored vessels. *Caesar, Venerable, Audacious,* and *Spencer* also anchored and engaged. *Hannibal,* farthest east of the British formation, was not yet in action.

Into the mind of Sir James Saumarez popped the memory of the Battle of the Nile. Here was a chance to duplicate Nelson's brilliant maneuver in doubling up on the French line. The *Hannibal* was signaled to swing around the *Formidable*'s bow and engage from inshore. Cheerfully, her captain tried to oblige.

Rear Admiral Linois was also familiar with the Battle of the Nile, and he had anticipated the British move. No sooner was the *Hannibal*'s purpose clear than he hoisted sails and weighed anchors, wearing his ships sharply inshore while continuing a heavy fire. *Hannibal*, trying to wedge herself inshore of this new position, ran hard aground. *Pompée* was badly battered. The dismayed Saumarez promptly pulled his squadron out of action and ran across the bay to Gibraltar, leaving the *Hannibal* at the mercy of the French. She was presently forced to surrender.

It was an amazing thing! A small French squadron had defeated a larger British force!

While Sir James Saumarez was frantically repairing his damaged ships at Gibraltar, the odds swung heavily against him. Six Spanish ships-of-the-line under Admiral Juan Moreno entered Algeciras roadstead, thus bringing the allied force up to ten, including the captured *Hannibal*. Now, the odds were two to one the other way.

On the evening of July 12—nearly two weeks after the battle off Algeciras—the French-Spanish fleet set sail for Cadiz, where facilities for repair were far better than at Algeciras. Saumarez at once came out in pursuit, determined to erase the stain of his recent defeat. In the midst of a stormy sea and a jet-black night, his ships overhauled the lumbering monsters of the allied fleet.

The last ship of the French-Spanish formation was the *Formidable*. As the leading British ships opened fire, her alert captain noted that each of them was marked by three vertical lanterns at the maintop. Promptly, he hoisted a similar string of lights. At once, the firing ceased, as Saumarez' ships forged ahead in search of other prey. This proved to be the *St. Antoine*, which was quickly dismasted and forced to strike.

Largest of the allied squadron were two Spanish 112's, the *Real Carlos* and the *San Hermenegilde*. The *Real Carlos* received a British broadside and immediately lashed out in the darkness in reply. Instead of hitting the enemy, her broadside tore into the *San Hermenegilde*. The battle which ensued between the two Spanish giants became a major tragedy for the allied fleet. Both took fire and both blew up, going down with all hands.

The allied squadron crawled into Cadiz minus two great ships sunk and one captured. Those vessels which remained were in no condition to fight or even to breast the swells of the open sea. Saumarez' British fleet, intact and in good condition, settled down to a tight blockade. Sir James had more than made up for his poor performance off Algeciras.

During August, naval hero Nelson provided a pair of anticlimactic actions. Twice, he attempted to attack the French "invasion port" of Boulogne, and twice he was driven off with far heavier losses than the enemy experienced. Boulogne remained as much of a menace as ever.

Both sides needed a breathing spell before the next round of conflict. Napoleon had proved at Marengo and elsewhere that his armies were supreme upon the Continent of Europe. Nelson had proved that the British fleet was supreme upon the seas. In 1802, the Peace of Amiens was signed, establishing peace between Britain and France on the basis of returning everything to the way it had been before the beginning of hostilities.

4.

The Peace of Amiens could not last. The provisions of the treaty did nothing to settle the basic causes of the war, and, in any event, the provisions were not fully observed by either side. Napoleon had promised to withdraw from the Netherlands and the British from Malta. The French troops did not depart from the low country; on the contrary, they showed every sign of remaining permanently on a basis of annexation. Accordingly, the British fleet kept its grip on Malta.

Napoleon Bonaparte had now made himself Consul for Life, with the privilege of naming his successor. France was in his hands. Dreaming of a great colonial empire, he sent an expedition to the West Indies under his brother-in-law, General Charles Leclerc, to restore French rule in Haiti, which had been seized by the Negro inhabitants under Toussaint L'Ouverture. Though the Negro leader was captured by an act of treachery, resistance went on under other able men. Leclerc died, and the French expedition failed disastrously. Balked in his colonial venture, Napoleon turned sharply about. Not only did he give up his attempts to subdue Haiti; he also abandoned his elaborate plans for the great French province of Louisiana and sold the entire vast area to the United States for a pittance.

Having failed in the New World, the French leader renewed his efforts in the Old. Work was begun to convert Antwerp into a formidable naval base. French shipyards were set to work constructing many new ships-of-the-line. Large numbers of gunboats and barges were built and gathered at Boulogne, the widely publicized "invasion base." Such saber-rattling was not intended to lead immediately to war. It was for the purpose of frightening the British into abandoning Malta and into yielding to Napoleon's wishes in various fields. To clinch the matter, the Consul issued an ultimatum: "Malta or war." To his dismay, Great Britain took him at his word and declared war on May 18, 1803.

5.

Scarcely had the ink dried on the declaration of war when the British navy swung into action. Under the able direction of the Earl of St. Vincent, squadrons were sent at once to blockade the key French bases and prevent the enemy fleet from uniting. The quickness of the move caught the French unprepared. The Boulogne flotilla and the six Dutch ships-of-the-line at Texel found themselves checked by Admiral Keith, with eleven ships-of-the-line and more than a hundred smaller warships. The Brest squadron of twenty-one French ships under Admiral Ganteaume was pinned down by Admiral Cornwallis with twenty-five. Admiral Calder, with ten British ships, kept an eye on the fifteen French and Spanish vessels in the neighboring harbors of Ferrol and Corunna. Admiral Orde, with five, guarded Cadiz, where seven French and Spanish warships lay at anchor. The eleven French ships at Toulon were guarded somewhat more loosely by Nelson, whose thirteen ships were based at Maddalena Island, near Sardinia. Only Rochefort, containing five French ships under Missiessy, and Cartagena, containing five Spanish vessels, were not actively blockaded.

In the West Indies, Commodore Samuel Hood (younger cousin of the admiral) took an imaginative step which proved highly effective in countering French strength. Hood's squadron of two ships-of-the-line and a few smaller craft, based at St. Lucia, was inadequate to blockade the important French base of Fort Royal on Martinique, the next island to the north. An extensive calm area, in the lee of Martinique's mountains, made it necessary for ships to pass south of the island to reach Fort Royal. About a mile off the southern shore stood Diamond Rock, a tall, cliff-girt island, difficult to scale and easy to defend. In a surprise move, Hood landed men, cannons, and supplies on the rock, which promptly became a stationary warship, H. M. S. *Diamond Rock*. French vessels could not now pass south of Martinique without suffering damage from the guns on the rock or swinging so far to the south that they could be captured by ships from St. Lucia. The men on the lofty rock, moreover, could keep a close watch on all French activities and could quickly communicate by semaphore with a British picket vessel stationed in the channel between Martinique and St. Lucia. Little Diamond Rock, with its garrison of 120 men, became a most painful pebble in the shoe of Napoleon Bonaparte.

6.

Thanks to the jealousy and incompetence of Minister of Marine Denis Decrès, France now had only two really competent admirals, Eustache Bruix at Boulogne and Latouche-Tréville at Toulon. Neither was destined to hold his position very long.

In July, 1804, Napoleon—now Emperor Napoleon of France—visited Boulogne in order to watch a rehearsal for launching the invasion of Britain. Admiral Bruix refused to order his men into the barges, for he could see that a severe storm was brewing. Both the emperor and the admiral lost their tempers, and the admiral also lost his job. Another officer took over, and the exercise proceeded. So did the storm. More than fifty of the barges were swamped and hundreds of men were drowned.

Lord Nelson, in the Mediterranean, intentionally kept a loose hold on Toulon, hoping to tempt the French fleet out to sea where he could defeat it. He was not familiar with the new French commandant at Toulon, Admiral Latouche-Tréville, but assumed that he was as timid and inept as other French admirals he had met. Overconfidence made Lord Nelson careless. Venturing too close with five ships-of-the-line and some frigates, he suddenly found himself pursued by eight French ships emerging from Toulon. The odds were not prohibitive, but the French held the wind gauge and the British squadron had opened up too much to form an effective battle line. Nelson had to flee, much to his embarrassment and rage.

Here was a fighting French admiral—one not afraid to come out and offer battle. He might have done much with Napoleon's growing fleet. Unfortunately, he was also a dying man, suffering from a fever which he had brought back from the tropics. In August, 1804, he died, being replaced by Admiral Pierre Villeneuve, who lacked, among other things, confidence and ability.

7.

There has never been any doubt that Napoleon Bonaparte was a master of military maneuver. The favorite tools of his trade were the proved fighting ability of his troops and the speed with which his armies could move when "traveling light." Knowing that his enemies on the Continent usually followed the Austrian "cordon system" of opposing every French force with a counterbalancing force of equal strength, he delighted in moving his units quickly and secretly so as to bring two French forces against one of the enemy. It was by this simple but effective means that such victories as that at Ulm were achieved.

Why not apply the same method to war at sea? Napoleon pored over his maps and came up with a master plan by which, he felt, the scattered British blockading forces could be bypassed or overcome and overwhelming French naval strength unexpectedly concentrated in the narrow seas about the British Isles. "Masters of the Channel for six hours, we shall be masters of the world!"

The plan, after numerous revisions, emerged as follows: Villeneuve will slip out of Toulon with his twelve ships-of-the-line and sail to Cartagena, where he will be joined by six Spanish ships. With his eighteen, he will sail to Cadiz, where he will break Orde's blockade and free the eight French and Spanish ships in Cadiz Harbor. His force will now include twenty-six ships-of-the-line, with which he will head westward for the West Indies. At the same time, Admiral Missiessy is to slip out of Rochefort with his five ships and sail to join Villeneuve in the West Indies. Admiral Ganteaume is to seize the first opportunity to slip out of Brest with his twenty-one ships and sail to the West Indies rendezvous. All three admirals are to avoid battle or contact with the British fleet. If Villeneuve and Ganteaume manage to combine their forces in the West Indies, they are to sail rapidly for the English Channel, there to appear unexpectedly in overwhelming numbers, while their enemies are widely scattered in vain search of the "missing" French fleets. If one of the main forces does not make the West Indies, the other is to wait for thirty days, then sail for Ferrol, overcome the blockading squadron there, release the twelve French and Spanish ships, and sail for the Channel. In either case, the British will be confounded and the narrow seas secured for the necessary few hours or days.

On paper, it was a brilliant plan—a typical Napoleonic master-piece. How did it work out in practice?

Villeneuve made a false start on January 17, 1805. There was a gale from the north, which had forced Nelson to retire with most of his squadron to his anchorage at Maddalena. By the time a frigate had found Nelson and had delivered the news that the French were out, Villeneuve's ships, mauled by the weather, were limping back to Tou-lon. Nelson did not know this. At once, he started on a wild goose chase that took him to Naples, Algiers, Greece, Malta, and, finally, Alexandria. This useless excursion gave Emperor Napoleon a great deal of satisfaction, for it was exactly what he had predicted Nelson would do when he found that the Toulon fleet was out. "The man has a mania concerning Egypt." Unfortunately for the emperor's master plan, Villeneuve was able to do nothing with the providential oppor-tunity.

On March 30, Villeneuve came out again. This time, Nelson did not rush off to Egypt, but he did station his fleet near Sardinia in order to intercept the expected eastward thrust. Naturally, he saw nothing of the French squadron, which had turned westward, directly away from him.

Villeneuve reached Cartagena on April 7 and received a setback. The Spanish admiral was polite but would not release his six ships without direct orders from Madrid. Would Admiral Villeneuve wait as his guest while messengers were sent? Knowing that Nelson would be hot upon his trail, Admiral Villeneuve would not. Disappointed, he departed for Cadiz with his original force. One cog of the emperor's intricate machine had broken at the very beginning of the operation.

In the Strait of Gibraltar, the French squadron sighted the single British ship-of-the-line *Renown* (74), returning from a convoy mis-sion. Of greater importance, the French were sighted by the *Renown,* which fled toward Cadiz bearing a message of warning to Admiral Orde of the British blockading squadron. Bowing to the odds and thankful for the warning, Orde took his five ships and sailed north, to bolster the Channel defenses. Villeneuve was able to enter Cadiz un-opposed and to add eight French and Spanish ships to his squadron. With nineteen ships-of-the-line, plus anxiliaries, he then set out west-ward across the Atlantic.

Meanwhile, Admiral Missiessy had been able to take advantage of stormy conditions and low visibility to slip out of Rochefort undetected and head westward, considerably in advance of Villeneuve's squadron. When at last British Admiral Graves found that he was gone, he emulated Orde and fell back to the north to strengthen the defenses of the Channel, rather than indulging in useless pursuit. This conservative activity of Orde and Graves, which was practically standard operating procedure for British admirals of that day, further fouled up the emperor's predictions, as he had not foreseen it.

By early May, Lord Nelson reached the conclusion that Villeneuve must have headed for the West Indies, since he was obviously not in the Mediterranean and had not been reported anywhere north of Cadiz. On May 12, a full month behind his quarry, he started westward across the ocean in pursuit.

Villeneuve arrived at Fort Royal, Martinique, on May 16, only to learn that Missiessy had been there, had waited, and had returned to Rochefort. There had as yet been no sign of Ganteaume and the Brest squadron. To utilize his time while waiting, Villeneuve made surprise attacks on Dominica and three smaller British outposts, taking all four. The most intense resistance came from the smallest point attacked, H. M. S. *Diamond Rock,* whose 120 men held out for three days and two nights against the full might of the French battle fleet before being forced to surrender.

Villeneuve was under instructions to wait in the West Indies until June 20, in the hope that Ganteaume and the Brest squadron would be able to join him before that date. The combined fleet was then to sail directly for the Channel, to cooperate with the invasion flotilla from Boulogne. If Ganteaume did not appear by June 20, Villeneuve was to take his fleet to Ferrol, drive away Calder's British blockading squadron, free the French and Spanish ships in Ferrol and Corunna, then turn north to the Channel, to open the way for the invasion.

Ganteaume did not appear. He did not, in fact, even start for the West Indies, being tightly blockaded in Brest by Admiral Cornwallis with eighteen ships-of-the-line. The French admiral, having twenty-two ships in the port, wanted to go out and attempt to scatter the blockaders, but he could not get permission. Napoleon wanted no frittering away of his sea power for the sake of nominal victories. He was, moreover, extremely doubtful if the Brest squadron could win any victory, nominal or otherwise. The British ships, though fewer, were larger, on the average, and they were equipped with new and heavier carronades with which to smash opponents at close range. In Napoleon's words, the lighter carronades on the French vessels were merely "little pistols, that do nothing but spit."

Villeneuve waited in the West Indies with growing apprehension. There was no sign of Ganteaume, but alarming rumors reached him that Nelson's squadron was hot on his trail. On June 9, eleven days early, he hauled up anchor and set sail for Europe, following a far northerly route that carried him past Nelson without being detected.

8.

Lord Barham was now First Lord of the British Admiralty. Though past eighty, he had lost little of his energy and none of his intelligence. Word reached him that a large French fleet had been sighted in mid-Atlantic, bearing steadily toward the Bay of Biscay. At once he ordered the fleets of Cornwallis and Calder to cease their tight blockades of Brest and Rochefort and to cruise off the Bay of Biscay and the Spanish and Portuguese coasts in the hope of intercepting this fleet which, Barham knew, could only be the missing unit commanded by Villeneuve.

For his part, Admiral Villeneuve, forging steadily eastward, wanted only to get home without a battle. Scurvy and other maladies had reduced the effective manpower of his fleet, and wear and weather had weakened his ships. There was no powder to spare for gunnery practice. Only in one area did he make any preparations for an encounter with a British squadron. Frequent conferences were held aboard the flagship *Bucentaure* (80) for the purpose of briefing his subordinate officers on the type of attack which might be expected. The British, he pointed out, would not be content to sail on parallel or opposite courses and cannonade in the time-honored formalist manner. They would bear in, tightly grouped, for the purpose of massing on the allied center and rear. What should be done to counter this move? An eloquent, Gallic shrug was the only answer.

Toward noon on July 22, 1805, British Admiral Calder, with fifteen ships-of-the-line, was cruising off Cape Finisterre when a large French fleet was sighted to the southwest, following a northerly course. Despite the facts that Villeneuve had the weather gauge and had five more ships-of-the-line, Calder grouped the fourteen British ships that had been sailing in double column into a single battle line and bore in steadily toward the French formation. Meanwhile, the single British ship *Dragon* (74), which had been scouting to the southeast, hurried to find a place in line before the firing should start.

Calder and his captains made a well-trained team. The original advance, if pursued, would have brought the head of the British line across the stern of the last French ship. Before this point was reached, signals flew from the *Prince of Wales* (98), and at once the captain of the leading ship *Hero* (74) tacked to starboard and headed for the middle of the allied line. The other British ships followed in perfect formation.

Aboard the leading allied ship, *Argonauta* (80), Spanish Admiral Gravina saw the British line turn and realized at once that this would lead to the dreaded massing attack, which Villeneuve had predicted. On sudden inspiration, he wore his ship around 180 degrees and headed south, with the allied battle line following him. He was on time. The *Argonauta* bore down on the *Hero* almost bow to bow, forcing both ships to veer off to the southwest, cannonading furiously. Both fleets followed their leaders, the battle developing into a classic formalist duel in spite of Calder's original intention to mass.

A sudden fog complicated the battle, alternately hiding and revealing the ships of the opposing lines. The leading British ship, *Hero,* staggered out of formation and went drifting downwind out of action, badly damaged. Not long afterward she was followed by *Ajax* (74). On the other side, the Spanish *San Rafael* (80) and *Firme* (74) suffered similarly, drifting straight into the British formation to leeward and being captured. Nightfall brought an end to the fighting after nearly eight hours of maneuvering and cannonading.

Dawn revealed both fleets badly scattered. Neither admiral attempted to renew the struggle. Villeneuve still stuck to his wish to reach a friendly port with as many ships as possible. Calder, mirroring the earlier complacency of Hotham, felt that he had done well to stave off a larger fleet and capture two ships-of-the-line and contented himself with shadowing the allied force until he was certain that it could not reach Ferrol and join forces with the French and Spanish squadrons there. Once this was determined, he clapped on sail and resumed his blockading activities off Ferrol.

Villeneuve, balked in his efforts to reach Ferrol, groped his way down the coast and into Vigo. Here he found none of the dockyard facilities he so badly needed. After a wasted week, he took advantage of a southwesterly gale and sailed for Ferrol, hoping against hope that he could get into port without a battle. To his joy and amazement, he found only eight British ships on patrol, as Calder had dispatched the rest of his command on a fruitless errand to blockade Rochefort. Brushing aside the blockaders, he sailed into port, thus successfully fulfilling his orders by uniting the two allied fleets.

Calder, with some justification, received the blame and was court-martialed. The members of the court felt that if he had persisted in renewing the battle, the union of the enemies' fleets would have been made more difficult and less effective—perhaps prevented entirely. He was censured but not otherwise punished.

9.

When Napoleon heard of Villeneuve's arrival at Ferrol and of the successful uniting of the allied fleets, he once more dreamed of conquering Great Britain. Orders were sent to the admiral to bring his full might north into the Channel. The messenger, arriving at Ferrol, found that the bird had flown, not north to the Channel but south to Cadiz. The French emperor threw a tantrum, damning all his admirals in general and Villeneuve in particular. He then broke up his Boulogne invasion force, renamed it the *Grande Armée,* and sent it marching eastward to win startling victories over the Austrians and Russians at Ulm and Austerlitz.

In Cadiz, Admiral Villeneuve presently received two communications. One was a set of orders to take aboard all available troops and sail through the Strait of Gibraltar to Naples. The other was an unofficial report incorporated in a personal letter, stating that Admiral Rosily was on the way to supersede him. His only chance to retrieve anything of his honor and his reputation was to sail at once, before Rosily's arrival. Accordingly, he loaded his troops aboard his ships and set sail on October 19, 1805, determined, as he said, "to win a victory, or to lose everything."

Unknown to Villeneuve, a significant change had taken place in the blockading squadron. The Frenchman knew that six of Collingwood's thirty ships-of-the-line had been sent to Gibraltar for supplies and repairs, thus reducing the British force to nine fewer ships than he himself commanded. What he did not know was that three more ships had arrived from Britain—the *Victory* (100) and two 74's—and that aboard the *Victory* was none other than Vice-Admiral Horatio Nelson, who was to supersede Admiral Collingwood in command. In the interests of secrecy, Nelson had issued orders that no salute should be fired in his honor.

Villeneuve's emergence from port was made without resistance, though adverse weather made it a difficult maneuver which could not be completed until nearly noon of the 20th. No British blockading ships were to be seen—merely a few frigates, which made off to the southwest. Grouping his thirty-three French and Spanish ships into five short columns, the admiral set sail for Gibraltar.

Knowing that the enemy was safe as long as he remained in port, Nelson had withdrawn some fifty miles to the southwest, leaving scout frigates to keep an eye on Villeneuve's activities. One of these presently informed him that the French fleet was out. At once, Nelson led his ships to the Strait of Gibraltar, checking to be sure that Villeneuve had not arrived there ahead of him. Seeing that he had not, Nelson then set sail to the north to meet the advancing allied fleet.

The two fleets came within sight of one another in the late afternoon of October 20. By this time, Villeneuve had changed his formation into a long, single column of ships, French and Spanish vessels roughly alternating in the formation. He himself commanded the center, with Spanish Vice-Admiral Alava in charge of the van and French Vice-Admiral Dumanoir le Pelley directing the rear. Attached to the van was a separate group of five fast ships under Spanish Admiral Gravina, who was instructed to keep his eye on the action and employ his ships at the point of greatest need, in order to defeat any British attempts at massing or doubling.

Nelson had often expressed the opinion that it is impossible for an admiral to organize his fleet and fight a formal action to a decision within the limits of a single day. Consequently, he had worked out a daring and unorthodox plan of attack to bring on what he called "a pell-mell battle," to bring quick and decisive victory to one of the fleets involved and defeat to the other. His plan, which he had often explained informally to one or another of his captains, involved two parallel columns of sixteen British ships each and a separate squadron of eight, much like Gravina's, to fight where needed. This required forty ships. Since he now had only twenty-seven, he dispensed with the group of eight and divided the others into two columns, one of twelve ships led by his flagship *Victory* (100) and one of fifteen, led by Admiral Collingwood in the *Royal Sovereign* (100). The exact procedure was explained to his captains in a night meeting aboard the *Victory*.

During the night, Villeneuve groped steadily to the southwest, still hoping to round Cape Trafalgar and reach the Strait of Gibraltar. Nelson gradually drew nearer, keeping contact and waiting for daylight, which came shortly after six o'clock on October 21, 1805.

The wind was very light, puffing fitfully from west by northwest. What little of it there was favored the British. Seeing this, Villeneuve hoisted signals directing his entire fleet to wear together, thus changing his course from south to north and placing the former rear of his formation in the van and the former van in the rear. The chief advantage of this shift was that it would keep the allied fleet upwind from Cadiz, thus making it easier for battered French and Spanish vessels to reach a safe haven. The maneuver took ninety minutes and was raggedly executed. At its conclusion, the allied battle line resembled a shallow crescent, bending eastward, away from the British, at its center. Gravina's special squadron, which was supposed to sail a little to the lee of the van, was now at the extreme rear, where it formed an extension of the line. Disregarding all of his admiral's signals, Gravina held this out-of-the-way position, in which his ships could do nothing to bring help to distressed sections of the allied line.

While the allies were reversing course, the two parallel columns of British ships were bearing steadily down upon them from the west. The lightness of the wind kept the speed down to a bare three knots, making the closing a long, slow process. Nelson, leading the more northerly column, headed for the center of the allied line, which was crawling northward with bare steerageway, at less than one knot, with the light wind abeam. Collingwood led his column toward the twelfth ship from the end of the enemy battle line. So, during the long morning, the fleets drew slowly together.

At 11:40, as the leading ships of the British columns neared extreme cannon range, a string of flags on the *Victory* informed the fleet: "England expects that every man will do his duty." The message was greeted with cheers. There was one more signal: "Close Action."

Collingwood's column was somewhat ahead of Nelson's. At 11:50, the French ship *Fougueux* (74) fired at the *Royal Sovereign*. Almost immediately, the great *Santa Ana* (112) brought her port batteries into action. Collingwood did not reply but forged steadily onward, toward the gap between the *Santa Ana* and the *Fougueux*. Men were killed beside the silent guns of the *Royal Sovereign,* but Collingwood knew what he was about. At 12:10, after a full twenty minutes of raking fire, *Royal Sovereign* passed through the allied line and cut loose with her 100 guns, each double shotted. Aboard the *Santa Ana,* 400 men died as the heavy balls crashed through from stern to bow. *Fougueux* swung to starboard to avoid being raked and managed to loose a broadside of her own, but she received heavy damage in the exchange.

Royal Sovereign, being fast and having crowded on all sail, was well ahead of her column when she swung through the allied line and opened the action. For the next five minutes, she fought alone, exchanging broadsides with six allied warships. Then, at 12:15, the second ship, *Belle Isle* (74), passed through and delivered her broadsides. Thereafter, the battle between the British southern column and the allied rear became general.

To the north, Nelson's column was drawing near to the allied formation. The admiral had his eyes and his intentions fixed on the middle of the enemy line, but he permitted the *Victory* to bear to the northeast, as though to strike somewhere in the van. Not until some of the van ships opened fire on him did he swing sharply to starboard, making for the huge *Santissima Trinidad* (130) and for Villeneuve's flagship *Bucentaure* (80), immediately astern. This deceptive action kept the van ships from doubling back to the assistance of the allied center, which did not seem to be in danger of attack.

At 12:20, the *Bucentaure* fired at the *Victory,* but the shots fell short. Five minutes later, hits were scored. Other French vessels now opened up on the silent British flagship, steadfastly leading her eleven followers ever closer. More than fifty men died aboard the *Victory* as she bore in. One was Nelson's personal secretary, who had his head carried away by a cannon ball as he stood talking to Captain Thomas Hardy. Another shot demolished the quarterdeck steering wheel, making it necessary to steer the ship from a gun room below decks, orders being sent down by messenger.

At one o'clock, *Victory* reached the allied line. Nelson had intended to pass through between *Santissima Trinidad* and *Bucentaure,* but the gap between them closed, so he changed course to go through the rapidly closing gap astern of *Bucentaure. Victory* crashed through, raking the French flagship from astern and at the same time causing the next allied ship, *Redoutable* (74), to swing hard to starboard to avoid collision. Spars and rigging tangled, and *Victory* and *Redoutable* clung together in mortal combat, the great guns blasting away at wooden sides a ramrod's length away.

It so happened that Captain Jean Lucas of the *Redoutable* was one of the few French commanders who had devoted time and effort to the training of his crew. The men of his ship had spent long hours practicing not only with the big guns but also with small arms, which Lucas felt would be of value should his ship come near enough to an enemy to make boarding practical. The fighting tops of the *Redoutable* were full of trained sharpshooters. One of these, peering through the smoke, saw a British officer in full uniform, his chest bright with ribbons and medals. Carefully he aimed, then squeezed the trigger.

On the quarterdeck of the *Victory,* Vice-Admiral Horatio Nelson staggered, then fell heavily to his knees. Captain Hardy caught him and tried to hold him up. "They have done for me at last," said Nelson, gasping painfully. "My backbone is shot through."

They carried him below and made him as comfortable as possible. He had just three more hours to live.

Aboard the *Redoutable,* Captain Lucas was frantically trying to organize boarding parties with which to seize the British flagship. He was thus engaged when the British *Temeraire* (98)—the famous "fighting *Temeraire*"—attacked from the starboard side. *Redoutable* was overwhelmed and soon surrendered.

From end to end, the battle degenerated into a *melee* as one British ship after another crashed through or into the allied line. The main fight broke up into twenty fights or more as ship battled ship with single-minded intensity. Near the center, *Santissima Trinidad,* the greatest warship in the world, swapped cannon fire with five British ships and was reduced to a dismasted, helpless hulk. The British *Tonnant* (80) grappled with the French *Algésiras* (74), leading to more than half an hour of arms-length slugging with the heavy guns, interspersed with attempts at boarding. A wave of French boarders tried to reach the *Tonnant*'s quarterdeck, but only one man lived to get there. Then the British boarders went over. Both ships were aflame from the close-up cannon flashes, but British fire-fighting crews succeeded in putting out the fires on both even before their boarders had completed the capture of the *Algésiras.*

Aboard the *Bucentaure,* Admiral Villeneuve, seeing possible victory slip away, sought death in battle. Men died beside him, but he remained untouched. His flagship was now a helpless wreck, but he could not transfer to another because all of his small boats had been smashed. At last, when the British *Conqueror* (74) came alongside and boarders swarmed on his decks, he proffered his sword in surrender. Captain Israel Pellew of the *Conqueror* was amazed to learn whom he had captured.

Admiral Nelson had set his heart on capturing twenty allied ships. As he lay dying, his officers brought him news of the battle. At 2:30 —an hour after his wound—he knew that a victory was in the making, with at least a dozen enemy ships in British hands. At 4:00, Hardy was able to report to him that the battle was well in hand. Though it was hard to see all ships clearly, he hazarded a guess that fourteen or fifteen of the enemy had struck their colors.

"That is well," said Nelson, then, after a pause, "but I bargained for twenty."

Half an hour later, Captain Hardy again came down and bade a final farewell to his admiral. "Thank God I have done my duty," said Horatio Nelson, shortly before he closed his eyes in death.

Had Captain Hardy been able to see more clearly through the smoke, he could have reported that seventeen, rather than fourteen or fifteen, allied ships had surrendered. An eighteenth, the *Achille* (74), was burning furiously, and presently blew up with the loss of her entire crew. Four of the van ships, under Rear Admiral Dumanoir le Pelley, were fleeing westward, out to sea. Eleven of the rear division, gathered by mortally wounded Vice-Admiral Gravina, were in flight toward Cadiz, some so badly damaged that they were beyond repair or further use.

In the end, Trafalgar was a greater victory than even Nelson had anticipated. Dumanoir le Pelley's four fugitives were subsequently captured by a four-ship squadron under Captain Richard Strachan. Though two of the crippled British prizes were retaken two days after the battle by a sortie of five ships from Cadiz, four of the five-ship squadron were storm-wrecked while out. Two other British prizes were lost when their prize crews, unable to control the ships in the storm, gave them up to their original crews, who managed to get them safely into Cadiz. That meant a total bag for the British fleet of twenty-two enemy vessels sunk or captured, reducing the allied fleet from thirty-three prime ships-of-the-line to eleven, of which seven were battered hulks. Only eight of the ships captured by the British survived to reach Gibraltar and safety, seven being scuttled or burned because they were beyond repair and the rest, including the *Santissima Trinidad* and the *Bucentaure,* going down in the great storm which blew up on the 22nd.

Not a single one of the twenty-seven British ships in the battle had been lost, either to the enemy or to the elements.

The dead and wounded at Trafalgar included approximately 7,600 seamen, of which 1,700 were British, 2,400 were Spanish, and 3,500 were French. It was a heavy toll for four hours of fighting.

Admiral Villeneuve was the last casualty of the battle. Captured when the *Bucentaure* surrendered, he was carried to England as a prisoner of war. Six months later, in April, 1806, he was exchanged and sent back to France. Hoping that the emperor would forgive him, he eagerly questioned his friends about the attitude which Napoleon had expressed. The news was bad, the prospect bleak. Fearful and discouraged, Pierre Charles Villeneuve lay down upon his bed and drove a dagger through his heart.

10.

Trafalgar was the high point of the naval war against Napoleon. The little that came afterward was anticlimax.

There were ten years more of war, practically all of it fought on the battlefields of Europe, far from the sea. This did not mean that British naval power could not be used; it merely meant that it was largely unopposed. Control of the sea permitted Great Britain to strike where and when she pleased and to cooperate with any seaside country menaced by Napoleon or resentful of his arrogance as an ally. It was difficult to guard against such omnipresent strength. The emperor himself expressed it well: "With 30,000 troops in transports at the Downs, the British can paralyze 300,000 of my army."

There is no need to go into details concerning the following activities—some successful, some unsuccessful—in which the British navy took part between October, 1805, and June 18, 1815, when Napoleon was finally defeated at Waterloo.

In November, 1805, a British naval expedition successfully landed an invasion force at Cuxhaven, at the mouth of the Elbe River in Germany. When the invasion failed in its purpose to bolster Prussia against Napoleon, the navy successfully removed the troops and carried them back to Britain.

In January, 1806, a small British squadron under Commodore Sir

Home Riggs Popham carried to South Africa an invasion force of 6,400 men under General Sir David Baird. In spite of heavy surf, a landing was made in the lee of a beached transport, which served as a breakwater. The Dutch defenders were unable to withstand the British invaders, who were well supported by naval gunfire. South Africa passed into British hands, thus assuring control of the sea route to India and the East.

From June, 1806, until July, 1807, a British expeditionary force, with naval support, tried unsuccessfully to gain control of Spain's colonies in South America. Though Buenos Aires was captured and briefly held, the entire expedition was eventually abandoned.

In July, 1806, a British naval force under Admiral Collingwood and Sir William Sydney Smith, cooperating with British troops under General Sir John Stuart, prevented the conquest of Sicily by a strong French force under Napoleon's brother, Joseph Bonaparte.

A British attempt to force the Dardanelles and capture Constantinople failed in February, 1807. With eight ships-of-the-line, Vice-Admiral Sir John Duckworth sailed deep into the strait and there was almost trapped, as the Turks set up strong batteries on the shores behind him. Heavily bombarded, Duckworth was fortunate to be able to fight his way clear and reach the Aegean. An interesting detail of this expedition was the successful use by the Turks of ancient fifteenth-century cannons firing 700-pound stone cannon balls weighing more than a third of a ton.

The Russians, meanwhile, were learning at Jena, Auerstadt, Eylau, and Friedland that they could not beat Napoleon. Since they could not beat him, they joined him in the summer of 1807 and set about the forming of an anti-British coalition including Portugal, Denmark, and Spain. In this emergency, the British government took energetic steps. Admiral James Gambier was sent to Denmark with twenty-two ships-of-the-line, a large fleet of smaller warships, and an army of 20,000 men under Lord Cathcart. Following an unsuccessful attempt to woo the Danes away from the alliance, Gambier and Cathcart launched combined naval and military operations against the greatly strengthened defenses of Copenhagen. The defenders held out stoutly for three weeks, finally surrendering on September 7 only because British shells and rockets had started uncontrollable fires, which threatened to destroy the city. Fifteen Danish ships-of-the-line and fifteen frigates were among the items taken by the British.

From a military-naval point of view, the taking of Copenhagen was a successful endeavor. Diplomatically, it was a blunder, for it turned the Danes more strongly against Britain and toward Napoleon and made the narrow straits a weapon in the French-Russian arsenal.

The rockets used against Copenhagen had been developed by Sir William Congreve and first employed a year earlier, with little success, against Boulogne. Basically, they were oversized skyrockets, containing explosive charges in their heads. Some large warships were equipped with slanting chutes, through which the rockets could be discharged obliquely upward from below decks. Since their firing involved no recoil, they could be fired equally well from small boats or from improvised chutes set on the ground. Their fiery trails through the air were counted on to weaken the enemy's morale. To quote Congreve himself: "Their explosion will clear the way for the boarders, both by actual destruction and by the powerful operation of terror among the crew." Crude and ineffective as was Congreve's "Rocket System," it was the forerunner of the ballistic missile system of today.

Forty miles west of Denmark and thirty miles north of the German coast stands the cliff-sided island of Helgoland, in 1807 a Danish possession. On the day Copenhagen was surrendered, the British ship-of-the-line *Majestic* and the frigate *Quebec* visited the island, overawed the inhabitants, and claimed this strategic spot for Great Britain. The original intention was to use it as a base for trade with Germany during times when the Danish straits were closed. The strategic importance of Helgoland was as yet completely unrealized.

Early in 1808, Russia and Denmark, backed by Napoleon, went to war with Sweden. Taking advantage of the fact that Denmark still lacked a fleet of major warships, the British sent a squadron of thirteen ships-of-the-line under Sir James Saumarez to patrol the Baltic waters and help protect the Swedes against their enemies. Most of the action was against small, oar-driven gunboats, well suited for the shallow, island-dotted areas where they were used, but there was one battle involving major warships. A squadron of two British and ten Swedish ships-of-the-line, under Sir Samuel Hood, encountered nine Russian ships-of-the-line, under Admiral Hanichof, in the eastern Baltic. The Russians fled, and a chase developed. Presently the two British ships, being copper-sheathed and hence less fouled below water than the Swedish vessels, left their allies out of sight behind. Now it was two against nine, but the Russians still retired. The *Vsevolod* (74), last ship in the Russian line, was overhauled by the British *Implacable* and, after a sharp action, hauled down its flag. At this, Hanichof bore back, drove off the *Implacable,* and rescued his ship. The pursuit continued. That evening, the Russians anchored off the Estonian coast, and *Implacable* once more attacked *Vsevolod*, which again surrendered and was burned where she lay.

At various times during the post-Trafalgar period, the French sent out small raiding squadrons from Brest, Dunkirk, and other seaports. Invariably, these were traced down and either taken or dispersed by stronger British squadrons.

When Napoleon established his Continental System in 1806 and tried, for six years, to close the ports of continental Europe to all British shipping, it was British sea power that made possible the exploiting of such weak spots in the Emperor's solidarity as Portugal, Spain, and, eventually, Russia. British armies came and went, and there was nothing that Napoleon could do about it.

French attempts to build up naval power and naval bases were constantly menaced by British naval or amphibious attack from the sea. In April, 1809, a sudden descent of British fireships and bomb vessels on Aix Island broke up a concentration of French vessels and destroyed a number of them. In August of the same year, a British landing on the island of Walcheren threatened the new French naval base at Antwerp. To Napoleon and to his Minister of Marine, Denis Decres, it began to appear useless to try to develop French naval power. Wherever the first flowerings of success appeared, the British were sure to arrive by sea and undo the work.

We should not leave our consideration of the Napoleonic Wars without some mention of a small but brilliant action fought on March 13, 1811, in the Adriatic Sea. With eleven French and Venetian vessels, French Commodore Dubordieu left the harbor of Ancona to occupy the island of Lissa, off what is now the coast of Yugoslavia. Near the island, he encountered a squadron of four British frigates under Commodore Sir William Hoste, who had gained much naval lore by serving under Nelson in the battles of Cape St. Vincent and the Nile.

Dubordieu had also learned something from Nelson, for he employed the exact plan of attack which the great British admiral had used at Trafalgar. The larger and more numerous French and Venetian ships were divided into two columns and were sent at right angles against the British line, for the purpose of splitting it as Nelson had done to the French and Spaniards six years earlier. This time, it did not work. Keeping his four frigates close together to prevent gaps,

Hoste raked the enemy as they approached. Foiled in his attempt to break through, Dubordieu tried to lead his starboard column across the bow of Hoste's leading ship. Instead, he ran his own flagship, the frigate *Favorite,* on the rocks, where she stuck fast and presently took fire.

The battle now degenerated into a *melee,* in which the British vessels had all the better of the fighting. The colors on three French frigates came down almost simultaneously, leading Hoste to believe that all three had surrendered. Two had, but in the case of the third vessel there still remains the disputed question whether the flag had been lowered or shot away. In any event, this ship, the frigate *Flore,* made good her escape during the excitement which followed the explosion of the French flagship's magazines. Commodore Dubordieu and most of his crew were killed in the blast.

It was, in all respects, a most satisfactory day for Sir William Hoste. Outnumbered eleven vessels to four, outgunned 265 cannon to 124, he had destroyed the enemy's flagship, captured two of the largest remaining vessels, and driven the others away in flight, all without loss or serious damage to any of his own ships, though his casualties had been high. He had saved the strategically situated island of Lissa from capture and occupation by the 500 French-Venetian troops carried by Dubordieu's squadron. In recognition of his achievements, he was presently made a baronet.

Once more, it had been proved that mere superiority in size, armament, and numbers is no guarantee of victory. Skilled leadership can more than redress the balance.

Napoleon might be supreme upon the land, but his power was circumscribed. When at last disaster came at Waterloo and the French Empire fell apart, much of the credit could be attributed to the British fleet. As Mahan so well expressed it: "Those far-distant, storm-beaten ships, on which Napoleon's soldiers never looked, stood between them and the dominion of the world."

Unlike his soldiers, Napoleon himself eventually became more than a little familiar with British warships. When the fighting was over and his enemies were closing in, he sought refuge aboard the ship-of-the-line *Bellerophon,* where he was courteously treated as a distinguished prisoner of war. Later, another ship-of-the-line, the *Northumberland,* took him to his perpetual exile at St. Helena.

13 THE WAR OF 1812

⚓

1.

It was inevitable that the United States should sooner or later become involved in the titanic struggle being waged between Great Britain and Napoleonic France. For a time, though, there was a real question of which nation would be the ally and which the enemy. Both gave plenty of offense.

Britain was Queen of the Seas. Her navy, increasingly feeling its strength, acted as though all the waters of the world were British property. A tight blockade was clamped upon the continent of Europe in an attempt to weaken the grip which Napoleon maintained upon many allied countries. Neutral ships were systematically stopped and seized, sometimes on the mere suspicion that they were headed for ports controlled by France.

Napoleon struck back by creating the Continental System, which closed the ports of Europe to all British trade. It was his feeling that the British were "a nation of shopkeepers," who would soon be brought to their knees by the loss of their European markets. He also issued the Berlin Decree, placing a paper blockade around the British Isles, and the Milan Decree, declaring that any neutral ship that had touched at a British port or had been searched by a British crew was to be confiscated.

The British government replied by issuing the Orders in Council, forbidding all trade between ports owned or controlled by France or her allies and declaring a blockade of "all the ports and places of France and her allies, or of any country at war with His Majesty."

As might have been expected, numerous American ships were taken and their cargoes confiscated by both sides in the European struggle. American tempers flared hotly against both France and Great Britain. Of the two, the British incurred by far the greater wrath. Comparatively few French warships managed to slip through the British blockade, so most American ships taken on the high seas were taken by the British.

The greatest single source of irritation was the taking of American seamen to serve aboard His Majesty's warships. This "impressment" was nothing new, nor was it strictly limited to the British navy, but the shortage of competent sailors to man the hundreds of British warships and the close resemblance in language and customs between British and American sailors made it both tempting and easy for British captains to think of plausible reasons for taking whatever American sailors they wanted. The glib statement, "Once an Englishman always an Englishman," was made to cover a multitude of sins.

2.

The quarrel over impressment first arose in November, 1798, when the American corvette *Baltimore* (20) was stopped off Havana by three British ships-of-the-line and two frigates. The British commodore curtly informed Captain Isaac Phillips of the *Baltimore* that no fewer than fifty-five of his men were British deserters and must be surrendered. Captain Phillips protested, but in the face of the overpowering force surrounding him he did no more. All fifty-five of the men had to be surrendered, despite the fact that most if not all of them were American citizens. Captain Phillips was subsequently court-martialed and was dismissed from the service.

An even more serious affair took place in June, 1807, when the United States frigate *Chesapeake* (38) encountered H. M. S. *Leopard* (50) off Cape Henry. The American ship had been newly reconditioned, and her guns had not yet been equipped for action. *Leopard* stopped her and demanded the surrender of three sailors, alleged to be deserters from a British man-of-war. Knowing that the three men were American citizens, Captain James Barron refused to surrender them. The *Leopard* then fired a broadside into the defenseless *Chesapeake,* following it up with three more. In the quarter of an hour of one-sided action, three Americans were killed and twenty-one wounded. Shortly before the flag was hauled down, an angry American officer, Lieutenant Allen, picked up a live coal from the galley and, despite the pain to his fingers, used it as a match to fire a single shot of protest in the general direction of the *Leopard.* Then the British came aboard and took the three men in question, plus a fourth not previously mentioned. One of the four was promptly hanged; the other three were flogged through the fleet.

Anger flared throughout the United States. In many quarters, there was a demand for war. President Thomas Jefferson, however, thought he knew of a better way to bring the British to their senses. He would stop both the British and the French abuses on the high seas by keeping all American ships at home. Accordingly, Congress in 1807 passed the Embargo Act, prohibiting all ships from leaving American ports except foreign-owned vessels carrying no cargo.

Undoubtedly, the Embargo Act did cause some hardship to Britain and to France, through the loss of American trade, but it caused much more harm to the United States. The resulting shortage of foreign goods lowered the American standard of living and crippled manufacturing, while the shipping and trading industries were almost completely ruined. The unpopularity of the law was reflected in a growing hostility to Jefferson and his Democratic-Republican party. Alarmed by this, the President induced Congress to bring the Embargo to an end early in 1809.

Jefferson was followed in office by his fellow Democratic-Republican, James Madison. At the suggestion of this new President, Congress passed the Non-Intercourse Act soon after the repeal of the Embargo. This law forbade American ships to visit British or French ports, and it also forbade British or French ships to visit American ports. All other trade was permitted. The law proved easy to circumvent. Ships sailed for neutral ports, then changed their destinations when safely at sea. The Non-Intercourse Act was repealed in May of 1810.

3.

The American measures had no appreciable effect upon British policy at sea. In May, 1811, the British frigate *Guerriere* (38) stopped the American bomb-brig *Spitfire* (12) and took a crew member. This comparatively minor offense brought a major reaction, for the *Guerriere* had been one of the most active of the British raiders and had earned for herself a most unsavory reputation.

Exasperated beyond endurance, President James Madison ordered the U. S. frigate *President* (44) to hunt down the *Guerriere* and get back the kidnapped American. On May 16, off the New Jersey coast, Captain John Rodgers of the *President* sighted a British warship which he took to be the *Guerriere*. Before Rodgers could close, night had fallen. Nevertheless, the American ship bore in and fired a warning shot. The British replied with a broadside. That was all that Rodgers needed. His broadside batteries blazed, then blazed and blazed again. The British ship was hit hard. Her captain hailed to say that he surrendered. It was well he did, for his vessel had thirty-one casualties aboard and was in a sinking condition. As it happened, she was not the *Guerriere* at all but the sloop *Little Belt* (24).

Great Britain's vehement protest over the *Little Belt* affair was coldly rejected by the United States, whose people were willing to back their government to the limit in resisting British aggression on the seas. A willingness, even a desire, for war was sweeping the United States. A significant change had taken place in Congress. Many of the members who had favored the use of peaceful methods had been defeated in the Congressional election of 1810. Their places had been taken by more violent members, the so-called War Hawks, who loudly declared that the United States must go to war with Great Britain not only to defend American rights upon the seas but also to make the United States supreme in North America.

Supposedly, the principal cause of America's growing war feeling was Great Britain's abuse of the freedom of the seas—the seizure of American ships and the impressment of American sailors. Yet, strangely enough, the demand for war did not come from the New England states, where the shipping interests were strongest. The New England shippers did not want war. In spite of the nuisance of blockade, seizure, confiscation, and impressment, they were prospering. The extremely high profits to be made by slipping cargoes through to the warring powers more than offset the loss of an occasional ship. If war came, the British navy would put a quick stop to this trading prosperity and would sweep the American flag from the seas.

It was the southern and the western states whose people called most belligerently for "Free Trade and Sailors' Rights." Though these inland people had little real interest in the sea, the war which loomed ahead promised an opportunity to end the Indian menace, which depended upon British support; to conquer Canada; and possibly to take Florida as well. Henry Clay, a War Hawk from Kentucky, loudly boasted that a thousand Kentucky riflemen could quickly take Canada without any outside assistance.

Eventually, the War Hawks had their way, though the reasons for going to war with Great Britain were rapidly vanishing. The impressment of American seamen was falling off, for Napoleon's navy had been beaten at Trafalgar and the need for British sailors was far less acute than it had been. Russia was beginning to turn against Napoleon, which would mean the end of the Continental System and would permit the loosening of the British blockade. The leading British statesmen were openly urging a more friendly attitude toward the United States, a fact which remained unknown in America, since the American minister had returned home. On June 16, 1812, the British government officially discontinued the Orders in Council, thus removing the last real cause of war. There was no way for the news to reach the United States in time. On June 18, Congress officially declared war against Great Britain.

4.

We should pause here to note a fateful meeting in a Washington tavern. Captain Charles Stewart and Captain William Bainbridge were both in the capital seeking command of a ship for the coming war with Great Britain. Both were dismayed at the news that the President and his Cabinet had decided that the odds were too great and that America should make no attempt to meet British power on the seas. All American warships were to remain in port, inactive and unmanned!

Filled with indignation, the two captains went the next day to see President Madison. Their vehemence and their deep sincerity swayed him. At his suggestion, they repaired to their lodging house and prepared a paper, setting forth the reasons why the United States Navy should be strengthened and actively employed during the war. The paper was read to the Cabinet. It turned the trick. The policy of inactivating the navy was summarily dropped.

The United States would undertake to meet Great Britain on the sea!

5.

The outbreak of war found Vice-Admiral Sawyer of His Majesty's Navy ready, willing, and able to begin action against "that handful of fir-built frigates with bits of striped bunting at their mastheads, manned by bastards and outlaws," as the London *Times* described the American Navy. At his base at Halifax, Nova Scotia, the admiral had the ship-of-the-line *Africa* (64) and the frigates *Shannon* (38), *Guerriere* (38) and *Aeolus* (32). He would send these fanning down the coast to take what American warships could quickly be snapped up. By separating his force in this way, he could do the greatest possible damage in the shortest time.

On June 26, Admiral Sawyer's plans underwent an important and necessary modification. A fourth British frigate, *Belvidera* (36), came into Halifax, showing unmistakable signs of battle damage. Three days before, she had encountered an American squadron, made up of the frigates *United States* (44), *President* (44), and *Congress* (44), the sloop *Hornet* (18), and the brig *Argus* (16). As the Americans had advanced, the *Belvidera* had fled, finally escaping as a result of an accident aboard the *President*—the bursting of one of the big guns. Even so, *Belvidera* had had to jettison much valuable equipment in order to get away.

The news that an American squadron was at sea, seeking individual British warships and endangering the huge West Indies plate fleet then en route to Britain, forced Admiral Sawyer to keep his ships together, thus eliminating much of the danger to stray American ships, many of which were able to slip safely into port during the next few days. All five British warships were sent south together under Commodore Philip Broke in search of the American squadron, which had now taken a course for Europe in the vain hope of overtaking the plate fleet. Commodore John Rodgers, in command of the American ships, was having a most unpleasant and difficult voyage; the cannon explosion, which had killed sixteen of his men aboard the *President,* had broken his leg.

Commodore Broke did not find Rodgers' squadron, but his search was not without results. Off New York, he encountered the little American brig *Nautilus* (14), which blundered in among his ships in a strong gale and could not run away from the frigates with their greater spreads of canvas. From *Nautilus'* captain, Broke learned that Rodgers and his squadron had turned eastward, toward Europe. It was accurate information, but the imparting of it did the United States more good than it did Great Britain. Fearing for the safety of a second plate fleet en route from Jamaica, Broke gave up his ideas of commerce raiding and sailed south in order to provide protection for the menaced shipping.

On July 17, the day after the capture of the *Nautilus,* Broke's squadron made a most important contact. Four of his ships were proceeding south along the New Jersey coast, close to the shore. The fifth ship, the frigate *Guerriere,* was farther at sea, out of sight over the horizon. Just as night was falling, Captain Dacres of the *Guerriere* sighted a strange sail to the south. At about the same time, a hail from the lookout on the masthead informed him of the sails of four other ships on the horizon to the west, just off the shore. Were these the other four ships of Broke's British squadron, or were the five ships the members of Rodgers' American squadron, which was known to be at sea? In the fading light, Dacres could not be sure.

A similar uncertainty was plaguing Captain Isaac Hull of the U. S. frigate *Constitution* (44). He had sailed from the Chesapeake five days before with a green crew and with orders to join Rodgers' squadron, which he expected to find somewhere off the New Jersey coast. Were these Rodgers' four ships, which he now saw dimly near the shore? And what of this fifth ship, far at sea? Was she British or American? On a hunch, Captain Hull sent his men to battle stations and set a course to seaward, away from the unknown four.

During the night, *Constitution* and *Guerriere* passed within long cannon range of one another. Each hoisted an identification signal of lanterns and thus discovered the other ship to be an enemy. Darkness and distance made it impractical to open fire. Besides, each captain was uncertain of the nationality of the four ships on the horizon. If they were enemies, engagement in a single-ship duel would be disastrous.

Dawn revealed the wisdom of Hull's cautious maneuvers. Astern of him, but dangerously close, were four enemy frigates and a ship-of-the-line. It was well that the *Constitution* was a fast ship under canvas! No sooner had this thought brought comfort to Captain Hull than the wind died out entirely.

Now began one of the most frustrating and exhausting chases in the history of the sea. At all costs, *Constitution* must get away from the five ships, which lay just out of cannon range astern! The ship-of-the-line alone or any two of the four frigates would be far more than a match for the American vessel. Boats were put over, the sailors laboring at the oars to inch the big frigate southward away from the enemy. At the same time, four 24-pounder guns were moved astern, two to fire through cut-away gaps in the taffrail, two to fire through punched-out stern cabin windows. The towing maneuver accomplished little, for the British soon detected what was being done and adopted the same maneuver. The ships remained in the same relative positions, just out of cannon range, as the *Shannon* conclusively proved by trying some long-range shots.

As the morning wore on, it became evident that two of the British frigates were gaining, *Shannon* on the starboard quarter, *Belvidera* to port. The other ships had contributed boats to these two, for faster towing. This closed the gap somewhat, though Hull promptly served warning that it might be dangerous. Some 24-pounder balls from his improvised stern battery splashed not far ahead of the towing flotillas.

Lieutenant Charles Morris now made a suggestion which Captain Hull seized with alacrity. The water was shallow—not more than 150 feet in depth. *Constitution*'s spare cable was spliced into two half-mile lengths, and an anchor was attached to an end of each long cable. A small boat was sent out ahead, bearing one of the anchors. Half a mile ahead, the anchor was dropped. Immediately, members of the frigate's crew began a parade around a windlass, winding in the cable and "walking" the ship forward toward the emplaced kedge anchor. Another small boat, meanwhile, was moving a second anchor out ahead, to be dropped as the first one was taken up. Thus, alternately, the two kedge anchors and the two long cables were used to move the *Constitution* away from her pursuers.

Of course, the British kedged too, but they were hampered by the ever-present danger from the 24-pounders which Hull had mounted astern. The small boats bearing the British kedge anchors dared not come within range.

From time to time, there were little puffs of wind. Captain Hull must have done some fine training during his five days at sea, for his crew handled the ship like veterans. As the sails billowed full, the small boats up ahead were picked up on the move, without the loss of precious time, and without the loss of a single boat. Meanwhile, members of the crew were swarming aloft, hauling up pails of water with which to soak the sails, the better to hold the light and tricky winds. Then, just as the *Constitution* would start to draw ahead, the wind would die, and the back-breaking towing and kedging would be recommenced.

All that day and all the next the relentless pursuit continued, with the all-too-powerful British squadron close astern. A single mistake, the slightest slackening of effort, would bring those guns into range and mean certain disaster. Despite exhaustion, panting lungs, aching muscles, and raw and bleeding hands, the crew had to keep laboring around the clock. The British crews could relieve one another, but there was no rest for the Americans.

On the third day, a light wind brought some relief. *Constitution* gained a little, partly because of her superior sailing qualities, partly because Hull had sacrificed ten tons of drinking water to lighten ship. The situation, though, was still desperate, with the two nearest British frigates still only about three miles away.

At this point, an American merchant ship appeared on the horizon, sailing slowly toward the six warships. Broke, hoping to take an easy prize, had the nearest frigate, *Belvidera,* hoist the American flag. The unsuspecting merchantman drew nearer, sailing into the trap. Suddenly, all watchers saw her veer away. Hull had hoisted the British colors on *Constitution!*

The decisive break occurred in the late afternoon of July 20. Far ahead, Hull saw a rain squall coming. It was only a little storm, but as the storm bore down he sent his men aloft to reef canvas, as though to withstand a mighty blow. The more distant British captains saw the frantic activity and followed suit, furling and reefing. *Constitution* sailed into the squall under the lightest of sails. No sooner did the rain hide her from the British than Hull spread every sail. The ship almost leaped ahead. By the time the cautious pursuers had reached and passed the storm front, *Constitution* was hull-down on the horizon and rapidly disappearing.

Only one of the six pursuing warships was ever to see her again.

6.

When Rodgers' squadron set out on its none-too-successful cruise, the light frigate *Essex* was left behind, undergoing repairs. She was a freak ship, armed with forty 32-pounder carronades and only six 12-pounder long guns. She could thus deliver crushing broadsides at close range, but was almost helpless at the longer distances usually favored for frigate duels. As Captain David Porter was well aware, any captures made by *Essex* would have to be preceded by elaborate maneuvering to bring the enemy into extremely close range. This involved exceptional teamwork, which Porter nourished by the unusual procedure of taking his crew into his confidence before going into action.

On July 3, 1812, *Essex* set out on a lone cruise in search of prizes.

The hunting was good. On the eighth day out, she encountered H. M. S. *Minerva* (32) convoying seven transports from Barbados to Quebec. The contact was made at night, in dim moonlight. Before the British knew that there was a raider about, Porter had cut out a transport with 197 soldiers aboard. Having extracted his first prize, he sailed back to fight *Minerva* and, if possible, take the rest. It was not possible. The *Minerva*'s captain, not knowing of Porter's short-range armament, prudently refused to come out and fight, but kept his convoy tightly grouped. *Essex* had to be content with her single capture. In the nine weeks which followed, there were to be nine more.

On August 13, *Essex* sighted a British sloop-of-war, H. M. S. *Alert* (20). Knowing that this smaller vessel would not dare approach an enemy frigate and could probably escape in the light winds then blowing, Porter resorted to guile. The guns were run in and the gun ports closed. All sails were set, but drags were hung astern to slow the frigate's speed. A course was set directly away from the *Alert*. The general effect was that of a sluggish merchantman trying to escape.

Alert did not live up to her name. She came sailing boldly up to make a capture, discharging a ragged broadside, which did little damage. Her crew cheered as she drew alongside, then gasped in dismay as the gun ports opened and they found themselves staring at the ugly snouts of *Essex*' heavy carronades. A single broadside left *Alert* a shattered wreck—the first British warship to be captured in the War of 1812.

7.

Captain James Dacres of His Majesty's navy was not popular with Americans. In the seizing of ships and cargoes and in the impressment of seamen who might possibly have been British, Dacres and his frigate *Guerriere* had consistently gone beyond the call of duty. Disdaining modesty, he had boasted far and wide, in the years before the war, that his ship was the best frigate in the world and that he and his crew could beat any American warship and compel its surrender within fifteen minutes. In the salons of Baltimore, he had offered the wager of a fine hat with any American captain who thought that his ship could contend with the *Guerriere* for a quarter of an hour.

On the afternoon of August 19, 1812, *Guerriere* was sailing along the coast of Nova Scotia, inbound for Halifax. A frigate was spotted to the north—a frigate which came on so boldly that Captain Dacres concluded that it could not be an American ship but must be Dutch. "The better he behaves, the more honor we shall have by taking him."

The approaching frigate was U. S. S. *Constitution* (44), commanded by Captain Isaac Hull, one of "Preble's Boys." Hull was risking more than his naval reputation, more than defeat and death or capture, in sailing along the hostile shores of British Canada. There was also the matter of a probable court-martial. In Boston, he had heard reports that all American warships were to be held safely in port until further notice. Closing his eyes and ears to all such suggestions, he had put to sea a mere matter of minutes before the unwanted instructions, now in the form of official orders, could be served upon him.

As *Constitution* sailed serenely toward the *Guerriere,* Captain Dacres prepared to deliver a raking broadside into the bow and across her deck. Just as the order to fire was given, the American ship yawed and swung sideways, widening the range and spoiling the aim. Quickly, *Guerriere* came about to present her port battery. Once more, *Constitution* yawed, spoiling the effect. Apparently, this Yankee skipper was too smart to sail straight into raking fire. Very well! *Guerriere* straightened her course, prepared for activity broadside-to-broadside.

Constitution's guns, meanwhile, had remained ominously silent. Now, as the ships surged along side by side, Isaac Hull gave the order for which his crew had been eagerly waiting. "Now, boys," he yelled, "pour it into them." At the same time, he leaped high in the air, splitting his tight uniform pants. All of the starboard guns roared as one.

Guerriere reeled from the blow, her decks strewn with dead and dying men. Another broadside, and her towering mizzenmast went by the board, dragging in the sea and pulling the bow around to starboard. "Damn it, Jack," called a gunner, "we've made a brig of her. Give her another and make her a sloop."

"No!" shouted Hull. "No! No! No! Aim for the yellow streak, where her guns are. Hull her, boys!"

Hull's boys hulled her. *Guerriere*'s sides were smashed, her guns dismounted, her men killed. As *Constitution* forged ahead, Hull brought his ship across the opponent's bow, raking heavily with his starboard batteries. Yawing, he came back, raking with his port guns. So close were the vessels at this point that *Guerriere*'s bowsprit became fouled in the rigging of *Constitution*'s mizzenmast. Men on both ships gathered for boarding but were unable to do it because of the rough weather and the heavy volume of musketry fire.

Swinging in the wind, the ships parted. As they did, *Guerriere*'s foremast toppled and fell, dragging with it the mainmast. She was now a helpless hulk, rolling heavily in the troughs of the waves and taking water through her gun ports. *Constitution* drew off briefly to make repairs, then came back to complete her conquest. As she crossed her opponent's bow, preparing to rake, the British colors came down in surrender.

Captain Dacres, himself painfully wounded, came aboard the *Constitution* and proffered his sword to Captain Hull. "No, no, Captain," said Hull, "I'll not take a sword from one who knows so well how to use it. But—I'll trouble you for that hat."

To Hull's distress, *Guerriere* was too badly shattered to be taken in as a prize. She was a sinking wreck. After a few unsuccessful attempts at salvage, she was set afire and abandoned. Presently, she blew up and was seen no more.

Word of the battle was received with joy in Boston and with dismay in London. The Lords of the Admiralty were thunderstruck. Such things could not be! Since the beginning of the war with France, two hundred British ships had won sea fights against opponents of approximately equal power without a single loss to the enemy. This could be no mere frigate that had defeated *Guerriere!* The official reports paid Humphreys a subtle compliment by speaking of the frigate he had designed as "a disguised ship-of-the-line."

The real answer to *Constitution*'s victory lay in careful preparation. Captain Hull had trained his men well in gunnery, devoting precious powder to target practice. This was a "wasteful" activity which the British navy at that time would not countenance. It was this factor, rather than the comparatively small difference in weight of broadside, that accounted for the much greater damage to the British ship and to the fact that *Guerriere* suffered 79 casualties to *Constitution*'s 14.

A word should also be said for the stout live-oak planking on *Constitution*'s sides. Observing a British cannon ball which bounced off and fell into the sea, one of the American gunners called out, "Look, boys! She has sides of iron!"

From that time on, the U. S. frigate *Constitution* was familiarly known in the navy as "Old Ironsides."

8.

There was soon to be more bad news for the Admiralty and for the readers of the London *Times*.

Out of Boston went Commodore Rodgers with the two frigates *President* and *Congress*. Their cruise along the Canadian coast was a disappointment, for the hunting proved to be poor. Only one prize proved really significant—the Royal Mail packet *Swallow,* carrying the governor's pay chest with $80,000 in cash. The news of this capture infuriated the British. Their blockading warships off the American coast were called north to guard the approaches to Canada. This was a mistake. Certain tightly contained United States warships seized the occasion to slip out to sea and do a little hunting of their own.

Among the ships thus freed was the sloop-of-war *Wasp* (18), commanded by Jacob Jones, one of "Preble's Boys." Jones slipped out of Chesapeake Bay and headed north, taking two British freighters almost at once. He then encountered a storm which broke his jib-boom, and was busy making repairs when a British convoy hove in sight guarded by the brig *Frolic* (20). At once, Jones hoisted sail and bore down on the British warship, which as resolutely came on to meet him.

This was no battle of elaborate maneuver. The sea was heaving with the terrific swells left from the storm, thus precluding precise operation and accurate long-range gunnery. Beam to beam, so close that the cannon rammers of one ship sometimes touched the side of the other, the two slugged it out. Captain Whinyates of the *Frolic,* following rule-of-thumb, ordered his broadsides fired on the up-roll. Jones, trying something new that he and Isaac Hull had devised, fired on the down-roll. As a result, *Wasp*'s rigging was soon in bad shape, with the upper parts of her two after masts shot away, while *Frolic*'s hull was badly battered from the destructive plunging fire of Jones's cannons.

Little by little, despite her damaged masts, *Wasp* edged ahead until she was able to swing across her opponent's bow. A raking broadside swept the *Frolic*'s deck; then the American boarders swarmed across the rail. An awesome sight met their eyes. On the brig's deck stood only four living men—the steersman at the wheel and three wounded officers, who hastened to throw down their swords in token of surrender. The down-curving fire of the down-roll broadsides had been effective beyond the wildest dreams of its inventors.

Jones's triumph was short-lived. Over the horizon came the British ship-of-the-line *Poictiers* (74). Wrecked *Frolic* was quickly recaptured, and crippled *Wasp* was run down after a short chase. Her next trip to sea would be as H. M. S. *Peacock.* The spoils went to the British, but much of the credit went to Jacob Jones and the men of the gallant *Wasp.*

9.

Meanwhile, the frigate *United States* (44), under Captain Stephen Decatur, was cruising in the vicinity of the Canary Islands. On October 25, 1812—exactly one week after the *Wasp-Frolic* duel—she encountered His Majesty's frigate *Macedonian* (38), commanded by Captain Samuel Carden, a martinet famous for his zeal in impressment. Both frigates were new and in prime condition, the American vessel having a slight advantage in size and in weight of broadside.

At the very outset, Carden made a serious error; he mistook the *United States* for the light frigate *Essex,* which he knew to be principally armed with short-range carronades. Being to windward and having the faster ship, he would stay at a distance and cut this helpless foe to pieces with his own long 18-pounders. It was with this thought in mind that he fired his first broadside at maximum range.

The hour which followed was a time of horror for everyone on the British ship. Extreme range for Carden's 18-pounders was easy distance for Decatur's 24's. Well-trained American gunners, firing carefully by divisions, as Decatur had taught them, systematically battered every part of the *Macedonian.* A British gunner later testified: "It was like some tremendous thunderstorm, whose deafening roar is attended by incessant streaks of lightning, carrying death in every flash. Only, in our case, the scene was rendered more terrible by the presence of torrents of blood."

Realizing his error, Carden tried to close with this dreadful opponent who was murdering his ship at long range. On he came, subjecting his ship to the horrors of raking fire in order to get close enough to strike back with effect. It was a vain effort. *Macedonian*'s sails were cut to ribbons; her mizzenmast cracked, her main-topmast, mainyard, and fore-topmast brought down; her hull splintered; her crew a company of dying men. Decatur, having faded away to keep the range open, now brought *United States* into close quarters, sailing across the enemy's unprotected stern. The anticipated raking broadside never came. It was not needed. Carden had understood the implied message to surrender or be blasted from the sea. He lowered his flag.

An American lieutenant came aboard, recognizing at once a British naval surgeon whom he had known before the war. "How do you do, Doctor?"

"I have enough to do. You have made wretched work for us with your guns."

"May we send some of our surgeons to help you?"

The Briton looked up, startled. "I should think they would have work enough tending to your own wounded."

"Oh, no. There were only seven, and their injuries were dressed long ago."

"Seven! Dear God, we had at least a hundred!"

Later, aboard the *United States,* Captain Carden was in despair. "I am undone! The first British officer to strike his flag to an American! What will they do to me?"

Decatur had the pleasure of telling him of Dacres' surrender of the *Guerriere.* As neither captain yet knew about the *Wasp* and the *Frolic,* that engagement could not enter their conversation. But, for what consolation it could give him, Carden learned that he was not the first!

Wailed the London *Times,* "A national disgrace! In the name of God, what was done?"

In the seaport cities of the United States, joy reigned supreme. Not only had Decatur beaten *Macedonian;* he had brought her home. She came sailing into Newport Harbor with the stars and stripes flying above her British flag. "A bird in the hand is worth two in the bush, and a frigate brought home for all to see is worth two sunk in distant waters." When once again *Macedonian* sailed, she was an American frigate under Captain Jacob Jones, who had recently been exchanged and brought home from England.

10.

The honeymoon was not yet over.

Captain William Bainbridge now had the *Constitution.* Isaac Hull had been removed from command by Congressional order after he had sailed from Boston in apparent violation of instructions and before word had been received of his victorious contest with *Guerriere.* A good man had been lost to the navy, but at this point good men were more plentiful than good ships. There was nothing wrong with William Bainbridge except his luck, which had been consistently bad to date.

Early on the morning of December 29, 1812, *Constitution* was coasting along the Brazilian shore, near the equator. A distant sail was sighted, H. M. S. *Java,* (38), formerly the French *Renommée,* one of the fastest ships in the world. Being on the edge of neutral territorial waters, Bainbridge set his course to the southeast, away from land. Veteran Captain Henry Lambert of the *Java* followed, gaining rapidly on what he took to be a fleeing vessel.

The firing opened at long range. It did not take long for Captain Bainbridge to realize that he was up against a bold and skilful opponent sailing a much faster ship. *Java* was to windward. Under the reduced battle sails on the two ships, she gained steadily on the *Constitution,* crawling ahead and threatening to sweep around the American's bow for raking action. Bainbridge boldly countered by hoisting additional—and vulnerable—large sails and by skilfully sailing an inside course to keep broadside opposed by broadside.

As the action continued, both vessels were hit hard. A musket ball wounded Bainbridge in the hip, but he would not leave his post. *Java*'s sides were being splintered by the heavy blows of the American 24-pounders, but she continued to maintain a rapid rate of fire as her captain sought once more to outfoot *Constitution* in order to gain a raking position. A British cannon ball screeched across *Constitution*'s quarterdeck, shattering her wheel, killing the steersman, and sending a heavy copper bolt singing like a bullet deep into Bainbridge's leg. Despite his agony, the captain managed to hold himself upright against the rail while he shouted directions to the men two decks below to steer by the tiller ropes. It was an awkward arrangement, and it might have proved fatal had not *Java* received a compensating wound; her jib boom and the end of her bowsprit were shot away, making her hard to bring about.

The climax came when Captain Lambert tried to turn his vessel into the wind. *Java* hung in stays, bow to the wind, her sails flapping. Quickly *Constitution* slid across her opponent's bow, firing one raking broadside, then another. As *Java* picked up a little forward motion, Lambert tried to swing her bow against *Constitution*'s side in order to board. The ships brushed and parted, while Lambert and many of his men went down before the rifles of the American Marines. At about the same time, *Java*'s foremast tottered and plunged overside. A few more broadsides and the mainmast went, then the mizzenmast. *Java* was a helpless hulk. She surrendered with 161 casualties to *Constitution*'s 34. So badly was she shattered that Bainbridge found it necessary to burn her where she lay.

The news struck Great Britain like a portent of doom. Cried the London *Pilot:* "The Public will learn, with sentiments which we shall not presume to anticipate, that a third British frigate has struck her flag to an American. This is an occurrence that calls for serious reflection—this and the fact that Lloyd's list contains notices of upwards of five hundred British vessels captured in seven months by the Americans. Five hundred merchantmen and three frigates! Can these statements be true? Anyone who had predicted such a result of an American war this time last year would have been treated as a madman or a traitor. He would have been told that long ere seven months had elapsed the American flag would be swept from the seas, the contemptible navy of the United States annihilated. Yet up to the present not a single American frigate has struck her flag."

Echoed the staid London *Times,* "Good God! Can such things be?"

Insult was added to injury in February, 1813. Captain James Lawrence, commanding the U. S. sloop-of-war *Hornet* (18), encountered the British brig *Peacock* (18) off the northern coast of South America. The first broadsides were fired as the ships passed in opposite directions. So accurate was the American gunnery that Captain William Peake of the *Peacock* quickly abandoned the idea of a gunnery duel and swung in to attempt a boarding. He was raked as he tried it, then raked twice more as *Hornet* swung around his stern. Captain Peake himself was torn in two by a cannon ball, and a third of his crew were down. The British flag was lowered, then quickly raised upside-down as a signal of distress.

The British signal was in no way misleading. *Peacock* was in bad shape, hulled in numerous places along the waterline. Scarcely had the boats from *Hornet* reached her than down she went, taking with her nine of her crew members and three men from the *Hornet,* who had just come aboard.

11.

Americans everywhere were intoxicated by the unexpected successes scored by their little navy. The fact that these were small, individual warships—frigates, sloops, and brigs—was widely overlooked. They were American ships, and they were beating comparable units from the hitherto-all-winning British navy. Hurrah for America, the new Queen of the Seas!

Even Congress caught the contagion. Money was appropriated for new war vessels, including four mighty ships-of-the-line. If individual American warships could defeat British units, what was to prevent American fleets from sweeping the British from the seas?

Actually, there was much to prevent any such outcome. A few well-designed, well-built, well-handled units of the new American navy had won startling victories over slightly inferior units of the vast, complacent, and overconfident British navy, still principally preoccupied with the continued suppression of the sea power of Napoleonic France. But Britain was still the ruler of the seas, with a navy incomparably stronger than any other. Now that she knew the danger and the ability of the foe she faced, she would be unlikely to repeat her earlier mistakes.

It was well for the morale of the United States that the encouraging victories upon the sea had been won. On land, the story was very different. General William Hull (Isaac's uncle) had surrendered Detroit without the firing of a shot. American armies under Generals Dearborn and Van Renssalaer, attempting to invade Canada, had been driven out unceremoniously. Henry Clay's boast about his thousand Kentucky riflemen had been made to look more than a little silly.

Now, upon the waters of the deep, a chastened and angry Great Britain was preparing to put an all-too-successful upstart nation in its place.

12.

James Lawrence, hero of the *Hornet*'s victory over the *Peacock,* was rewarded by being given command of the frigate *Chesapeake* (38), being refitted in Boston. His was a green and untried crew, but he had orders to put to sea at once. He also had a challenge from Captain Philip Broke, aboard H. M. frigate *Shannon* (38), lying outside Boston Harbor. Broke had an experienced, well-seasoned crew, trained (against specific Admiralty orders) in the use of the ship's guns.

The challenge was accepted on June 1, 1813. *Chesapeake* found

Shannon waiting for her outside the harbor. Knowing that he would probably be outmaneuvered if he tried fancy tactics, Lawrence drove his ship directly for his enemy. Broke waited for him. Fire was opened at close range with the two ships sailing side by side, *Chesapeake* to windward. From the very outset both ships suffered heavily.

The windward position proved to be more of a handicap than advantage to the *Chesapeake*. The smoke from the broadsides, drifting downwind, hid the men on the *Shannon*'s deck from the riflemen in *Chesapeake*'s fighting tops, while the men on the American decks made clear targets. Lawrence himself was hit in the hip, and many of his men fell from the accurate fire of the British sharpshooters.

Far more important were the effects of *Shannon*'s excellent artillery fire. *Chesapeake*'s forestays were carried away, causing her headsails to collapse. Her head swung away, exposing her stern to vicious raking fire. In the hurricane of shot which came aboard, most of the men on the quarterdeck were felled. The ship drifted helplessly, her stern quarter coming to rest against the *Shannon*'s bow. Led by Broke himself, the British crew came leaping aboard, cutlasses aswing. "Come on, *Shannons!*"

Just as the boarders came over the rail, Captain Lawrence went down with a bullet through his abdomen. He was carried below, while the surviving members of the *Chesapeake*'s crew gathered themselves at the waist of the ship under Second Lieutenant George Budd to organize what defense they could.

Below decks, Lawrence became aware of the cessation of firing from *Chesapeake*'s guns. Despite his agony, he tried to struggle up and give commands. There was no one to hear him but the surgeon's mate who was attending him. "Leave me," the dying Lawrence cried. "Go on deck. Tell the men to fire faster and not give up the ship. The colors shall wave while I live."

"Don't give up the ship!" It was a motto destined to endure, to be adopted by the American navy. But on this day, it could not be honored. Lieutenant Budd and his men fought furiously, cutlass against cutlass. Budd himself struck down Captain Broke, wounding him so seriously that the British officer's active naval career ended on the *Chesapeake*'s deck. It was to no avail. Budd was killed, his men subdued. Fifteen minutes after the firing of the first gun, *Chesapeake* was a captured vessel.

Unlucky *Chesapeake!* First the *Leopard,* then the *Shannon*—two of the toughest frigates in the entire British navy!

13.

Out from New York, carrying a new American minister to France, went the U. S. brig *Argus* (20), commanded by William Allen. She crossed without incident, landed her passenger, then embarked on a spectacular raiding voyage in the waters surrounding the British Isles.

Argus did well, taking nineteen prizes within sight of the British shores. The twentieth proved to be her undoing. It was a merchant-man loaded with rare wines. The temptation proved to be too great. Officers and crew imbibed heavily and became more than a little tipsy. They were in this rosy state when H. M. brig *Pelican* (20) came upon them.

It seems probable that, had it not been for the wine, Captain Allen would have avoided battle with this armed and equal opponent, as a good raider should. Instead, he awaited *Pelican*'s approach down the wind. As the ships exchanged broadsides, Allen went down with a shattered thigh. No sooner had Lieutenant Watson taken charge than he, too, went down. Second Lieutenant James Allen took over, han-dling the ship brilliantly. As *Pelican* tried to rake, Allen swung *Argus* squarely across her bow. A well-directed broadside at this point might have brought victory, but the ragged little burst put out by *Argus*' tipsy gunners was anything but well directed. Lieutenant Allen fell, struck by a musket ball, and at the same time *Argus* went out of control, her after braces shot away. *Pelican* raked her again and again, making casualties of more than a quarter of her crew. Then the ships came together, and British boarders swept across the rail. With no officers left to organize hand-to-hand resistance, the crew surren-dered.

Britain had taken two American warships in succession, thus clos-ing the gap and evening the score somewhat. Far more important, British warships now appeared in large numbers off the coast of the United States, tightening the blockade and threatening to smother the United States Navy in its home ports.

14.

"Lucky little *Enterprise*," once the fastest ship in the American navy, had meanwhile been undergoing some highly questionable tinkering in the Portsmouth navy yard. Her fast and effective fore-and-aft schooner rig had been replaced by the slower and more ponderous sail equipment of a brig. In partial compensation, her striking power had been increased. Instead of the twelve 6-pounders which she had once carried she now had two 9-pounders and fourteen 18-pounder carronades. Her new commander, Lieutenant William Burrows, was by no means sure that he liked the alterations. Early in September, 1813, he took *Enterprise* out to see what she could do.

On September 5, off the coast of Maine, Burrows encountered the British brig *Boxer* (14), under Commander Samuel Blythe.

William Burrows was not a man to rush blindly into combat. For two hours he sailed a parallel course to the enemy ship, fading away when Blythe tried to close, carefully evaluating the performances of the two vessels. For the double purpose of improving *Enterprise*'s trim and widening her angle of fire, he had one of his long 9-pounders moved aft and run out through one of the windows in his stern cabin. These maneuvers troubled his crew, who sent him a written memo of their willingness to fight.

The crew need not have worried. Burrows was one of Preble's Boys, and was willing enough to give battle when he felt that conditions were right. After his two-hour test, he concluded that the time had come. Instead of continuing to veer away, *Enterprise* headed for *Boxer,* which could be seen coming on sturdily while crew members nailed her colors to the mast.

Both ships withheld their fire until they were side by side, at a distance of only thirty feet. Simultaneous broadsides crashed out. Commander Blythe was killed instantly by a ball from an American carronade. Burrows took a grapeshot in the thigh, which severed an artery. Though dying, he insisted upon issuing orders as he lay in his blood upon the deck.

The plan of action which Burrows had drawn up in advance worked to perfection. *Enterprise,* slightly the faster ship, forged slowly ahead. As she cut at a slight angle across *Boxer*'s bow, the stern 9-pounder raked the deck of the British ship. Taking advantage of the resulting confusion, *Enterprise* swung around and raked her opponent with a broadside from bow to stern, then repeated the maneuver on the other tack. *Boxer*'s main topmast came down. With more than a third of her crew dead or wounded, she surrendered.

Boxer's surrender was done by hailing, since her nailed-up colors could not be lowered. Seeing the enemy's flag still flying, the dying Burrows murmured a wish to have it. A sailor, sent over in the first boat, climbed the *Boxer*'s rigging, tore loose the flag, and brought it back to his captain.

Together, *Enterprise* and *Boxer* put in to Portland, Maine. There, the two dead captains were buried side by side, with a single commemorative stone for both graves. In later years, Henry Wadsworth Longfellow was much impressed by this stone, uniting in death two former enemies. In his poem, "To My Lost Youth," he wrote sadly of "the sea-fight far away."

15 .

While the United States Navy was experiencing its early successes on the salty seas and its later strangulation from blockade, affairs of some importance were taking place on the Great Lakes. These fresh-water seas were effectively insulated by land from the overwhelming might of British sea power. The British in Canada and the Americans in the United States had to start virtually from scratch in their struggle for the control of the vital inland waterway upon which the fate of a continent might well depend.

The Duke of Wellington, busily employed in Europe combating the armies of Napoleon, nevertheless took time to write some words of sage advice concerning this distant area of war: "Any offensive operation founded upon Canada must be preceded by the establishment of a naval superiority on the Lakes. . . . The defense of Canada and the cooperation of the Indians depends upon the navigation of the Lakes."

Both the British and the Americans would have done well to have heeded the words of the Iron Duke.

For the British, access to the upper Great Lakes was practical only by way of the St. Lawrence River and Lake Ontario. This lake—the lowest and most easterly of the chain—can logically be considered the key to the entire Great Lakes area. The British possessed two bases on Ontario, one at Kingston, where the St. Lawrence enters the lake, the other at York (now Toronto), near the lake's western end. The Americans had their principal base at Sackett's Harbor, on the eastern shore, and had a fort at Oswego.

When the war began, the British had on Lake Ontario a fleet of six warships, including the corvette *Royal George* (22), two sloops, and three schooners. On July 19, 1812, this fleet, under Commodore Earle, appeared off Sackett's Harbor, demanding the surrender of the town under penalty of its complete destruction.

In the harbor lay the brig *Oneida* (16), the only American warship on Lake Ontario. Her commander, Lieutenant Melancthon Woolsey, had wisely been providing for the impending attack long before the British ships appeared. Knowing the folly of opposing the eighty guns of the six British ships with the sixteen guns of his own slow-sailing *Oneida,* he had wisely anchored his ship with her port battery commanding the harbor mouth. The eight guns of her starboard battery he had taken ashore and emplaced, thus effectively doubling his ship's firepower. He had also refurbished the town's only fort, restoring to usability a long-neglected 32-pounder, two 9's, and two 6's. By these moves, he had stretched his thin resources for defense to the utmost.

Had Commodore Earle acted boldly and aggressively, it is hard to see how Sackett's Harbor could have held out for long. Neither the artillery nor the manpower was sufficient to withstand an all-out assault. Earle, however, played his cards poorly. For two hours, his ships lay off the harbor mouth, conducting an ineffective cannonade. The defenders replied as best they could. The siege ended when the *Royal George* was carelessly permitted to swing her stern toward the fort. A well-aimed ball from the 32-pounder raked her from stern to bow. At that, Earle withdrew his fleet, leaving Sackett's Harbor untaken and virtually undamaged. Melancthon Woolsey had served his country well.

16.

Soon after the successful defense of Sackett's Harbor, Commodore Isaac Chauncey was put in charge of the American forces on the Great Lakes. He proved to be an excellent builder and organizer, quickly providing a formidable little fleet made up of the sloop *Madison* (20), the brig *Oneida* (14), and eleven armed schooners of from one to ten guns each. In spite of some similar activity on the part of the British, the balance of power on Lake Ontario now favored the Americans.

Unfortunately for the American cause, Chauncey proved to be timid in using the fine force he had built up. Knowing that Kingston was the vital point upon which British control of the lake depended, but fearing groundlessly that the base might have been reinforced without his knowledge, he decided to pass up Kingston in favor of a raid on York. This was a minor objective but was known to be weakly defended.

On April 27, 1813, Chauncey's flotilla appeared before York and began a spirited bombardment of the forts. Thus beset from the ships, the garrison was unable to prevent the landing of the assault force of 1,700 American soldiers under General Zebulon Pike, supplemented by about 400 sailors from the fleet. The 700 British defenders were driven back, and the town was taken.

The American casualties, to this point, had been very light. Ironically, with resistance all but wiped out, they suddenly became enormous. The magazine of a captured British fort blew up, killing no fewer than 250 Americans, including General Pike. The result of this misfortune was a burst of vindictiveness on the part of the victors. The government buildings in York were set afire, as were some ships in the stocks. There were looting and brutality. A seed of bitterness was sown.

Advancing to the Niagara region, Chauncey was in the midst of launching a promising campaign when he received word that a British force from Kingston was besieging his home base at Sackett's Harbor. Back he rushed, hoping to arrive in time to save his base and his largest vessel, the corvette *General Pike* (24), which was under construction there.

Commodore Chauncey might far better have continued his Niagara campaign, for he was not needed at Sackett's Harbor. The attack, launched by a British squadron under Sir James Lucas Yeo and an expeditionary force under Sir George Prevost, had already failed before the American squadron could arrive. As Prevost's regulars had landed, the American militia had fled, but the American regulars had not. These had defended their little blockhouse and stockade so vigorously that Prevost's men had quickly become discouraged and had sailed for home. The sole result of the attack on Sackett's Harbor had been to take the pressure off the British garrisons in the Niagara region.

The remainder of the war on Lake Ontario consisted of indecisive naval brushes, which should not be dignified by the name of battles. Several times, the fleets of Chauncey and Yeo met on the surface of the lake. Each commander, it seems, had acquired an exaggerated respect for the other. As a result, whenever they met both tended to "edge away" toward safety. Nothing decisive happened in any of these "actions."

In May, 1814, the British made what might have been an important move, had it been followed up. A five-ship squadron under Yeo appeared unexpectedly off Oswego, bombarded the fort, and landed an 800-man expeditionary force. The American garrison was driven inland, away from the town. The American fort was destroyed, the barracks burned, and a damaged American warship raised, repaired, and taken. With victory in his hands, Yeo then sailed away, leaving Oswego open to immediate American reoccupation.

The rest of the war was spent by the British at Kingston and the Americans at Sackett's Harbor rushing work on rival ships-of-the-line, neither of which was ever to see service.

17.

The fate of Lake Erie and of the upper lakes beyond was supposed to depend upon victory by one side or the other on Lake Ontario. When such a victory failed to materialize, the center of gravity shifted to the shores and waters of Lake Erie.

At the beginning of the war, the only American warship on Lake Erie was the small brig *Adams,* armed with fourteen 6-pounders. When General William Hull surrendered Detroit, the *Adams* fell into the hands of the British, who named her *Detroit,* after the location of their bloodless victory. She was subsequently moved to Fort Erie, near the eastern end of the lake, where she was joined by the smaller brig *Caledonia,* mounting three swivel guns.

Within sight of Fort Erie, on the other side of the mouth of the Niagara River, was a small American base at Black Rock (now Buffalo). Here a group of men under Commander Jesse D. Elliott was hard at work converting four lake schooners into gunboats. Before dawn on October 8, 1812—the day after the arrival of the British warships at Fort Erie—Commander Elliott took a force of men in two large rowboats to make a surprise attack on the brigs. The men aboard the *Detroit* were caught unawares and could put up no resistance, but those on the *Caledonia,* alerted by the noise, resisted strongly before they, too, were overwhelmed.

It proved easier to take the two brigs than to remove them safely. Wind and current were adverse. After much hard labor and some excitement, *Caledonia* was worked back near enough to Black Rock so that she could be beached under the protection of the American guns there. *Detroit,* though, ran aground at a point within the range of both the British and the American batteries. Moving all his guns to the side facing the British, Elliott maintained a vigorous cannonade until his ammunition was exhausted. The British, having a plentiful supply, kept right on firing, forcing the Americans to abandon the vessel, taking some of her cannons with them in their boats. Presently, boats from Fort Erie reached the stranded brig, and the British had her once again. It did them little good, though, for the batteries at Black Rock opened up on them and forced them out. In the end, the *Detroit* was completely destroyed.

18.

Having begun on such an auspicious note, Commander Elliott naturally expected that he would retain the American command on Lake Erie. To his vast disappointment, he did not. During the winter of 1812–13, a new commodore, Oliver Hazard Perry, made his appearance, having been appointed by President Madison at the earnest urging of a Senator from Rhode Island. Naturally enough, Elliott did not relish the prospect of being placed under the command of this newcomer.

Perry established his headquarters at Presqu' Isle, the crescent-shaped peninsula which now forms the harbor of Erie, Pennsylvania. Here, an energetic master builder named Noah Brown was hard at work on two American brigs. Brown had no seasoned timber, so he cut his beams and planks from green forest trees. He had no nails, so he used wooden pegs. The important thing was that he made progress. What little time he and his men had left over was devoted to converting three little lake schooners into gunboats. Perry gave Brown all the support and encouragement he could, while sending frantic messages east and south for men, arms, and equipment.

The British were now definitely ahead in the arms race on Lake Erie. At Detroit and nearby Malden, Trafalgar veteran R. H. Barclay had the sloop *Queen Charlotte* (17); two brigs, *Lady Prevost* (13) and *Hunter* (10); a schooner, *Little Belt* (3); and a sloop, *Chippeway* (1). They had, in addition, a nearly completed sloop, the *Detroit* (20). This force was all together, and was largely ready. Perry's was still in process of formation and was divided between Presqu' Isle and Black Rock.

The forces on the lake had their counterparts on the shore. British General Henry A. Procter held Detroit. Facing him, a little to the south, was the American army of William Henry Harrison. Until naval control of the lake should be secured, Harrison dared make no move toward the enemy. It would be all too easy for the British fleet to land forces in his rear and cut him off.

In the early spring of 1813, American control of Lake Erie seemed at best an idle dream. Barclay's British fleet controlled the lake, and unless he blundered the British commander seemed assured of continued domination. At this stage, it would be easy enough for him to take lightly held Presqu' Isle and destroy the American preparations there. Even if he did not do this, a tight blockade would keep the forces at Black Rock from joining Perry's little fleet. Finally, there was the question of the bar across Presqu' Isle harbor's mouth. The American vessels would have to be moved across this in stripped condition, gunless and defenseless, easy prey for Barclay's squadron. Not one blunder but three were necessary for American supremacy!

To get Elliott's ships safely away from Black Rock, it was necessary to drive the British from Fort Erie, at the southern end of the Niagara River. This, in turn, involved dislodging them from the supporting stronghold, Fort George, near the river's northern end. With the assistance of Chauncey's Ontario fleet, fresh from its raid on York, Perry and his men were able to take Fort George by assault on May 27, 1813. Fort Erie was abandoned the next day without a fight.

There was still a calculated risk to be taken. Barclay's British fleet was prowling Lake Erie with more than ample force to overwhelm and destroy the five little ships. Wind and current failed to cooperate. It was necessary to tow the ships up the river and along the lake shore with teams of oxen. Perry, seriously ill with fever, lay aboard one of the ships. Foot by plodding foot the ships crept along the shore while the American officers scanned the horizon, hoping against hope that Barclay's sails would not appear.

On June 1, still undetected, Perry's little flotilla reached Presqu' Isle. One by one, the ships were unloaded and floated over the shallow bar. The last schooner was passing over when a patch of white appeared on the horizon to the north. Barclay had arrived too late!

The British commander still had an opportunity to take Presqu' Isle and destroy the nascent American flotilla. With this in mind, he consulted with General Procter. Procter, however, was involved in a project of his own—an attack on Fort Meigs, some distance east of the end of Lake Erie. The attack on Meigs was a failure. By the time it was over, Perry had received some reinforcements, so that his base was no longer defenseless. Once more, Barclay had missed an opportunity.

In time, the American brigs *Lawrence* and *Niagara* were completed at Presqu' Isle. In ships and guns, Perry's force was now better than equal to Barclay's. The trouble was that he couldn't use it. To cross the bar at the entrance to Presqu' Isle Harbor, the ships had to be lightened by the removal of all guns, stores, and munitions and then carefully hauled and worked across the shallow section. While in transit, every ship would be as helpless as an unarmed fat man worming his way through a tight-fitting cellar window. There, off the harbor mouth, lay Barclay's squadron, ready to pounce at the first sign of activity on the part of the trapped Americans.

On August 2, for reasons which have never been made clear, Barclay committed his third blunder by sailing away. At once, Perry swung into action. The *Lawrence* was stripped of all heavy equipment and towed to the bar. As she still would not pass over it, Perry resorted to a trick which he had picked up years before in a Dutch shipyard—the use of "camels." Two large scows were sunk to the very tops of their hulls, one on either side of the brig. Timbers were run through the warship's gun ports and across the decks of the scows. When the scows were pumped out, they raised the *Lawrence* high enough for passage. With frantic haste, the same method was applied to the other warships.

When Barclay returned on August 5 to resume his blockade, he found all of the American squadron except the *Niagara* outside the bar and apparently ready for action. Discouraged at the formidable appearance of his enemies, he fired a few long-range shots, then sailed away to the west, leaving Perry free to get the *Niagara* out without interference.

Commodore Barclay had obligingly made the three errors necessary to give Perry a chance to contest for mastery of the lake.

19.

During the next two weeks, Oliver Hazard Perry put his fleet into condition for action against the British. In this, he received splendid cooperation from Commodore Chauncey, who sent him more than 200 seamen, and from General Harrison, who sent him 100 Kentucky riflemen. On August 18, he sailed westward, directly to the British base at Malden. Barclay saw him but did not come out to fight. Not venturing to attack the enemy's fleet and its protective forts at the same time, Perry then sailed south about thirty miles to the Bass Islands, where he instituted a tight blockade of the western end of Lake Erie.

It did not take long for Perry's blockade to have the desired result. Deprived of supplies brought down the lake, Procter's troops at Detroit and Barclay's sailors at Malden began to suffer from shortages of food and other necessities. Either Barclay must come out and try to win control of the lake or the British must give up their strategic outposts and their stranglehold on the upper lakes. True to the traditions of the British navy, Barclay came out to fight.

In mid-morning of September 10, the fleets sighted one another north of Put-in Bay. The British line consisted of the *Chippeway* (1), the *Detroit* (19), the *Hunter* (10), the *Queen Charlotte* (17), the *Lady Prevost* (13), and the *Little Belt* (3). To counter this formation, Perry headed his line with the *Scorpion* (2) and the *Ariel* (4), to dispose of the *Chippeway*. Next came his flagship *Lawrence* (20), to engage Barclay's flagship *Detroit*. The *Caledonia* (3) was to take on the *Hunter*. The *Niagara* (20), under Elliott, was to match broadsides with the *Queen Charlotte*. At the end of the line, the *Somers* (2), the *Porcupine* (1), the *Tigress* (1), and the *Trippe* (1) were to try to contend with the *Lady Prevost* and the *Little Belt*. The Americans had three more ships, but the British had nine more guns, though they averaged smaller in size and in weight of projectiles.

For well over an hour, Perry maneuvered in an unsuccessful attempt to gain the windward position. At last, despairing of the effort, he set a converging course toward the British from leeward. "To windward or to leeward, they shall fight today!" Scarcely had he said this than the wind shifted to the southeast, giving him the windward position he desired.

Perry's excellent disposition of his ships did not hold up as the battle began. *Scorpion, Ariel, Lawrence,* and *Caledonia* held to their approaching course, but *Niagara* and the four little ships behind her veered off and ran parallel to the British line at extreme range. It has been alleged, though never proved, that Elliott, jealous of Perry, wished to dash into action at the eleventh hour, wrest victory from defeat, and gain the glory for himself. Perhaps timidity accounts for his actions, perhaps ineptness. Whatever the cause, his long-range activities accomplished little during the early stages of the battle except a waste of American ammunition.

Barclay was quick to take advantage of the break in the American line. As the *Lawrence* approached, the *Detroit* fired a ranging shot which fell short. Five minutes later, at 11:50 A.M., she fired again, scoring a telling hit. This was excellent gunnery, especially when one considers that the cannons of the newly built *Detroit* were not equipped with firing locks but had to be discharged by snapping pistols over the loose powder on the touch holes.

Detroit's second shot set loose the thunders of the battle. The small vessels in both lines were entirely ignored as targets in order to concentrate fire on the larger vessels. As a result, the *Lawrence* soon found herself swapping broadsides with the *Detroit* and the *Hunter* and also receiving an occasional hurtful blow from *Chippeway*'s single 9-pounder. The small American vessels *Scorpion* and *Ariel,* meanwhile, had taken advantageous positions off the head of the British line and engaged in raking fire until *Scorpion*'s 32-pounder, carelessly overloaded, smashed its own carriage and went crashing down a hatchway, while one of *Ariel*'s 12-pounders blew up and killed its gunners.

Seeing no sign of effective antagonism on the part of the *Niagara,* the captain of the *Queen Charlotte* now brought his vessel into the group which was pouring destruction into the *Lawrence.* Perry found his flagship's twenty guns opposed by forty-six on his three principal antagonists. Thanks to Elliott's failure to support, the original American superiority in armament had become a definite inferiority. The situation became still worse when the *Lady Prevost* added her thirteen guns to the arc of death.

Seldom has a crew received such punishment as did the men aboard the *Lawrence.* The sides of the ship were smashed and splintered. All but one of the guns in the starboard battery were put out of action. Of the 103 men aboard, 83 were casualties. There was no place of safety on the ship. Wounded men, awaiting the surgeon's attention, were wounded again, and some were killed, in the hospital ward. Unattended dead lay everywhere. The reddened decks were slippery, despite the sand which had been sprinkled over them. The shortage of able-bodied men at last became so serious that Perry had to send back into action any wounded who had enough life left in them to pull a line.

Amazing as it seems, the *Lawrence* was still fighting back against the circle of her foes after two hours and forty-five minutes of frantic action. Nor had she left her enemies unscathed.

Far to windward, virtually untouched, lay the reluctant *Niagara,* playing only a token part in the struggle. As the *Lawrence* came to the end of her resources, Perry—miraculously unwounded—took his twelve-year-old brother Matthew and a handful of sailors into a small boat and set out across the shell-splashed water. As his boat pulled away, Lieutenant Yarnell, to whom Perry had relinquished command of the *Lawrence,* threw down to him the blue-and-white battle flag bearing the motto, "Don't give up the ship!"

Aboard the *Detroit,* Commodore Barclay thought that he had won. Though the *Lawrence*'s American flag still flew, he felt that the hauling down of the battle flag and the evident move to abandon ship meant that the enemy had surrendered. Only when he saw that Perry was headed for the *Niagara* did he realize his mistake. A number of the British ships fired on the small boat, but only a single grapeshot took effect, tearing a hole in the planking and starting a small leak which Perry was able to check with the rolled-up fabric of his cloak.

Reaching the *Niagara* safely, Oliver Hazard Perry went into immediate action. Captain Elliott was sent in a small boat to organize the American gunboats and bring them into battle. Perry himself took over the *Niagara,* abruptly checking her retirement from action and driving her under full sail toward the heart of the battle.

The arrival of the fresh and unblooded *Niagara* spelled disaster for the battered British. Disdaining the raking fire to which she was subjected as she approached bow-on, the new American flagship sailed at right angles through the British line, followed by the four little gunboats under Elliott. Broadsides from her port battery raked *Hunter* and *Lady Prevost* from stern to bow. Off to starboard, *Detroit* and *Queen Charlotte* were trying frantically to maneuver so as to present their broadsides to this new enemy. Instead, they ran afoul of one another and drifted in helpless entanglement. *Niagara*'s starboard battery raked them from bow to stern, the heavy carronades causing tremendous damage at this short range. Meanwhile, the Kentucky riflemen in the *Niagara*'s fighting tops were pouring a devastating small-arms fire upon the British decks.

Such punishment could not be long resisted. Only eight minutes after Perry pierced the line, a hail from the *Detroit* announced her surrender. At about the same time, *Hunter*'s and *Lady Prevost*'s flags came down, and someone aboard *Queen Charlotte* was observed waving a white cloth on the end of a pike. *Chippeway* and *Little Belt* tried to escape in the confusion, but they were pursued by the busy little *Scorpion* and were brought back before nightfall.

An American officer, boarding the shattered *Detroit,* found Commodore Barclay in his cabin, suffering from three wounds. The British commander looked up sadly. "You are sent for my sword, sir."

"No, sir. I have come to take possession of the ship."

There was a moment of silence. "Well, sir," said Barclay, at last, "I would not have given sixpence for your squadron when I left the deck."

Using a flat cap for a desk, Commodore Oliver Hazard Perry dashed off an urgent message to General William Henry Harrison: "We have met the enemy and they are ours: two ships, two brigs, one schooner, and one sloop. Yours, with great respect and esteem, O. H. Perry."

The Battle of Lake Erie was the first naval conflict in which a battle line of American warships had contended formally with an enemy battle line. It was the first naval battle in which the British navy had lost an entire squadron to an enemy of comparable strength. Far more important, it broke Britain's hold upon the upper lakes and ruined a British plan to extend the borders of Canada southwestward through control of the western rivers.

Following receipt of Perry's note, General Harrison was able to launch an immediate attack on the British forces controlling the waterway between Lakes Erie and Huron. Proctor was driven from Detroit, was brought to bay at the Thames River, and was signally defeated. Among the British dead in this battle was Tecumseh, leader of the British-allied western Indians. The elimination of this powerful tribal leader considerably lessened the danger of Indian raids on American settlements. Thus the strengthening of the frontier against hostile redmen may be regarded as an important by-product of Perry's victory on Lake Erie.

20.

On October 28, 1812, the United States frigate *Essex,* Captain David Porter commanding, sailed from the Delaware in the hope of joining Bainbridge's squadron in the south Atlantic. The *Essex* was a strange ship, armed with forty 32-pound carronades but only six long guns, all 12-pounders. Like a short-armed prize fighter, she could deliver heavy blows at close range but was almost helpless against an opponent who chose to duel at a distance.

For a month and a half, *Essex* forged steadily southward, without incident. On December 12, a sail was sighted. She proved to be the British mail packet *Nocton,* laden with letters and with a very welcome cargo of $55,000 in gold and silver coins. This prize was sent home with a skeleton crew, but it never arrived, being retaken by the British on the way.

Two days after taking the *Nocton,* the *Essex* reached Fernando de Noronha Island, a remote British outpost. Disguising herself as a British merchantman, the American frigate boldly approached and sent an officer ashore in civilian clothes. He learned that a frigate and a sloop, flying the British flag, had lately visited the port and had left a letter addressed to Sir James Lucas Yeo. The letter was picked up. In itself, it said nothing, but when exposed to heat it revealed a secret postscript, written in lemon juice. It was from Bainbridge, setting a new point of rendezvous at Rio de Janeiro.

Bainbridge was not at Rio. Later, speaking a Portuguese brig, Porter learned why—learned of *Constitution*'s victory over *Java* and of *Hornet*'s destruction of *Peacock.* Since there was now little chance of making contact, Porter imaginatively launched out on an Odyssey of his own designing.

Still farther south drove the *Essex,* heading for dread Cape Horn and the "shrieking sixties." The weather was frightful—day after day of storms which sent white water and green across the pitching decks. Through four weeks of torture, *Essex* inched south, then west, with the crewmen fighting to keep her afloat and themselves alive. At last, the weather cleared and the *Essex* lay at peace off the Isle of Mocha—the first American warship ever to sail the waters of the Pacific Ocean.

It was necessary to get supplies at Valparaiso. This worried Porter, for Spain, the mother country, was an ally of Great Britain. To his relief and amazement, he found that Chile had revolted against the Spaniards and that the Chileans were friendly and helpful. He learned, however, that the Peruvians to the north were of quite another mind. Their Viceroy was sending out privateers to prey upon American merchant vessels, and particularly upon American whalers. In this, the Viceroy was receiving help and encouragement from the British, who had armed a number of their own Pacific whalers in order to eliminate the rival American whaling fleet.

Early in April, 1813, the *Essex,* flying the British flag, encountered the Peruvian privateer *Nereyda,* escorting two captured American whalers into port. At Porter's invitation, *Nereyda*'s captain came aboard, eager to boast about his raids on American shipping. To his horror, he found himself in American hands. His ship was stripped of her stores, guns, powder, and most of her sails and was sent limping home, bearing a stern message to the Viceroy. The American whalers and their liberated crews were added to Porter's force.

In the early years of the nineteenth century, the Galapagos Islands formed a meeting and provisioning center for the world's Pacific whaling fleets. Cruising among the islands in late April and early May, Porter captured five British whalers, one being the sound and well-armed *Atlantic*. Her armament was increased to twenty guns, all of them small. Renamed *Essex, Junior,* she was placed under the command of Lieutenant John Downes.

Essex, Junior, was sent down the Chilean coast to look for British shipping, while the frigate headed westward for the Marquesas Islands and a much-needed overhaul. On the way, four more British whalers were taken—the last four in the Pacific. These were entrusted to the command of various under-officers, one going to a thirteen-year-old midshipman by the name of David Glasgow Farragut.

While *Essex* was being careened, patched, and repaired with the help of friendly natives, *Essex, Junior* arrived at the Marquesas. She, too, underwent repairs.

The natives, though cooperative, had to be kept friendly through gifts of iron scraps, which were convertible into tools and spear points, and through American help in two little native wars. In each case, the "thunder tubes" of the American sailors quickly brought victory to the local citizenry.

Porter's four months in the Marquesas formed an idyllic period for his crew. Much hard work was done, careening and repairing the ship and smoking out the rats; taking on supplies; and establishing the little naval base at Nukahiva, complete with fort and town. There was, however, ample opportunity for the men to enjoy the soft leisure of the tropics and the favors of the friendly natives. When at last the time of departure came, Porter's task was not unlike that of Odysseus when trying to leave the Land of the Lotus-Eaters.

David Porter left Nukahiva with a new purpose in mind. He had driven British commerce from the eastern Pacific. Now he wished to defeat a British warship, preferably a frigate, thus duplicating the deeds of Hull, Decatur, and Bainbridge. It is easy to criticize the decision as "glory seeking" and to point out the far greater advantage of continuing an elusive cruise, thus spreading the British cruiser forces far and wide. It is also easy to understand why he decided as he did.

On February 3, 1814, *Essex* and *Essex, Junior,* reached Valparaiso, where officers and crew were royally received by the population. Five days later, sails were sighted, the British frigate *Phoebe* (36) and the sloop *Cherub* (20). Into the harbor they came, *Phoebe* making straight for the anchored *Essex* as though to ram or board. At once, Porter piped his crew to the deck and issued cutlasses. "Stay clear!" he shouted through his speaking trumpet. "Stay clear!"

The British ship came on. From her deck rang a voice: "Captain Hillyar's compliments to Captain Porter, and hopes he is well."

"Very well," shouted Porter. "If you touch a rope-yarn of this ship, I shall board you instantly."

Hillyar looked at the crowded decks and the gleaming cutlasses. At the last second, he swung his ship aside, his yardarms barely missing those of the *Essex*. *Phoebe* and *Cherub* came to rest near the American anchorage.

The situation was a ticklish one. Since Chile was neutral, international law forbade either force to attack the other in Chilean waters, that is, within three miles of the shore. Conflict within Valparaiso Harbor would be especially bad, since Chilean citizens were certain to be killed and Chilean property destroyed by stray cannon balls. Two complicating factors were the weakness of the new Chilean government, which was quite unable to enforce neutrality, and the still-existent claim of Britain's ally, Spain, to Chilean sovereignty.

While their ships lay at anchor, Captains Porter and Hillyar met ashore and discussed the situation. There is no record of what they said or of any agreements they may have made. Subsequent events seem to indicate that they must have agreed to rule out Valparaiso Harbor as a battleground, but that no other binding promises were given. This must remain conjecture.

After several tense days, the two British ships hove up anchor and left the harbor, patrolling back and forth across the entrance in constant blockade. Porter was anxious to try conclusions with either British ship alone, but he knew it would be folly to fight them at the same time. A constant watch was kept, but *Phoebe* and *Cherub* never separated. Stalemate!

On March 28, Nature took a hand. A sudden storm from the south swept across the anchorage, snapping one of *Essex'* cables and causing the other anchor to drag. On sudden inspiration, hoping to escape the blockade, Porter cut his remaining cable and hoisted sail. For awhile it looked as though the swift-footed *Essex* might get away, as she scudded for the tip of the dangerous Point of Angels with *Phoebe* and *Cherub* trying to head her off. Just as the point was passed, a sudden fierce gust carried away Porter's main topmast. Escape was now out of the question. Hoping against hope that Chilean neutrality would be respected, Porter swung into a little cove and dropped an anchor.

Chilean neutrality was not respected. *Phoebe* and *Cherub* entered the cove and carefully took positions, one off the bow, the other off the stern, just out of reach of Porter's carronades. For two hours and twenty minutes it was long guns against long guns—six American against forty-two British. Perhaps "execution" would be a better term than "battle." *Essex* was systematically cut to pieces. Her crew, knowing it was helpless, served their guns until at last Captain Porter hauled down his flag to prevent further loss of life. Of her crew, 58 were dead and 65 wounded. *Phoebe* and *Cherub* together had only 5 dead and 10 wounded.

Thus ended in disaster the epic voyage of Captain David Porter and his frigate *Essex*. The survivors were paroled and sent back to New York in the *Essex, Junior,* effectively out of the war on their own words of honor. Some of the Lotus-Eaters left in the Marquesas staged a mutiny and took over the Nukahiva naval base. Four loyal officers—Lieutenant John Gamble and three midshipmen—gathered what non-mutinous men they could and escaped in the *Sir Andrew Hammond,* one of the captured British vessels. In time they reached the Sandwich Islands (now the State of Hawaii). Another idyll was in prospect when the *Cherub* unexpectedly appeared and scooped up the entire company as prisoners of war.

Brief as the visit was, the United States had had its first official contact with the Hawaiian Islands.

21.

In spite of the tightness of the British blockade, an occasional American warship managed to slip out of port and to go raiding in the seas which Britain regarded as her own. Especially noteworthy were the sloops-of-war *Peacock, Frolic,* and *Wasp,* all 22-gunners, designed by William Doughty to outsail and outfight the current British brigs and war sloops.

A fair share of the credit must go to a civilian—to William Jones, President Madison's new Secretary of the Navy. It was Secretary Jones's intention to keep the British navy off balance by a series of lightning raids. He received splendid cooperation from the navy.

Not all of the raiders were successful. The first to sea in 1814, the light frigate *Adams* took a number of prizes, then became trapped and blockaded in the Penobscot River. Though the blockading ships could not or would not go up the river after her, a landing force of British marines and regulars handled the affair with ease. Following the banks of the river, they were faced with a gathering of militia. A few volleys were fired. As usually happened when militia met trained fighting men, the militia ran away. *Adams*' commander found it necessary to burn his ship to keep it from falling into the enemy's hands.

In March, 1814, *Frolic* successfully ran the blockade and got out of Boston. Her luck was bad from the start; most of the ships she encountered were British warships so large that she was the one which had to flee. Only one prize was taken, and that was so badly damaged that it had to be burned. In the Caribbean, she encountered a semipiratical Venezuelan privateer, out to prey on American shipping. The privateer's captain had the bad judgment to resist. As a result, he, his ship, and about one hundred of his crew went down before *Frolic*'s well-directed broadsides.

In the Florida Strait, *Frolic*'s captain, Joseph Bainbridge (younger brother of William) sighted two sails. Had the luck turned at last? No! They proved to be the British frigate *Orpheus* and the armed schooner *Shelburne*. It was a bad combination, for *Frolic* could not defeat the frigate or outrun the schooner. Bainbridge made every effort to escape, jettisoning guns, anchors, and other equipment and starting his water supply. It did no good. The schooner was able to draw ahead and interfere with flight, while the frigate came relentlessly on astern, like a symbol of doom. As the heavy guns of the pursuer came into range, Bainbridge surrendered. "A remarkably fine ship," wrote the captain of the *Orpheus* in his log, "and the first time of her going to sea."

Peacock, meanwhile, had managed to get to sea, running the New York blockade in March, 1814, under cover of a heavy storm. She was supposed to rendezvous with the *Hornet* and the frigate *President,* neither of which managed to get out. While waiting for her missing companions, she cruised the seas between Florida and the Bahamas, looking for prizes.

On April 27, off Cape Canaveral (now Cape Kennedy), the look-out on *Peacock*'s masthead sighted four sails to the northeast. Three were British merchant ships, which made all haste to flee. The fourth was the sloop-of-war *Epervier* (18). Apparently in the hope of cover-ing his charges' flight, *Epervier*'s captain headed directly toward the oncoming American sloop.

The two ships closed rapidly, bow to bow. Thinking to rake the enemy, Captain Lewis Warrington (one of Preble's Boys) turned the *Peacock* sharply to starboard. Much the same thought must have gone through the mind of *Epervier*'s captain, for at the same instant he swung to port. As a result, the ships passed on opposite courses, can-nonading heavily. Both received heavy damage to their rigging, mak-ing precise maneuvering impossible. From this point on, it had to be a slugging match.

The Americans, thanks to persistent gunnery practice, had all the better of the slugging. Three quick broadsides smashed *Epervier*'s hull and rigging, while most of the British cannon balls hit only ocean water. Desperate at the carnage he could see about him, *Epervier*'s captain swung toward his adversary in the hope of boarding. As the ships closed, another broadside raked his deck. The would-be board-ers lost their zest, threw down their weapons, and ran for cover with the cry, "She's too heavy for us!" *Epervier*'s flag came down.

Warrington and his men had a hard struggle saving their shattered prize—a prize indeed, with a gold horde worth $125,000 in her flooded hold. Save her they did. She and the *Peacock* were patched up and set out together for Savannah. On the way, they found themselves dogged by two British frigates. *Peacock* led one away and lost it by faster footing. *Epervier* had more trouble. She was overtaken by a calm with the enemy not far astern. Neither ship could move, but the frigate put out boats which came crawling up with the evident purpose of assault. Lieutenant J. B. Nicholson and his prize crew of sixteen men had little chance of resisting successfully. Where force would have failed, bluff succeeded. Managing to wear his ship around with the aid of an errant puff of wind, Nicholson shouted, "Now, boys, give them a broadside!" The British boatmen heard, believed, and fled back to the protection of their frigate. *Epervier,* still with her treasure intact, made Savannah Harbor safely.

After a brief stay in port, *Peacock* got out again. This time she headed for the Bay of Biscay, where she took fourteen fat prizes in a few months' time before returning home, safely, through the blockade.

22.

Long after *Frolic* and *Peacock* had run the blockade to begin their voyages, their sister sloop *Wasp* lay tightly corked in Portsmouth Harbor. Said Captain Johnston Blakely, "The *Peacock* has spread her plumage to the winds, and the *Frolic* is taking her revels on the ocean, but the *Wasp,* I fear, will remain a dull drone in the waters of her country." It was a sad prediction, and a most inaccurate one. An April storm drove the blockaders to shelter, and the *Wasp* came out of her nest.

Blakely (another of Preble's Boys) headed boldly for the spot where the hunting would be best—the waters about the British Isles. In a month he took twelve prizes, while the British press screamed, the insurance rates mounted, and His Majesty's warships swarmed out to sea. It was the devastating raid of the *Argus* all over again.

On June 28, *Wasp* was pursuing two British merchantmen when she sighted the brig *Reindeer* (18) and abandoned her quarry for this more dangerous game. And, indeed, the *Reindeer* was dangerous, for her captain, William Manners, was a brave and resourceful man who had trained his crew into a smoothly working team of sailors and gunners.

As the ships approached bow to bow, *Reindeer* drew first blood. Though none of the broadside guns of either ship would bear in this position, the resourceful Manners had mounted a 12-pound carronade on the forecastle to fire directly forward. Slowly and deliberately, his well-trained gunners put five solid shots into the *Wasp*'s bow as the distance between the vessels shrank. To these repeated blows, *Wasp* was able to offer no return.

The two ships were less than fifty yards apart when Blakely brought his ship up into the wind and opened fire. Now it was broadside to broadside, with both ships taking grievous hurts. Captain Manners, coolly assessing the results of the duel, saw the tide of battle turning against him as a result of *Wasp*'s heavier armament. At his command, the *Reindeer* was swung in against the *Wasp*'s side, while the pipes squealed the call for boarders. In an instant, British and American seamen and marines were engaged in a desperate hand-to-hand struggle along the railings.

Captain Manners was both brave and conspicuous—too brave and too conspicuous to remain alive for long. Even before the ships touched, he was twice wounded, with a musket ball through both thighs and a more serious wound from a cannon ball that ripped the flesh from the calves of both his legs. Nevertheless, he held himself erect against the rigging and shouted his boarders on. When he saw his men fall back, he managed to pull himself onto the railing, calling for his men to follow. They tried, but even as they rallied to advance they saw their wounded captain collapse with a bullet through his body and another through his brain.

Now it was the Americans' turn to board. Over they swept, carrying all before them. The British resisted stubbornly, seeking to hold their ship against the superior number of their foes. When at last surrender was forced upon them, the highest officer left alive was the captain's clerk. It was he who finally struck the flag.

So badly smashed was *Reindeer* that she had to be burned where she lay. *Wasp,* too, had suffered. For several weeks she lay in the French port of L'Orient, having her damages repaired.

In August, Blakely and his ship were out again. Two easy prizes were taken off Brittany. Then a convoy of ten was sighted, being shepherded along by the ship-of-the-line *Armada* (74). Like a wolf around a buffalo herd, the raider circled, avoiding the powerful but clumsy guardian. At last a prize was taken, a most desirable one laden with cannons and military stores.

On September 1, four British brigs were sighted just at dusk. Selecting the one farthest to windward, Blakely closed. A close-range battle was fought in the darkness of the night—an inferno of brilliant flashes and jet blackness intermixed. *Wasp*'s men were better gunners, even under such conditions. One by one, the British guns fell silent. When at last there were no more flashes from his target, Blakely called across to ask if the enemy had struck. A single cannon shot supplied an answer. *Wasp* fired one more broadside, and a voice called out in surrender.

During this time, the three other British brigs had been beating slowly upwind toward their embattled sister. Now they were close at hand, their sails looming grayly in the dark. *Wasp* could not fight all three, so she fled—fled so quickly, indeed, that her captain never learned that he had defeated the brig *Avon,* and in so doing had damaged her so badly that she sank even as her sisters arrived upon the scene.

Never learned? Why *never?*

Twelve days after her battle with the *Avon,* the *Wasp* took the

British brig *Three Brothers,* stripped her, and scuttled her. Two days later—September 14, 1814—she did the same for the brig *Bacchus.* A week later, she captured the brig *Atlanta* (8), and sent her into Savannah with a prize crew. On October 9, she stopped the Swedish brig *Adonis* and took from her two American officers from the *Essex,* traveling to England as paroled prisoners of war. Then she disappeared—an unsolved mystery of the deep.

There have been rumors aplenty—picturesque and implausible rumors, for the most part—but no man knows for sure the fate of the gallant little *Wasp.*

23.

The raids of the American warships were more daring and brilliant than important. In spite of them, Britain controlled the seas—most of the seas most of the time, at least—and was able to concentrate overwhelming naval power when and where she pleased. In 1814, she tried invasion at a number of places along the Atlantic coast of the United States.

The raid up the Penobscot, in which the *Adams* was destroyed, was part of a successful invasion of Maine. Bangor and Eastport were taken, and much of the coast was controlled. At the time, it had the look of a successful edging south of the eastern end of the Canadian boundary.

More spectacular was the attempt to invade Connecticut. Following a probing action up the Connecticut River in April, in which a battery and twenty-two American vessels were destroyed, the British came in force in August. It was an impressive naval force which Rear Admiral Sir Thomas Hardy—erstwhile captain of Nelson's flagship *Victory*—brought against the little town of Stonington on August 9, 1814. Besides the seventy-four-gun ship-of-the-line *Ramilles,* the admiral had the frigate *Pactolus* (44), the brig *Despatch* (22), and the bomb-ketch *Terror,* giving him a total of some 141 guns, though the 74 aboard the flagship were of little use because the shallowness of the water kept the great ship far from shore. To these, the defenders could oppose but three old guns—two 18-pounders and a 4-pounder—mounted behind a crude earthwork.

The attack started at dusk and lasted for nearly four hours. The ships' cannons hurled solid shot into the town. The high-angle mortar in the bomb-ketch hurled "carcasses" or "stinkpots," filled with what historians have delicately dismissed as "fetid substances." Some of the ships discharged Congreve rockets, which went hissing through the streets of the town trailing sparks and smoke. It was a spectacular bombardment, the chief result of which was to attract to Stonington every weapon-bearing man for miles around, including a company of militia from Mystic, under a skilled artilleryman, Captain Jeremiah Holmes, who promptly took charge of the three little guns behind the earthwork.

At dawn, the firing recommenced. The Americans, aiming carefully, managed to hull the *Despatch* a few times, forcing her to draw away to a position of greater safety. When the defenders' ammunition was exhausted, they spiked their guns and prepared to abandon the earthwork. Then somebody found six more kegs of powder, the local blacksmith drilled out the spikes, and the firing was resumed. A brief truce brought a lull in the afternoon, but at eight the next morning the guns opened up again. *Despatch* received some more hits; so did *Pactolus*. That was enough for Admiral Hardy. He hauled up his anchors and sailed away.

What was the result of this three-day battle of three guns against 141? The British had lost twenty men killed and fifty wounded; the Americans had had one man mortally wounded and about forty less seriously injured. Two British warships had been seriously damaged; so had two houses in Stonington, where there was other, minor damage here and there. When the excitement was over, the thrifty inhabitants actually managed to realize a profit by gathering and selling much of the lethal material that had been hurled against them. From the point of view of the attackers, the whole affair had been an expensive fiasco.

24.

Far more important and successful was the British naval campaign in the area of Chesapeake Bay. As early as February, 1813, Rear Admiral Sir George Cockburn had seized the mouth of the bay as an anchorage for his formidable fleet of four ships-of-the-line and eight frigates. Later, this force had been materially increased by the arrival of five more ships-of-the-line and eight more frigates under Vice-Admiral Sir Alexander Cochrane, who now assumed over-all command. Against this armada, the single American frigate *Constellation* and the two little squadrons of gunboats under Tarbell and Barney could offer no opposition at all.

For the dual purpose of gaining supplies from the Americans and "rendering the war so onerous to them that they will come to terms," Vice-Admiral Cochrane sent Rear Admiral Cockburn to conduct a series of raids against the bayside settlements. Towns whose people meekly surrendered supplies were spared further punishment, but those which showed defiance were chastised. In this spirit, Dover and Lewiston, Delaware, were bombarded, and Havre de Grace, Maryland, was taken and burned. An amphibious assault on Norfolk, Virginia, was beaten off by the inspired gunnery of the American defenders. Enraged by this, Admiral Cockburn took and destroyed the neighboring town of Hampton. Unfortunately, the attacking force got out of hand, inflicting on the people of Hampton a series of atrocities that infuriated Americans everywhere and tarnished the admiral's reputation.

The Americans fought back as best they could. Whenever possible, the gunboats took advantage of their shallow draft and oar-activated mobility to damage or drive off venturous units of the British fleet. A case in point was the pursuit of H. M. armed schooner *St. Lawrence,* which was saved from capture by gunboats only by the timely appearance of the ship-of-the-line *Dragon.* On another occasion, the frigates *Loire* and *Narcissus,* helpless in a calm, were damaged by gunboats. The ship-of-the-line *Poictiers* (74), venturing into unfamiliar waters, had her bottom stove in by an underwater explosive device planted by an American inventor named Elijah Mix. Such minor gestures could have no important results. The British squadron continued to control the waters of Chesapeake Bay.

Early in August, 1814, the British naval force was reinforced by Brigadier General Robert Ross, accompanied by four battalions of Wellington's veteran British troops, fresh from their victorious Spanish campaign against Napoleon. Something more significant than raiding for supplies was now in prospect.

On August 17, the British flotilla moved quietly up Chesapeake Bay. Troops and marines were landed at the mouth of the Potomac and at the head of the Patuxent, to proceed overland in a two-pronged advance toward Washington. American Commodore Joshua Barney, backed into a corner, had to burn his gunboats to keep them out of British hands. He and his men fell back on foot from the head of the Patuxent to Bladensburg, Maryland, where they joined a force of 7,000 American militia, hastily gathered to block the way to the national capital.

The "battle" of Bladensburg, fought on August 24, reflects little glory on American arms. At the first volley, the militia broke and ran, leaving the defense of the capital to Barney and his 400 sailors. These resisted as best they could, twice driving back British attacks before being overwhelmed. Barney himself was wounded and captured. The British forces marched on in triumph.

In Washington, all was confusion. President Madison and his family left the White House, their dinner but half eaten, and fled barely in time to escape capture. In the dockyard, the new sloop *Argus* (18) and the nearly completed frigate *Columbia* (44) were burned by panic-stricken Americans, thus saving the British the trouble. The Capitol, the treasury building, and the "President's Palace" were burned at Admiral Cockburn's orders, in retaliation for the earlier American burning of the public buildings at York. These things accomplished, the invaders retired unhurriedly to their fleet, re-embarking on the 29th.

Elsewhere in the Chesapeake area, things went less well for the British. To provide a diversion and, if possible, to draw American troops from the defense of Washington, Captain Peter Parker took H. M. frigate *Menelaus* up Chesapeake Bay to Kent Island. Observing some American militia on the shore, the captain led a landing party for the double purpose of seizing provisions and of enjoying "a frolic with the Yankees." The Yankees, it developed, had rough ideas about frolicking. Parker and his men were enticed into an ambush, in which he and a number of his men were killed by point-blank blasts of buckshot. His body, suitably preserved in a cask of Jamaica rum, was later returned to England for burial.

The easy conquest of Washington led Vice-Admiral Sir Alexander Cochrane to plan for the taking of Baltimore, a notorious nest of American privateers. This time, he, himself, took charge. On September 11, his fleet lay off the mouth of the Patapsco River. From his flagship, H. M. S. *Tonnant* (74), the admiral was able to survey the spires of Baltimore and unpretentious little Fort McHenry, the city's main defensive unit. Against Cochrane's fifty warships, the fort did not seem much of an impediment.

On the morning of the 12th, General Ross and a large body of troops went ashore at North Point, with the intention of driving up the peninsula to Baltimore. Again, nothing but militia stood in the way of the regulars. This time, the militia fought a little better, deriving a toll of the attackers who were forcing them back toward the city. A strong, well-led attack would almost certainly have taken Baltimore, but the man who should have led it was among the 350 British casualties who lay along the way. General Ross was dead, struck down by a sniper's bullet. Without him, the attack lost its momentum. The British fell back to their ships.

Now it was the navy's turn. In the predawn darkness of September 13, the British warships opened a heavy long-range bombardment of Fort McHenry. Solid shot, explosive shells, and the new Congreve rockets were hurled at the fort, which replied with some small effectiveness. It was a magnificent spectacle. Among the thousands who watched it was Francis Scott Key, a young Baltimore attorney who was being temporarily detained aboard one of the British men-of-war. Excited by the bombardment and anxious over the fate of his city, he composed a poem set to a then-popular tune, "To Anacreon in Heaven." "Anacreon" has long been forgotten, but the new song, "The Star-Spangled Banner," lives on as the national anthem of the United States.

The bombardment, for all its picturesque qualities, failed to silence the fort. A halfhearted landing failed when the militia uncharacteristically stood their ground. On September 14, the British fleet dropped back down the Chesapeake, and Baltimore was safe.

25.

While the British were raiding along the coast, they were sowing the seeds of a far more dangerous invasion out of Canada. Again, as in the Revolution, the Champlain Valley was to be the gateway into the heart of the United States. With the approval of the great Duke of Wellington, Sir George Prevost laid his plans for an excursion up the Richelieu from Quebec, then down Lakes Champlain and George and the Hudson River to New York City. New England would be cut off and the most populous parts of New York occupied. The United States would be forced to sue for peace.

It all depended upon the control of Lake Champlain. Could Sir George maintain naval control of the waters and at the same time drive the Americans out of Plattsburg and other strong points on the shores? Sir George thought he could. Once given control of the lake, he could outflank and cut off any fortified posts beside it.

Early in 1813, the Americans had controlled the lake with their three sloops, *President, Growler,* and *Eagle,* each mounting eleven guns. Against these, the smaller British galleys operating from the north end of the lake had little chance. Then, dramatically, the odds shifted. On June 1, *Growler* and *Eagle* chased some rowing galleys into the Sorel River and became entrapped by adverse winds. The galleys turned about and opened a long-range bombardment while British troops moved artillery into position along the banks. Ignominiously, the two sloops were forced to surrender. They became H. M. S. *Finch* and *Chubb.* Now it was the turn of the British to sweep the lake, the turn of the Americans to flee and to hide.

The new American commander on Lake Champlain was Lieutenant Thomas MacDonough, one of Preble's Boys, who had played a brilliant part in the burning of the *Philadelphia* in Tripoli Harbor. Though he was helpless for the moment, he did not plan to remain so indefinitely.

Well up Otter Creek, on the Vermont shore of Lake Champlain, MacDonough established a snug little naval base, protected by emplaced batteries near the lake. Here there was intense and intelligent action aplenty, as Henry Eckford designed ships and Noah and Adam Brown rode herd on the workmen who were whipping them together out of virgin timber. The little *President* was judged unserviceable as a warship. She was sold to a private buyer. Her guns, plus many others, were used to equip other ships: the *Saratoga* (26), the *Eagle* (20), the *Ticonderoga* (17), the *Preble* (7), and ten one-gun row-galleys.

The British, too, were busy. Montreal was alive with veteran soldiers, fresh from action against Napoleon on the battlefields of Europe. Given a chance, they would sweep through the American defenses as through a wall of paper! All they needed was control of the lake. To assure this, Prevost had abuilding the frigate *Confiance* (38), the brig *Linnet* (16), and a dozen row-galleys. He already had, ready for action, the eleven-gun sloops *Finch* and *Chubb,* taken from the Americans the year before.

On September 7, 1814, Sir George Prevost made his move. Down along the western shore of Lake Champlain he led his army toward Plattsburg, which was defended only by a skeleton force under Alexander Macomb. Paralleling the troops came the ships, some with workmen still aboard. From the southeast came MacDonough and his squadron, also with workmen still applying finishing touches to many of the vessels. The Americans reached Plattsburg Bay before the British were in sight.

Commodore Thomas MacDonough was not a man to throw away an advantage. Within the curve of Plattsburg Bay he set out his squadron with care and foresight. From north to south, *Eagle, Saratoga, Ticonderoga,* and *Preble* were anchored across the bay, from Cumberland Head to Crab Island. On the island was installed a battery of American field artillery. This battery, shoal waters, and a strong north wind combined to make it impossible to turn the flanks of the anchored ships. Behind the line, evenly spaced, were the ten row-galleys. The larger ships were not only anchored; they had springs on their anchor cables and supplementary kedge anchors, so placed that they could swing about and even turn completely around without the raising of a sail.

Prevost and his army arrived before the American defenses on September 10 and encamped to await the arrival of his ships under Commander George Downie. Early the next morning, Downie reached Cumberland Head and signaled his presence by the firing of a cannon. As the British troops on the shore began their attack on the American defenses, the sixteen vessels of Downie's squadron rounded the point and came tacking in to engage the fourteen American vessels awaiting them.

Downie's plan was a good one and would probably have worked against an opponent less thorough than MacDonough. The British vessels were to advance abreast, with the large ships on the right and the row-galleys on the left. As the squadrons engaged, the shallow-draft galleys were to pass through the shoal waters and outflank the American line. In the meantime, powerful *Confiance* was to anchor and use her heavier armament to overwhelm *Saratoga. Chubb* and *Linnet* were to double-team *Eagle* and knock her out with their combined fire. *Finch* was to lead the British row-galleys against *Ticonderoga,* little *Preble,* and the American gunboats.

As the British squadron rounded the point, *Eagle* fired a single shot, which fell short. Linnet replied with a cannon ball which demolished a chicken coop on the *Saratoga,* releasing a little rooster which stood on a gun carriage, flapped its wings, and crowed defiance. Those of the flagship's crew who saw this incident took it as an omen of victory. *Saratoga* then drew first blood with a ball from a long 24, which traveled the length of the *Confiance*'s deck, killing several men and wounding many.

As the firing grew general, the British plan appeared to be working. *Confiance,* anchoring as planned, opened a heavy fire which severely damaged *Saratoga* and set her on fire. Some of the frigate's guns were also brought to bear on *Eagle,* which was already being heavily pounded by *Linnet.* As the punishment became unbearable, *Eagle* cut her cables and drifted down behind the American line. *Linnet* slid into the gap and opened a deliberate raking fire on *Saratoga*'s unprotected bow. At the southern end of the line, little *Preble* was unable to match *Finch*'s eleven guns with her own seven and was hammered into helplessness. Cut loose from her anchorage, she drifted ashore.

But the Americans were giving as well as receiving. *Chubb,* exposed to raking fire as she advanced bow-on toward *Eagle,* became uncontrollable, drifted through the American line, and was captured. *Confiance* suffered increasingly from *Saratoga*'s deliberate, well-aimed fire, which continued as her own newly installed and untested guns began to work loose in their mounts. Fifteen minutes after the battle began, Downie was killed by a round shot from the *Saratoga. Finch* and the row-galleys were roughly handled by *Ticonderoga*'s gunners and by the battery on Crab Island. As the schooner drove hard aground, four of the row-galleys turned to flee.

It was at this point that MacDonough's forethought paid him golden dividends. *Saratoga*'s starboard battery had been reduced to impotence, and she should have been through as a fighting unit. Her crew was down to less than half. Yet this battered remnant pulled itself together. The spring cables were hauled in, and the flagship slowly spun around to present her undamaged port broadside to the enemy. Frantically, the crew of the *Confiance* tried to improvise a similar maneuver. The frigate swung halfway and stopped, with her vulnerable bow turned toward *Saratoga*'s thirteen broadside guns. A few raking volleys, and it was all over. The British flag came down. *Chubb* and *Finch* had already surrendered, and *Linnet* did so a few minutes later, just as she was going down. The four row-galleys which had fled early were the only British vessels which got away.

On the shore, Sir George Prevost had been going through the motions of an attack, saving the real blows for the time when the victory of Downie's squadron would give him control of the water and a chance to flank. That time, he could now see, would never come. Control of the lake had been irretrievably lost. As the surviving row-galleys limped northward, the invading army followed along the shore. Plattsburg had been saved, and with it the northern United States and perhaps the country as a whole.

26.

In Ghent, Belgium, an American commission headed by Albert Gallatin had been discussing possible terms of peace with a British commission, since August 8, 1814. Though both nations ardently wanted an end to hostilities, it did not appear that any agreement could be reached. British demands, which included the cession of parts of New England and upper New York State and complete British control of the Great Lakes and the St. Lawrence River, were far too high for American acceptance. Conversely, Britain's prospects for winning the war were far too good to justify any yielding on the demands. In Europe, Napoleon was on the run, and it seemed certain that the British government would soon be able to unleash trained and experienced armies that would make short work of the American armed forces. Until something should happen to change the situation, the negotiators were faced with an enduring stalemate.

In October came electrifying news. Cochrane's fleet and Ross's army had been repulsed at the very gates of Baltimore. A British attack on the Niagara frontier had failed. Downie's fleet had been shattered on Lake Champlain, and as a result Prevost's army had been forced to retire into Canada. Though the mighty British fleet still ruled the salty seas, victory now seemed neither so near nor so easy as it had short weeks before.

The negotiations were resumed in a more conciliatory spirit by the members of both commissions. Britain dropped her demand for territory, and the Americans decided to forget their earlier requirement that impressment of sailors be disavowed as a part of British naval policy. On December 24, 1814, the Treaty of Ghent was signed. It provided for nothing but an end of hostilities. All unsettled questions were left for later discussion and negotiation, provided either side cared to bring them up again.

At once, by courier and sailing ship, the news began to spread. It was a slow process. Much was to happen in distant parts of the world before the news arrived that this Christmas Eve had brought tidings of more than one kind of peace.

27.

While the peace negotiations were in progress, Britain was preparing the greatest blow of the war. This was to be an attack on New

Orleans, to seize control of the mouth of the Mississippi and to provide the basis of a British-dominated Indian territory west of the Appalachian Mountains. A formidable fleet and a vast army headed by Sir Edward Pakenham were sent to make sure that the conquest could not fail.

Inadvertently, the American privateer *General Armstrong* (14) did much to spoil the British plans. On September 25, 1814, this little ship, commanded by Captain Samuel Reid, was lying peacefully in the neutral harbor of Fayal, in the Azores, when three British warships appeared—*Plantagenet* (74), *Rota* (38), and *Carnation* (18). Captain Lloyd, in command of the three, had every good reason to leave the little privateer alone. The laws of neutrality demanded it. More important, he was under orders to rendezvous at Fayal with the frigates *Thais* and *Calypso* and then to proceed directly to the Louisiana coast, where the buildup for the invasion was about to begin. Nothing so unimportant as the elimination of a privateer should be allowed to jeopardize this mission.

Captain Lloyd thought otherwise. He hated privateers and could not pass up an opportunity to capture or destroy one. Four well-manned boats from the *Carnation* tried to sneak up on the *Armstrong* and take her quietly by assault. They were quickly spotted. Captain Reid himself aimed the Long Tom that sent them back, battered and with their crews decimated.

Very well! Now came twelve cannon-armed barges from *Rota* and *Plantagenet*. Again the Long Tom spoke, but the barges kept on coming, firing their own guns as they approached. They reached the privateer's side, and the British tars and marines went swarming up onto the deck, crying "No quarter! No quarter! Kill the pirates!" That cry was a mistake, for it drove the *Armstrong*'s crew into a battle of desperation. The boarders were forced over the side and driven off, leaving behind four of their boats and thirty-four dead.

If boats and barges couldn't do it, ships could! The *Carnation* ran out her guns and moved into range. Three hours later, she moved out again, her main topmast down, her bowsprit shattered, and fifteen of her men dead.

But the string had run out. All three of the ships were coming in now, bent on annihilating the saucy little privateer. Captain Reid was a brave and resourceful man, but he could see no chance of resisting 130 guns with 14. The *General Armstrong* was scuttled where she lay, while Reid and his crew made for the safety of the shore. There they commandeered an old castle and prepared to sell their lives dearly. They were attacked no further.

Captain Lloyd had made a serious mistake. He had lost 65 men killed and 117 wounded. *Carnation* was so badly damaged that she could not proceed. *Thais* and *Calypso,* when they arrived, had to be used for transporting the wounded to British bases. The invasion had been delayed nearly a month.

It was a vital month. During the time so providentially provided, General Andrew Jackson had time to reach New Orleans, to gather and organize his rag-tag defensive forces, and even to make an unnatural alliance with Jean Lafitte, the pirate. The American defenders were pathetically few and deplorably weak, but they were now as ready as they could ever expect to be.

28.

The great British armada, bearing an army of 10,000 men, reached the Louisiana coast on December 8, 1814. Rather than advance up the swift-flowing river, Pakenham sent his men by barges through the bayous below New Orleans. A little group of American gunboats delayed the advance but was then swept aside as the barge flotilla wormed its way northwestward.

General Andrew Jackson, meanwhile, was gathering whatever men he could get and was putting up earthworks and cotton-bale defenses south of the city. No federal reinforcements were sent to him. Instead, he had to raise the rawest of militia from among the civilians and slaves of New Orleans, supplemented by Lafitte's pirates and a trickling of volunteers from Tennessee and Kentucky. Only about 800 of his men were regulars.

By December 23, the advanced units of the British army were near enough to their objective so that Jackson was able to begin molesting them. Night raids were made, to reduce morale and increase nervousness. From time to time, the little American schooner *Carolina* (15) dropped down the river and used her guns effectively on groups camped along the water's edge. In time, she made such a pest of herself that the British brought up heavy guns, shelled her, and blew her up. A second American warship, the corvette *Louisiana* (14), carried on where the *Carolina* had left off, using her guns to cover Jackson's right flank, along the river.

After several days of intermittent bombardment by guns and rockets, the British made their assault on the morning of January 8, 1815. Ten thousand veteran troops, hardened on the battlefields of Europe, moved forward confidently against Jackson's 5,500 strangely varied defenders. The men behind the barricade knew how to shoot, and with Jackson there to lend them courage they held their lines and spilled out lead. First Jackson's thirteen artillery pieces cut swathes through the advancing lines. The regulars came on grimly, increasing their pace as they neared the American line. When the range was down to one hundred yards, the rifles and muskets blasted forth. The ranks melted. The survivors tried to carry forward, then broke and gave ground, leaving windrows of redcoated dead behind them.

Once more the British came on, redcoats and highlanders this time, led by Sir Edward Pakenham in person. Again they were blasted, shattered, driven back. Sir Edward's body was among those left upon the field. More than 2,000 Britons had fallen. The American losses were but eight men killed and thirteen wounded.

On January 18, ten days after the Battle of New Orleans, the invaders re-embarked and left Louisiana. Three weeks later they landed at Mobile, captured an American fort, then learned for the first time that the war was over. Their efforts and their sacrifices had been in vain.

29.

Last of all did the tidings of peace reach the far-flung warships of the two warring navies.

On January 14, 1815, a strong westerly gale forced the British warships of the New York blockade to leave their station off Sandy Hook and seek shelter. Commodore Stephen Decatur, noting the gale with satisfaction, decided to take advantage of the situation to bring out the American frigate *President* (44) on a long-planned raiding voyage to the East Indies.

Decatur's luck was bad. Outside the harbor he ran upon a sandbar. For nearly two hours, the unfortunate frigate was hammered mercilessly by wind and wave before the crew managed to work her free with her frame hogged, her masts twisted out of true, and a dangerous leak in her forward planking. She should have returned to port but could not because of the strong westerly wind. The one chance was to carry on, hoping to get to sea before the blockaders should return. She almost made it, but not quite. By the first rays of the morning light she was sighted by the ships of the returning blockade squadron—the *razee Majestic* (56) and the frigates *Endymion* (40), *Pomone* (38), and *Tenedos* (38).

Decatur did everything possible to get away, jettisoning boats and other equipment and starting his frigate's water supply. It availed him nothing. Foot by foot, nimble *Endymion* overhauled the half-crippled American vessel. The chase lasted all day. As dusk settled, the pursuer opened with her bow chasers, *President* replying with her stern guns, the only ones which would bear. Captain Hope of *Endymion* handled his ship well, using his superior speed to yaw and fire broadsides and to veer away whenever Decatur tried to do likewise. Aboard the *President,* the enemy-inflicted damage, though still slight, continued to increase.

Though it meant losing ground by permitting the other pursuers to set an intercepting course, Decatur at last swung hard to starboard and forced *Endymion* to exchange broadsides. Now the Americans were giving out more than they were taking, slamming solid shot into the British hull. It was a dangerous game. *Endymion*'s guns swung up, to cripple *President* aloft. Should she succeed, all would be over, with the other three pursuers so close at hand. Decatur, too, changed and aimed high, using whirling dismantling shot to rip the British sails to pieces, shatter yards, and part halyards. In less than half an hour, *Endymion* was out of it, drifting helplessly, her motive power gone.

But the game was up. *Pomone* had now forged ahead, and *Tenedos* and *Majestic* were drawing into range behind. Gunfire from the pursuing frigates was beginning to score on the battered *President.* Reluctantly, to save the lives of his crew, Decatur ordered the flag hauled down. "One-fifth of my crew killed or wounded, my ship crippled, and more than fourfold force opposed, . . . without a chance of escape left, I deemed it my duty to surrender!" He might have added that he himself was suffering from two wounds.

Nine days after the *President* had sailed—and while her fate was still unknown in New York City—another westerly gale gave the sloops-of-war *Peacock* and *Hornet* a chance to get out. They did so with alacrity, heading for a presumed rendezvous with *President* at Tristan da Cunha Island in the South Atlantic.

The *Hornet,* under Captain James Biddle, reached the rendezvous point first. There she found, not the *President,* but the British brig

Penguin (18), an improved model carrying heavier guns than the earlier British war brigs. *Penguin* came on bravely to the attack but was soon taking heavy punishment from the better-served guns of her opponent. Her captain died in the opening minutes, cut in two by a cannon ball. Nevertheless, she came on into the teeth of *Hornet*'s broadsides, ramming her bowsprit through the *Hornet*'s shrouds and piping her boarders forward for hand-to-hand action. American musketry stopped them in their tracks, lacing the decks with red. Thinking that the British had struck, Captain Biddle leaped to his vessel's rail, only to receive a British musket ball in the neck. Fortunately for all, it was not a fatal wound. He was presently able to call off his men, who were swarming to the *Penguin*'s deck with slaughter in their hearts. *Penguin* was so badly damaged that she had to be burned.

The flames of the burning *Penguin* guided the *Peacock* to the rendezvous. With her came an American privateer brig, bringing news of the *President*'s capture. There was nothing now to hold the two sloops-of-war at Tristan da Cunha. Off they went around the Cape of Good Hope, headed for India and the East Indies.

The hunting was poor. On April 27, after two weeks of fruitless cruising, they sighted their first sail and went boldly in to make a capture. It was a costly mistake. The supposed East Indiaman turned out to be the ship-of-the-line *Cornwallis* (74). The sloops fled, parting company as they did so. *Peacock* got away cleanly, but *Hornet* spent a miserable two days trying to shake her pursuer, who was surprisingly fast and handy for so large a ship. At last Biddle escaped, but only after jettisoning so much of his equipment that he was unable to continue his cruise and had to head for home.

Constitution, meanwhile, was also at sea, having slipped out of Boston Harbor under cover of dirty weather. Captain Charles Stewart had a sharp and well-trained crew and a battle-tested ship armed with forty-four guns, most of them long 24's. Of all American ships, this was the one which British Admiral Sir George Collier least wanted to have roaming free over the sea lanes. As promptly as possible, he organized a squadron to go in pursuit.

At dusk on February 20, 1815, *Constitution* was prowling in the vicinity of Madeira when she sighted two British warships. They were the light frigate *Cyane* (32) and the corvette *Levant* (20). Neither, alone, was a match for their American opponent, but together they should have the advantage if their teamwork was good and if they

14 POTPOURRI

⚓

1.

Although Russia had her earliest beginning as a naval power, in the days of the Varangians and their long ships, by far the greater part of her history has been associated with affairs upon the land. Neither the geography of the country nor the nature of its people has inclined the Russian government to seek, with any consistency, the dominion of the deep, blue waters of the world.

In a very real sense, Peter the Great (1682–1725) may be regarded as the Father of the Russian navy. When only a boy, still holding the throne jointly with his half-brother Ivan under the regency of his older half-sister Sophia, he began his studies of ships and shipping. In an old Russian storehouse, he came upon a small English sailboat with a fore-and-aft rig. Russian boats at this time were all square-rigged. When he learned that this novel craft from the west could tack upwind, nothing would do but that he learn to sail it himself. He did so. Transferring his boat to Lake Pereiaslavl, he established there a small shipyard in which he built and experimented with somewhat larger vessels.

Peter's dawning naval ambitions for Russia were thwarted by the facts of geography. The Russian seacoasts to the north were ice-locked for most of every year. The Baltic Sea, not far from his borders on the northwest, was controlled by the Swedes. The Black Sea, to the south, joining the waters of the Mediterranean through the Bosporus and Dardanelles, was under Turkish control. These facts do much to explain the almost incessant warfare against the Swedes and the Turks, during the century and more which followed.

Peter's first attempt at conquest was aimed at the Turks in 1695. His army, advancing south toward Azov, was supposed to be accompanied down the Don by a large fleet of two-masted sailing ships called saics and by two Dutch-built frigates. The ships did not sail, not being ready, and the army bungled its first attempt at a siege and was forced to withdraw.

The next year, Peter tried again. This time, his fleet was ready and accompanied the army. Its presence proved decisive. A fleet of Turkish saics, trying to carry supplies to the defenders of Azov, was beaten by the Russian warships and was driven away, several Turkish vessels being taken. The city was starved out and surrendered on July 29, 1696.

For the sake of the record, we should note that many of the officers and the greater part of the seamen aboard the Russian saics were Venetians, veterans of numerous naval wars in the Mediterranean. While they were winning this victory for Peter, they were also teaching his seamen a great deal about the successful conduct of naval warfare.

Now that he had Azov, Peter the Great set about making it into an important naval base. The fortifications were strengthened, the harbor was dredged, and a permanent picket flotilla of thirty-two saics was assigned for its defense. More important was the construction of shipyards, in which work was soon begun on a large fleet of sailing warships based on western designs. At the same time, he issued orders that the Cossacks living nearby should build fleets of small boats in which they could make raids for the purpose of discouraging the Turks and Mongols and edging them out of the entire Crimean region.

Having the greatest admiration for western European civilization, Peter in 1697 and 1698 made a long trip, incognito, through a number of western countries. This remarkable ruler was no mere tourist and sightseer. First-hand knowledge was what he sought and what he got. In the Netherlands and in England, he served for some weeks as a common shipyard laborer, learning to do, and actually doing, all of the steps necessary for the building of a sound ship. Similarly, he later entered first his own army, then his navy, working himself slowly upward, rank by rank, under the guidance of experienced officers. There was little about his armed forces that he did not soon come to know at first hand.

2.

The signing of a peace treaty with Turkey in 1700 freed Peter the Great to cast his eyes northward, toward Sweden. He liked what he saw. King Charles XI had recently died, leaving his throne to his eighteen-year-old son, Charles XII. A boy so young could certainly do little to defend his borders against attack. Peter hastily made an alliance with Augustus II of Poland and Frederick IV of Denmark to defeat and partition their northern neighbor.

Charles XII proved to be one of the most underrated monarchs in history. Scarcely had the Great Northern War begun than his armies invaded Denmark and knocked her out of the war. Three months later, in November, 1700, he beat Peter's Russian army at Narva, though he failed to crush it as utterly as he might have. Poland was next. Augustus, his armies routed, was replaced on the throne by Stanislaus I, who favored Charles.

We need not concern ourselves with the details of the Great Northern War, which dragged on until 1721. Peter the Great, shorn of his allies, fought on alone. By 1703, Russian armies had forced their way to the easternmost tip of the Gulf of Finland. Here would be Peter's "window to the west." Conscripting laborers throughout Russia, he rushed the building of the new seaport-city of St. Petersburg, his new capital.

Slowly, very slowly, Sweden's brilliance gave way before Russia's might—the clever boxer worn down by the slugger. Finding things going badly in the north, Charles led his armies in an epic campaign across the enemy's homeland, deep into the Ukraine, hundreds of miles to the south. In 1709, at Poltava, the Swedes were disastrously defeated. Surrender? Not Charles! With what was left of his forces, he fought his way into Turkey and succeeded in persuading the Sultan to join him against the Russians. Five years later, when the Turks had lost heart and abandoned him, he managed to make his way back across Europe to the Swedish stronghold of Stralsund, near the southern shore of the Baltic Sea in the German state of Pomerania.

The presence of the Swedish king and Swedish armed forces on German soil caused a new alliance to be formed, including Russia, Denmark, and Prussia. The objective was the capture of Stralsund and the ejection of the Swedes from the mainland of Europe. Though Stralsund could be besieged from the land, it appeared too strong to be taken unless its sea-borne supplies and reinforcements from Sweden could be cut off. This, in turn, could be done only by taking the nearby island of Rugen, past whose shores the supply ships must pass in order to reach Stralsund. Capture of Rugen depended on gaining control of the sea.

For nearly a century, the powerful Swedish navy had dominated the Baltic. In 1714, the Swedish fleet outnumbered the Danish by thirty ships-of-the-line to twenty-four; the Russians had thirteen and the Prussians none. Though the Danish and Russian ships together outnumbered the Swedes, Sweden's central position kept their enemies from uniting on the sea. As long as Charles XII played his cards right, he could overpower either enemy fleet which came against him.

Charles did not play his cards right. Like Alexander the Great and Napoleon, he was more at home on the land than the sea and did not use his navy nearly so well as he used his army. A series of bad mistakes destroyed his advantage.

The trouble started in July of 1714, when a squadron of Russian galleys attacked and defeated a small Swedish squadron off Hango, at the southwestern tip of Finland. Charles reacted by dividing his fleet, sending nineteen ships-of-the-line and some smaller vessels east to blockade the Gulf of Finland, retaining four at Stralsund, and sending the rest to defend his capital, Stockholm.

When the allies moved by land against Stralsund, Charles made his second mistake. Angrily, he ordered Rear Admiral Count Wachtmeister to take his four ships-of-the-line westward "to take prizes and fight the enemy." Against his better judgment, Wachtmeister followed orders, engaging a Danish squadron of eight ships-of-the-line and a frigate under Rear Admiral Gabel off Fehmarn Island on April 24, 1715. Everything favored the Danes, who not only had numbers on their side but also had the weather gauge and were able to trap their enemies against a lee shore. All four Swedish ships were driven aground, one of them in flames. The other three were captured and became units of the Danish fleet, which now outnumbered the total Swedish fleet by one ship-of-the-line. Even the recall of the squadron blockading Russia could not redress the balance.

Because of a shortage of trained seamen, the Danes were at first unable to take full advantage of their newly won superiority. The fleet which Admiral Raben took to sea on July 15, 1715, included only sixteen ships-of-the-line, to protect a large flotilla of shallow-draft vessels under Vice-Admiral Sehestedt, intended for use in the shoal waters off Rugen. At the same time, a Swedish squadron of twenty-one ships-of-the-line, under Admiral Sparre, sailed for Stralsund, on what amounted to a collision course with the Danes.

The collision did not occur, thanks to the vigilance of Danish frigate captain Peter Wessel, who sighted the Swedish warships and bore the word to Admiral Raben. Raben made a quick decision, turning his squadron back as the Swedish sails appeared on the horizon. Vice-Admiral Sehestedt did not follow his protector but carried on toward Rugen with his smaller vessels. Fortunately for him, Sparre hoisted his battle flags and pursued Raben, ignoring this lesser game. In a nip-and-tuck chase, Raben got away.

Failing to overtake the Danish ships-of-the-line, Admiral Sparre doubled back to bag the shallow-draft vessels. He found that they had taken refuge in shoal water off Usedom Island, some seven miles southeast of Rugen. There they were safe from the guns of the Swedish ships-of-the-line, which were forced to remain about a third of a mile at sea, and they had little to fear from Swedish frigates, because several of them carried larger guns than the frigates did. They had little protection, though, from some batteries of Swedish field artilley on Usedom until a Prussian army unit commandeered some fishing boats and crossed to Usedom, driving the artillerymen away.

On August 8, the Danish fleet came back. It now numbered twenty-one ships-of-the-line, making it approximately equal to the Swedish squadron. Shortly after noon, the two fleets formed line of battle, in the formalist tradition, and began an artillery duel which did not end until both forces ran out of ammunition in the early evening. No ships were sunk, though a number were badly damaged. When one of the Danish ships-of-the-line was forced to drop out, bold Captain Wessel filled the gap with his frigate, in violation of custom, for frigates were presumed to lack the strength and the armament to hold a place in a battle line. Considerations such as this never deterred Captain Peter Wessel.

There was no clear-cut victory, and casualties totaled about the same, but the advantage clearly rested with the Danes. Admiral Sparre took his battered Swedish fleet back to the naval base at Karls-krona for extensive and badly needed repairs, leaving the waters around Rugen to the Danish squadrons under Raben and Sehestedt. It would be fully eight weeks before the major Swedish force would again be ready for action.

The eight weeks were decisive. During this time, Sehestedt's shallow-draft vessels managed to force their way into the coastal waters behind Rugen and Usedom, where they eliminated the minor Swedish naval units which remained there. In the meantime, young King Frederick William I of Prussia had been organizing a powerful assault force and gathering transport ships and barges.

On November 15, 1715, the allied invasion force approached the shores of Rugen Island in 337 transports and 300 barges. By plan, the transports dropped anchor off shore, while the barges, bearing picked assault troops, headed for the beaches. As each barge neared shore, the men aboard crowded into the stern, thus lifting the bow high and permitting a close approach before grounding. The men then went over the bow quickly, holding their weapons and powder above their heads, and waded ashore to secure a beachhead.

Not until one o'clock the next morning were enough Swedish soldiers on hand to launch a counterattack. It was then much too late. King Charles XII himself led the Swedish assault, which was beaten back with heavy losses, the king being among the wounded. Two days later, the island was in allied hands, and the strangulation of Stralsund had begun. For more than a month, the wounded king defended his stronghold, seeing the walls gradually reduced to rubble. It appeared that Charles XII was at last in the hands of his enemies.

King Charles was not an easy man to take. On December 22 he embarked in a small boat, succeeded in chopping his way clear of the ice-choked harbor, and managed to reach the Swedish galley *Hvalfisken* some miles off the coast. A few days after he reached Sweden, Stralsund surrendered, and the Swedes had lost their last foothold south of the Baltic.

The career of King Charles XII came to a dismal end in 1718. The first nine years of his reign had been marked by brilliance and success, the second nine by indecision and disaster. He now crowned his misfortunes by a colossal blunder. Although Russia and her allies were still undefeated and dangerous, he undertook to invade and conquer Norway, which was then a Danish possession. Frederickshald was placed under siege, hemmed in between Charles's veteran army and a Swedish fleet of forty-four vessels.

Out of nowhere came a Danish squadron of seven ships under Captain Peter Wessel—now a nobleman with the title of Tordenskjold ("Lord Thundershield"). Despite their numbers, the Swedish ships, caught unawares and unprepared, were all captured or destroyed. For his part in eliminating the Swedish fleet, Tordenskjold was made a rear admiral. The next year, after another victory, he would be a vice-admiral. The year after that, "Admiral Thundershield" would die in a duel, the senseless destroyer of so many able men.

Undeterred by the elimination of his fleet, King Charles XII persisted with his siege. His troops suffered dreadfully in the bitter northern winter. Then, one Sunday morning, the king's body was found lying across a parapet, a musket ball through his head. No one would admit to having seen him die, and the exact circumstances of his death are still shrouded in mystery. The siege was abandoned, and the army returned home, bearing the body of their leader.

Charles XII was followed on the Swedish throne by his sister Ulrica. Encouraged by a hint of aid from King George I of Great Britain, Queen Ulrica demanded that Peter the Great surrender all of the lands which Russia had gained at Swedish expense. Peter, by way of reply, sent out a squadron of warships under Admiral Siniavin and captured two Swedish ships-of-the-line and a brigantine which were bringing grain supplies to Stockholm. This minor move was followed by far greater activity. No fewer than 180 Russian warships and 300 barges, laden with 40,000 soldiers, were sent to ravage the Swedish coasts.

The arrival of a British fleet under Sir John Norris created a tense situation. Would the British come to the aid of the Swedes? Czar Peter sent a blunt message to Admiral Norris, demanding the answer. When the admiral hedged and pleaded absence of orders, Peter determined to ignore him. Destructive raids were carried out before the eyes of the British, who did nothing to interfere. The discouragement which this caused in the Swedish court did much to hasten the end of the war. It was a Russian victory, involving important territorial cessions. Peter's "window to the west" was now secure.

3.

While the long war with Sweden was in progress, intermittent warfare was also being waged between the Russians and the Turks. Here, Czar Peter experienced less success.

In June, 1711, the Czar and a small segment of his army found themselves trapped between the Pruth River and five times their number of Turks. With the Russian army were the Czarina Catherine and a number of her women. The Czar was considering a desperate effort to cut his way through the Turkish lines when his wife, with or without his knowledge, took things into her own hands. Gathering up her jewelry and that of all her women, she sent it as a bribe to the Turkish commander, with a request for a truce. The bribe was taken, and the request was granted. Bargaining replaced fighting. Peter had to give up his lands along the Black Sea, including his naval base at Azov and the newly developed harbor at Taganrog, but his life and liberty were saved, and he was left free to carry on his war against Charles XII and the Swedes.

The career of the Czarina Catherine deserves a few words in passing. She was no Russian but a Livonian orphan girl, Martha Skavronskaya by name. At the age of fifteen, she became a bride and widow on the same day, marrying a Swedish soldier who was killed within the next few hours while trying to defend his city of Marienburg against the Russians. The weeping child-widow caught the eye of Russian General Bauer, who took her into his home and made her his mistress. A year later, Prince Alexander Menshikov took the girl away from the general, only to lose her within a year to the Czar himself.

Czar Peter saw real worth in little Martha Skavronskaya, who was still only seventeen. He was a lonely man, having recently divorced his wife, Eudoxia. For seven years, the Livonian girl served as royal mistress, steadily gaining a hold over the mind and heart of the Czar. They were secretly married in 1707. Four years later, after adopting the Greek Orthodox religion and after changing her name to Catherine, she openly became the Czar's wife. In 1724, she became co-ruler. Upon Peter's death in 1725, she succeeded him as sole ruler of Russia —Empress Catherine I.

With the possible exception of Theodora, no woman in history has risen so high from such unpromising beginnings.

4.

There was little war and no important naval activity in Russia during the reigns of Catherine I (1725–27), Peter II (1727–30), Anna Ivanovna (1730–40), Ivan VI (1740–41), Elizabeth (1741–62), or Peter III (1762). It was not until the reign of Catherine II—Catherine the Great—that Russia once more turned her eyes seriously toward the sea.

Like Catherine I, Catherine II was a foreigner, born outside of Russia. She was the daughter of the ruler of the minor German state of Anhalt-Zerbst. Empress Elizabeth of Russia, wishing a German princess as a wife for her dissolute playboy-nephew Peter, asked Frederick the Great of Prussia to contribute his sister Ulrica. Frederick refused indignantly. He sent, instead, the least attractive and most insignificant German princess he could find—Princess Sophia-Augusta of Anhalt-Zerbst. At the time, it seemed an excellent joke on Elizabeth and Peter.

It turned out to be a good joke on Frederick, as well. Demure little Sophia-Augusta underwent one of the most complete transformations in human history. She changed her name to Catherine, her religion to Greek Orthodox, her language to Russian, and her nature to imperious. When Elizabeth died in 1762 and Peter III started misruling the country for his own pleasure, she had him deposed and later murdered and took over the government as sole ruler. Frederick the Great of Prussia suddenly found himself faced by a strong rival of his own creation, Empress Catherine the Great of Russia.

Catherine governed the country through a combination of her own whims and the machinations of her favorites. There were many of these. The empress was a woman of fierce appetites. The royal bedroom became a combined workshop and playground for an amazing number of self-seeking courtiers.

5.

Although Russia had long had designs on the Black Sea region, Catherine's first attempts at conquest in this area came about more by circumstance than by deliberate plan. The Poles were responsible. Accurately foreseeing the partition of their country by Russia, Prussia, and Austria, a group of Polish patriots made an alliance with Sultan Mustapha III of Turkey. This gave the empress an excuse to send her military and naval forces against the Turks. Goaded into action by the approach of his enemies, Sultan Mustapha declared war late in 1768, with his country still woefully unprepared.

While the Russian and Turkish armies were battling indecisively on the land, Empress Catherine sent her fleet from the Baltic through the North Sea, around Europe, and into the Mediterranean by way of the Strait of Gibraltar. The purpose of this maneuver was to aid and encourage the people of Greece, who had seized the opportunity to revolt against their Turkish masters. The squadron consisted of twelve Russian ships-of-the-line under the command of Rear Admiral John Elphinstone, borrowed from the British navy to help make up for the lack of experienced Russian officers.

A hastily gathered Turkish fleet, larger in numbers but smaller in size of ships, set out through the Dardanelles to meet and destroy the menace. On July 7, 1770, the fleets came together in the narrow channel between the Island of Chios and the mainland of Asia Minor. Four hours of cannonading produced no decided advantage for either side. Suddenly, almost as parts of the same explosion, the rival flagships blew up. Elphinstone was not killed; the Turkish admiral was. In confusion and dismay, the Turks broke their formation and fled to the shelter of the harbor of Tchesme.

Admiral Elphinstone, whose losses to date had been greater than those of the Turks, was quick to take advantage of the situation. Two fireships, manned by volunteers, were sent boldly into the harbor. The Turks could easily have destroyed them but did not do so. Somehow, the idea spread through the Turkish fleet that these two little vessels were loaded with deserters from the Russians, coming to lend help in the defense of the harbor. The two ships were welcomed into the heart of the fleet, where their crews set about systematically binding them to the nearest enemy vessels. There were sudden explosions. Flames burst from both fireships, spreading rapidly through the crowded anchorage. All efforts to check the fire were in vain. Before the last wisp of smoke circled up, every Turkish ship in Tchesme Harbor was a charred and sunken wreck.

The destruction of the Turkish fleet at Tchesme laid Turkey open to immediate and devastating attack from the sea. Admiral Elphinstone realized this and urged a naval invasion through the unguarded Dardanelles. He was overruled by Alexis Orlov, one of the current favorites of Empress Catherine the Great. Orlov insisted on an invasion of the island of Lemnos. While this misguided campaign was going on, the Turks pulled themselves together and fortified the Dardanelles, with the aid of Baron François de Tott, a French military genius.

The Russians had passed up the elephant in order to shoot the rabbit, and even the rabbit got away. While the fighting men landed by the Russian fleet were subduing Lemnos, the Turks launched a daring countermove. Four thousand soldiers in small boats, without artillery, put out from the mainland and crept past the Russian warships under cover of darkness. Discovery would have meant annihilation, but they were not discovered. They appeared on Lemnos in the morning and at once opened fire on the Russian invaders. The very unexpectedness of the maneuver assured its success. The Russians fled to their boats and sought the safety of their fleet. Lemnos was saved.

So much for the naval activity of the Russo-Turkish War of 1768–74. On land, the scales of fortune gradually swung in favor of the Russian army. By the Treaty of Kuchuk-Kainardji, signed July 17, 1774, the Turks acknowledged a Russian victory. Catherine gained Kerch and Yenikale in the Crimea, commanding the entrance to the Sea of Azov; the fortified position of Kinburn at the mouth of the Dnieper; nominal control of the Tatars and Cossacks of the Crimea; a protectorate over all Greeks of the Orthodox faith; and the right to send her shipping unhindered through Turkish waters.

Fo the first time, the Russian government had clear control of a warm-water exit to the seas of the world.

6.

The signing of the Treaty of Kuchuk-Kainardji did not mean an end of Catherine's intrigues against Turkey. Indeed, these increased. Aided and abetted by a new favorite, "Prince" Grigori Alexandrovich Potemkin, she laid careful plans for the complete dismemberment of the Turkish Empire. Toward this end, in 1781 she made a "defensive" alliance with Emperor Joseph II of Austria. Two years later, she boldly annexed the entire Crimea, installing Potemkin as its ruler. From this point on, her policy was one of constant small irritations and aggressions, with the purpose of goading Turkey into a declaration of war. This was at last achieved in 1787. At once, the alliance with Austria was invoked to help repel the Turkish "attack."

As in the previous war against the Turks, Russia had to depend heavily on foreign naval officers to make up for the inexperience of her own. Many of these were British. One, the Prince of Nassau-Siegen, was French. One, surprisingly, was the well-known American citizen, John Paul Jones, who had come to Russia in search of the admiral's commission that his own government had denied him.

Rear Admiral John Paul Jones had been given to understand that he would be in supreme command of the Russian naval forces in the Black Sea. He was vastly disappointed to learn that this was not true. He was in command only of the fourteen largest ships—the so-called Squadron. All of the smaller ships—the "Flotilla"—were under the independent command of Nassau-Siegen. Both co-equal commanders were under the whims of Potemkin, who stood between them and the empress, from whose favor was derived all of the real authority. An understood part of the policy, it soon developed, was the claiming of small victories where there had been defeats and of great victories where there had been small ones. Jones's refusal to play this game aroused the displeasure of both Potemkin and Nassau-Siegen.

The scene of the Black Sea naval activity was the broad bay, known as the Liman, into which both the Dnieper and Bug Rivers discharge their waters. The Kinburn Peninsula, south of the Liman, was in Russian hands. Kherson, at the mouth of the Dnieper, was a Russian base. West of the Bug, the northern shore of the Liman was Turkish, nailed down by the important base of Oczakow, on the northern shore of the entrance to the Liman. A Russian army under Potemkin was stationed just east of the Bug. The Kinburn Peninsula was under the command of Russian General Suvarov.

As a first step, John Paul Jones advised General Suvarov to emplant strong batteries on the tip of the Kinburn Peninsula, thus restricting free Turkish use of the entrance to the bay. Suvarov could see the advantage of this and did as suggested, installing not only the batteries but also a strong blockhouse.

Late in May, 1788, Jones and Nassau led out their naval forces for the purpose of cooperating with Potemkin's army in its advance upon Oczakow. Such cooperation proved to be impossible, for the prince not only did not advance but also failed to inform his naval associates of any plans at all. For more than a week, the Squadron and the Flotilla maintained their diagonal formation across the Liman. Farther west, a Turkish naval force maintained a roughly parallel formation, keeping between the Russians and Oczakow.

On June 6, following a conference with Jones, Nassau took the shallow-draft ships of his flotilla westward, for the purpose of cutting off a part of the Turkish fleet. At the first gunfire, Nassau's vessels turned back and retreated rapidly, pursued by an inferior Turkish squadron. This so encouraged the Turks that they brought up the remainder of their ships in order to fight a decisive action.

The battle was fought on June 7. Seeing the bold advance of the Turks, Nassau gave way to panic and advised the scuttling of the Russian fleet to keep it out of Turkish hands. When his advice was not heeded, he deserted his own smaller vessels in order to take refuge on Jones's flagship *Vladimir,* where he complicated the rear admiral's problems by rushing about and shouting contradictory orders. It became necessary for John Paul Jones to assume the command of both the Squadron and the Flotilla.

Directed by Jones, the combined Russian fleet advanced upon the Turks in an oblique formation, with the intention of enfolding the enemy. As the close-range gunfire increased, the Capitan Pacha of the Turkish fleet saw with consternation the disaster which threatened. He ordered an immediate retreat. Fifty-five of his vessels bore away toward Oczakow, leaving two burning briskly on the surface of the water.

After the battle, Potemkin wrote to Empress Catherine: "Nassau was the real hero. To him belongs the victory."

7.

Lack of cooperation did much to destroy the efficiency of the Russian fleet in the Liman. Potemkin would not advance with the army when the fleet was in position to help him. Russian Admiral Woynowitch, who commanded a second fleet at Sevastopol, would not bring his ships around to the Liman to entrap the Turks from behind. Nassau would not employ his light-draft vessels in conjunction with Jones's Squadron. Only the Turks seemed to cooperate, and in their case it was inadvertent.

Since he could not get any cooperation for an advance, John Paul Jones deployed his ships east of a shoal area in the hope that the Turks would try to attack across it. On June 16, they obliged. The Turkish fleet came on, under full sail, showing every evidence of an all-out attack. The Russians were girding to meet them, when suddenly the Capitan Pacha's flagship ran hard aground. At once, the other Turkish ships dropped their anchors, to prevent similar disaster. Jones, having the wind in his face, could do little but inaugurate a broad tack at the left of his line as the first step in an enfolding operation.

During the night, the wind shifted. With the first daylight, Jones got his ships under way, toward the Turks, who promptly cut their cables and fled. The flagship was no longer aground, but as the *Vladimir* bore down with guns run out the Turkish crew once more grounded their vessel. Jones and his Squadron continued on in pursuit of the remaining enemy, followed at a slow pace by Nassau and his Flotilla.

The reluctance of Nassau to keep up with the Squadron presently brought about a danger to Jones and his fourteen large vessels. Off to the right lay shallow water where the ships of the Squadron could not go. It was one of Nassau's duties to protect this area, using his light-draft vessels to check the similar vessels of the Turks. In Nassau's absence, Turkish galleys armed with special guns for throwing fire-bombs approached the unguarded flank. The frigate *Little Alexander* was struck by such a bomb, and went down in flames. Even after this, Nassau, whose Flotilla had come up on the left of the line instead of the designated right, refused to send his vessels into the menacing shallows.

In spite of the lack of cooperation in the Russian fleet, the Turks once more decided that they had had enough and turned to flee. A second one of their large ships went aground, but the remainder managed to get away and to disappear in the general direction of Oczakow.

The two grounded Turkish frigates would have made a welcome addition to the Russian Squadron. Since both were in water too shallow for his large ships to traverse, Jones sent Nassau and the light-draft Flotilla out to seize the helpless warships, which were canted at such an angle that none of their guns would bear. Even so, Nassau took no chances. In spite of the pleas of the Turkish crews, who were eager to surrender, he had his ships lie at a distance and lob incendiary missiles into the grounded frigates. Hundreds of Turkish seamen were burned alive, and two valuable prizes were destroyed.

8.

Now that he had the enemy on the run, John Paul Jones had no intention of letting him escape. Presumably, the Turkish vessels now lay safe in the harbor of Oczakow, under the protection of many heavy guns. Nevertheless, Jones took his fleet to the Turkish stronghold and personally conducted a night reconnaissance in a small boat with muffled oars, much to the delight and admiration of the handful of Russian sailors who went with him.

Back aboard the *Vladimir,* Rear Admiral Jones received tidings of great importance. While retiring from the action of June 16, the Turkish fleet had blundered within range of the unsuspected batteries on Kinburn Point. Suvarov's gunners had promptly opened fire, causing the Turks to flee so hastily that six of their ships had run aground. These six ships now lay helpless on the shoals of Kinburn Point.

Unfortunately, the Prince of Nassau-Siegen also received the news. Here was an opportunity to outdo his glorious victory of two days before! Over the bitter opposition of John Paul Jones, the glory-seeking Nassau took most of the ships of the Flotilla into the shallows where Jones's Squadron could not go. The same barbaric slaughter was re-enacted, the helpless Turks being shelled with firebombs despite their efforts to surrender. Returning, Nassau reported to Potemkin: "My Flotilla fought alone. We have detroyed six vessels, of which the crews of four are burned." In his report of the following day, Nassau listed the numbers of ships which he had destroyed in battle as "four vessels of 64 guns, five great frigates of 36 to 40, a sloop of 30, a brigantine of 14, and three small boats, all of which were led by the Capitan Pacha, who had three or four times as great a force as I possessed. . . . I always acted against the advice of the commander of the Squadron, who has achieved nothing. Paul Jones has learned that there is indeed a difference between commanding a privateer and a squadron."

Whether or not Potemkin believed his friend's report, he forwarded it to the empress without correction.

9.

Now that the Russians had gained naval command of the Liman, Prince Potemkin saw fit to move his armies across the Bug and to advance upon Oczakow. As an aid in the capture of this important stronghold, Jones and Nassau were instructed to destroy the Turkish vessels lying in the harbor. This was definitely a task for the Flotilla, for the large ships of Jones's Squadron could not traverse the shallow waters to the Turkish anchorage. Nassau, however, flatly refused to take his vessels in. There was too much danger!

Danger never deterred John Paul Jones. Using only the small boats from the ships of the Squadron, he personally led a night raid on the Turkish fleet. Five Turkish galleys, moored at the outer fringe of the anchorage, were his immediate objective. To reach them, he had to traverse a stretch of water which was presently whipped into foam by shells from both the Turkish and the Russian warships. Despite losses, he and his men kept on. One galley was taken and towed out of action. A second—the new flagship of the Captain Pacha himself—was assaulted and captured, though the Turkish commander himself managed to escape. Here was a prize worth having! The command of the flagship was turned over to a young officer, to be kedged out of danger, while Jones went after the other galleys.

From his position outside the harbor, Nassau beheld the capture of the Turkish flagship. It would never do for John Paul Jones to have such a feather for his cap! A boat was sent out, with instructions to burn the captured vessel. The young officer was browbeaten into submission, the torch was set, and the galley and most of its crew were consumed by the flames. Technically, at least, Nassau had established grounds for claiming the destruction of the enemy's flagship.

The attack by the small boats, without the aid of the Flotilla, could not succeed, despite the individual bravery of the participants. In all, one Turkish vessel was taken and six were destroyed. The greater part of the naval forces in Oczakow Harbor remained undamaged. The city itself was still untaken. Nevertheless, both Potemkin and Nassau received rewards and decorations of the highest order, while Jones got only a minor award. The officers of the Flotilla, who had taken no part in the battle, were advanced in grade and were given decorations and cash awards; those of the Squadron were ignored.

By this time, it was clear to John Paul Jones that his neglect at the hands of the United States Navy had been as nothing compared to his deliberate mistreatment at the hands of Potemkin and Nassau. He faced the Prince and protested loud and long. Potemkin, for his part, came to the conclusion that little more selfless activity could be expected from "that pirate." John Paul Jones was relieved of his command and sent to St. Petersburg, for attachment to Russia's Baltic fleet.

10.

Sweden, meanwhile, had come into the war against Russia. There were two excuses, neither very convincing. A trade treaty with the Turks was cited, though this contained no mention of military assistance. There was also the question of a bridge over the River Kimmene, joining Russian and Swedish territory. The existence of the bridge was not disputed. The quarrel arose over whether it should be painted in the Swedish or the Russian national colors! The real reason for the war was the conviction of King Gustavus III of Sweden that the time was propitious for avenging previous Russian aggressions. Neither the Swedish people nor their parliament shared the king's enthusiasm for the war.

Immediately after the declaration of war, the Swedish fleet put to sea under the king's brother, Duke Charles of Soldermanland. It was an imposing fleet, consisting of fifteen ships-of-the-line and five frigates. North of the island of Gothland, it encountered three Russian ships-of-the-line, making for their home base of Kronstadt. The Russians, understandably enough, made no effort to attack the superior Swedish squadron. Duke Charles, for his part, did not attack the Russians but contented himself with shadowing them. He was reluctant to fire the first gun of a war for which he personally felt little zeal.

Trouble had meanwhile developed at the Russian base at Kronstadt. John Paul Jones was there, having reported for duty with the Russian Baltic fleet. Admiral Greig, in command of the fleet, was an Englishman; so were most of his highest officers. This group, understandably, felt no love for John Paul Jones, the "despicable pirate" who had caused Britain such grief during the American Revolution. A written ultimatum was sent to the empress. If Jones remained with the fleet, the British officers would all refuse to serve. John Paul Jones was promptly removed, and the Russian fleet put to sea.

Off Hogland, on July 17, 1788, the Russian fleet from Kronstadt came upon Duke Charles's Swedish ships and the three Russian vessels which they were shepherding homeward. The numerical odds now favored the Russians, who had seventeen ships-of-the-line to the Swedes' fifteen and seven frigates to the Swedes' five. Admiral Greig had no compunctions about opening hostilities. His ships promptly formed in line of battle and opened fire.

After more than an hour of cannonading and some spirited hand-to-hand action, the Swedes withdrew and sought safety in the harbor of Sveaborg. They had not suffered actual defeat, having lost one ship-of-the-line and having captured another to replace it. Nevertheless, the numerical odds had begun to tell. The Russians promptly established a tight blockade off the harbor mouth.

Despite the immobilization of his fleet, Gustavus III was determined to prosecute the war against Russia and force a decision. He himself led a land expedition aimed at Friedrichsham, a key point defending St. Petersburg. The army arrived before the walls but refused to attack, as officers and soldiers alike were opposed to the war. At the same time, a group of peace-minded nobles in Sweden were negotiating a truce with the Russians. King Gustavus found, to his embarrassment, that his cherished war had come to a halt.

When news of the truce was received, the king withdrew his invading forces and returned home. At about the same time, the Russians withdrew their blockading squadron from Sveaborg to Copenhagen, thus permitting the bottled-up Swedish fleet to regain the open sea.

11.

In the spring of 1789, the war was resumed. An attempt by Gustavus to burn the Russian fleet in the harbor of Copenhagen was frustrated by the vigilance of the Russians and the Danes. A land campaign in Finland was ruined by the efforts of the amateur warrior, Gustavus III, to direct the actions of his professional soldiers. Swedish naval raids in June, August, and September were driven off by Russian squadrons under Admiral Tchitchakov, ably assisted by borrowed foreign officers. Among those present was the Prince of Nassau-Siegen, who once more, characteristically, claimed credit for the victories which others had won.

Early in 1790, dogged King Gustavus returned to the attack. The idea of taking St. Petersburg and of driving Empress Catherine from her capital seemed to blind him to all other avenues of action. The Russian Baltic fleet was divided at this time, fifteen ships-of-the-line with their auxiliaries lying at Kronstadt and another fifteen ships-of-the-line, plus auxiliaries, at Reval. The Swedish fleet under Duke Charles contained nineteen ships-of-the-line, twenty-seven galleys, and a large number of shallow-draft gunboats. It was thus superior to either segment of the Russian Baltic fleet but decidedly inferior to both segments combined. Common sense dictated great care to keep the Russians disunited.

For three days, Duke Charles maintained his strategic position between Kronstadt and Reval, thus holding the Russian naval forces in check. Then, on June 6, 1790, he made the obvious mistake of withdrawing his ships to Viborg Sound, a semilandlocked bay some distance to the north. At once the Russians united their squadrons, throwing a tight cordon of thirty ships-of-the-line, plus numerous smaller vessels, across the mouth of the sound. The Swedes were neatly bagged.

With the Russians was an experienced French officer, Captain Pelissier, who had served in numerous campaigns. He went at once to Admiral Tchitchakov and to the Prince of Nassau-Siegen, pointing out the importance of constant vigilance and of a close, careful arrangement of the Russian warships so that the entrance of the sound could be swept with an annihilating volume of fire should the Swedes try to emerge. How dare a mere captain offer advice to an admiral and a prince! Pelissier was sent away, his advice unheeded. Nothing daunted, he went next to Russian generals Suchtelen and Soltikov, urging that heavy batteries be emplaced on both shores of the entrance to the sound. Again he was sent away, with heavy sarcasm. The original Russian disposition remained unchanged.

Within Viborg Sound, the Swedes were beginning to suffer from shortages of food. Duke Charles and many others wanted to capitulate, but the king would not hear of it. On July 3, a desperate attempt was made to break out of the trap. Thanks to the looseness of the Russian formation, the Swedish ships were not destroyed one at a time as they came out but managed to pass through the entrance and to engage in battle as a body. Though the odds against them were great, twelve ships-of-the-line managed to fight their way free and escape. Seven were sunk or captured, together with three frigates and upwards of thirty small craft. The rest of the small Swedish vessels were forced to turn back and to seek refuge in the rock-strewn waters of Suenske Sound, where the largest Russian ships could not get at them.

The Prince of Nassau-Siegen, in charge of the Russian light-draft ships, saw in the situation an opportunity for honors and for glory. Surely the fragment of the Swedish force hiding in Suenske Sound could not be capable of much dangerous activity! Without taking time for much reconnaissance, he ordered an assault by his vessels. The Swedes fought with valor, and the uncharted rocks took their toll from the advancing Russian formation. Fourteen thousand Russians were lost as fifteen of their ships went down and fifty-five were taken in this, the greatest naval defeat in Russian history.

Both Russia and Sweden were weary of the war. On August 14, 1790, the Treaty of Varela brought an end to hostilities, without a gain for either side.

12.

What of John Paul Jones?

Discredited in the Black Sea area, despite the brilliance of his services, and denied an opportunity to serve in the Baltic, he was to experience still more humiliating treatment at the hands of Empress Catherine and her favorites. There must be an excuse to get rid of this man on such terms that no one else would wish to snap up his services. Since such an excuse could not be found, one was manufactured.

John Paul Jones suddenly found himself the victim of the ancient and dishonorable "badger game." A young girl testified that she had been abused and assaulted by Jones when she went to his apartment to deliver some cheese. The charges were heard and accepted. The defense was summarily rejected on the ground that it had been expressed in English rather than in Russian, which Jones did not know how to speak. Despite the absurdity of the charges and the mass of contradictions in which the prosecution soon involved itself, John Paul Jones suffered a completely undeserved muddying of his character.

The empress, however, was not quite ready to release all holds upon her imported naval genius. Word reached her that Sweden would like his services. To avoid having him pass into the hands of her enemies, she granted him a two-year "leave of absence" from the Russian navy, paying him just enough to keep him feeling that he was a member of the Russian team. He went to France, expecting to be recalled to active duty at any time. There he became ill of Bright's disease, and there he died, plunged face down upon his bed, fully dressed, with his shoes on and his feet planted firmly on the floor.

John Paul Jones had been badly used by his own country and used much worse by Imperial Russia.

13.

The Austro-Russian war against Turkey continued. There was fighting aplenty, practically all of it upon the land. Austria dropped out in 1790, but Russia carried on alone, with Suvarov winning the victories and Potemkin claiming the credit for them. The favorite's reputation flourished until he made the mistake of entrusting an army to a less servile general, Repnin. This worthy had the bad taste to win a smashing victory at Matchin in July, 1791, at a time when Potemkin was too far away to be able to claim the victory. It was a devastating blow to the Prince.

The neutral nations of Europe had been watching the course of the war with deep concern. It would never do for Russia to win too great a victory at Turkey's expense. The Russian bear was powerful enough, as it was. As a result, Great Britain and other nations offered their good offices and applied pressure for a moderate settlement without absolute victory.

They had their way. On January 9, 1792, the Treaty of Jassy was signed, granting the Russians the fortress city of Oczakow, the land between the Bug and Dniester rivers, and a protectorate over Georgia.

Catherine had extended her borders, but not nearly to the extent which she had hoped.

Potemkin did not live to see the signing of the treaty. Seized with a fever, he disregarded all advice and continued to eat and drink immoderately. His death occurred at Jassy, only a few days before the conclusion of the peace.

14.

During the War of 1812, the Algerian pirates had once more become active against American merchant vessels. Knowing the might of the British navy, the Dey of Algiers had leaped to the conclusion that never again would American warships sail the seas. American vessels would therefore make the safest of prizes to take. The British authorities did nothing to discourage these activities.

With the end of the war, the United States took immediate steps to correct the situation. Commodore Stephen Decatur sailed for the Mediterranean with a squadron consisting of the frigates *Guerriere* (flagship, 44), *Constellation* (44), and *Macedonian* (38), two sloops, three brigs, and two schooners. A second squadron, under Commodore William Bainbridge, sailed somewhat later.

Arriving at Gibraltar early in June, 1815, Decatur learned that an Algerian squadron had recently passed eastward through the strait. He set out in pursuit, and on June 17 sighted a large vessel off Cape de Gata, on the southern coast of Spain. Hoping to lull this supposed enemy into a false sense of security, Decatur ordered all ships to hoist the British colors. An error was made, and *Constellation* displayed the Stars and Stripes. At once the quarry made off, revealing that she was indeed an Algerian vessel.

After a long chase, the frigate *Guerriere* and the sloop-of-war *Epervier* drew up within range of the enemy, which proved to be the frigate *Mashuda* (44). The Algerian gunners proved to be no match for their American counterparts. Two broadsides from *Guerriere* and one from *Epervier* killed thirty men, including Admiral Reis Hammida, commander-in-chief of the Algerian navy. The flag came down.

Two days later, on June 19, Decatur's squadron sighted the Algerian brig *Estedio* (22). The brig fled, closely pursued. As the American vessels closed the distance, *Estedio*'s captain turned his ship toward the shore and ran her aground. Many of the Algerian crew escaped, but the *Estedio* was taken and was eventually refloated.

There being no sign of the remaining vessels of the Algerian squadron, Decatur sailed directly for Algiers to enforce a suitable treaty. The Dey was deeply shocked at the news that two of his vessels had been taken and his admiral killed. At first he tried to play for time, but Decatur put an end to that maneuver by announcing that if the Algerian fleet should appear before a treaty had been signed he would attack and either destroy or capture it. Thus stimulated, the Dey agreed, in writing, to cease all claims for tribute from the United States, to release all American captives, to restore all seized American property, to pay $10,000 for an American merchant brig which one of his ships had taken, to grant permanent freedom to any Christian slave who should manage to escape to an American vessel, and to treat all future American captives as prisoners of war and not as slaves. Later, the American commodore managed, without the necessity of fighting, to wring somewhat similar terms from the rulers of both Tunis and Tripoli.

The fate of the American captives released from Algiers was sad and ironic. All were placed aboard the sloop *Epervier* for transportation home. They never arrived. Somewhere in the Atlantic, the *Epervier* foundered in a storm, taking down with her both her crew and her homeward-bound passengers.

Scarcely had the American warships departed from the harbor of Algiers when the Dey sent his Prime Minister hurrying to the British consulate with a reproachful message: "You told us that the Americans would be swept from the seas in six months by your navy, and now they make war upon us with some of your own vessels, which they have taken." [1]

The British consul could only say that he was sorry—as indeed he was.

15.

The Dey of Algiers had been wrong in his assumption that Great Britain would continue to condone the practice of piracy. When hostilities against the United States and France came to an end in 1815, the British government aligned itself solidly with the forces of law and order by taking part in an international meeting at Vienna to consider the suppression of piracy, and by volunteering the use of its navy to enforce the decisions of the commissioners.

---

[1] Actually, the frigate *Macedonian* and the sloop-of-war *Epervier* were captured British vessels. The frigate *Guerriere* was named after the British frigate which Isaac Hull and the *Constitution* had destroyed early in the War of 1812.

As a first step, Great Britain demanded that Algeria give up immediately and for all time the enslaving of Christians. The Algerians flatly refused. To make their refusal more striking, they sent out a raiding expedition to seize and enslave a group of fishermen from Naples, a British protectorate. That did it! Without further ado, the British Admiralty sent Admiral Viscount Exmouth with six ships-of-the-line, and a few frigates and bomb vessels. At Gibraltar, the squadron was joined by five Dutch frigates and a corvette, under the command of Vice-Admiral Baron de Capellan. The expedition was thus truly international in makeup.

The harbinger of the expedition was Captain Warde of H. M. S. *Banterer,* sent to Algiers in advance to try to gain concessions from the Dey in order to avoid hostilities and also to observe the defenses of the town. The Dey would not see him, but Warde was able to see the defenses very clearly, noting the disposition of the 220 guns on the masonry mole and also noting that few of these guns could be brought to bear on vessels lying close-in to the south and southeast of the mole. This information was duly reported back to Admiral Exmouth.

The squadron reached Algiers on August 27, 1816. As the ships lay off the port, a final effort was made to extract an agreement from the Dey. When no reply was received after three hours, the ships moved in close to the southeastern face of the mole and anchored. Exmouth's flagship *Queen Charlotte* (100) lay only half a cable's length from the mole's southern end, the fifty heavy guns of her starboard broadside bearing in perfect position for raking, or enfilading, fire. From the flagship's quarterdeck, Exmouth could see that the mole was crowded with soldiers. Vainly he tried to wave them away from their exposed position. Though the defenses must be destroyed, he hoped to accomplish this purpose without unnecessary loss of human life.

The soldiers on the crowded mole paid no attention to Exmouth's signals, but continued to gaze at the silent warships. Long minutes of nerve-wracking tension followed, broken at last by a cannon shot from the mole. A solid ball crashed into the side of the ship-of-the-line *Superb*. Then Exmouth gave the order to fire, and the guns of the British warships blasted forth, almost in unison.

For the better part of five hours the carnage continued, while the heavy masonry defenses of Algiers slowly crumbled into dust. The Algerians fought well, doing much damage and attempting far more. Early in the battle, a fleet of thirty-seven gunboats issued from the harbor and made for the *Queen Charlotte* and the *Leander* (50), with intent to board. Fast, accurate fire sank all but four, which retired quickly. Heavy damage was done to the ship-of-the-line *Impregnable* (98), which had anchored too far to the north to be protected by the "blind spot" which Warde had discovered. There were 210 casualties on this ship alone. But the damage done by the British and the Dutch far outweighed that which they received.

Night brought an end to the bombardment. The defenses of Algiers were gone, and the shipping in the harbor was aflame. Nearly 7,000 Algerians were dead, most of them struck down on the mole by the opening broadsides from the ships. The Dey was heartsick and penitent. The next morning he eagerly signed the agreement which he had scorned so short a time before.

It would be pleasant to record that the successive blows by the American and the British-Dutch expeditions put an end to piracy in the Mediterranean. Such was not the case. Whenever they dared, the seagoing inhabitants of the North African coast seized passing ships, confiscated them and their cargoes, and held passengers and crew for ransom, despite all treaties and agreements to the contrary. Undoubtedly the blows struck against them had a deterrent effect, but the best that can be said is that the pirate raids became less frequent. Not until the advent of steam-driven merchant ships, which could not be overtaken by pirate sailing craft, did the business of piracy cease to flourish.

16.

There have been many wars without naval battles. Far rarer are naval battles without a war.

The defeat of Napoleon was followed by a period of reaction in Europe. Under the guidance of Prince Metternich of Austria, the so-called Concert of Europe was organized to maintain the status quo. Freedom of expression was crushed everywhere, even in comparatively liberal Britain. Armies were sent to put down budding revolutions in Spain, in Italy, and elsewhere. The Concert of Europe was thought of as a sort of fire department, ready to dash anywhere to quell the fires of revolt.

Trouble developed for the Concert of Europe when the Greeks revolted against their Turkish masters. To be consistent, the members of the Concert should have put down this revolution, too. The Greeks, however, were Christians, and the people of western Europe had little stomach for a fight waged against Christians in behalf of Mohammedans. In addition, Russia, an important member of the Concert, had long been trying to stir up the Greeks against the Turks and could see little point in turning around and helping the Turks put down the revolt which she herself had helped foment. Piously, the nations of the Concert twiddled their thumbs, hoping that the Greeks would be able to free themselves without help or interference.

For a while, it looked as though the Greeks might manage. A semi-piratical Greek navy was organized, which supported itself by piracy while fighting bravely against the Turks. When the Turkish flagship was rammed and sunk by a Greek vessel, Sultan Mahmud II appealed to Mehemet Ali of Egypt for help. Since Mehemet Ali was technically Mahmud's vassal, he did not feel that he was in any position to decline.

A strong Egyptian naval and military expedition was sent to southern Greece, under the command of Mehemet's son Ibraham. While the army raided, raped, and massacred on the land, the fleet put in at the port of Navarino on the western shore of the Peloponnesus. Here Ibraham's ships were joined by those of the Sultan, making a powerful combined fleet of nearly one hundred vessels, headed by three ships-of-the-line. This force was to be used for the double purpose of annihilating the little Greek navy and of landing troops at many points along the coast to extend the rapine already inaugurated.

The people of western Europe did not share their governments' indifference to the fate of the Greeks. To many who regarded Greece as the cradle of human freedom, the struggle for Greek independence became almost a holy crusade. Lord Byron was only one of many who volunteered to help the Greeks wage their unequal campaign. Increasingly strong pressure was brought to bear on various governments to do something to stop the Turkish atrocities.

In July, 1827, representatives of Great Britain, France, and Russia met and drew up the Treaty of London, in which they expressed the determination to intercede unless both the Turks and the Greeks should agree to an immediate armistice and to arbitration, with the three great powers to serve as arbitrators. The British Mediterranean Fleet, under Vice-Admiral Sir Edward Codrington, was dispatched to Navarino, where it was to be joined by French and Russian naval units. The instructions given to Codrington, to French Admiral De Rigny, and to Russian Admiral Heiden called for the maintenance of peace, if possible, but for the use of force if necessary to prevent activity against the Greeks by the powerful Turko-Egyptian fleet. The British and French admirals were also instructed to prevent the receipt of supplies by the invaders.

Arriving at Navarino, Admiral Codrington disposed his little force across the harbor mouth to create a blockade. He had, at this time, only the ship-of-the-line *Asia* (84), a frigate, a corvette, and a brig—four ships against one hundred, 172 guns against 1,270! Nevertheless, he at once assumed control, informing Ibraham that the Turkish and Egyptian ships must remain in the harbor. The Mohammedan leader was much upset by this, for the Greeks had recently extended their field of operations south of the Gulf of Corinth, and he wished to use his ships to effect a countermove. In defiance of Codrington, he weighed anchor and started out with his entire force.

Though the odds were suicidal, Admiral Codrington had no doubt of what must be done. He cleared his four vessels for action and prepared to oppose the mass of armed shipping which he could see bearing toward the harbor entrance. Nothing, it seemed, could avert hostilities and the quick destruction of the little British squadron.

At the last moment, with gun about to answer gun, the Turko-Egyptian fleet halted and began a retirement into the harbor. Far off on the western horizon were white sails. It was De Rigny's French squadron, coming to reinforce the British. For the moment, at least, the situation had been saved.

The arrival of De Rigny's ships gave Codrington ten warships and brought the odds against him down to a mere ten to one. Thus reinforced, he took the *Asia* into the harbor, and he and De Rigny went to see Ibraham. The Egyptian leader promised faithfully not to move his fleet without further instructions from Cairo or Constantinople. Thus reassured, the allied commanders went back to their ships, buoyed by a hope for peace.

The appearance of the Russian squadron further increased the allied fleet. Now it contained twenty-six vessels, of which ten were ships-of-the-line, *razees,* frigates, or corvettes. Though the numerical odds were still about four to one against Codrington, he now had a clear advantage in first-class fighting ships.

Ibraham lived up to his promise in the most literal of senses. Not a ship was moved. The crews, however, were sent ashore and were used for conducting raids far and wide against Greek towns and villages. Pillars of fire by night and of smoke by day marked the Turkish activities, while pitiful stories of rape and murder came seeping out from the inland areas.

Admiral Codrington, meanwhile, was among the busiest of men. Before he could bring peace to the Greeks, he had to establish it among his allies. The French and Russian admirals hated and despised one another and were most unwilling to cooperate. Russian Admiral Heiden, moreover, was under instructions to remain friendly to the Austrians, who were busily furnishing the Turkish forces with supplies. It took tact, patience, and a fine brand of salesmanship to weld the three disparate squadrons into a reasonably unified fighting force.

When he felt that he had established as much cooperation among his allies as was possible, Admiral Codrington took the next step. He sent a resourceful British officer, Colonel Cradock, to try to extract a further pledge of cooperation from Ibraham. The colonel was unable to see Ibraham, who was away with his raiders, but he seized the opportunity to sketch the disposition of the Turko-Egyptian fleet in the harbor.

Following the advice of a borrowed Frenchman named Letellier, Ibraham had arranged his ships ingeniously. The hundred vessels formed a great crescent, three tiers deep, curving from the two headlands to a point deep within the harbor. The largest ships were in the first row, the next largest in the second row, the smallest in the third. Those in the second and third rows were anchored in such a position that they could fire through gaps in the first row. The ends of the crescent were secured by fireships, anchored between the main body of the fleet and the land. A fleet entering the harbor would be at the focal point of the fire of 1,270 guns.

Though he clearly recognized the danger, Admiral Codrington did not hesitate to act. Early in the afternoon of October 20, 1827, he boldly led his little fleet into the trap which had been prepared for it. Doubtless he believed that Ibraham, having once been bluffed, would not fight. A message from the shore proclaimed that Ibraham had issued no orders for the allied fleet to enter the harbor. Replied Codrington: "I am not come to receive orders but to give them. If any shot be fired at the allied fleet, the Turkish fleet will be destroyed."

As the tension grew, the allied fleet came in past the silent land batteries and began to anchor, each ship in its carefully preselected place. *Asia* took her position between the Turkish and Egyptian flagships, each less than a cable's length away. *Genoa* (76) anchored opposite a 74-gun Turkish ship. The *razees,* frigates, corvettes, and smaller units went at once to their assigned places within the semicircle of death. Not only did the allied ships anchor; each of the crews hastily rigged springs on the cables, to permit the vessels to be turned quickly with the use of winches.

The anchoring was still incomplete, the Russian squadron still drifting into position in a dying breeze, when the spark dropped into the powder barrel. A small boat was sent out from the frigate *Dartmouth* to request a Turkish fireship to shift its position. A trigger-happy Turk raised his musket and killed a British seaman. The small boat and the *Dartmouth* herself returned the small-arms fire.

A frantic hail from the Egyptian flagship *La Guerriere* besought Admiral Codrington not to fire. Hoping to avoid a general engagement, Codrington at once sent his interpreter in a small boat to reassure the Egyptian vice-admiral. There was more musket fire, and the interpreter died between the ships. Elsewhere in the harbor, cannon fire crashed out. It was too late now to avert the holocaust.

So be it! *Asia*'s starboard batteries blazed into action, and the Turkish flagship crumbled into helplessness. With the aid of her springs, *Asia* swung slightly to bring her port battery to bear on the frigate *La Guerriere.* As they saw the frowning rows of guns swinging toward them, Vice-Admiral Moharem Bey and his French adviser Letellier went over the side. It was well for them that they did, for the first broadside was devastating. Shattered and burning, the frigate tried to move away from the great opponent which was destroying her. Flight was hopeless. *La Guerriere* ran aground, then blew up.

Meanwhile, Admiral De Rigny's flagship *Syrene* (60) was engaged in conflict with three enemy frigates. One blew up so horrendously that *Syrene* herself was badly damaged. For the remainder of the battle, *Trident* served as De Rigny's flagship.

As the Russian ships entered the fray, the battle became a formless *melee,* impossible to describe. The entire surface of the harbor was covered with ships, firing, receiving fire, fleeing, or pursuing. All afternoon and into the early evening the carnage continued. There was no darkness, but by the time when the light of the setting sun was replaced by the red glare of burning ships the issue had been settled.

The Turko-Egyptian fleet had been destroyed. The allied squadron had lost not a single ship.

The world gasped as the news of Navarino spread far and wide. Would there not now be a dreadful holy war—a new crusade of Christians against Mohammedans? What would the rulers of Turkey and Egypt do in reprisal? As the weeks went by, the tension evaporated. Nothing happened—nothing at all! The sample of Western warfare had been enough.

The most important single result of Navarino was the gaining of Greek freedom. Without sea power, the Turks were unable to control sea-girt Greece. It was a blow to Turkey, and it helped to kill the Concert of Europe, but it brought joy to freedom-loving people everywhere.

In considering the events which took place in the harbor of Navarino we should throw into the scales one fact which we now know, but which Codrington did not. The semicircle of ships had indeed been intended as a trap. Plans had long been laid for the destruction of the allied fleet, should it enter the harbor. At the stroke of midnight, all one hundred Turkish and Egyptian ships were to open fire simultaneously. When midnight came, there were no Turkish or Egyptian ships to carry out the plan.

17.

As an aftermath of the Napoleonic wars, which had weakened Spain and had loosened her hold upon her colonies, most of the Spanish possessions in the New World shook off the control of the mother country during the second and third decades of the nineteenth century. Among the important newly independent countries was Mexico, which gained freedom in 1821 and established a republican government in 1823.

Shortly before the winning of Mexican independence, an American citizen named Moses Austin had gained permission from the Spanish authorities to lead immigrants from the United States into the thinly settled section of northern Mexico known as Texas. Neither the ending of Spanish sovereignty nor the death of Moses Austin was permitted to interfere with this migration. The colonizer's son, Stephen F. Austin, led the first group of Americans southward across the Red River in 1821. In the years which followed, several other groups also settled in Texas. The legal status of the settlement was reconfirmed when

Stephen F. Austin went to Mexico City and negotiated an agreement with the new Mexican government.

It was not long before the governing authorities in Mexico City began to regret the agreement so hastily made. More and more Americans were swarming across the border, bringing with them their slaves and various kinds of Protestantism, of which the Mexicans did not approve. Worst of all, the new immigrants were rapidly making Texas far more American than Mexican in language, background, customs, and sympathy. If something were not done quickly, Texas might soon slip completely out of Mexican control.

An attempt was made to correct the situation. Laws were passed prohibiting slavery, restricting further American immigration, limiting trade with the United States, and providing that only bona fide Mexican citizens of the Catholic faith could own land.

The moves were made too late. The Texans resisted by force of arms. What started as a little war for the regaining of rights soon acquired bitterness when Mexican President-General Antonio Lopez de Santa Anna captured the Alamo in San Antonio and massacred all of its defenders. "Remember the Alamo" became the war cry of General Sam Houston's hard-fighting Texans.

Though most of the battles for Texas independence were fought upon the land, a Texas navy was soon created and saw no little service. The original force, scraped together from a variety of sources, included four armed schooners, a smaller armed vessel spoken of merely as "the raider *Flash*," and three privateers. These eight vessels carried the Lone Star flag of the newly proclaimed Texas Republic out upon the waters of the Gulf of Mexico, searching for ships flying the Mexican colors.

While the three privateers contented themselves with seizing unarmed Mexican merchant vessels and waxed prosperous by doing so, the five warships went looking for bigger game. Little *Flash* provided the most valuable service, dashing in to a point on the coast where a group of Texans, including Provisional President David Burnet, had become entrapped between the Mexican army and the Gulf. Burnet and his companions were rescued and whisked away, under the very eyes of their would-be captors. Without this bold maneuver, carried out by Captain Luke Falvel, the entire Texas revolt might have come to a premature end.

The schooner *Liberty,* under Captain Jeremiah Brown, raided commerce successfully and, when trapped by Mexican warships, succeeded in fighting her way free. Two other schooners were less fortunate. Commodore William Brown and his flagship, *Independence* (8), were captured by the Mexicans. The *Invincible*'s captain, C. E. Hawkins, had the bad judgment to fly the American flag in the presence of a United States warship. His ship was seized, and his crew was charged with piracy, taken to New Orleans, and imprisoned.

Two very different events combined to bring the activities of the little Texas navy to a halt. On April 4, 1836, the rag-tag army led by Sam Houston turned upon the Mexicans at San Jacinto and defeated them, taking President-General Santa Anna a prisoner. When deprived of narcotics, to which he was addicted, the Mexican leader became an abject figure. In order to secure the drugs he craved, he willingly signed an armistice, ending the Mexican campaign to conquer Texas, though not the war. At about the same time, Texas Secretary of the Navy S. Rhoades Fisher was caught taking graft and was dismissed. The remaining Texas ships were recalled to port, and a period of inactivity ensued.

18.

Most of the citizens of the newly freed Republic of Texas hoped and expected to become a part of the United States without delay. This did not happen. Slavery had become a major issue in United States politics, and the free states of the North were not willing to see their influence weakened by the admission of another state permitting slavery. Most Americans were also anxious to avoid the war with Mexico which was certain to occur if Texas were annexed. Consequently, the Lone Star Republic was left, for the time being, on its own.

For its own defense, Texas needed a navy. One was created in 1839 by the legislature, at the urging of President Mirabeau B. Lamar. The sum of $800,000 was appropriated, which was well expended for the 20-gun brig *Austin;* the smaller brigs *Archer* and *Wharton;* the schooners *San Antonio, San Bernard,* and *San Jacinto;* and the small, paddle-wheel steamboat *Zavala* (8). The new Commodore, in charge of all naval operations, was Edwin W. Moore of Virginia, a veteran of the United States Navy.

Mexico, too, had been building up a fleet, including two brigs, two schooners, and an armed steamer named the *Regenerador*. More important were two steam frigates, the *Guadaloupe* and the *Montezuma,* which presently came from Great Britain. Both were driven by paddle wheels. The larger *Montezuma* was a wooden ship of 1,164 tons mounting a 68-pound swivel gun and six 32's. The *Guadaloupe,* of 775 tons, had only two 68-pound swivel guns, but her hull was of iron. She was the first ironclad warship to see action in the Western Hemisphere.

Technically, Texas and Mexico were still at war, though there had been no important fighting since the signing of the armistice in 1836. Occasionally one of the Texas warships picked up a Mexican merchant ship and brought it in as a prize. Such prizes became scarce in 1842 when a revolution within Mexico greatly reduced the number of Mexican ships on the sea. Between two days, the Texas schooner *San Antonio* slipped away from her anchorage and left the fleet, her crew turned pirates. The *San Bernard* ran on a reef off Galveston and was lost. Distressed by the misfortunes of his fleet, Commodore Moore sailed to New Orleans for supplies and recruits.

San Houston had meanwhile become president of Texas for a second time. Fearing what his desperate and unpredictable navy might do next, he ordered Moore and his squadron to return to Galveston for decommissioning. The commodore disobeyed. He had received word that the Mexicans in Yucatan were willing and anxious to hire his fleet for use in their revolution against the Mexican government. The lure of action, excitement, and possible gain drew him southward. Houston, angry, denounced Moore and his men as pirates and renegades.

On April 30, 1843, the seven vessels of the Mexican fleet lay off Campeche, Yucatan. Admiral Don Tomas Marin had no thought of action against other naval units; he was merely interested in cooperating with the army in rounding up rebels and ending the Yucatan revolution. By way of improving his own mastery of sea warfare, he had been holding a series of conferences with his two British officers-on-loan, Captain Charlewood of the *Guadaloupe* and Captain Cleaveland of the *Montezuma.*

Suddenly, out of nowhere, appeared the four little vessels of the Texas squadron. The element of surprise favored the Texans. Numbers and weight of armament favored the Mexicans. There was a brief exchange of cannon fire, doing little damage to either side. Then the Texan fleet drew away, and the indecisive skirmish was over.

Less than three weeks later, on May 16, the Texans were back.

This time Admiral Marin was not taken by surprise. Out to sea he led his fleet, seven ships against four, to pursue and destroy this audacious enemy. Pursuing and overtaking proved not to be difficult, but destroying was a different story. The guns of the wooden Texas warships were well and accurately served, particularly the 24-pounders of the flagship *Austin*. Steam should have vanquished sail, and iron should have proved better than wood. The results were otherwise. When the shooting was over, the ironclad *Guadaloupe* went limping out of action with forty-seven dead and with five huge holes in her hull. After her came the *Montezuma,* badly battered and with forty dead. The other Mexican ships were sunk or captured. The dead aboard the Texas squadron numbered five.

Having destroyed Mexican sea power, Commodore Moore belatedly came home to face the music. The city of Galveston gave him a hero's welcome, but President Houston was less enthusiastic. The commodore was tried for mutiny. Though he was acquitted, his days at sea were over. Dejectedly, he made his way across the border and into the United States, where he lived and eventually died in obscurity. His crews were dispersed, and his ships lay idle at their piers until the United States annexed Texas in 1845 and took them over as part of the United States Navy.

19.

Reform, badly needed in all navies, was slow in coming. Training was haphazard. Promotion was slow and uncertain. Thinking was ultraconservative. Punishment was often brutal. Certain archaic practices persisted—dueling, for one. Some of these weaknesses had to be worn away by time and gradual evolution. A few were erased with dramatic suddenness.

Commodore James Barron, U.S.N., hated Commodore Stephen Decatur. It was a quarrel of long standing, dating back to 1812, when Decatur had reluctantly served as president of the court-martial which had removed Barron from command for his part in the *Chesapeake-Leopard* affair. Fuel had been added to the fire when Decatur had sided with Oliver H. Perry rather than with Barron's friend Elliott in the dispute over Elliott's lack of cooperation on Lake Erie. Barron and Elliott blasted Decatur, and Decatur blasted right back. As a result, he was challenged to a duel.

Stephen Decatur was no stranger to dueling, but this was an affair for which he had no stomach. He felt that he had only done his duty, without rancor or fervor. He had no wish to kill Barron, and even less wish to be killed by Barron. His quiet statement, "I have never been your enemy, sir," was ignored. The duel had to be fought.

The pistols went off early in the morning of March 22, 1820. Decatur fell to the ground, dying. Barron was also wounded. Though he later recovered, his naval career was ruined. A barbarous custom had cost the United States Navy two fine officers. Belatedly, the navy prohibited dueling. Great Britain followed suit in 1844. To some extent, the custom still exists in the services of certain other nations.

20.

Before the 1840's, the training of officers for the United States Navy was anything but thorough. Midshipmen went to sea and learned as they could by observing and by doing. There was little formal schooling, though some of the larger warships did carry civilian schoolmasters to instruct the midshipmen. Though many good officers were developed, a very large number were seriously deficient in certain aspects of training and character development.

As an experiment in training, the navy instituted special instructional cruises in which small naval vessels were manned by apprentice seamen and midshipmen under veteran officers. It was on such a cruise that Commander Alexander S. Mackenzie took out the brig *Somers* (10) in 1842, manned by some 130 young seamen and officers-in-training.

Commander Mackenzie was a harsh seaman of the old school. He had had little contact with high-spirited boys, and he had absolutely no patience with their inevitable pranks. Flogging was his solution for any serious irregularity, and a great deal of heavy flogging was experienced by the boys during their voyage from Brooklyn to the African coast and back. Naturally, there was resentment.

Among the angry young men was a somewhat unbalanced character named Philip Spencer, whose father happened to be the Secretary of War. Philip had pranked and loafed his way out of college and out of the navy. Reinstated in the service through his father's influence, he had been included among the boys on the training cruise. Now he was grumbling with the rest and fashioning vivid daydreams of wished-for revenge on certain of the stricter officers.

A member of the crew reported to Commander Mackenzie that he had heard Spencer speak of leading a mutiny, seizing the ship, and taking up piracy as a way of life. The next day, Spencer was seen whispering to Seaman Small and Bosun's Mate Cromwell. In Spencer's seabag was found a list, written in Greek, naming all crew members and designating certain ones "To Be Killed." The three boys were arrested and charged with mutiny. Spencer swore that the list and the talk of mutiny were only parts of a joke. The other two attested that they knew nothing of any plan for mutiny. Mackenzie didn't believe them. He had all three handcuffed to the rail with bags tied over their heads—treatment usually reserved for the most dangerous of criminals. The next day, he hanged all three from the yardarm before the eyes of the entire crew, "to make a beneficial impression on the disaffected."

In order to prevent the complete disintegration of authority afloat, a shocked court of inquiry found it necessary to exonerate Commander Mackenzie. Nevertheless, immediate steps were taken to prevent a repetition of the tragedy. The power of life and death was taken from the hands of ship captains. In today's navy, no death sentence can be carried out without the specific approval of the President of the United States.

If voyages under hardened veteran officers were not the answer, how should midshipmen be trained? Secretary of the Navy George Bancroft thought he had the answer, though he suspected that Congress would not support him. The opportunity to try his plan arrived in 1845. During the absence of the Secretary of War, Bancroft found himself in charge of both departments. Taking full advantage of the situation, he transferred from army to navy administration old Fort Severn, at Annapolis, Maryland. At the fort, he established a school for the training of naval officers. Franklin Buchanan, an experienced officer, was the first commandant. Four instructors were hired, plus an officer to teach gunnery and engineering. When the school opened on October 10, 1845, the United States Naval Academy had come into being.

When Congress reconvened, it was too late to do anything but approve the new school. In view of the possibility of war with Great Britain and the probability of war with Mexico, the academy was permitted to carry on its work. Perhaps the results would be beneficial, as were the results of the older French naval academies at Toulon, Rochefort, and Brest; the British Royal Naval Academy at Dartmouth; and the United States Military Academy at West Point.

21.

Rumors were rife in 1842. Despite Santa Anna's earlier defeat, Mexico was still at war with the Texas Republic. Not only Texans but all citizens of the United States were objects of dislike and suspicion south of the Rio Grande. It was widely believed that the British and Mexican governments were hatching a plan by which large areas of Mexican land on the Pacific coast of North America would be deeded to Great Britain in exchange for the cancellation of all or part of the very considerable debt which the Mexicans owed to the British. Such rumors had a disquieting effect on the United States, whose own eyes were firmly fixed on those Pacific lands. The high-sounding term "manifest destiny" was already beginning to be heard.

On September 6, 1842, an American squadron lay in the harbor of Callao, Peru. It consisted of the frigate *United States* (44), the sloop-of-war *Cyane* (20), the brig *Dale* (16), and the schooner *Shark* (12), all under the command of Commodore Thomas ap Catesby Jones. Both Jones and American Chargé d'Affaires Pickett were deeply concerned over the rumors they had heard and over the definite news that a French fleet had seized the Marquesas Islands. Their agitation increased markedly when an additional rumor was received that the United States and Mexico were at war. It reached the boiling point when the British frigate *Dublin* put out to sea on a mysterious errand. Where were the British going? Jones and Pickett jumped to the conclusion that they were going to take over California before the Americans could do so.

Out to sea went Jones's squadron, headed north under full sail to beat the British warship to the coveted prize. As an afterthought, the *Shark* was detached and sent back to Callao to allay suspicion, while the *Dale* was sent eastward toward Panama with a hastily written communiqué for the American government. *United States* and *Cyane* continued onward toward Monterey, California, which they reached on October 19.

Evidently the two American warships had outfooted the *Dublin,* which was nowhere to be seen. So much the better! The guns were run out, and a peremptory message was sent to the Mexican governor, demanding immediate surrender. Being a sensible man, the governor did not try to match the 64 guns on the ships with his few outdated cannons. He quickly surrendered and stood by while the Mexican flag was hauled down and was replaced by the Stars and Stripes.

Forty-eight hours later, a very different situation prevailed. The Mexican flag was once more flying from its staff. Commodore Thomas ap Catesby Jones, very red of face, was apologizing to the governor and to other officials and was rejoicing that there had been no resistance and hence no bloodshed. Word had arrived that the United States and Mexico had not gone to war after all. Whatever the *Dublin*'s mission, she had not gone to California to take possession. The whole affair had been a wild goose chase.

Farther south, at San Diego, the same embarrassing thing happened a few days later. Captain Phelps of the American merchant ship *Alert* heard of Jones's seizure of Monterey, and he also began to suspect that the Mexican authorities were going to take his ship. Though the *Alert* carried only four 6-pounder guns, Captain Phelps boldly led his men ashore, spiked the guns in the Mexican fort, and took possession of the town in the name of the United States. When the truth finally overtook the rumors, he, too, had the unhappy task of trying to restore the status quo.

It is interesting to note that the United States government took no punitive steps against Commodore Thomas ap Catesby Jones. In the interests of peace and international amity it was necessary to remove him from command of the Pacific squadron, but he was never court-martialed, never reprimanded, never penalized in any way for his enterprising action. It was only his timing that had been at fault.

22.

When the United States annexed Texas in December 1845, war with Mexico became inevitable. It did not, however, start automatically and at once. An excuse was needed. In the weeks that followed annexation, each of the two countries was provided with an excellent one.

When Texas had been a part of Mexico, the southern border of Texas was the Nueces River. With the gaining of independence, the Texans claimed that their southern border was the Rio Grande. The area between the rivers was thus claimed by both the United States and Mexico. When American troops under General Zachary Taylor crossed the Nueces into this no-man's land, the Mexicans regarded it as an invasion of Mexico and resisted by force of arms. When American soldiers were killed in the fighting that followed, President Polk felt justified in calling for war on the grounds that "Mexicans have shed American blood on American soil." To most Americans, it seemed to make little difference that the soil in question was of highly doubtful ownership.

The Mexican War (1846–48) is sometimes spoken of as "the war without a naval battle." In a very literal sense, this was true. Thanks to Commodore Moore and the Texas navy, Mexico had few warships left. Two that had survived were the steam-driven frigate *Montezuma* and the ironclad steamboat *Guadaloupe*. These were at Vera Cruz at the outbreak of the war. To counter this threat, the United States dispatched two steam-driven fighting ships, the *Mississippi* and the *Princeton,* to Vera Cruz, where some sailing warships were already maintaining a partial blockade. Here, the world might well have witnessed the first real naval battle between fleets of steamboats. It did not happen. Learning of the approach of the *Mississippi* and the *Princeton,* the captains of the *Montezuma* and the *Guadaloupe* availed themselves of a dead calm, easily skirted the motionless blockading squadron, and made for Havana, where they turned over their two warships to the British, from whom they had originally secured them.

With war actually declared, General Taylor moved to cross from the no-man's land between the rivers into Mexico proper. It seemed possible that the Mexican army might use the Rio Grande as a formidable barrier to invasion. Accordingly, Taylor asked help from Commodore David Conner, whose American squadron was located just off the river's mouth. A flotilla of small boats was dispatched up the river as far as Barita, a Mexican town fifteen miles from the Gulf. The landing of the sailors, under Captain Aulick, was the war's first invasion of undisputed Mexican soil. There was no resistance. The Mexicans had already fallen back, so the beachhead was easily secured.

In the Gulf, the navy found much valuable work to be done, but no fighting afloat. Transports and supply ships were guarded against the few Mexican privateers that managed to get to sea. The various ports were tightly blockaded. Troops and special equipment were carried to key points. But only by going ashore on special assignment could the marines or sailors of the fleet find action against the enemy, and the opportunities for this were very limited.

23.

The year 1847 brought an important change. General Zachary Taylor's heavy-handed but generally successful campaign in northern

Mexico was brought to a conclusion after his smashing land victories at Ciudad Monterrey and Buena Vista. The tremendous distance to Mexico City and the ruggedness of the intervening terrain were cited, but an equally important reason was friction between the presidency-minded general and the Polk administration. The new general in charge was Winfield Scott. The new plan was a sea-borne invasion, to land at or near Vera Cruz and to strike directly inland to Mexico City.

This was to be the first large-scale amphibious operation in American military history. Up and down the coast in the little steamer *Petrita* went Commodore Conner, General Scott, and their staffs. The shore was examined almost foot by foot, and the advantages and disadvantages of every alternative were debated. The plan, as it finally emerged, was largely the product of Conner's fertile mind.

Anton Lizardo was the staging point for the projected invasion. This coastal town, ten miles south of Vera Cruz, had been seized some time earlier by Conner and had been converted into a secondary naval base, much nearer and more convenient than the official base of operations at Pensacola. Scott's troops, 12,000 in number, were carried to Anton Lizardo in transports and were there transferred to the warships of the American squadron.

Early on the morning of March 9, 1847, Commodore Conner's squadron appeared off the coast at a carefully selected spot about three miles south of Vera Cruz, where the island called Sacrificios shields a sandy beach. Since it seemed likely that strong Mexican forces were waiting behind the dunes to attack the disembarking troops, the steamboats *Spitfire* and *Vixen* and the schooners *Bonita, Falcon, Petrel, Reefer,* and *Tampico* swept in close and opened a heavy covering fire. All that was flushed out was a handful of Mexican cavalry, who rapidly departed. The landing was made without opposition.

It was one thing to make a landing; it was quite another to take heavily fortified Vera Cruz. The Mexicans were confident that the place could not be taken. The walls were thick. The garrison was strong. The guns were large and numerous. Just off shore loomed the powerful island fort of San Juan de Ulloa. More important than any of these was the plague—*El Vomito,* "Yellow Jack," "King Death in His Saffron Robes." The susceptible northerners would perish miserably.

General Scott slowly moved his forces forward and enfolded the city. On March 18, his artillery, under the able direction of Captain Robert E. Lee, opened fire on the walls. Lee's primary purpose was to disable the Mexican artillery. He knew just where to aim, for a few days before the little *Spitfire* had run boldly into the harbor to draw the fire of the defenders. Every gun that opened up on her had promptly been marked down on charts.

Two days after the opening of the bombardment, the *Mississippi* arrived from Pensacola, where she had been sent in July with a cargo of yellow-fever victims. On board was Captain Matthew Calbraith Perry, returning to duty after a bout with the disease. With him he bore orders placing him in charge of the squadron as commodore and taking Conner north for a well-earned rest.

On March 21, General Scott called Perry to him and freely confessed that the army's guns were too light to breach the walls. What he wanted was six of the heavy naval guns. Would Perry lend them to him? "Certainly, General," replied Perry, "but I must fight them. Wherever the guns go, their officers and men must go with them."

The guns were landed—three 68-pounders and three 32-pounders —and were emplaced behind sandbags. Double gun crews were assigned to each. They opened fire on the morning of the 24th and did so much damage that the Mexicans concentrated on them every battery that would bear. To take pressure from his land-based guns, Perry then ordered the *Spitfire* and the *Vixen,* each towing two gunboats, to enter the harbor and hammer the walls. The raid was carried on with great daring, the little *Spitfire* under Commander Tattnall boldly sailing within 800 yards of the walls in spite of the tremendous volume of fire directed at her. Not one of the six little ships was seriously damaged.

On the 25th, the Mexican commander at Vera Cruz asked for an armistice. Three days later, the city was unconditionally surrendered.

24.

The taking of Vera Cruz brought General Scott face to face with a knotty problem. The way was now open to Mexico City. He could, and in fact should, start westward immediately. Every day spent in the steaming coastal lowlands meant more men down and more men dead with yellow fever. But the army was pinned down by a shortage of mules and horses. There were three times as many wagons laden with equipment as there were animals to pull them.

Someone recalled that the land around Alvarado, thirty miles to the south, was a pasturing ground for vast herds of horses. Commodore Perry was given the assignment of taking Alvarado and holding it until troops could come by land to round up the horses. Since Alvarado had twice withstood attacks from the sea, Perry took his entire squadron, ready for an all-out assault.

Anticlimax! Arriving off Alvarado, Perry's squadron encountered no opposition at all. In the harbor lay a single little American gunboat, the *Scourge*. The town had surrendered meekly to Lieutenant Hunter, the gunboat's skipper, who had not even known of the impending invasion.

Commodore Perry was neither pleased nor amused. Since he could not charge Lieutenant Hunter with making him look ridiculous, he charged him with acting without the permission of his superior officer and with scaring the horses away and thus spoiling the purpose of the raid. Hunter was court-martialed and dismissed from the navy. Fortunately, President Polk had a better sense of humor than Commodore Perry. The findings of the court-martial were reversed.

Somehow, somewhere, General Scott managed to collect some horses. Slowly his army crawled westward and upward, away from the seacoast and toward Mexico City and ultimate victory.

25.

The departure of the army did not mean that Perry's work was done. Several spots on the coast still had to be secured and nests of guerrilla resistance wiped out. These jobs the squadron tackled with vigor.

The river port of Tuxpan was a center of resistance. During the previous summer, the brig *Truxtun* had tried to take the place but had run aground and had been battered into helplessness by Mexican artillery. The *Truxtun*'s guns had been brought ashore and used to equip a strong new fort, which was currently manned by 650 Mexican troops under General Cos.

On April 17, 1847, Commodore Perry's squadron arrived off the river's mouth. Because of a bar, only the smaller vessels could go farther. Perry transferred his flag to the *Spitfire,* which led a column of little gunboats upstream. Below Tuxpan, a landing party went ashore under Captain Samuel L. Breese. When the Mexican batteries opened up, the ships returned the fire, meanwhile steadily drawing closer.

Then Breese launched his land attack, catching the Mexican defenders in the flank. General Cos and his men retreated, and Tuxpan was secured, at a cost of only fourteen American casualties.

At Coazacoalcos, Perry's squadron was fired on by a coastal fort mounting twelve heavy guns. The ships blasted back, and the fort was silenced and taken.

Tabasco was the next point of attack—a strongly held town some distance up a winding river. As at Tuxpan, Perry had to leave the large ships off the river mouth and proceed with the smaller vessels. This time, the *Scorpion* served as his flagship. She and *Spitfire,* being steamers, were able to tow the bomb brigs and other vessels upstream. Though frequently fired on from the banks, the little squadron continued on until they reached a crude fort, called La Comena. Here the Mexicans had obstructed the channel to make further progress impossible.

Though the ships apparently could not advance, men afoot might be able to do so. Perry's men went ashore and succeeded in dragging their field guns up the almost perpendicular 30-foot banks that lined the river. Small Mexican detachments were brushed aside and the El Comena fort was assaulted from the rear and taken. On went Perry and his men, slogging overland toward Tabasco.

Lieutenant David Dixon Porter, who had been left in charge of the gunboats, did not waste his time waiting for the landing party to return. The barricade in the river looked vulnerable, so Porter blew it up and sailed through. Near Tabasco, he was fired on by heavy guns in Fort Iturbide. Very well! Porter landed with sixty-eight men and took the fort by assault.

When Commodore Perry and his weary men emerged from the jungle at Tabasco, the gunboats were already there, and the town was in American hands. Perry's squadron had succeeded in securing complete control of the entire Mexican east coast.

26.

Along the Pacific coast, meanwhile, small-scale events of enormous importance had been taking place. California, nominally under Mexican control, was virtually independent of the central Mexican government. It was, moreover, divided. Monterey was held by General José Castro, the military commandant. Farther south, the civil governor, Pio Pico, controlled the area about his capital city of Los Angeles. The two men were bitter rivals.

The delicate situation within California was further complicated by various disciples of American "Manifest Destiny." Long before the declaration of war, Secretary of the Navy George Bancroft had sent secret orders to the American Pacific squadron under Commodore John D. Sloat. As a result, the little war fleet of five vessels had moved north from Callao, Peru, to Mazatlan, Mexico, in order to be near the scene of desirable activity. Obviously, Jones's grab of 1842 was to be repeated, this time on a legal basis. At about the same time, a little group of adventurers, headed by explorer John C. Frémont, had headed west across the Rockies under the guidance of Kit Carson, famous scout and Indian fighter.

Frémont reached California too soon. No war had been declared. General Castro took a dim view of his presence and ordered him out. The American group was in the act of withdrawing into Oregon when they were overtaken by a government courier, Lieutenant A. H. Gillespie of the United States Marines. Gillespie brought orders and definite tidings of war. As a result, Frémont turned back, gathered up all the Americans he could find in the area north of San Francisco, and organized a government, with himself as president. The flag of the new Republic of California was white with a red stripe and bore the picture of a bear—hence the term "Bear Flag Republic." From his new capital at Sonoma, President Frémont led his men against San Francisco, placing the city under loose siege and taking the fort on the southern point of the Golden Gate by the end of June, 1846.

Commodore Sloat, meanwhile, had dispersed his squadron to strategic points along the coast. On July 2, his flagship *Savannah* (44) joined the *Warren* (32), the *Cyane* (18) and the *Levant* (18) at Monterey. Five days later, he demanded and received the surrender of the town. On the 9th, the *Portsmouth* (20) appeared off San Francisco. Commander John B. Montgomery ran out his guns, and the town was surrendered without resistance.

Brief hope flared in the hearts of the native Californians on July 11, when the British sloop *Juno* (18) appeared at San Francisco, and on July 15, when H. M. ship-of-the-line *Collingwood* (74) put in at Monterey. Would the British help their Mexican friends against the Yankee imperialists? The British would not. The tension eased, and the British ships departed.

Affairs presently grew far more complicated. On July 15, the frigate *Congress* (44) arrived at Monterey, bearing Commodore Robert F. Stockton. Sloat had refused to cooperate with the Bear Flag forces, but Stockton was inclined to do so. There was disagreement, which came to an end when Sloat, an ill man, turned over control of the squadron to Stockton and sailed east on the *Levant* for medical attention. Then, in December, 1846, General Stephen W. Kearney of the United States Army arrived, and there were more questions of rank, seniority and sovereignty. There was also a good deal of fighting on the land, much of it being carried on by men from the Pacific fleet, battling on foot far from their native element. In California, as in Mexico, the superior training and equipment of the United States forces insured eventual victory.

Whether or not the Mexican War can be defended on moral and ethical grounds, no one can deny its importance to the United States. A clear title to Texas was secured. Farther west, a vast area, including the present states of California, Nevada, Utah, Colorado, Arizona, and New Mexico, came under the American flag. Most important of all, from a naval point of view, the United States acquired a Pacific coast and with it all the problems connected with creating and maintaining a two-ocean navy.

27.

Far to the east, the European pot was boiling again. Czar Nicholas I had inherited from his predecessors the old Russian urge to expand and to secure a warm-water exit to the Mediterranean. As this could be done only at Turkish expense, he sent his troops in the summer of 1853 to invade the lands about the western end of the Black Sea where Rumania now is.

The situation was far more complicated than a mere struggle over territory between Russia and Turkey. France was interested both because she feared the expansion of Russian influence and because she was currently engaged in a dispute with the Czar's government over the question of which nation should protect Christian shrines in the Holy Land. Great Britain was interested because she feared that a Russian foothold in the Mediterranean would menace her lifeline to India. Strong British and French naval squadrons were sent into the Sea of Marmara, the water gateway to the Black Sea, in the hope that their presence and their strength would inhibit Russian naval action.

The Turks shared the hope of the British and the French. In spite of the presence of strong Russian naval units in the bases along the northern shore of the Black Sea, Turkish ships went confidently along the southern shore, carrying supplies and equipment to support a guerrilla band operating against the Russians in the Caucasus region just east of the Black Sea. Units of the Turkish fleet also used this southern route in perfect confidence.

Late in November, 1853, a Turkish squadron of seven frigates and eight smaller craft was caught in a storm while en route from Constantinople to the eastern Black Sea. The fleet scattered, each ship for itself, but later managed to get together in the lee of the peninsula at Sinope, midway along the southern shore. Here they were discovered by Admiral Pavel S. Nakhimov, on patrol with three Russian ships-of-the-line.

Admiral Nakhimov was not a man to rush in blindly. Though his three large ships were superior to the enemy's fifteen smaller vessels, he wanted to make assurance doubly sure. Retiring, he sent a small steamboat scooting north for reinforcements. While awaiting their arrival, he set out a string of picket vessels along the southwestern Black Sea coast to bear early warning of the approach of the French and British watch-dog squadrons.

Early in the morning of November 30, Admiral Nakhimov approached Sinope under cover of fog. His force now consisted of six ships-of-the-line, ranging from the flagship *Empress Maria* (84) to the tremendous *Grand Duke Constantine* (120), plus five frigates. Because of the poor visibility, the Turks had no warning. Their first indication of danger was the materializing of monstrous shapes in the fog, less than half a mile away. Their second was the crash of broadside cannon. Trapped between the Russian fleet and the shore, the Turks had no possible course but to fight to the death. One small ship, and one alone, managed to escape.

More than mere weight of broadside was involved in the battle which followed. The Russians had done much experimenting with explosive shells, and their ships were armed with these improved projectiles. A Russian hit was almost certain to be followed by a devastating concussion and by a fire. Hits by the solid Turkish cannon balls were relatively ineffective. The Turkish fleet was quickly and methodically destroyed, even the survivors in open boats being massacred. The batteries on the shore were then silenced, and the town of Sinope was shelled and set afire. Before the last gun was fired at four in the afternoon, approximately 3,000 Turks had been killed, as opposed to 37 Russians. Few naval battles have been as one-sided as was the Turkish defeat at Sinope.

Sinope was also a defeat for the Russians, though in a very different sense. At the very time when the battle was fought, diplomats from France, Great Britain, Russia, and Turkey were making satisfactory progress in peace talks being held at Vienna. Now there could be no thought of peace. Russia had disregarded the implied warning issued by Britain and France in sending their squadrons into the Black Sea region. Russia had violated naval custom by permitting her ships-of-the-line to turn their cannons on helpless smaller vessels. Russia had outraged the world by the slaughter of helpless men in the water. The so-called massacre of Sinope was used to turn world opinion against the czar's government.

This was the window dressing. These are the excuses. Russian diplomats could point out that the British and French had also turned the guns of ships-of-the-line against lesser vessels at Navarino, not many years before. They could call attention to the fact that the "massacre" was in reality the elimination of a hostile though inferior battle fleet, in the midst of war. What they could not explain away was Russia's growing power and the menace which it presented to the British and the French. This was the real reason for the subsequent outbreak of the Crimean War of 1854–55, in which Britain, France, Turkey, and Sardinia would defeat Russia and set back the czar's plans of conquest.

15 AGAIN, TRANSITION

⚓

1.

The picturesque age of sails in naval warfare came to an end in the middle years of the nineteenth century. Like the dinosaurs, the great ships-of-the-line and their lesser bretheren of the wind were doomed long before the fact of death became self-evident. When James Rumsey and John Fitch built their first crude steamboats in 1787, the handwriting was on the wall. When Robert Fulton attached a steam engine to a paddle wheel and the *Clermont* proved her practicality in 1807, the message was unmistakable. When John Ericsson made the first efficient screw propeller in 1836, sailing warships were already obsolete. It took nearly twenty years for naval authorities to recognize the fact.

For a long time, sails still enjoyed advantages over steam. Few steamships of a hundred years ago could outfoot the clipper ships. Wind, though somewhat unpredictable, was everywhere; it did not have to be carried along, taking up valuable cargo space, or stored in distant fueling stations. Wind cost nothing; coal was expensive.

Still, it *was* handy to have steam power available. When the great ships-of-the-line were becalmed, a little paddle-wheel tug could quickly get them under way and take them to needed points. Men thought hard about such epic chases at sea as the one in which the *Constitution* had escaped the British squadron off New Jersey. How either side could have profited by having a single tug that day! Events such as the escape of the Mexican steam gunboats from Vera Cruz made their impression. As the Russians proved before Sinope, messages were more likely to get through on time if carried by steamboat.

More and more, puffs of smoke were seen about harbors and above the small auxiliary vessels with the fleets. It was only a question of time before major naval units would be steam-driven.

2.

As in most historical transitions, it is not possible to pinpoint the exact moment at which the change from sail to steam took place. The United States built a steam-driven ship-of-the-line during the War of 1812, yet it saw no action, and the war at sea and on the lakes was a war of sails. We have seen minor uses of steam during the Mexican War of 1846–48 and during the preliminaries to Sinope in 1853. Again, though, these were primarily sailing actions.

There is good reason to choose the end of 1853 as the best of several possible points of transition.

Sails were used in the Crimean War, which broke out in 1854, yet this was, in the main, a war of steam-driven navies. The American War of Secession, or Civil War, 1861–65, was still more clearly a war of steam warships, though a number of large sailing craft saw service. Even as late as World War I, a few German raiders made use of sails to circumvent their navy's chronic lack of fueling bases. Yet no one would speak of this as a war of sails.

No, 1853 was the turning point. From that time on, the great ships-of-the-line and the frigates, with their towering clouds of sail, grew fewer and fewer—mere isolated remnants of a once-proud genus going down the long road to extinction.

BIBLIOGRAPHY

ABBOT, WILLIS J. *The Naval History of the United States* (2 vols.), P. F. Collier, New York, 1896.

ABSHIRE, DAVID M. "The Naval Battle of Navarino, 1827," *United States Naval Institute Proceedings,* Annapolis, Maryland, January, 1959.

ALBION, R. G., and POPE, J. B. *Sea Lanes in Wartime, 1775–1942,* W. W. Norton & Company, Inc., New York, 1942.

ANDERSON, R. C. (ed.). *Journals and Narratives of the Third Dutch War,* Navy Records Society, London, 1946.

———. *Naval Wars in the Baltic, 1522–1850,* Gilbert Wood, London, 1910.

———. *Naval Wars in the Levant, 1559–1853,* Princeton University Press, Princeton, New Jersey, 1952.

BALLARD, G. A. *Rulers of the Indian Ocean,* Houghton Mifflin Company, Boston, 1927.

BASSETT-LOWKE, W. J. and HOLLAND, GEORGE. *Ships and Men,* George G. Harrap and Company, Ltd., London, 1946.

BRYCE, VISCOUNT *et al. The Book of History* (7 vols.), The Grolier Society, New York, 1914–1921.

BURNE, ALFRED H. *The Noble Duke of York,* Staples Press, London, 1949.

Cambridge Mediaeval History. Cambridge University Press, Cambridge, England, 1936.

CASSON, LIONEL. *Illustrated History of Ships and Boats,* Doubleday and Company, Inc., Garden City, New York, 1964.

CHAPELLE, HOWARD I. *The History of the American Sailing Navy,* Bonanza Books, New York, 1949.

CLARK, G. R. *et al. A Short History of the United States Navy,* J. B. Lippincott Company, Philadelphia, 1939.

CLARK, GEORGE N. *The Dutch Alliance and the War Against the French Trade, 1688–97,* Oxford University Press, Oxford, England, 1934.

CORBETT, JULIAN S. *Drake and the Tudor Navy* (2 vols.), Longmans, Green, and Company, London, 1899.

————. *England in the Seven Years' War* (2 vols.), Longmans, Green, and Company, London, 1918.

————. *The Campaign of Trafalgar,* Longmans, Green, and Company, London, 1913.

COSTAIN, THOMAS B. *The Conquerors,* Doubleday and Company, Garden City, New York, 1949.

————. *The Magnificent Century,* Doubleday and Company, Garden City, New York, 1954.

————. *The Three Edwards,* Doubleday and Company, Garden City, New York, 1958.

————. *The Last Plantagenets,* Doubleday and Company, Garden City, New York, 1962.

COWBURN, PHILIP. *The Warship in History,* The Macmillan Company, New York, 1965.

CREASY, E. S. *The Fifteen Decisive Battles of the World,* Thomas Y. Crowell and Company, New York, 1851.

CULVER, HENRY B., and GRANT, GORDON. *The Book of Old Ships.* Garden City Publishing Company, Garden City, New York, 1924.

————. *Forty Famous Ships,* Garden City Publishing Company, Garden City, New York, 1938.

CURRY, EDWARD H. *Sea Wolves of the Mediterranean,* Frederick A. Stokes Company, New York, 1929.

DE LA VARENDE, JEAN. *Cherish the Sea,* The Viking Press, New York, 1956.

DOWDELL, VINCENT J., JR. "Captain Mugford and the Powder Ship," *United States Naval Institute Proceedings,* Annapolis, Maryland, November, 1956.

DOWNY, FAIRFAX. *Sound of the Guns,* David McKay Company, New York, 1956.

DUFFY, JAMES. *Shipwreck and Empire,* Harvard University Press, Cambridge, Massachusetts, 1955.

EHRMAN, J. *The Navy in the War of William III,* Cambridge University Press, Cambridge, England, 1958.

FATTORUSSO, JOSEPH. *Kings and Queens of England and France* (2 vols.), Giuseppi Fattorusso, Florence, Italy, 1953.

FORESTER, C. S. *The Age of Fighting Sail,* Doubleday and Company, Garden City, New York, 1956.

GILLIGAN, ARTHUR E. "The Battle of Valcour Island," *United States Naval Institute Proceedings,* Annapolis, Maryland, October, 1967.

GOLDER, F. A. *John Paul Jones in Russia,* Doubleday, Page, and Company, Garden City, New York, 1927.

GREEN, J. R. *A Short History of the English People* (4 vols.), Harper and Brothers, New York, 1893.

GUIZOT, F. *The History of France* (8 vols.), American Publishers' Corporation, New York, 1869.

HAKLUYT, RICHARD. *Voyages and Discoveries of the English*, Alfred A. Knopf, New York, 1926.

HALLAM, HENRY. *History of the Middle Ages* (4 vols.), John B. Alden, New York, 1888.

HOLLAND, RUPERT S. *Historic Ships*, MacRae, Smith, and Company, Philadelphia, 1926.

JAMES, SIR WILLIAM. *Old Oak: The Life of John Jervis*, Longmans, Green, and Company, London, 1950.

KNOX, DUDLEY W. *A History of the United States Navy*, G. P. Putnam's Sons, New York, 1936.

LANDSTROM, BJORN. *The Ship*, Doubleday and Company, Garden City, New York, 1961.

LE VAN, HOWARD A., JR. "The Continental Navy Frigate *Raleigh*," *United States Naval Institute Proceedings*, Annapolis, Maryland, December, 1959.

LEWIS, CHARLES L. *Admiral de Grasse and American Independence*, United States Naval Institute, Annapolis, Maryland, 1945.

————. *Famous American Naval Officers*, L. C. Page and Company, Boston, 1948.

————. *Famous Old World Sea Fighters*, Lothrop, Lee, and Shepard Company, Boston, 1929.

LLOYD, CHRISTOPHER. *Ships and Seamen*, World Publishing Company, Cleveland, 1961.

LORENZ, LINCOLN. *John Paul Jones*, United States Naval Institute, Annapolis, Maryland, 1943.

LOVETTE, LELAND P. *Naval Customs, Tradition, and Usage*, United States Naval Institute, Annapolis, Maryland, 1939.

LUDWIG, EMIL. *Napoleon*, Boni and Liveright, New York, 1926.

MACLAY, EDGAR S. *A History of the United States Navy, 1775–1901* (3 vols.), D. Appleton and Company, New York, 1906.

MAHAN, ALFRED THAYER. *The Influence of Seapower upon History, 1660–1783*, Hill and Wang, New York, 1957.

————. *The Influence of Sea Power on the Wars of the French Revolution and Empire* (2 vols.), Little, Brown, and Company, Boston, 1901.

————. *The Life of Nelson* (2 vols.), Little, Brown, and Company, Boston, 1907.

MAINE, RENE. *Trafalgar*, Charles Scribner's Sons, New York, 1957.

MAPS, JAMES. "The Battle of Ushant—and After," *United States Naval Institute Proceedings*, Annapolis, Maryland, March, 1964.

MARCUS, G. J. *A Naval History of England—The Formative Centuries,* Little, Brown, and Company, Boston, 1961.

MEANS, P. *The Spanish Main,* Gordian Press, Brooklyn.

MELVILLE, COL. PHILLIPS. *"Lexington—Brigantine of War, 1776–1777,"* *United States Naval Institute Proceedings,* Annapolis, Maryland, April, 1960.

MERRIMAN, R. D. (ed.). *Queen Anne's Navy,* Navy Records Society, London, 1961.

MOLYNEUX, THOMAS M. *Conjunct Expeditions,* R. & J. Dodsley, London, 1759.

MONTROSS, LYNN. *War through the Ages,* Harper and Brothers, New York, 1944.

MORAN, CHARLES. *The Sea of Memories,* Charles Scribner's Sons, New York, 1942.

MORDAL, JACQUES. *Twenty-five Centuries of Sea Warfare,* Clarkson N. Potter, New York, 1965.

MORISON, SAMUEL E. *John Paul Jones,* Little, Brown, and Company, Boston, 1959.

MOTLEY, JOHN L. *History of the United Netherlands* (4 vols.), Harper and Brothers, New York, 1860.

————. *The Rise of the Dutch Republic* (4 vols.), John B. Alden, New York, 1899.

New Cambridge Modern History (12 vols.), Cambridge University Press, Cambridge, England, 1957.

NORMAN, C. B. *The Corsairs of France,* Edward J. Clode, Inc., New York, 1929.

NOWELL, CHARLES E. *A History of Portugal,* D. Van Nostrand Company, New York, 1952.

OWEN, JOHN H. *War at Sea under Queen Anne, 1702–1708,* Cambridge University Press, Cambridge, England, 1938.

PENGELLY, COLIN. *The First Bellerophon,* John Baker, London, 1966.

PENN, C. D. *The Navy under the Early Stuarts and Its Influence on English History,* J. Hogg, London, 1920.

PEPYS, SAMUEL. *Diary,* Random House, New York, 1946.

PERKINS, JAMES B. *France in the American Revolution,* Houghton Mifflin Company, Boston, 1911.

POTTER, E. B. *et al. The United States and World Sea Power,* Prentice-Hall, Inc., Englewood Cliffs, New Jersey, 1955.

————. Nimitz, Fleet Admiral Chester W. *et al. Sea Power,* Prentice-Hall, Inc., Englewood Cliffs, New Jersey, 1960.

PRATT, FLETCHER. *Empire and the Sea,* Henry Holt and Company, New York, 1946.

————. *The Battles that Changed History,* Hanover House, Garden City, New York, 1956.

————. *The Navy,* Garden City Publishing Company, Garden City, New York, 1941.

RAWSON, EDWARD K. *Twenty Famous Naval Battles* (2 vols.), Thomas Y. Crowell and Company, New York, 1899.

RICHMOND, H. W. *The Navy as an Instrument of Policy, 1558–1727,* Cambridge University Press, Cambridge, England, 1953.

————. *The Navy in India, 1763–1783,* Ernest Benn, Ltd., London, 1931.

ROBERTS, W. A., and BRENTANO, L. *The Book of the Navy,* Doubleday and Company, Garden City, New York, 1944.

ROBISON, REAR ADMIRAL S. S., and ROBISON, M. L. *A History of Naval Tactics from 1530 to 1930,* United States Naval Institute, Annapolis, Maryland, 1942.

ROOSEVELT, THEODORE. *The Naval War of 1812,* Charles Scribner's Sons, New York, 1926.

ROSCOE, T. *et al. Your Navy,* Navpers 10600, Bureau of Naval Personnel, Washington, D. C., 1946.

ROSCOE, T., and FREEMAN, F. *A Picture History of the U. S. Navy,* Charles Scribner's Sons, New York, 1956.

RUGE, VICE-ADMIRAL FRIEDRICH. "Beachhead 1715," *United States Naval Institute Proceedings,* Annapolis, Maryland, December, 1966.

SCHILLER, FREDERICK. *History of the Revolt of the Netherlands,* S. E. Cassino & Company, Boston, 1884.

SOUTHEY, ROBERT. *The Life of Horatio, Lord Nelson,* J. M. Dent and Sons, London, 1906.

STEVENS, WILLIAM O., and WESTCOTT, ALLAN. *A History of Sea Power,* Doubleday, Doran, and Company, Garden City, New York, 1942.

SWANSON, NEIL H. *The Perilous Fight,* Farrar and Rinehart, New York, 1945.

TUNIS, EDWIN. *Oars, Sails, and Steam,* World Publishing Company, Cleveland, 1952.

————. *Weapons,* World Publishing Company, Cleveland, 1954.

VERE, FRANCIS. *Salt in Their Blood,* Cassell and Company, London, 1955.

VILLIERS, ALAN *et al. Men, Ships, and the Sea,* National Geographic Society, Washington, D. C., 1963.

WARNER, OLIVER. *A Portrait of Lord Nelson,* Reprint Society, London, 1958.

————. *Great Sea Battles,* The Macmillan Company, New York, 1963.

————. *The Sea and the Sword,* William Morrow & Company, New York, 1965.

WEDGWOOD, C. V. "The Golden Age of the Dutch Republic," *Horizon,* Heritage Publishing Company, New York, September, 1948.

WELLER, JAC, and HERVEY-BATHURST, SIR FREDERICK. "His Majesty's Stationary Sloop of War," *United States Naval Institute Proceedings,* Annapolis, Maryland, April, 1959.

WESTCOTT, ALLAN (ed.). *Mahan on Naval Warfare,* Little, Brown, and Company, Boston, 1941.

———— *et al. American Sea Power Since 1775,* J. B. Lippincott Company, Chicago, 1947.

WILLIAMS, HENRY SMITH *et al. The Historians' History of the World* (27 vols.), The Encyclopaedia Britannica Company, Ltd., London, 1926.

WILLIAMSON, JAMES A. *The Age of Drake,* Barnes and Noble, New York, 1960.

————. *The English Channel,* World Publishing Company, Cleveland, 1959.

ADDITIONAL SOURCES OF INFORMATION

Boston colonial newspapers for 1743–48—*Weekly Post-Boy, News Letter, Evening Post,* and *Gazette*—for hitherto largely neglected details of King George's War and the Boston impressment riot of 1747, consulted at Massachusetts Historical Association, Boston.

Personal visits by the author to museums, harbors, fortifications, naval bases and exhibits, and points of historic interest in the Balearic Islands, Belgium, the Canary and Cape Verde Islands, Egypt, England, France, Gibraltar, Greece, Italy, Lebanon, Madeira, Malta, Mexico, the Netherlands, North Africa, Portugal, Scotland, Sicily, Spain, Turkey, and Yugoslavia; to the decks of H.M.S. *Victory;* and, nearer home, to Boston, Canso, Fort McHenry, Louisburg, New Orleans, Port Royal (Annapolis), Quebec, the United States Naval Academy, Washington, Yorktown, and the decks of U.S.S. *Constitution* and *Constellation.*

INDEX

Semicolons separate groups of references to different people, ships, or places of the same name. References in Italic type in parentheses are to maps, as (*M. 2*), or to pictures, as (*P. 4*).